THE EAST-WEST CENTER, established in Hawaii by the United States Congress in 1960, is a national educational institution with multinational programs. Its purpose is to promote better relations and understanding among the nations and peoples of Asia, the Pacific area, and the United States through their cooperative participation in research, study and training activities.

Fundamental to the achievement of the Center's purpose is the cooperative discovery and application of knowledge, and the interchange of knowledge, information, ideas and beliefs in an intercultural atmosphere of academic freedom. In Center programs, theory and practice are combined to help current and future leaders generate, test, and share knowledge about important world problems of mutual concern to people in both East and West.

Each year about 1,500 scholars, leaders, public officials, mid-level and upper-level managers, and graduate students come to the Center to work and study together in programs concerned with seeking alternative approaches and solutions to common problems. For each participant from the United States, two come from the Asian/Pacific area. An international, interdisciplinary professional staff provides the framework, content, and continuity for programs and for cooperative relationships with universities and other institutions in the Center's area of operations.

Center programs are conducted by the East-West Communication Institute, the East-West Culture Learning Institute, the East-West Food Institute, the East-West Population Institute, and the East-West Technology and Development Institute. Each year the Center also awards a limited number of "Open Grants" for graduate degree education and research by scholars and authorities in areas not encompassed by the problem-oriented institutes.

The East-West Center is governed by the autonomous board of a public, non-profit educational corporation—the "Center for Cultural and Technical Interchange Between East and West, Inc."—established by special act of the Hawaii State Legislature. The Board of Governors is composed of distinguished individuals from the United States and countries of Asia and the Pacific area. The United States Congress provides basic funding for Center programs and for a variety of scholarships, fellowships, internships and other awards. Because of the cooperative nature of Center programs, financial support and cost-sharing arrangements also are provided by Asian and Pacific governments, regional agencies, private enterprise and foundations.

The Center is located in Honolulu, Hawaii on 21 acres of land adjacent to the University of Hawaii's Manoa campus. Through cooperative arrangements with the University of Hawaii, the Center has access to University degree programs, libraries, computer center and the like.

THE EAST-WEST CULTURE LEARNING INSTITUTE seeks to develop more effective methods of helping persons from different cultures to understand other cultures as well as their own. In particular, the Institute is concerned with ways and means by which cultures may come in contact with each other for the mutual benefit of persons in those cultures while individual and national identities are maintained. For program purposes, it conducts cooperative research, study and training in four main areas: cultural identity, language in culture, cultures in contact, and thought and expression in culture learning.

Verner C. Bickley, Director

Editorial Board
    Mark P. Lester, Chairman   Larry Smith
    J. G. Amirthanayagam   Gregory Trifonovitch
    Jerry Boucher   John Walsh
    Richard Brislin   Karen Watson-Gegeo
    Krishna Kumar   David Wu

CHILDREN OF THE DISPOSSESSED

CHILDREN OF THE DISPOSSESSED

A consideration of the nature of intelligence, cultural disadvantage, educational programs for culturally different people, and of the development and expression of a profile of competencies

Barry Nurcombe

A Culture Learning Institute Monograph
EAST-WEST CENTER
The University Press of Hawaii

Copyright © 1976 by The University Press of Hawaii
All rights reserved
Manufactured in the United States of America
Book design by Roger J. Eggers
Composition by
Asco Trade Typesetting Limited, Hong Kong

Library of Congress Cataloging in Publication Data

Nurcombe, Barry, 1933–
Children of the dispossessed.

(A Culture Learning Institute monograph)
Bibliography: p.
Includes index.
1. Australian aborigines—Education.
2. Socially handicapped children—Education—
Australia.   3. Nature and nurture. I. Title.
II. Series: East-West Center. Culture Learning
Institute. A Culture Learning Institute monograph.
LC3501.A3N87   371.9'67'0994   75-35981
ISBN 0-8248-0362-0

For Alison

CONTENTS

FIGURES — xi

TABLES — xiii

FOREWORD — xvii

PREFACE — xxi

Chapter One: What Is Intelligence? — 3
    Historical Background
    The Evolution of the Concept of Intelligence
    Intelligence: General or Specific?
    That Elusive Definition
    Cross-cultural Applications
    Problems in Cross-Cultural Testing
    Different Types of Intelligence
    A Spectrum of Competencies
    Summary

Chapter Two: The Great Debate — 21
    The Different Faces of Ignorance
    The Jensenist Heresy
    Explicit Issues
        The Comparison of SES Groups
        Language Deprivation
        Health and Nutrition
        Heritability
        Evidence from Australian Studies
    Implicit Issues
    Science and Social Responsibility
    Summary

Chapter Three: Deprivation, Disadvantage, or Difference? — 51
    The Evolution of the Notion of Deprivation
    Health and Nutrition

CONTENTS

    Personality and Motivation
        Low Self-Esteem
        Stigma
        Lack of Basic Trust
        Impulsiveness
        Aspirations and Values
    Cognition
    Restricted and Elaborated Codes
    Culture and Dialect
    The Central Function of Language
    Summary

Chapter Four: Early Childhood Education: Success or Failure?   77
    Historical Background
    The Westinghouse Evaluation
    How to Describe and Assess a Preschool Program
        Educational Philosophy
        Objectives
        Systematic Planning
        The Staff
        The Children
        The Parents
        The Primary School
    Experimental Programs That Work
        Infant Education Programs
            Day-care Programs
            Home-teaching Programs
        Preschool Programs
            Structured Programs
            Semistructured Programs
            Child-centered Programs
            Multiple Programs
    Discussion
    Conclusions
    Predictions

Chapter Five: Cultural Disadvantage in Australia   103
    Aboriginal Social Groups
    The Historical Background of Bourke
    Class, Status, and Social Organization in Part-Aboriginal
        Communities
    The Culture of Poverty: Australian Version
        Relationship to Larger Society
        Social Organization
        The Family
        The Individual
    Cultural Difference and Scholastic Adjustment
    Summary and Conclusions

Chapter Six: An Australian Preschool   122
- *History*
    - The Ecology of the Arid Zone
    - Early Rationale and Establishment
- *Action Research: Design*
    - Objectives
        - Affective Objectives
        - Perceptual-Motor Objectives
        - Language and Cognitive Objectives
    - Selection
    - Attendance
    - Methodology
    - Teaching Strategies
        - Wave I
        - Wave II
        - Wave III
        - Wave IV
    - Evaluation
        - ITPA
        - PPVT
        - WPPSI
        - DAP
        - Nixon Test
        - Boehm Test
    - Summary
- *Action Research: Results*
    - Wave I, 1970
    - Wave II, 1971
    - Wave III, 1972
    - Wave IV, 1973
    - Follow-up
    - Summary of Results
- *Action Research: Discussion*
    - The Staff and Observers
    - The Parents
    - The Children
    - Integration
    - Validity
    - Durability and Follow-Through
    - Transfer
- *Action Research: The Future*
- *The Rationale and Ethics of Intervention*

Chapter Seven: Potential, Competence, and Performance—   189
                A Conceptual Framework
- *From Observation to Theory*
- *Potential*
    - The Biological Rudiments of Cognition

The Development and Function of Language
Summary
Realization
  Maturation
  Equilibration
  Environment
  Modal Cultural Themes and Socialization
  Sensitive or Favorable Periods
  Summary
Competence
  Synchronicity
  A Spectrum of Competencies
  A Multidimensional Model of the Structure of Competence
  Competence and Performance in Generative Linguistics
  Deep and Surface Structure in the Spectrum of Competencies
  Summary
Expression and Performance
  Expression, Context, Strategy, Feedback
  Cultural Relativism
  Ecological Functionalism
  Summary
Assessment and Evaluation

Chapter Eight: Questions and Assumptions   232
Questions
Assumptions
In Conclusion

APPENDIX: Extended Experience Program: 1973–1974   237

BIBLIOGRAPHY   243

INDEX   261

FIGURES

1.1	The hierarchy of intellectual functions (after Vernon 1969)	8
1.2	Potential, competence, and performance	19
2.1	The distribution of IQ scores in a population	25
4.1	Types of preschool program	82
4.2	Systematic planning	85
6.1	Wave I: ITPA profile means for unstructured traditional classes, Aborigines and whites combined	146
6.2	Wave I: ITPA profile means for structured BEP classes, Aborigines and whites combined	147
6.3	Wave I: follow-up into 1971 of structured and traditional classes on PPVT IQ	168
6.4	Wave I: follow-up into 1971 of structured and traditional classes on WPPSI vocabulary	169
6.5	Wave I: follow-up into 1971 of structured and traditional classes on ITPA grammatic closure	170
6.6	Wave I: follow-up into 1971 of structured and traditional classes on ITPA auditory association	171
6.7	Waves I, II, III, IV: mean results of Aboriginal children on PPVT, Bereiter-Engelmann technique	172
6.8	Waves I, II, III, IV: mean results of Aboriginal children on ITPA auditory association, Bereiter-Engelmann technique	173
6.9	Waves I, II, III, IV: mean results of Aboriginal children on ITPA grammatic closure, Bereiter-Engelmann technique	174
7.1	Potential: tool use and social relations	191
7.2	Basic schema: language, tool use, and social relations	193
7.3	Extended schema: language, tool use, and social relations	194

FIGURES

7.4	Realization	204
7.5	The spectrum of competencies	211
7.6	Profiles of primary abilities of four ethnic groups (modified from Stodolsky and Lesser 1967)	215
7.7	Language, egocentric speech, and thought	221
7.8	The internalization of egocentric speech	221
7.9	Expression and performance	224
7.10	Evaluation	230

TABLES

2.1	IQ correlations empirically discovered (r) and theoretically expected on the basis of inheritance alone (ρ)	26
4.1	Mean IQ scores of children in five programs at beginning and end of preschool and at the end of the first two years of primary school (Karnes et al. 1970a)	97
4.2	Results on Stanford-Binet IQ test of three treatment groups of four-year-old children (Weikart 1967)	99
4.3	Results on Stanford-Binet Intelligence Test of three treatment groups of three-year-old children (Weikart 1967)	99
5.1	PPVT scores of Aboriginal and white preschool children in Bourke, 1969	115
5.2	Mean difference scores between chronological and language ages on ITPA of Aboriginal and white preschool children in Bourke, 1969	115
5.3	Mean PPVT IQ scores of different groups of Australian children (de Lacey 1971)	116
5.4	Index of frequencies of different transformations in either standard or Aboriginal English used by white and Aboriginal four-year-old children (Hart 1973)	118
6.1	Experimental methodology of comparison between teaching techniques	129
6.2	Correlations of scores on Nixon Test with PPVT (from de Lacey 1971)	142
6.3	Wave I: mean results on PPVT, WPPSI vocabulary, and WPPSI geometric design of Aborigines and whites combined, unstructured traditional and structured BEP classes compared	144
6.4	Wave I: mean results on composite ITPA scaled scores, Aborigines and whites combined, traditional and structured BEP classes compared	145

TABLES

6.5	Wave I: mean scaled score results on ITPA subtests, Aborigines and whites combined, unstructured traditional and structured BEP classes compared	145
6.6	Wave I: mean results on PPVT, WPPSI vocabulary, and ITPA for unstructured traditional classes, Aborigines and whites compared	147
6.7	Wave I: mean results on PPVT, WPPSI vocabulary, and ITPA for structured BEP classes, Aborigines and whites compared	148
6.8	Wave I: mean gain scores on PPVT, WPPSI vocabulary, and ITPA of whites and Aborigines in the structured BEP classes	148
6.9	Wave I: mean results on PPVT, WPPSI vocabulary, and ITPA for structured BEP classes, two teachers T_1 and T_2 compared	149
6.10	Wave II: mean results on intelligence and language tests for all, for Aboriginal, and for white subjects in the structured BEP	151
6.11	Wave II: mean results on perceptual-motor tests for all, for Aboriginal, and for white subjects	151
6.12	Wave II: mean results on perceptual-motor tests for all children, FP and BPMP compared	152
6.13	Wave II: mean results on DAP IQ, for the FP and the BPMP, Aborigines and whites compared	152
6.14	Wave III: mean results on all tests in both programs (BEP–FP and EEP–BPMP) for total group, Aborigines and whites combined	153
6.15	Wave III: mean scores of Aborigines and whites on all tests in both programs (BEP–FP and EEP–BPMP) combined	154
6.16	Wave III: mean scores of Aborigines and whites combined on all tests, structured BEP–FP and semistructured EEP–BPMP compared	155
6.17	Wave III: mean scores of Aborigines on all tests, structured BEP–FP and semistructured EEP–BPMP compared	156
6.18	Wave III: mean scores of whites on all tests, structured BEP–FP and semistructured EEP–BPMP compared	157
6.19	Wave III: mean gain scores (SD in parentheses) of Aborigines in perceptual-motor tests, FP and BPMP compared	158
6.20	Wave III: mean gain scores (SD in parentheses) of whites in perceptual-motor tests, FP and BPMP compared	158
6.21	Wave IV: mean results on all tests in both programs for total group, Aborigines and whites combined	159
6.22	Wave IV: mean scores of Aborigines and whites in both programs, structured and semistructured combined	160

6.23	Wave IV: mean scores of Aborigines and whites combined on all tests, structured and semistructured programs compared	161
6.24	Wave IV: mean scores of Aborigines on all tests, structured and semistructured programs compared	163
6.25	Wave IV: mean scores of whites on all tests, structured and semistructured programs compared	164
6.26	Mean ages of all preschool and non-preschool samples in 1970, 1971, and 1972	165
6.27	Follow-up comparison of mean scores of unmatched 1970 non-preschool, 1971 Wave I preschool, and 1972 Wave II preschool children on PPVT and Nixon Test	166
6.28	Follow-up comparison of mean scores of 36 non-preschool and 36 matched preschool children from Wave II on PPVT, ITPA, and Nixon Test in mid-1972	166
6.29	Follow-up comparison of mean scores of 15 Aboriginal non-preschool and 15 matched Aboriginal preschool children from Wave II on PPVT, ITPA, and Nixon Test in mid-1972	167
6.30	Follow-up comparison of mean scores of 21 white non-preschool and 21 matched white preschool children from Wave II on PPVT, ITPA, and Nixon Test in mid-1972	167
6.31	Follow-up comparison of mean scores of 15 Aboriginal and 21 white preschool children from Wave II on PPVT, ITPA, and Nixon Test in mid-1972	167

FOREWORD

I am greatly honored by the opportunity to write the foreword to this imaginative and constructive volume. At issue here is one of the major problems of our time in education—how to incorporate and utilize our vast and growing amount of relevant knowledge in the *service* of education. Research directly related to education has been growing at a terrific pace for the last fifteen years in psychology, linguistics, anthropology, and sociology—each discipline having important things to say about human growth and development with significant implications for the socialization of young people in our schools. The information tends to be fragmented, each specialist appealing to his or her own reference group. The psychologists write for and to each other, and not always to all of *them*; and so do anthropologists, linguists, and the rest. Yet each is directly concerned with enhancing our knowledge of human development. There is need periodically for revision and reorganization of our knowledge here, with a fresh look to create order out of the chaos. Dr. Nurcombe has done just such a service—not only for his colleagues in his native Australia, but also for the professionals on an international level.

By providing a conceptual model that is broad yet direct, one that encompasses the significant dimensions of development and is presented in a constructive spirit, Dr. Nurcombe offers a paradigm which is applicable to a wide array of educational contexts. The form of the model he provides has potential for universal applicability since he does take into account the idiosyncrasy of particular cultures. Sensitivity to the valuing of cultures is critical in these days of Western cultural imperialism, where with sophisticated technology and political power, we of the West have been in the process of destroying indigenous cultures in the United States, Australia, Canada, Africa, and elsewhere. Whether the destructive trend can be halted or whether the destructive aspects of so-called progress can be converted into constructive growth experience are questions which

Foreword

will be answered in due time. For me, Dr. Nurcombe has contributed significantly in the latter case, to avoid the evil consequences of the former.

My point is this. The science of education has to evolve in a context that takes into account the place and kind of the *to-be-educated*, intertwined with the objectives of the educator. Ignoring the potential by destroying the foundation from which the to-be-educated come is to deny their integrity as human beings. Applying Western models of education to "native" peoples creates the danger of destroying the very roots and identities of those "to be saved." In effect, intervention programs may create marginal individuals—rootless and alienated. The responsibility for the educator is considerable. Of course, there are those who would justify such a policy by operating from the principle of integration into the majority society. To take the integration theme seriously requires societal changes beyond education. It requires a society that truly accepts its minority members—an unrealistic expectation in 1975 anywhere. The "melting pot" theory has not worked in the United States, where it had 200 years to evolve; in America this theory was conceptualized for various ethnic groups—but never for racial groups. In fact, miscegenation was a dread and, until recently, in some states an illegal social act.

For racial groups, then, the problem is clear: how to make it as a black person in a white society. The black needs to live in two cultures, and one can only do that, I believe, if one culture provides a *security blanket*. The Bourke project appears to be providing that security blanket for Aboriginal children. It offers them skills and strategies to enhance their learning without destroying their origins or respect for themselves as individuals. The task is formidable but possible—especially with the honest participation of the white community.

How does the Bourke project fit the elegant competence-realization model developed by Nurcombe? Although he does not make the connections as explicit as I would like, it seems clear that his conception of the Bourke preschool project is to formulate the development of competence in a constructive way to enable the children to develop options as to how, where, what they might do. The children's style of dealing with problems, their fluency in so doing, and whether they do so in school or not—these are potential outcomes from a preschool experience. More important perhaps, and also of considerable interest, Dr. Nurcombe and his colleagues employed ideas from the United States but adapted them to the Bourke environment.

This poses the crucial question of transferability of programs from one culture to another; the validity of a Piaget-based program for Aborigine children is moot, as is a Bereiter-Englemann approach. Dr. Nurcombe and his colleagues are sensitive to this issue. Their research

Foreword

results will have theoretical value regarding the viability of specific cognitive function, as well as having educational value—if it works, all to the good. Since the program does seem to make some difference, at least in the short run, there seems to be some generality for growth and development. How long will these effects last, and in what form? This is an open question. Do these effects spiral, serving as catalysts setting up subsequent changes? Only time will tell. Whatever the outcome, Dr. Nurcombe deserves our thanks for sharing his scholarship with us in a lucid and exciting style, helping us gain perspective in working with compensatory education programs.

A final note. I once had the pleasure of meeting Barry Nurcombe in person. I found in that meeting the commitment, the concern, the humanism so evident in his writing about so complex a set of issues. I feel this is a personal book and it is this quality which gives it strength. And although this volume will be of value to an array of professionals, my fervent hope is that public policy makers will read it also.

Irving E. Sigel
Senior Research Psychologist
Educational Testing Service

PREFACE

As the world shrinks and technologically sophisticated nations grow more powerful, the glaring distance between rich and poor widens. Education is one means by which the economic gap may be reduced. No nation today can afford to waste human potential or to turn its back on technology. For better or worse we are all headed in roughly parallel directions, albeit by different paths. This book is about pathways and directions; but it is mainly about the underbrush that must be cleared before the paths can be surveyed.

The book starts with a review of the evolution of the notion of intelligence. Beginning with the work of Galton and Spencer in the nineteenth century, and applied in the form of ability tests, the concept of intelligence has dominated the educational field. It has diffused into everyday language in such a way that people use the term as though it were as concrete and defined as "height" or "temperature." The problems of definition and of application are discussed, along with the dominant current trends of thought in this field, in chapter 1. There it is suggested that the meaning of "intelligence" has become hopelessly confused. Alternative terms are introduced and defined to clarify the contemporary semantic muddle.

It has long been a matter of controversy whether the gap between rich and poor people in one society, or between rich and poor societies, is due to differences in innate potential. Do different individuals have different potential? Are there limitations upon the degree to which different kinds of intelligent behavior can be fostered, educationally, in different social and racial groups? Are the differences in measured intelligence between those in the one group, or between different groups, due predominantly to genetic or to environmental factors? For some years, a liberal viewpoint has prevailed: although within any group there is a variation in potential determined, in part, by the genes, all human races

PREFACE

have the same fundamental capacity if environmental influences are favorable and comparable. In 1969 an article by an eminent psychologist reopened the issue. A. R. Jensen suggested that compensatory education for disadvantaged—especially black—children, in the United States, has been misguided; there may be innate differences in intellectual potential between black and white, and, if so, these differences should be taken into account in educational planning. Jensen's article detonated a fierce and acrimonious dispute that still continues. The controversy is reviewed in chapter 2.

In the 1950s and 1960s the concepts of cultural deprivation and disadvantage gained currency. Poor children, especially those from culturally excluded minority groups, were described as lacking certain crucial experiences—particularly language experiences—necessary for learning in primary school. These theoretical concepts were closely related to the historical forces prevailing in North America at that time: the civil rights movement and pressure for racial integration. The emergence of a new sense of identity among minority groups has forced a realization of the ethnocentrism of the deprivation hypothesis and a revision in terms of *cultural difference*. Recent linguistic evidence has strengthened this viewpoint. The various approaches to environmentally determined differences in cognitive performance are discussed in chapter 3.

In the early 1960s the writings of Robert Havighurst, Benjamin Bloom, J. McV. Hunt, Martin Deutsch, and others fostered a resurgence of the preschool movement in the United States. Perhaps cultural disadvantage could be overcome by a concerted compensatory effort in the preschool period. A national effort was mounted—Project Head Start. A thousand flowers bloomed; and many withered. A sober stock-taking of gains and losses is now possible. Are there any criteria which apply to those programs that had success? How are programs to be planned, implemented, and evaluated? Are the successes durable or do they fade out with time? Is preschool, after all, the most appropriate period for educational intervention? Is intervention but one more attempt of a spiritually bankrupt dominant society to impose its will on the oppressed? These controversial issues are the subject of chapter 4.

The shock waves of the great educational debate have been felt beyond North America. In Australia, a new but affluent country of 13 million people, there is a depressed minority group of about 150,000 Aborigines who live in different social settings varying from traditional and tribal to the outcast fringes of the dominant white society. On the whole, Aborigines do poorly in school and economically. A new sense of Aboriginal identity is beginning to emerge, only now. The history, cultural setting, and educational difficulties of this people are discussed in chapter 5.

In chapter 6 the history, rationale, and results of an Australian preschool in the outback, established for part-Aboriginal children, are described. The way in which systematic educational planning allows for the deliberate incorporation of new, alternative ideas is clarified. The need for eclecticism is stressed. The preschool is seen as part of—integral to—a broader approach of community development. Formal education is a contract between families, social group, and educators. Education, as a whole, is not restricted to the environs of the school; nor is it limited to the years between five and sixteen.

Experience in the field and the need to interpret empirical data allow one to view theory from a new perspective. It becomes apparent that much of the controversy about cognitive development originates from a lack of clarity about the factors involved. Chapter 7 deals with theoretical issues. What is the meaning of internal *structure* and *schema*? What is the significance of hierarchy for cognitive performance? How are emotions and motives associated with knowledge, skill, and their application? What is the significance of language development for intellectual competence?

About each of the topics discussed in the previous chapters of this book, fierce controversies rage. Psychometricians and Piagetians argue about the nature and evaluation of intelligence. Those who suggest that there may be innate racial differences in intellectual potential are subject to vilification, threat, and physical attack by their opponents. Those who adhere to the idea of cultural deprivation are seen as naïve environmentalists on the one hand or as patronizingly ethnocentric on the other. Acrimonious battles are waged in print or in the lecture hall on the most appropriate preschool strategies for minority groups. The highly directed, convergent teaching techniques of Bereiter and Engelmann, for example, are seen as crushing spontaneity; whereas open, child-centered approaches are pilloried as being based on rhetoric rather than knowledge and wasteful of valuable time. The very heat of the arguments indicates the crucial nature of the issues at stake, the lack of empirical data available and, above all, the absence of an overall view, a "road map," which schematizes the issues involved, indicates where knowledge is lacking, and interrelates aspects of the gestalt of potential, competence, performance, and evaluation. Chapter 7 aims to provide such an overview and to define the terms used in such a way as to counteract the fallacies promoted by a unidimensional concept of intelligence.

Such an overview leads directly to a consideration of the assumptions underlying, and of the questions raised by, the framework. What direction is future research likely to follow? How can the theoretical

PREFACE

framework described in chapter 7 be applied to educational and social problems in different societies? These topics are dealt with in chapter 8.

The controversy and contradictions inherent in the areas covered by this book are due partly to the different philosophies and training of the antagonists, partly to the formulation and brandishment of opinions based on insufficient evidence, and partly to the lack of a common vocabulary and a common overview of the very complex issues involved. It is little wonder that the young teacher, psychologist, psychiatrist, or social worker is daunted by the problem of coming to terms with such a chaotic battleground. Thus specialists become trapped in their own domains of knowledge (or ignorance) and are unable to interact, constructively, with others whose help or skills they need. The social and educational problems inherent in economic inequality, cultural difference, and technological change in emerging countries are enormous. Their solution will require interdisciplinary cooperation. Their urgency is such that national and international efforts are required. This book is a recognition of and a contribution to those who work with children and families toward the solution of these problems.

ACKNOWLEDGMENTS

The architect of the Bourke community project was John Cawte, of the University of New South Wales, the first Australian psychiatrist to work with Aborigines. From him and from Leslie Kiloh and John Beveridge, of the Schools of Psychiatry and Paediatrics, we have had constant support. Fred Katz, of the Tertiary Education Research Center, University of New South Wales, has provided us with invaluable consultative and practical help. In the first two years of Project Enrichment of Childhood, I collaborated with Paul Moffitt in the building of the school and the design and supervision of the experimental methodology. In 1972, I was assisted by Phil de Lacey and Lorne Taylor, of Wollongong University College. Since 1973 Phil de Lacey has been codirector of the Bourke Preschool.

Throughout the history of the project we have had the support of the Prince of Wales Hospital and the Darling Shire Council. Funds for the establishment and continuation of the Bourke Preschool have been provided by the Australian Mineral Industries Research Association and by the Australian Department of Aboriginal Affairs. We are indebted to Jim May of AMIRA, to Barrie Dexter and Jeremy Long of Aboriginal Affairs, and to John Tonkin and Peter Allen of COMALCO for their personal support. We have also been much stimulated and encouraged by Don McElwain and Betty Watts of the University of Queensland, by Max Kelly of Macquarie University, and by Lex Grey of the New South

Preface

Wales Van Leer Foundation. The people of Bourke welcomed the preschool, provided us with a building, and entrusted their children to us; we were fortunate in our choice of town. Dr. E. C. Coolican's support and advice have been invaluable. We have been fortunate, too, in the preschool teachers who have worked in the project: Esther Whitton, Ann McMillan, Megan Passmore, Pat Doolan, Rosemary Lawrie, Jan Condie, Elvira McIntosh, and Amada Oroczo.

This book was written while I was on sabbatical leave from the University of New South Wales, as a senior fellow of the Culture Learning Institute, East-West Center, Honolulu. The manuscript was typed by Karen Shiroma, and to her and to Hazel Tatsuno and Patricia Kim I owe my thanks. Verner Bickley, director of the Culture Learning Institute, has been continuously encouraging. I have been much aided in my preparation by consultation with Richard Brislin, Mark Lester, Tony Marsella, Tom Maretzki, and Arthur Jensen. I should like to pay tribute, finally, to John Money of Johns Hopkins Medical School who helped me see the world afresh, and to John Cawte who introduced me to cross-cultural work.

Barry Nurcombe
Honolulu, Hawaii

CHILDREN
OF THE
DISPOSSESSED

ALICE: Would you tell me, please, which way I ought to go from here?

THE CAT: That depends a good deal on where you want to get to.

Lewis Carroll

CHAPTER 1
WHAT IS INTELLIGENCE?

The tendency has always been strong to believe that whatever receives a name must be an entity or being, having an independent existence of its own. And if no real entity answering to the name could be found, men did not for that reason suppose that none existed, but imagined that it was something peculiarly abstruse and mysterious.

J. S. Mill

HISTORICAL BACKGROUND

All cultures have words that denote "intelligent." It is a matter of common observation that in any community there are individuals who stand out in wisdom, accuracy of prediction, ability to solve problems, craftiness, or in their accumulation of traditional knowledge and technical skills. Most people are not outstanding in competence. A few are so markedly backward that they may be called "dull." "Intelligent" connotes goodness, power, activity. In Western societies "dullness" connotes badness, impotence, passivity. Take these synonyms from *Roget's Thesaurus* (1965):

> Adj. *intelligent*, quick of apprehension, keen, acute, alive, brainy, awake, bright, quick, sharp; quick-, keen-, clear-, sharp-, -eyed, -sighted, -witted; wide awake; canny, shrewd, astute; clear-headed; far-sighted; discerning, perspicacious, penetrating, piercing, nimble-witted; sharp as a needle; alive to; clever; arch.
> Wise, sage, sapient, sagacious, reasonable, rational . . .
> Adj. *un-intelligent*, -intellectual, -reasoning; brainless; having no-head; not-bright; inapprehensible.
> addle-, blunder-, muddle-, pig-headed.
> weak-, feeble-minded; shallow-, rattle-, lack-brained; half-, nit-,

Chapter One

short-, dull-, blunt-witted; shallow-, addle-pated; dim-, short-sighted; thick-skulled; weak in the upper story.
Shallow, weak, wanting, soft; dull; stupid . . .

And so on.

Despite the ubiquity of the concept "intelligent," the particular astute behaviors that are most valued vary from culture to culture. Irvine (1969b) describes how in Rhodesian Shona society an individual's esteem rests upon the degree of cohesion his actions foster in his kin group. Intelligent behavior tends to incorporate a keen awareness of interpersonal relations. Force and life are imputed to words and natural objects, and the ancestral spirits of kinfolk are regarded as involved in personal transactions. The Shona equivalent for "act intelligently" is *ngware*, a word that connotes caution, prudence, and diplomacy. This is markedly different from—if not antithetical to—the Western ideal of independent, individual, competitive achievement. One culture values the judicious choice and application of traditional forms; the other, the creation of new forms of problem-solving. One stresses the group and its continuity with ancestral spirits and the world of nature; the other promotes the individual who masters nature and stands out from others.

In white Australia and rural America during the last century, the intelligent person was one who could improvise from limited natural resources the wherewithal to survive and prosper in a harsh environment. This person is likely to have had scant respect for a "book-learning" that had no clear applicability. Spatial, practical, and mechanical skills were highly valued. The education of the doctor was esteemed because of its clear relation to concrete needs; the education of the teacher was often held in contempt. *What's the use of it?* was the yardstick against which more abstract, literary, mathematical, or scientific pursuits were judged.

As Jensen (1970a) points out, the Western educational system has evolved from literary, verbal forms favored by the European upper classes of the eighteenth century. The first to be exposed to it were the sons of aristocrats, next the expanding middle class of industrial society, until finally it was universally applied. More recently it has been exported to other societies that are in the process of technological transition from traditional agriculture or hunting. In the Western system, the young begin at five or six years of age. They are taught in groups by an adult, predominantly in a showing-seeing and a telling-listening mode. This puts a high premium on the child's ability to attend, to inhibit random motor activity, to decode, store, and utilize verbal symbols, and to continue to work on material after it has been presented. The children of aristocrats and of the middle class in Western society already have the basis of these skills at the time they commence school; but the children of the poor and of other societies may not.

The predominantly verbal content and the passive teaching modes of Western education must often have seemed irrelevant to the working-class child; yet the arch-pedagogue of the nineteenth century, Thomas Arnold, extolled the virtues of Latin and Greek precisely because they were pure, irrelevant, and unsullied by practical applicability. The classical dons of the prestigious universities of England, until recently, looked askance at the intrusion into their cloisters of the "rude mechanicals" of science. The wonder is that, up to a point, the creaking system has worked, more or less; but since its extension to all social classes and—more recently—to other nations, its limitations have become increasingly apparent. The reasons why it is failing and what might be done about it are the burden of this book.

THE EVOLUTION OF THE CONCEPT OF INTELLIGENCE

It is a considerable conceptual leap from *intelligent* to *intelligence*, to an abstract something that some people have more of than others. The leap was historically coincident with the extension, at the turn of this century, of formal education to all people in industrial societies. Teachers found that many of their new pupils were struggling to learn fundamental reading, writing, and numerical skills. Perhaps they had too little of what it took to do so. The term *intelligence* gained currency. With some rapidity the word diffused into everyday language so that it is used, now, with most assurance by those who have least technical knowledge of its derivation. Give an idea a name and it begins to assume an existence.

Galton (1869) and Spencer (1895), in England, were the first to postulate a superordinate mental ability that was potentially measurable. But how to measure "it"? Galton attempted to do so by evaluating individual differences in sensory acuity. He did discover the principle of variation—discriminatory capacities in the various sensations were distributed in the population along the now familiar bell-shaped curve (the normal distribution)—but the measurement of intelligence eluded him as it did other psychologists who sought it along the blind alley of sensation.

Others involved in clinical work with psychotic and retarded people designed rough tests of memory, language, and attention to aid in the diagnosis of feeblemindedness; for the latter had only recently been distinguished from insanity. A similar pragmatism inspired Alfred Binet, a French psychologist. Why not measure intelligence—whatever it was—

directly? Intelligence seemed to have something to do with a diversity of functions: memory, comprehension, moral sentiments, imagery, force of will, and the like. So why not devise tests to measure the functions per se? For ten years after 1895, Binet and his associates labored to find problems that would discriminate between French schoolchildren at different ages. He looked for tests that would sort people into high, average, and low. Having found a problem that did so at a particular age, he could then establish its *norm*; for example, at six years of age, 50 percent of French schoolchildren could copy the shape of a diamond.

In 1904 the French Ministry of Public Instruction commissioned Binet to design a test to help schools detect slow learners in order to arrange special classes for them. Drawing on the norms he had established, Binet with his colleague Simon (1905) put together a series of items that were graded in difficulty. As expected, they found that at each age some children did better than, some worse than, and some as well as, the average child of that age. Binet and Simon arranged their test to provide at each age five problems that the average child of that age should be able to solve. The subject's performance could thus be rated in terms of *mental age*.[1] Binet had hit upon a means of describing performance in a quantified way. Later Stern, a German psychologist, pointed out that a thirteen-year-old child with a mental age of twelve years was better off than a three-year-old child with a mental age of two years; it was the relation that mattered, rather than the difference, between mental and chronological ages. To account for this relation Stern proposed the *intelligence quotient* or IQ— the relation between mental age and chronological age expressed as a percentage:

$$IQ = \frac{\text{mental age}}{\text{chronological age}} \times 100$$

The solidity of the figures thus derived has long been a support to those who would view intelligence as a unitary "thing" like water in a pitcher, a trend accentuated by the competitive nature of the prevailing educational ethos.

Binet's test proved very useful in the detection of retarded children. It was exported, translated, modified, and improved. The intrinsic notion that intelligence is the result of cumulative and consecutive development was highly appropriate to the educational setting. But the test's practicality and usefulness should not obscure the fact that Binet had been forced by circumstances to restrict the cast of his conceptual net.

1. That is, performance relative to the performance of the average child of different ages. Each of the five items at each age level was worth .2 of a year in mental age score.

What Is Intelligence?

Originally he had proposed to include in the test such matters as aesthetic appreciation, force of will, and imagery; but the difficulty of doing so defeated him. In final form the test consisted of an eclectic group of problems to do with coordination, comprehension, memory, recognition, sensory discrimination, concentration, verbal conceptualization, verbal fluency, and general knowledge. It was loaded with verbal items cast in a form similar to that of the conventional school syllabus—not unexpectedly, of course, in view of the origin, purpose, and validation of the test.

Binet had measured intelligence without saying what it was. He never did define it precisely, preferring to leave it open, but his writings make it clear that he saw it as encompassing comprehension, goal direction, invention, and self-evaluation. He was not able to incorporate all these elements in his test; but did that matter? The test "worked," and educators and psychologists have used it extensively to this day. It has been the progenitor of a host of general and specific ability measures.

Guilford (1967) has described how an increasing unease with Binet's test and its later versions arose as a result of the fact that the test items composing the various year levels differed from year to year. To overcome this, Wechsler (1958) introduced new scales in which the same items were given at all ages: firstly the Wechsler-Bellevue Intelligence Scale[2] for adults and, later, the Wechsler Intelligence Scale for Children and the Wechsler Preschool and Primary Scale of Intelligence—instruments designed for adults, and for children from six to fifteen and from two to six years of age, respectively. Wechsler's tests have been so constructed that the frequency distribution of the scores on his subtest items corresponds as closely as possible to the familiar bell-shaped curve of a normal distribution. The IQ, in Wechsler's tests, represents an index of rank order on a composite ability test converted to a standard score that has been related to a hypothesized normal distribution. As Layzer (1972) points out: "The inference that IQ is a measure of intelligence depends on certain assumptions, namely: (a) that there exists an underlying one-dimensional metric character related to IQ in a one-to-one way ... and (b) that the values assumed by this character in a suitable reference population are normally distributed."

Wechsler's tests sample a wide variety of abilities from the cognitive and psychomotor domains. They provide a standardized profile of the subject's scores, a verbal IQ, a performance IQ, and a full-scale IQ that refers to "overall" ability. As Guilford (1967) suggests, Wechsler

2. The most recent form of this scale is known as the Wechsler Adult Intelligence Scale (1958).

CHAPTER ONE

wanted to have his cake and eat it too: to pay homage to the concept of a unidimensional metric "intelligence" and yet to tap differential abilities. In doing so, Wechsler reflected the theoretical controversy that was current in academic circles concerning the general or specific nature of intelligence. Yet, as Guilford points out, both Binet's and Wechsler's tests redundantly overemphasize convergent thinking in the semantic domain while underrepresenting or ignoring other aspects of intellectual functioning.

INTELLIGENCE: GENERAL OR SPECIFIC

The successors of Galton and Spencer—Spearman, Pearson, and Burt—were much influenced by the preeminent British neurologists of the day. They conceived of intelligence as a "monarchic," superordinate ability related to the extensiveness of cerebral neuronal connections and organization and controlled by the genes.

To pursue the matter further, Spearman (1927), using a mathematical analysis of his own design, examined the results of a large number of people on a variety of ability tests. He extracted, from the intercorrelations of the test scores, a common factor that he entitled g and a number of more specific factors $s_1, s_2, \ldots, s_n$. Factor g was related to the monarchic concept: a quintessentially pure intellectual power, unadul-

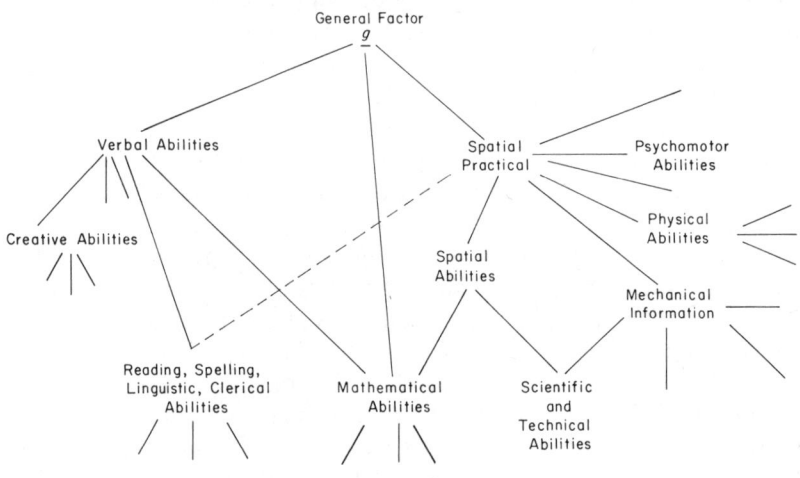

FIGURE 1.1 The hierarchy of intellectual functions (after Vernon 1969)

What Is Intelligence?

terated by emotion or values, that permeates all cognition. Factor g was also associated with a large number of subordinate special abilities that are involved in specific tasks. Learning to play the piano, for example, involves g; but it also requires s_{music}, a special musical ability, if the learner is to achieve high quality.

Spearman, Burt, and Vernon (see Figure 1.1) have described intelligence as a hierarchy of superordinate and subordinate functions, with g at the apex. These interpretations have been derived from the analysis of a wide variety of ability tests applied to Euro-American adults and schoolchildren. The pursuit of g has provided an abiding interest for British psychometricians during this century.

Across the Atlantic, on the other hand, psychologists such as Thorndike (1927), Thurstone (1955), and Guilford (1967) disputed the preeminence of g. The statistical evidence from their research pointed to a large number of specific abilities with a smaller number of more abstract second-order factors. Vernon (1969) suggests that the difference between the American and British findings was caused by the fact that the British applied their tests to a broader, more heterogeneous population whereas the Americans concentrated on more homogeneous college samples. In any case, as Butcher (1968) points out, it has become clear that statistical evidence alone cannot settle this dispute. The factor-analytic techniques introduced by Spearman are formal methods for classifying test performance; they should not, alone, be used to identify basic abilities (Vernon 1969). As this point became apparent, the controversy cooled off in stalemate.

THAT ELUSIVE DEFINITION

Other trends had become apparent by mid-century. Earlier "purist" behaviorists attempted to discard the concept of "intelligence," which they saw as a mentalistic fiction obscuring more than it illuminates. More recently, neo-behaviorists have attempted to employ computer analogues to explain complex thinking in terms of more molecular intermediate mechanisms. From another point of view, educational sociologists reacted against the idea of an immutable, inherent intelligence and pointed out the importance of early environment and schooling in shaping the abilities tapped by intelligence tests.

From about 1950, the internally consistent theoretical system of Piaget has been increasingly influential in the West. Piaget describes intelligence (operational thinking) as an adaptation evolving out of congenital, inborn, species-universal *schemata* or primordial behavioral organizations. Cognitive development is a spiral interaction between innate schemata, biological maturation, and the environment. It proceeds through an invariant sequence of recognizable stages toward increasing objectivity and abstraction. Intelligence in maturity should be regarded not as a continuous quantity, like water in a pitcher, but rather as the accumulation of stable, flexible, and interrelated *structures* of mental organization.

As the layman became more confident in the use of the term *intelligence*, psychologists became more confused. Those who agreed that the term had utility saw it as an abstraction, the broadest and most pervasive cognitive trait, involved in all intellectual skills. There was a general consensus that its unity should be more than merely statistical; it should refer to psychological function, a quintessentially high-level skill of integrative nature at the summit of the hierarchy of all other cognitive skills (Butcher 1968). But how was the skill to be defined? Here is a sample of attempts to pin down this elusive abstraction:

1. The ability to carry on abstract thinking (Terman)
2. The capacity to acquire capacity (Woodrow)
3. The eduction of relations and correlates (Spearman)
4. The power of good responses from the point of view of truth or fact (Thorndike)
5. Action in the process of formulation; the capacity to live a trial-and-error existence with alternatives that are as yet only incomplete conduct (Thurstone)
6. The aggregate or global capacity of the individual to act purposefully, think rationally, and deal effectively with his environment (Wechsler)

There are numerous others. Freeman (1940) divided them into those emphasizing power of adaptation, those emphasizing capacity for learning, and those emphasizing ability for abstract thinking.

As Butcher describes, there is a conflict between those who want an *open definition* and those who want an *operational definition*. An open definition is one that is broad, able to be modified in the light of new information, and capable of generating empirical research. The operational definition of a term specifies the procedure to be followed in its measurement (for example: "intelligence is the score in IQ on the Wechsler-Bellevue Adult Intelligence Scale"). Butcher points out that there are too many IQ tests for IQ to be considered a satisfactory operational definition of intelligence. Until psychologists have formulated laws of intellectual functioning that have predictive value, contemporary attempts at operational definition are arbitrary, narrow, and without sound scientific basis. As it stands, the operational definition refers to an ability to perform on a test the construction and implementation of which have been influenced by cultural factors.

CROSS-CULTURAL APPLICATIONS

The application of Western intelligence tests to other ethnic and cultural groups has been hampered by numerous problems aside from the theoretical and methodological issues already described. There are obvious language difficulties that defy translators. Correct performance in the usual test items requires exposure to a common educational system. Motivational factors are also problematical. Do the subjects comprehend and support the purpose of the test? Are Western subjects rendered "sophisticated" in test behavior by the achievement-oriented school system they have experienced? These issues are of more than theoretical importance. How are the authorities to select from a group of New Guinea village children those who are likely to benefit most from formal education when only a limited number of school places are available? How are candidates for officer training to be selected for Niugini's Pacific Island Regiment? The elitist trends of Western education are thus inherent in tests exported to foreign climes.

Attempts have been made to reduce the educational and cultural weighting of tests applied to non-Western people These "culture-free," "culture-fair," or "status-fair" tests have tended to emphasize spatial and quantitative reasoning items such as the solution of matrix-problems and two- and three-dimensional design problems (as in Raven's matrices, Koh's blocks, the Queensland Test, or Cattell's culture-fair tests).[3] None of these tests has been adequate to eliminate racial differences in IQ, or socioeconomic status (SES) IQ differences within Western societies.

Jensen (1970a) has reviewed the criteria of status-fair ability tests. Some tests have been designed—that is, their constituent items have been selected—in such a way as to minimize SES differences. Jensen takes issue with this approach since it is based on the assumption that there is no basic SES or interracial difference in cognitive ability. The assumption is unwarranted, according to Jensen, and unlikely. Jensen also suggests that Anastasi's (1964) criterion—a culture-fair test should control relevant cultural parameters—is too slippery. It can always be applied *post hoc:* how can the test designer ever know whether all relevant parameters have been controlled? Test results can always be rejected on this basis.

Jensen considers that a test which has low correlations with relevant environmental variables—parental income, occupation, education; quality of housing; size of family; educational attainment—is more likely to be status-fair. A test that is very resistant to improvement after practice is also likely to be more status- or culture-fair. Although it should

---

3. These tests are reviewed and described in Brislin, Lonner, and Thorndike (1973).

CHAPTER ONE

not be assumed that the mean scores for high-status, low-status, or different cultural groups should be the same, the statistically determined factorial structure of the test applied should be similar in both groups. In particular, the test results for both groups should be heavily and equivalently saturated with g, the general ability factor. As Jensen points out, no test that taps g in contrasting social or cultural groups has failed to show differences in mean scores for those groups. He therefore proposes a more basic theoretical criterion: A test is culture-free or culture-fair to the degree that it measures inherited potential. *Phenotype* is the physical or behavioral expression of *genotype* (innate, genetically determined potential) after interaction during development between genes and environment. Physical height in maturity, for example, is determined by many inherited genes and by the effect, upon genetically determined biological structure, of intrauterine environment, the process of birth, nutrition after birth, and freedom from (or exposure to) noxious diseases and adverse psychological experiences. Intelligence (that is, what IQ tests measure) is also determined by many genes which, in turn, interact with intrauterine, perinatal, and postnatal factors to produce the behavioral phenotype of IQ in maturity. According to Jensen, the genetic component of IQ can be determined by applying the mathematical formulas of population statistics to IQ correlations in close and not-so-close kin, a subject that will be discussed in chapter 2. (Note that Jensen has, essentially, adopted an operational definition of intelligence.) Accepting that this is so, it is theoretically possible to determine the degree to which the variance in the test scores of a given population is determined by hereditary factors. (Variance is a measure of the spread of scores in a population the individuals of which have been measured in some way along a continuous scale.) Jensen suggests that a test is fair to the extent that its results in a given population correlate with heredity. Technically speaking, the heritability or genotype/phenotype ratio should approximate 1; and the IQ estimated by the test, ideally, should be determined predominantly by hereditary in contrast to environmental factors.

PROBLEMS IN CROSS-CULTURAL TESTING

Unfortunately, there is many a slip between the cup of theoretical design and the lip of application. What are the *extrinsic* and *intrinsic* factors that hamper the application of culture-fair or status-fair tests?

A cross-cultural psychiatrist once asked a young tribal Aboriginal woman about the origin of babies. He wondered if she understood the connection between coitus and conception, and pursued the issue with a series of open questions. Yes, she agreed, babies come from the dreaming time, from the branches of totemic trees where they wait for the right time to enter the womb. Yes, the occasion for their entry is a dream, by the father, about having a baby; so the father, through the dream, provides the implanting force in cooperation with the spirit world. Other parallel traditional mythical explanations were elaborated until the young woman, getting the drift of the questions and exasperated by the persistence of the interrogator, said, disgustedly, "Course—you got to fuckim too!"

Earlier anthropologists who concluded that Aborigines had not connected coitus and conception had missed the point. Their investigation involved the questioning of dignified elders who assumed that the Westerners would, like sensible people, take the crassly obvious for granted. Their answers, therefore, were framed in broad, philosophical and spiritual terms, much in the way that the same question put to a Western physiologist or a priest would evoke answers to do with meiosis, hormonal levels, or divine design. Once, as a quite raw cross-cultural psychiatrist, I asked the same question of a group of "primitive" Aboriginal women, through an interpreter. They looked at me with some disbelief. One woman stifled her giggling as another nudged her in the ribs. Slowly, and with a broad smile, the spokeswoman of the group pointed to the heavens. They all burst into laughter. It was not the first time that the elaborate plodding gracelessness of white people has amused Aborigines.

The desire to evaluate knowledge or performance is a Western characteristic. The desire to achieve in an assessment test in competition with others is peculiarly Western. Motivational factors affect the data derived from evaluation techniques in the same way that they determine the context in which specific abilities will be expressed. Psychological tests may give us leads about what a person can do; but not about what that person *cannot* do (Cole et al. 1971).

Psychological tests attempt to evaluate a *sample* of performance in a *reliable* and *valid* way. It would not be possible to test all performances; the sample must be a representative one. From a (hopefully) valid and reliable estimate, usually expressed as some kind of measurement, comparisons between individuals can be made. From the evaluation of performance, conclusions about ability are drawn. If these conclusions are to have any weight, a complex and interacting variety of prerequisites must be satisfied. Some of the most important of these prerequisites are:

1. The sample of behavior that constitutes the test must be judiciously chosen—representative enough not to distort conclusions, yet economic enough to satisfy the practical exigencies of testing. This is known as *content validity*.
2. The test should have *predictive validity*. It should accurately predict (either now or in the future) what it purports to predict.
3. The test must be administered and assessed in a *standardized way* so

Chapter One

       that the same kind of performance sample is drawn from all subjects and evaluated by the same criteria.
4. Experience with the test should have proved it to be *reliable*: different testers, or the same tester at different times, should get comparable results from the same subject (provided the attribute being tested is stable).
5. The subject's performance should be *maximized*. This is a complex requirement involving the optimization of the tester-testee relationship, the elimination of extraneous variables (such as subject anxiety and fatigue), and the unequivocal motivation of the testee. Subjects should *want* to do their best. It is important to ensure that the content, the construction, the administration, and the purpose of the test are comprehensible to and accepted by the subject.
6. The test should have *construct validity*. Its contents should be based on empirically derived theoretical principles which it, in turn, puts to the test. If the empirically determined principles are sustained, then laws may be derived from which scientifically valid definitions and measures can be framed and designed.

Brislin, Lonner, and Thorndike (1973) ask certain questions of prospective cross-cultural testers along the following lines:

> What evidence is there to support the cross-cultural appropriateness of the items in the test?
> Can ethnographic evidence be produced to support the items selected?
> If the test is verbal and involves a different language group, can one be sure that the translation is adequate and comprehended in the way required?
> What is the best possible way to administer the test to the group in question? What are the problem areas?
> Has the content validity been checked? Is the test representative of the conceptual framework to be understood? Does ethnographic evidence support this?
> What is the natural range of the behavior being measured in this culture? Does the environment allow the development of extreme individual differences or at least a reasonable variation of performance?
> Has the construct to be measured been defined in a culturally appropriate and valid way?
> Have predictive and construct validity been clearly distinguished?
> Have (unbiased) norms been established for the culture in question? If multinational norms are used, has it been checked that they are based on similar parameters (for example, age and sex) for the cultures studied?

WHAT IS INTELLIGENCE?

These are stiff prerequisites. Keeping them in mind, one can critically examine the cross-cultural and subcultural applicability of intelligence tests.

The reliability and validity of most intelligence tests concern school performance. Designed initially to predict this, they have been validated, by circular logic, against each other and against school performance. IQ tests get at behavior valued by teachers. The relevance of this behavior for the world outside the classroom is a matter for conjecture, at least. Despite this, conclusions about general ability have repeatedly been drawn from such tests. Ability for what? It may be little more than aptitude for doing well on tests and playing the kind of word games that schools foster (McClelland 1973).

The degree to which the subject's performance is maximized is often open to question. Motivational factors are very important. Is the subject comfortable with a white, usually male, adult? Does the subject comprehend the content, construction, and purpose of the test? Does the subject concur with the purpose of the test? Does it make sense to the subjects to do their best under the circumstances of the test? These requirements are frequently (? usually) open to question with younger children in general and in all subjects from other than a white, middle-class, achievement-oriented, educationally sophisticated background.

In a cross-cultural or cross-status setting, content validity may be difficult to attain. Does the test evoke performance that is representative of the way the competence is expressed naturally? Does the child understand the language of the test? This may be a serious problem where a minority subcultural group such as Afro-Americans speak a dialectal variant of standard English and, in addition, are unfamiliar with the context in which they are expected to display their abilities (Labov 1970a).

The overriding criticism of IQ tests is of their construct validity. Intelligence tests are not based on empirically derived, empirically tested, and empirically stated theoretical laws of intellectual functioning. The operational definition employed by Jensen (1969a) is arbitrary. Jensen (1970a) compares the measurement of intelligence with an IQ test to the determination of temperature with a thermometer. But the latter is based on a scientific understanding of heat through the laws of thermodynamics; whereas the former has no such foundation. Indeed, Jensen's own work on different types of learning facility aims at deriving more fundamental and heuristic principles (Jensen 1968a). Until, through cross-cultural research, we have defined the fundamental spectrum of human abilities and the laws of their interaction and operation, intelligence tests and similar instruments should be restricted to the utilitarian purpose for which they were designed: to predict performance in a Western educational system.

CHAPTER ONE

Jensen (1968a, 1973c) himself is by no means unaware of the circularity of much of the rationale in this field. McClelland (1973) goes further, in a devastating attack on the practice of educational testing. Tests do, indeed, predict school performance. "The games people play on aptitude tests are similar to the games teachers require people to play in school." But it has not been universally easy to correlate school performance with other abilities (apart, of course, from doing well on tests). There is, as anticipated, a correlation between educational level attained (high school or college) and occupational status because certain qualifications open certain desirable career doors. McClelland questions whether society should continue to allow teachers and educational psychologists to determine who merits education, when the performance of interest to teachers has doubtful relevance to anything outside of school. There is, further, little evidence that the scholastic aptitude results of college students correlate with their later accomplishments. McClelland suggests that Terman's (1959) famous studies of the gifted and their development may mean little more than this: The power elite have children who are offered more opportunities and who do better in life. Terman's studies did not control for opportunity. In short, IQ tests—like black skin relative to white—are good predictors of school performance; but this is a far cry from a "general ability factor." Psychologists created serious fallacies when they induced the public to believe that mental tests had a wider validity.[4]

DIFFERENT TYPES OF INTELLIGENCE

The obvious confusion in the field of intelligence—in regard to definition, evaluation, and cultural differences—has stimulated a number of eminent scientists to impose some order on the contemporary chaos. Hebb (1949), for example, proposed a distinction between *intelligence A*, innate potential, and *intelligence B*, the product of an interaction between hereditary and environmental factors. Intelligences A and B are therefore equivalent to genotype and phenotype, respectively. As Vernon (1969) points out, intelligence B is not a universal single faculty which varies along one dimension in people and races (the water in a pitcher theory) but, rather, the name for an accumulation of different cognitive skills developed in, and valued by, different cultural groups. In the West one of the skills valued—particularly by teachers and psychometricians—has to do with abstract, verbal, symbolic, relational problem-solving (factor *g*). Aware of other confusions, Vernon adds a further intelligence—*intel-

---

4. McClelland goes too far in making his cogent point. A correlation of .40 to .60 between SES and IQ has consistently been found in industrial societies with universal education and social mobility (Jensen 1973c).

ligence C—to the previously mentioned A and B. Intelligence C refers to test scores which may, or may not, reliably reflect intelligences A and B.

Cattell (1963) has distinguished between *fluid general intelligence* and *crystallized general intelligence*: g_f and g_c. Intelligence g_f is a basic general brightness that can be applied to new learning situations. It is thought to be closely related to innate, genetic determinants. Intelligence g_c represents the outcome of the interaction between g_f and the culture in which the individual lives. The answer to the question *Who wrote Hamlet?* is heavily culture-loaded and thus more clearly relevant to g_c in English-speaking Western countries. The solution of a pattern-reproduction problem involving the manipulation of three-dimensional blocks is regarded as representative of g_f. Cattell has designed a culture-fair test that aims to tap g_f and, thus, intrinsic ability stripped of irrelevant cultural material.

Jensen (1961, 1963, 1966, 1969a) has attempted to pare away the culturally determined superstructure of cognitive abilities in order to investigate basic processes. He suggests that *learning rate* is the most simple definition of the biologically based ability underlying intelligence tests. In a series of experiments with retarded, average, disadvantaged, and advantaged children he has discriminated two types of ability, levels 1 and 2. His findings will be described in more detail in chapter 2; but, briefly, level 1 refers to associative, rote learning, and level 2 to abstract problem-solving. According to Jensen (1969a), these two types of ability have become differentially distributed in the population of the United States according to social class. Lower-social-class children perform as well as middle-class children on tests of level 1, but they are well below the more advantaged on tests of level 2. Jensen is currently attempting to investigate in more detail the cognitive components of levels 1 and 2.

A SPECTRUM OF COMPETENCIES

Within the ranks of cross-cultural psychologists a different interpretation of cognitive abilities has appeared. The workers associated with this approach have been influenced by anthropology and by experience in the field. Their work will be described in more detail in chapter 7, but a brief outline is useful at this point.

Irvine (1969b) has pointed out that different cultures value and emphasize different kinds of ability. Cole et al. (1971) assert that culture determines not only the different kinds of ability that will be emphasized but also the contexts and strategies of their expression. Berry (1973b) and Berry and Dasen (1973) describe how, whenever psychologists enter an alien culture or subculture, they do so with inescapable preconceptions about the nature of, say, intelligent behavior. Their initial aim should be

Chapter One

to study manifestations of the behavior in question from within the culture. The crude application of Western psychological tests associated with Western educational modes is a common example of the least satisfactory approach. The aim of psychologists should be to tap and assess behavior emphasized by that culture. If some of their preconceptions are confirmed, well and good; generalizations can be derived. If generalizations are confirmed across a number of cultures—for example, that the fostering of independence in child-rearing is related to the ability to analyze the detail of complex pictures—then tentative universal laws may be further derived for testing (Berry 1971). Whether or not different cultures foster different kinds of skill depends, ultimately, on ecological pressures. The notion of a universal unitary g fades like a mirage. It is an artifact of the ethnocentric glasses through which we view those alien to us. Factor g is most appropriately regarded as an ability to do with abstract symbolic problem-solving, and as but one of a broader spectrum of competencies that is of great importance in Western education and in some kinds of scientific, technological, and academic work. Its chief value inheres in the way it facilitates conceptual superordination, a matter that will be taken up in chapter 7.

Despite the ubiquity of its use in advanced countries, the concept of intelligence has become hopelessly confused. Under a freight of distracting semantic connotations, fragmented by different levels of interpretation (A, B, or C?; g_f or g_c?; level 1 or level 2?) the venerable concept is collapsing. In my opinion it would be better to discard it and use different terms to refer to specific issues. For this purpose, I propose the following definitions:

> *Potential*: The aggregate of those genetically determined possibilities that add together and interact with each other and the environment during maturation to produce competence. The interaction process is the process of *realization*.
> *Competence*: The aggregate at any point in time of the hierarchically organized and stabilized abilities that determine the quality and nature of performance. Competence is multidimensional. It denotes internal organizations—structures—and the strategies and tactics of their expression. It is best thought of as a multidimensional spectrum and profile, with depth and range.
> *Performance*: The manner in which underlying competence is expressed. Performance is behavior organized (1) in response to adaptive problems that have been mastered in the past and (2) resulting from the application of competence to novel problems.
> *Evaluation*: The technical instruments—tests—or the data from

What Is Intelligence?

Potential → Realization → Competence → Expression → Performance
evolves to   which is expressed as
                                              ↓ Assessment
                                              which is assessed as
                                              ↓
                                              Evaluation Data

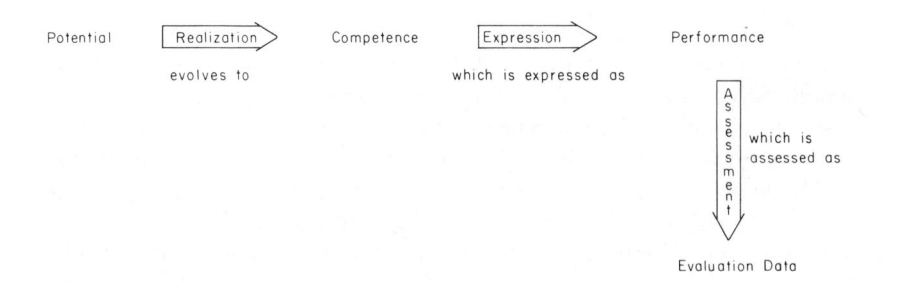

FIGURE 1.2 Potential, competence, and performance

them—evaluation data—or the technical processes—assessment—that aim to sample and measure performance and to provide inferences about competence.

Competencies are evolved, in time, from the realization of potential. Realization is the complex interaction between (1) genetic potential, (2) the pre- and perinatal environment, and (3) postnatal environmental stimulation, nutrition, and health on a backdrop of (4) genetically determined, phasic maturation. Potential, competence, and performance are multidimensional. Competence and potential can be inferred only after performance has been sampled in evaluation. Competence is expressed as performance. Performance is sampled in evaluation. The flow diagram in Figure 1.2 illustrates this discussion.

In this paradigm, potential and competence are equivalent to Hebb's intelligences A and B, whereas evaluation data correspond to Vernon's intelligence C. Cattell's g_f and g_c are different aspects of competence, g_f, theoretically, correlating more closely with the abstract-conceptual aspect of a complex potential. Spearman's g—abstract, symbolic, relational reasoning ability—is one kind of competence heavily stressed, though poorly fostered,[5] in traditional Western schooling.

I suggest that the use of this rational paradigm will clear the underbrush and eliminate much argument based on semantic confusion. The way it can illuminate contemporary research findings and lead to research predictions will be demonstrated in chapters 6, 7, and 8. In the rest of this book I will restrict myself, where possible, to the terms defined in this chapter and avoid such confusions as "intelligence" (A, B, or C), g, "capacity," "aptitude," "achievement," and "ability."

5. Engelmann (1970) makes this point. Western schools assume the basis for such thinking in those who enter at kindergarten level. They do little to promote it systematically. Engelmann describes how such skills can be objectified and taught.

CHAPTER ONE

SUMMARY

All cultures code the concept "intelligent" in some way, although there is a considerable variation in the specific behavior most valued and emphasized. There is a large gap between this notion and the Western scientific concept of "intelligence" which has roots in the literary, verbal, scholastic traditions of the eighteenth century and before. Thus verbal symbolic problem-solving is heavily emphasized in the West.

For this reason, the first intelligence tests were (and still are) saturated with symbolic reasoning. Factorial analysis of the results tended to produce a hierarchical structure of abilities surmounted by a quintessential factor g to do with abstract reasoning. Statistical psychologists tended to extract from their test results the factors (such as g) that they had built into the design of the test items (that is, learning and response styles emphasized in Western school systems). The preeminence of g was disputed, however, and various definitions of "intelligence" have shown confusing disparities. Operational definitions are rendered doubtful because of a failure to derive empirical laws of intelligent behavior.

Intelligence tests have been applied to different cultures and subcultures with limited success, despite a concerted attempt to devise instruments free of culturally loaded items. Jensen has discussed a number of criteria of "culture-fairness." He considers that the test with results which correlate most highly with heritability is the most likely to be culture-fair. In other words, a test is culture-fair to the extent that the variance of its scores in a given population is determined by heredity. But there are many extrinsic and intrinsic problems in the implementation of intelligence tests, especially in non-Western cultures. Stringent prerequisites must be satisfied before the test can be considered reliable or valid.

A number of writers have attempted to discriminate between different aspects or levels of intelligence. The resulting confusion between genetically determined potential, inferred competence, and evaluation data has rendered the field, and the very term *intelligence*, hopelessly confused. Thus I propose and define concepts that are intended to supersede this outmoded concept and clear the semantic underbrush for more fruitful work.

CHAPTER 2
THE GREAT DEBATE

There is not a scrap of silver in (Britain), nor any hope of booty except from slaves; but I don't fancy you will find any of them with literary or musical talent.

Cicero (54 B.C.)

The number amongst the negroes of those whom we should call half-witted men is very large. . . . The mistakes the negroes made in their own matters were so childish, stupid and simpleton-like as frequently to make me ashamed of my own species. I do not think it any exaggeration to say, that their c is as low as our e, which would be a difference of two grades. . . . The Australian type is at least one grade below the African negro.

Sir Francis Galton (1869)

THE DIFFERENT FACES OF IGNORANCE

Dominant peoples cannot but see themselves and their own cultures as on a pinnacle. From the heights, others are viewed as "savage", "barbarian", "childish", "primitive", or "underdeveloped". The prevailing, inescapable ethnocentric bias, dressed in the language of science, has sometimes permeated cross-cultural psychology. In this chapter, a recent revival of the nature-nurture controversy is discussed in regard to American blacks, together with some of the fallacies that pervade the arguments of those who have taken either side in a violent controversy.

All of us are chauvinists. Scratch the veneer, if there is a veneer, and one finds a fearful animal who shies away from or attacks those who are physically or culturally different, justifying his reaction by referring to skin color, physical characteristics, unacceptability of customs, or an inferred malevolence on the part of those rejected. Primitive revulsion is balanced by other forces: curiosity, wonder, pleasure at acceptance, and the desire to share and help, expressed, perhaps, in the form of philosophical systems such as Christianity and Buddhism that stress the common nature and potential of humanity. The problem is akin to that which seeks to find whether we are fundamentally good or bad. Are we fundamentally antagonistic or cooperative?

In Australia, in the nineteenth century, Aborigines were viewed by white colonists as repellent and irredeemable or as pests like the kangaroo. Their subhuman image enabled the hard men of the frontier to lend a hand in their extermination. There was only so much useful land and farmers, pastoralists, their livestock, Aborigines, and native animals were in competition for it. At least one of these groups had to go. The resulting unofficial policy of genocide was reflected in the popular literature of the era (Chase and von Sturmer 1973):

> The blacks of Australia are, with the exception of the Bosjeman, the lowest and most irreclaimable of the native tribes with which we are acquainted ... but although occasional instances of affection and fidelity are found amongst them, just as we meet with tame foxes and pheasants, they are as a race truly irreclaimable. [*Illustrated London News*, April 24, 1852:314]

> Without a history, they [the Aborigines] have no past; without a religion they have no hope; without the habits of forethought and providence they can have no future. Their doom is sealed. [Woods 1879:38]

> [They are] deceitful, suspicious, slippery time-servers or dissemblers. ... Judging from the number of their skulls in my possession, I should say that permanent improvement with grown individuals, if not impossible, is a very difficult achievement. [Victorian phrenologist]

As Chase and von Sturmer have pointed out, evolutionists reflected the prevailing ethos:

> If we take into account the creasing of the cerebral surface, the differences between the brain of a Shakespeare and that of an Australian savage would doubtless be fifty times greater than the difference between the Australian's brain and that of an orang-outang. [Fiske 1893:71–72]

Australia was viewed as an evolutionary backwater where

> ... many a quaint old-fashioned creature, many an antediluvian oddity, which would long ago have been rudely elbowed out of existence in more progressive countries, has been suffered to jog along in this preserve of Nature's own. [Frazer 1961:1023]

The Aborigines, in their timeless cul-de-sac, were Darwinian relics, like the duckbilled platypus, sadly but inexorably bound to wither away under the pressure of the more vigorous Anglo-Saxon race.

A closer acquaintance with their way of life revealed some unexpected facts. Their technology and resourcefulness were highly adaptive to a harsh environment. Their languages and social customs were

The Great Debate

very complex—in some ways, more so than those of the English. How could this be explained?

> The Australian natives exhibit a degree of mental activity which at first sight may be thought inconsistent with the childish position here assigned to them. ... This activity results from ... a development of the lower intellectual faculties. [Wake 1872:82]

Their complex tongue was explained, flip-flop, by a degeneration hypothesis. Aboriginal languages were rather

> ... remnants of a noble language than a tongue in the process of development. ... [They] must have descended to their barbarism from a state more nearly approaching civilization. [Taplin 1879:119]

Others took a more active approach. The Aborigines, though sunk in degradation, might be reclaimed through their children:

> Our chief hope now is decidedly in the children; and the complete success as far as regards their education and civilization would be before us, if it were possible to remove them from the influence of their parents.[1]

The reader may even detect distant echoes of the missionary approach in the later chapters of this book. None of us is untouched by the history of his society.

The popular contemporary stereotype of Aborigines is of a shifty, footloose, improvident, backward race, dispossessed of their land, and either hopelessly beyond help or desperately in need of it. In contrast with this static image, the stereotype of the American black is changing. The fun-loving, unreliable, gullible, musical caricature is breaking up under the influence of black political pressure and a new-found sense of pride in identity.

Psychologists, and other scientists, cannot avoid the *Zeitgeist*. The application of "culture-fair" tests to primitive peoples was claimed to reveal the undeveloped basis of their reasoning powers:

> Actually, the central Australians were only somewhat below the two ethnic groups with the best maze performances. ... The lowest scores were achieved by the Negritos of the Zambali mountains in Luzon, the Sakai-Jeram of the Perak coast regions and the Bushmen of the Kalahari. [Porteus 1961]

Anthropologists, on the other hand, pointed out the ethnocentric bias of such investigations. The very process of comparing races according to some preconceived scale (as well as the scale itself) is rooted in Western man's tunnel vision of the world. But lingering doubts remained. Could

---

1. From the South Australian Protector's report, July 1840, quoted in Rowley (1970).

CHAPTER TWO

there be genetically determined differences in cognitive potential, one race having more than another? By the middle of this century a decided reaction had set in. Most reputable scientists rejected the hypothesis of racial differences. In 1951, UNESCO stated:

> ... there is no proof that the groups of mankind differ in their innate mental characteristics, whether in respect of intelligence or temperament. The scientific evidence indicates that the range of mental capacities in all ethnic groups is much the same. [Klineberg 1951]

As Vernon (1969) has pointed out, it would have been more correct to say that there was no reliable evidence one way or the other. Any reference to racially determined differences in potential had become equivalent to uttering an obscenity. The liberal viewpoint of environmentalism had become an orthodoxy. Little wonder, then, that a recent detailed exposition of a heretical view was greeted with a shock similar to the fracas in Vienna when Freud first expounded his theory of infantile sexuality.

THE JENSENIST HERESY

In 1969, writing in *The Harvard Educational Review*, Arthur Jensen exploded a psychological bombshell the reverberations of which are still felt. The article in question presented a closely reasoned argument concerning possible racial differences in innate intellectual potential. It provoked a deluge of criticism, refutation, misrepresentation, threat, and even physical attack on those who lined up on Jensen's side. And the pitched battle that ensued has often done little credit to Jensen's adversaries. Jensen has asserted that there should be "no holds barred" in science; no question, properly and respectfully examined, should be sacrosanct. He referred here to the duty of scientists to investigate the most sacred of cows if need be—not to the acceptability of any weapon in a scientific dispute.

Jensen's hypothesis requires a close examination; it will be summarized in this section: The Jensenist Heresy (a colorful phrase coined by H. J. Eysenck). Jensen began by asserting that attempts to help disadvantaged—particularly black—children in the United States through preschool compensatory programs have apparently failed. He considers that there is evidence suggesting the reason may lie in an inherent difference in cognitive potential between blacks and whites. Intelligence is reliably and validly measured by various standard intelligence tests that intercorrelate highly. So measured, intelligence correlates highly with scholastic and occupational achievement. The general factor (g) that pervades intelligence tests and scholastic achievement is best described as a competence in abstract reasoning, logical problem-solving, and

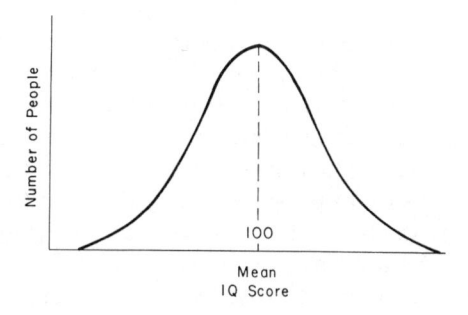

FIGURE 2.1 The distribution of IQ scores in a population

cross-modality transfer. Intelligence, therefore, should not be regarded as synonymous with "mental ability" but rather, as a particular kind of mental ability that is stressed in Western Education.[2] Intelligence is a concept derived from empirical data, analogous to the concept of the atom. Just as fluctuations in heat can be measured by a thermometer and expressed as "temperature," so can variations in g-type cognitive competence be measured by tests and expressed as "intelligence." Jensen therefore adopts an operational approach: Intelligence is defined by IQ score.

When the distribution of mental ability scores in a large population is examined, it is found to spread out over a *normal distribution* (see Figure 2.1). (Actually there is always a slightly greater than expected proportion of the population at each end of the IQ continuum. At the lower end this is due to an accumulation of those who have biological defects such as mongolism.) Another important phenomenon is known as *regression to the mean:* the progeny of parents who are low or high on the IQ continuum tend to have IQs closer to the mean. Bright parents have rather less bright children; dull parents have somewhat brighter children. These phenomena—normal distribution and regression to the mean—have been found by geneticists to be associated with polygenic inheritance: that is, the derivation of a phenotypic trait not from a single gene but from a number of genes. Normal distribution and regression are therefore consistent with the genetic theory of intelligence.

Population geneticists have proposed a number of mathematical formulas to derive the value of a factor known as heritability (h^2). Jensen himself has made original contributions to this field (Jensen 1967, 1969a).

---

2. In Jensen's terms (1973c), "intelligence cannot be equated with overall behavioral adaptability. It is but one aspect of the total spectrum of human abilities, albeit a uniquely important aspect in the industrialized world."

Chapter Two

The value of h^2 is derived from the differences between the IQs of different degrees of kin. It is defined as the proportion of the variance of IQ, in a population, that is determined by genetic in contrast to environmental factors. (Variance refers to the degree of spread of the distribution of population scores on a continuous scale; it is the average of the squared differences between individual measurements and the mean.) It varies from 0 to 1. If h^2 is .5, for example, then the balance, .5, is the proportion of the population variance due to environmental (postconceptional) factors. This is symbolized as e^2 ($e^2 = 1 - h^2$).

The simplest empirical derivation of h^2 is from IQ differences in twins. Monozygotic (MZ) twins are from one egg and therefore have the same genetic makeup. Dizygotic (DZ) twins are from two eggs and are therefore no more alike, genetically, than siblings. If MZ twins are reared together, theoretically they should have the same IQ since their environment and genes are identical. If MZ twins are reared separately, the difference in IQ between them should be accounted for by differences in environment. DZ twins reared together should have an IQ difference accounted for by the difference in their genes since, theoretically, their environments are identical. DZ twins reared apart should have differences in IQ due to their genetic difference plus the difference in environments. Note that this reasoning assumes a perfect world: that MZ and DZ twins are treated identically by their parents; that no physical factors such as intrauterine starvation or birth damage affect one twin more than the other; and that the genetic equipment of MZ twins is always identical.

Erlenmeyer-Kimling and Jarvik (1964) have surveyed fifty-two studies of IQ in different degrees of kinship. These studies were carried out in eight different countries, over a period of fifty years, using a variety of intelligence tests. They derived the correlations in Table 2.1. The marked consistency of such findings for these and other kinship correlations, in a considerable number of studies, provides strong support to the theory of genetic preponderance in the development of IQ.

TABLE 2.1 IQ Correlations Empirically Discovered (r) and Theoretically Expected on the Basis of Inheritance Alone (ρ)

	Median Correlation	
	Obtained (r)	Expected (ρ)
Siblings reared together	.49	.50
Siblings reared apart	.42	.50
DZ twins reared together	.53	.50
MZ twins reared apart	.75	1.0
MZ twins reared together	.87	1.0

MZ twins reared together should, theoretically, have perfect IQ correlation. If there were no environmental effect, MZ twins reared apart would share IQs. If there were an environmental effect then the correlation between the IQs of MZ twins reared apart should be reduced by a factor equivalent to e^2. Thus:

$$e^2 = 1 - r_{MZA} \qquad (1)$$

where r_{MZA} is the IQ correlation between MZ twins reared apart. Thus, from Table 2.1,

$$e^2 = 1 - .75 = .25 \qquad (2)$$

However, using the data of Burt (1958) the equation becomes

$$e^2 = 1 - .83 = .17 \qquad (3)$$

Jensen's formula for the derivation of heritability is

$$h^2 = \frac{r_{AB} - r_{CD}}{\rho_{AB} - \rho_{CD}} \qquad (4)$$

where: r_{AB} is the obtained correlation (corrected for test unreliability) in IQ between pairs of individuals of one particular degree of kinship

r_{CD} is the correlation between pairs of a lesser degree of kinship than AB

ρ_{AB} is the theoretical genetic correlation between pairs A and B

ρ_{CD} is the theoretical genetic correlation between pairs C and D

Applying formula (4) to the data in Table 2.1:

$$h^2 = \frac{r_{MZT} - r_{DZT}}{\rho_{MZT} - \rho_{DZT}} \qquad (5)$$

where: r_{MZT} is the obtained correlation for MZ twins reared together

r_{DZT} is the obtained correlation for DZ twins reared together

ρ_{MZT}, ρ_{DZT} are the theoretical correlations for the two degrees of kinship, reared together

Thus:

$$h^2 = \frac{.87 - .53}{1.0 - .50} = .68 \qquad (6)$$

CHAPTER TWO

Other calculations based on kinship data place the value of h^2 at about .8, and therefore that of e^2 $(1-h^2)$ at .2. Jensen thus concludes that genetic factors are about four times as important as environmental factors in determining the variance in IQ scores in a population. In other words, since variance and h^2 are derived from squared differences, h and e (the relative contributions of genetic and environmental factors to *actual individual differences* in IQ) are in a ratio of $\sqrt{4}$ to $\sqrt{1}$ or 2 to 1.

Jensen has discussed the significance of these statistics at length and in numerous later articles. In a review of Dobzhansky's *Genetic Diversity and Human Equality* (Jensen 1974a), for example, he elaborates on the former's important concept of *reaction range* of phenotype—the range (for example, of IQ) through which identical genotypes will vary given the amount of environmental variation presently found in the population. Two-thirds of all individuals with the same genotype for IQ will be found within a ±7 point range around the mean IQ of all such individuals; however, the range over which 99 percent of identical genotypes can vary is more than 30 IQ points. This range is attributable to nongenetic factors which are at present little understood. Jensen himself concludes that "prenatal and early postnatal biological and nutritional factors and subtle aspects of early child-rearing practices and the parent-child interaction seem the most likely places to seek an understanding of most of the nongenetic influences on IQ" (1974a:432).

There are at least seven other statistical complexities that Jensen has discussed. First: like tends to mix with and select like. Bright husbands tend to meet, mix with, and marry bright wives, increasing the favorable genetic loading of their children. Second: some intelligence-enhancing genes may be completely or partially dominant over other genes at the same chromosomal locus. Third: some of the genes at different loci may interact and multiply their individual effects (*epistasis*). Fourth: some genes may have a multiplicative interaction with certain environmental factors. Fifth: the factors of population attenuation and score error must be corrected for in calculations. Sixth: it is not uncommon for one twin to be at a biological disadvantage *in utero* and for his potential to be reduced. Seventh: merely living in the same environment does not guarantee identical experiences for both twins. All these factors are considered and, where possible, accounted for in the calculation of population statistics. It must be strongly asserted here that h^2 does not express the degree to which an individual's IQ has been determined by his or her genes. It is a *population statistic*. It refers to the degree to which the spread of IQ scores is determined by genetic in contrast to nongenetic factors, in a particular population at a particular time. The twin data quoted by Jensen and Eysenck are derived from samples of white European or American populations, of rather homogeneous environmental background, over a period of some years up to the middle of this century. They cannot validly be applied to other populations, or to the same groups at other points of historical time. As Jensen points out, if environmental conditions maximally favorable to intellectual development prevailed, h^2 would approximate unity. Actually, in both black and white populations, h^2 appears to be lower in the lowest socioeconomic group, the reason for which is unclear (Jensen 1973c).

Jensen has discussed the importance of the environment in IQ development. The study of Skeels (1966) has often been quoted as supporting the importance of environmental factors. Skeels described the favorable outcome in IQ development of a group of institutional children who were first mothered by retarded older girls and then fostered out to advantaged private homes. In a follow-up of their adult status, Skeels found that all these children had become self-sufficient (despite a mean IQ at eighteen months of 64) and that their children had a mean IQ of 104. In contrast, a control group who had remained institutionalized during childhood did poorly, making no IQ gains. Jensen, although critical of the data provided, originally postulated that the environment is important as a *threshold effect*.[3] Below a certain level of stimulation, IQ development will be markedly retarded. Above a critical level, further enrichment makes little difference. Jensen compared this to the effect of nutrition on height. Most studies of marked IQ change after environmental improvement are associated with extreme deprivation, far beyond that found in the population as a whole and not comparable to the alleged cultural deprivation of minority groups. More recently, Jensen (1973c) has pointed out that the threshold hypothesis was introduced to account for the effect of later enrichment on grossly deprived children; but no clear data have been gathered to support it. The best evidence would be the finding of significantly higher h^2 in the advantaged than in the disadvantaged. It is true that h^2 calculated from the IQs of those gifted parents and their children studied by Terman (1959) is very high—higher than that calculated from an American rural sample; but this is tenuous evidence. If the h^2 of IQ in American blacks were known to be appreciably lower than that of whites, it would clearly indicate that the scale of environmental effect is greater for blacks. Jensen (1973c) reviews the available heritability estimates of black IQ in America and finds them wanting, mainly on the

---

3. It is interesting to note that Vernon (1969) has apparently misinterpreted Jensen's threshold hypothesis, but in doing so has provided an alternative hypothesis: below a certain level of genetic potential, environment is markedly important; above it the importance of environment decreases insofar as the development of competence is concerned. There seems to be little evidence to support this hypothesis.

basis of inadequate sample size (Vandenberg 1970; Osborne and Gregor 1968). A study by Scarr-Salapatek (1971) does, however, suggest that lower-SES groups have a lower h^2 and thus offers some support to the threshold hypothesis.

Jensen originally suggested that the environmental factors of subnutrition, poor prenatal maternal health, and prematurity are more likely to determine environmental causes of low IQ than the unspecified and vague psychosocial factors imputed by environmentalists. (Although, as he points out [Jensen 1973b], a Dutch study has failed to show intellectual deficits in young men conceived and gestated during a period of widespread famine in Holland during World War II.) He reviewed a number of compensatory programs that have claimed IQ boosts in culturally disadvantaged children and points out that the improvements are subject to erosion after the program ceases; that the gains may be due to a greater familiarity of the children with test situations; and that elements of the test may have been taught in the program itself. Such claims of IQ boosting, therefore, are suspect.

Jensen has also discussed the question of "race," defining the term, ultimately, as referring to different populations that can be distinguished on the basis of different distributions of gene frequencies. Although American blacks have a significant (perhaps an average of 20 to 30 percent) admixture of Caucasian genes, he considers that it is valid to regard them as forming a distinct gene pool and, therefore, a separate race.

Numerous investigations (summarized in Shuey 1966) have demonstrated a lower mean IQ for American blacks in comparison with whites. There are differences between rural and urban, northern and southern, and male and female means but the upshot is to suggest that blacks, on the average, score about 15 IQ points below whites—equivalent to about one standard deviation. In other words, there is an overlap between the curves for black and white IQ distributions, but only about 16 percent of the black population exceed the test performance of the average white. Even when socioeconomic (SES) factors are stacked in the black child's favor compared to whites, differences remain. Shuey discounted the effect of low self-concept, lack of confidence with white testers, and poor motivation. Jensen (1973c) too reviews the evidence on self-concept and finds it ambiguous. Jensen (1973c) also questions the validity of the work of Rosenthal and Jacobsen (1968) on the effect of the self-fulfilling prophecy of the teacher's (and, possibly, the tester's) expectation on the child's performance. He is not alone in this doubt (Thorndike 1968).

At the time of Jensen's original article, in 1969, there had been no direct studies of h^2 in black populations. Nevertheless, Jensen concluded that the weight of evidence tended to support a predominantly hereditary basis for IQ differences between social classes and races. He pointed out that American Indians, though even more environmentally depressed than blacks, score higher on evaluation tests (Coleman 1966). Thus cognitive competence is not clearly related to environmental background; some additional factor must be postulated to account for the depression of black IQ scores.

Jensen has referred to the work of Lesser, Fifer, and Clark (1965) on the different *patterns* of abilities found in different ethnic groups in one American city. Within each group there was the expected SES differential; but the patterns that distinguished the ethnic groups were quite consistent regardless of SES. It is not possible to say whether these pattern differences are due to heredity; but Jensen considers that the possibility should be investigated.

Jensen himself has carried out important research on the nature of intelligence. He has suggested that IQ tests, to varying degrees, get at a fundamental competence which is best characterized as *learning rate*, a concept he has attempted to define precisely. At first (Jensen 1961) he compared dull and bright Anglo and Chicano children on their ability in recall tasks (estimated from an IQ test: dull [IQs around 80]; bright [IQs around 115]). He found that dull and bright Anglos differed, as expected, but that there was little difference between the two levels of Chicano children and that their scores were close to those of the bright Anglos. Other experiments on trial-and-error learning (Jensen, Collins, and Vreeland 1962) with different IQ groups revealed a small group of retarded children (IQ 50 to 75) who performed as well as gifted children (IQ 135+). All the low-IQ children who were fast learners came from a culturally disadvantaged background. Rapier (1968) compared upper-, middle-, and lower-class children, matched for IQ, on serial and paired-associate learning tasks. (For a criticism of the validity of matching in this way, see Campbell and Erlebacher [1970].) She found that correlations between the evaluation data and IQ were from .41 to .60 in the upper-SES groups, but only .01 to .22 in the lower group, findings which have been corroborated in other studies. These tests of associative learning appear to be getting at a competence that is blurred by conventional IQ tests. How are the results to be interpreted? Jensen has proposed alternative hypotheses:

> 1. Tests of associative learning tap the basic ability that is determined predominantly by genetic factors. IQ tests tap this ability but superimpose on it a verbal, symbolic problem-solving form of thinking that is

Chapter Two

determined predominantly by the environment. Lower-SES children have lacked this necessary input and therefore do less well on standard IQ tests.
2. Mental competence is hierarchical. Level 1 competence involves short-term memory and simple *concrete-associative* learning; level 2 competence—*abstract-conceptual* reasoning—is closely akin to *g* (see chapter 1). The genetic determinants of levels 1 and 2 are independent and have become differentially distributed in the world according to race and social class. Level 1 ability is required for survival in any environment. Level 2 bestows an advantage mainly in technologically advanced societies. Level 1 ability is necessary but not sufficient for the development of level 2.[4] Level 1 is causally independent of level 2.

Jensen (1968a) finds the evidence inconclusive, but tends to reject the first hypothesis. On the basis of the hypothesis of environmental causation, it would be difficult to explain the high h^2 of IQ in the middle class.[5] Why do some deprived children and not others quickly acquire average IQ when their environments are enriched? Why is it that learning ability correlates so poorly with IQ in the culturally disadvantaged? Why do some deprived children have a high IQ despite the fact that their backgrounds seem no more favorable than those of their less gifted fellows?

In summary, Jensen considers that the weight of evidence is in favor of the second hypothesis. If it were true that there are racially—and socioeconomically—determined genetic differences in the potential for abstract thinking, as Jensen postulates, it would be of great educational importance. Jensen (1970b) has suggested methods by which this could—and should—be investigated. He is aware of the strong emphasis on *g*-type thinking in Western schools, asserts that this places the less endowed at a further disadvantage, and recommends more individualized teaching techniques.

Jensen's papers reveal a statistical grasp, a knowledge of a breadth of literature and personal research of high order. His conclusions are properly qualified—the relevance of the heritability statistics to the black population is regarded not as proved but as highly suggestive. His current position (Jensen 1973b) is that it is a reasonable and potentially testable hypothesis that genetic factors are involved in the average white-black IQ difference; his conclusion from available research studies is that the preponderance of the evidence is more consistent with a genetic hypothesis, which of course does not exclude the influence of the environment and its interaction with genetic factors. Jensen deserves a comprehensive

---

4. In a recent study of white and black elementary-school pupils in California, Jensen (1974b) concludes that the amount of dependence of level 2 on level 1 is only slight.

5. Actually, the value of h^2 increases in a trait in which both genetic and environmental factors are important if the environment is relatively uniform in its favorability *or* unfavorability. The former may be the case in middle-class children.

critique. Such a commentary can be approached from two viewpoints: criticism of issues *explicit* in his articles; criticism of issues not mentioned in the articles but *implicit* in Jensen's rationale.

EXPLICIT ISSUES

THE COMPARISON OF SES GROUPS

Jensen relies heavily on the work of Shuey (1966), who summarizes over 400 publications that overwhelmingly point to large IQ differences between blacks and whites. It should be noted that the mean black IQ in the southern United States is 80, whereas it is 88 in the north. Black girls and women compared to boys and men do better both on IQ tests (by 3 or 4 points) and educationally (45 percent of girls finish high school but only 34 percent of boys). Both phenomena suggest significant and differentiating environmental effects within the black group. Irvine (1969b), commenting on the problem of intercultural comparisons, points out that it is not statistically meaningful to compare two samples by using mean scores unless item difficulty, subtest correlation matrix, and factorial structure within each sample are comparable. Detailed work of this nature has not been done; the bulk of the studies cited by Shuey rely on the crude comparison of mean IQ scores.

Jensen (1971a) has reviewed the data concerning white and black sex differences in occupational attainment, educational achievement, and ability tests. In all of these, black female means exceed the male by a factor equivalent to .1–.3 of a standard deviation, or about 3 IQ points. This is a small but highly consistent and significant difference. Jensen reviews evidence that the male is biologically less well buffered than the female against adverse environmental influences. Since the black population is exposed to a more suppressive environment than the white, it is reasonable to propose that the black male will suffer more greatly, statistically speaking, and that this will be reflected in IQ and its socioeconomic correlates. Jensen suggests that the reason for the vulnerability of the male generally is that his Y chromosome has relatively few gene loci and thus fewer genes to counteract undesirable recessive alleles on the X chromosome.

Jensen has considered socioeconomic status (SES) as an intervening variable. When black and white families are of comparable status, there are still 8 to 13 IQ points difference in favor of whites (Shuey 1966).[6] Arguments of this nature confuse a distant variable—SES—with the relevant one: the child's experiential environment. Jensen is correct in

---

6. A matching technique that involves an unacknowledged regression artefact (Campbell and Erlebacher 1970).

asserting that environmentalists are vague in their definition of the relevant variables; too little is known; but he has overlooked the important work of Bernstein (1961) on the sociolinguistic environment of lower- and middle-class children; of Hess and Shipman (1965) on mother-child interaction patterns and cognitive styles in black families of different social class; of Labov (1970a, 1970b) on major differences between black and white dialectal forms of English; and of Wolf (1963) on the correlation between school achievement and specified, socioeconomic environmental variables. These matters will be discussed in more detail in chapter 3.

Jensen doubts that factors such as low self-esteem, low motivation, and interpersonal difficulties between white tester and black testee significantly affect test scores. In this context, he has discussed (1973c) the important work of Katz (1968). In a series of experiments with black subjects and black and white testers, Katz showed that when a black is tested by a white it is likely to be stressful enough to reduce his performance, firstly because the white person tends to be viewed as socially threatening and secondly because the black tends to anticipate failure. In one complex experiment, southern black students, after a preliminary large-group test, were retested in small groups on a speed-of-performance test (a test liable to produce variance due more to distraction than to intelligence). The "tester" was either white or black, and posed as a psychologist from an educational testing service. Some students were told that their previous scores had been compared with freshman norms for their own black college; others were told that the scores had been compared with overall state (white) norms. Before the "test" the students were handed envelopes containing a fictitious probability percentage (10, 60, or 90 percent) that the individual would attain average status on the test. A control group received no "feedback." The students who did best of all were those who were (1) told they had 60 percent probability of success, were (2) tested by a white tester, and (3) expected to be compared with black norms. Those who did worst were those who were (1) told to expect success with 10 percent probability, were (2) tested by a white tester, and (3) expected to be compared with white norms. The performance of those (1) with no specified feedback, (2) tested by a white tester, and (3) expecting to be compared with white norms, however, was little better. In other words, blacks, even without feedback, anticipated poor comparative results. In another experiment it was demonstrated that blacks, compared to whites, rated their own performance unrealistically lower than did whites who had actually done comparably well on an ability test. In a more recent assessment of 9,000 black and white California schoolchildren by black and white testers, however, Jensen (1974c) could find no evidence—from

THE GREAT DEBATE

both group and individually administered tests of verbal and nonverbal abilities—that the race of the tester had a systematic effect upon the mean scores of either ethnic group. Jensen points out that the tests used by Katz were not comparable to *g*-based intelligence tests. Katz's experiments demonstrate variations in black performance on tests of concentration, not black-white differences in intelligence. The magnitude of the variations, moreover, is small and scarcely sufficient to account for the established black-white IQ differential. Some of Katz's experimental effects were in the opposite direction predicted and gave rise to ad hoc explanations.

LANGUAGE DEPRIVATION

In *Educability and Group Differences*, Jensen (1973c) tackles the explanation of SES IQ differences on the basis of impoverished language development. There are three competing theories in this field—*cultural deprivation*: the disadvantaged child has an impoverished vocabulary and syntax due to relative lack of stimulation; *cultural difference*: the black child, particularly, has a fully developed language but it functions by rules different from those of standard English (that is, it is a different dialect and the child is not naturally bidialectal); *inadequate expression*: the child has not been exposed to experiences that stimulate him to apply the "distancing" possibilities inherent in language to the kind of problems included in IQ tests. These theories, which are not mutually exclusive, are discussed in detail in chapters 3 and 5. Jensen is highly selective in the literature he cites on this topic; and he restricts himself to the cultural deprivation theory. He notes from Lesser, Fifer, and Clark (1965) and from Coleman et al. (1966) that blacks do better on "verbal" than "nonverbal" tests but fails to point out that there is an important verbal-educational factor involved in the so-called nonverbal part of the Wechsler tests, for example (Guilford 1967). He quotes one study (Entwisle 1970) which claims that black children are actually *precocious* verbally, at first-grade level, in terms of the quality of their word-association responses. The voluminous literature (reviewed by Cazden 1968) on maturational lags in black phonology, vocabulary, and syntax is not discussed. Baratz (1970) is quoted out of context, and her strong support of the cultural difference theory is not mentioned. Jensen relates the "precocity" of Negro children to the physical and motoric advancement reported in African and Afro-American babies compared to Caucasians (for example, Bayley 1965); sensorimotor advancement is thought to be negatively correlated with later intelligence. Whatever the merits of this theory and of the assertion of black verbal precocity, it should be noted that the sensorimotor advancement of Africans and Afro-Americans is restricted to the first two years, whereas Entwisle's isolated observation of precocity relates to a later age group. Jensen's current rather cursory treatment of language is disappointing in view of his earlier extensive review of the subject (Jensen 1971b).

HEALTH AND NUTRITION

Jensen (1973c) has considered the problem of subnutrition and the continuum of reproductive casualty (Kawi and Pasamanick 1958) associated with low socioeconomic status (especially among blacks), preeclamptic toxemia, antepartum hemorrhage, urinary tract infection, prematurity, and low birthweight. The contribution of these environmental, nongenetic factors is at present imponderable and probably varies considerably in different geographic regions and between different social groups in the United States. Jensen propounds the interesting theory that the high rate of reproductive casualty among blacks may be caused by genetic factors: in particular, the genetic heterogeneity[7] of black ancestral gene pools.

HERITABILITY

The core of Jensen's argument relies upon heritability estimates for IQ. This work has been carried out by a variety of researchers in Europe, Great Britain, and the United States. They have published comparable results which can thus be regarded as unusually well replicated. The variances in the IQ test scores of the samples of population tested, at the times of testing, appear to have been determined by a hereditary factor which is about four times as great as an environmental factor. A third factor—environment-heredity interaction—is calculated to be inconsiderable.

Bodmer (1972) and Cavalli-Sforza (1970) discuss some of the problems and implications inherent in population statistics. The variation within a population of a multifactorially determined phenotype is usually far greater than the average difference between populations. Moreover, the use of MZ and DZ twins to estimate the heritability of a trait is not without problems. The contrast between MZ and DZ tends to minimize both genetic and environmental differences, but each to an uncertain degree. It should be emphasized (as Jensen points out) that estimates of the heritability of a phenotype depend upon the extent of the environmentally and genetically determined variation in that phenotype which prevails in a particular population at the particular time of analysis. Such

---

7. A factor that operates in a direction opposite to the invigoration derived from hybridization. More distantly related gene pools have the potential for producing a greater *genetic imbalance* between gene loci on the chromosomes, producing lethal or sublethal effects.

estimates are not necessarily valid for other populations or for the same population at a different time. All heritability estimates for IQ, thus far, have been carried out on white Europeans or Americans. They have been limited, therefore, to differences among and within a small number of families from fairly homogeneous sections of the white population in the countries concerned. It is not valid to extrapolate from these figures to the American black population, since this would assume, without empirical basis, that the environmental variation within the races is comparable to the environmental variation between them.[8] Bodmer also points out that controlling SES and still finding mean IQ differences between the races (Shuey 1966) does not justify the conclusion that the IQ differences are genetically determined; comparable socioeconomic status (a rating usually based on parental education, income, and occupation) does not necessarily ensure equivalent environmental influence during development. No adequate heritability studies had been carried out on the black population of the United States at the time of Jensen's original (1969a) paper. Even if they had been, and even if the heritability of black IQ were conclusively established, this would not be relevant to the argument that the difference in mean IQ scores between the two races is caused by a difference in the gene pools. The key experiment would be to study the IQs of blacks adopted into white homes (and vice versa), a possibility that will be discussed later in this book.

Hirsch (1971), Li (1971), Ginsburg (1971), and Vandenberg (1971) have all pointed out that the heritability statistics quoted by Jensen should not be interpreted to mean that, from birth, an immutable proportion of IQ is determined by heredity. Work with monozygotic twins reared apart indicates that up to 20 points of difference in IQ may be found. Blacks and whites, moreover, do not form distinct, partitioned gene pools. Cavalli-Sforza (1970) points out that the time of earliest evolutionary split between Africans, Easterners, and Indo-Europeans was about 50,000 years ago (of the order of 2,000 generations). The production of an IQ difference of one standard deviation between whites and blacks in such a relatively short time—assuming that the rate of evolution is roughly constant in the different races—would suggest extreme selection pressures of a nature and extent for which no evidence is available. Biological evolution is slow, cultural evolution much more rapid. Agriculture began about 10,000 years ago (400 generations), Aristotle's formulation of logic

---

8. However, Jensen (1973c) asserts that the fact of substantial heritability of IQ in the white and (speculatively but probably) in the black populations does increase the a priori probability that the white-black IQ difference is attributable to genetic factors. As yet, no environmental factors have been proposed that could account for the magnitude of the 15-point IQ difference between American whites and blacks, according to Jensen's calculations.

CHAPTER TWO

2,000 years ago (80 generations), and universal education about 100 years ago (4 generations). Jensen (1970b) counters this argument by pointing to the large (approximately four standard deviations) difference in mean height between the pygmies and the Watusi in Africa. In other words, very large, genetically determined racial differences can be accounted for by different natural selection. However, wide variations in height may be evolutionary adaptations to different climatic circumstances; it is hard to see the evolutionary advantage of wide variations in intelligence (assuming that "intelligence" is a unidimensional metric).

Sanday (1972) has presented a detailed analysis of Jensen's argument and summarizes more recent work that does not support it. She argues that h^2 is not a measure of the magnitude of the genetic contribution to a trait—as she claims Jensen implies—but a measure of the extent to which the variability of a trait is determined by genetic relative to environmental factors.[9] The magnitude of the genetic contribution to a trait such as IQ cannot be measured by the methods currently available. Sanday criticizes recent articles by Osborne et al. (1968, 1969) on heritability estimates for black and white twins in regard to tests of spatial and numerical ability. These writers calculated a high h^2 in black twins by applying Jensen's formulas; but the size of their sample was small. In the case of black twins the difference between the within-pair variances of DZ and MZ twins was not significant, although Jensen himself considers this to be a prerequisite for calculating h^2. There is, in addition, some evidence supporting the operation of factors related to poor prenatal and postnatal care, resulting in an unusually high within-family variance for black twins. In any case, a higher h^2 estimate for black children might imply no more than that they are exposed to a more uniform—and more uniformly disadvantaged—environment.[10] Sanday reports a growing disillusionment among geneticists with the mathematical formulas available for calculating h^2 and, indeed, with the applicability of h^2 to human populations.

Studies by Golden et al. (1971) and Mercer (1971) attempt to refute Jensen and Shuey's (1966) claim that it has not been possible to produce comparable IQ scores for minority groups and white children by controlling SES factors. The relevant factors for Chicano children, in Mercer's study, were crowding of home, maternal educational aspirations for the child, the educational attainment of the head of the house, the

---

9. This is something of a straw man. Jensen has stated clearly that h^2 does not measure the magnitude of the genetic contribution to individual IQs.

10. The more uniform the environment, the greater h^2 will be. The more heterogeneous the environment, the lower h^2 will be, in any polygenically determined phenotype. The environment may be uniformly advantageous *or* disadvantageous.

language spoken in the home, and home ownership. The relevant factors for black children were family size, maternal aspirations, the marital state of the head of the family, home ownership, and the occupational level of the family head. When all five characteristics are held constant for Chicano children, their mean IQ is 104.4; for blacks it is 99.5. The significance of these observations is vitiated, however, by the fact that the control of SES factors causes the minority group to be highly selected as to intelligence and, presumably, intellectual potential. Thus the white and minority groups' parents are unfairly matched for IQ.

Sanday presents an explanation alternative to Jensen's. In her model the variation of IQ within population groups is due to the interaction of four factors: genetic potential; diet and prenatal and postnatal health; individual emotional and motivational factors; and degree and nature of contact with mainstream culture. Assuming that genetic potential is equivalent, the difference in mean test performance for black and white children is due to differences in the remaining influences. There is considerable evidence of a biologically suppressive environment in black children (see chapter 3). The content of conventional IQ tests is closely related to the cultural experience of upper- and middle-class children. To some extent, this aspect of mainstream culture has diffused down into minority groups, but imperfectly. In a biologically suppressive environment, h^2 estimates will be low; in a nonmainstream subculture, h^2 estimates will be inflated. The outcome of the concatenation of the two factors is imponderable.

The arena of this controversy was recently entered by Layzer (1972), a Harvard physical astronomer, who takes issue with Jensen on a number of scientific issues. Layzer's main points, and Jensen's (1973a) rejoinders to them, illustrate the technical sophistication required of those who would join the Great Debate. Consider the following points of contention.

First, Layzer considers that the high heritability of IQ scores reveals nothing of the educability of the children involved. Between ethnic groups, as between socioeconomic groups, there are systematic differences in developmental conditions that influence performance on IQ tests. Reported differences in IQ, therefore, tell us nothing about the existence of any average genetic differences. Even if they did, this would not settle the question of educability, since high h^2 can mean either (1) that the expression of a trait is insensitive to environmental variations or (2) that the range of relevant environmental variations is small. Jensen has assumed that (1) is the case without adequate consideration of (2).

Jensen disagrees. The high heritability of learning ability implies that if a number of individuals are given the same learning opportunities,

Chapter Two

they will differ from each other in their rates of learning. Changes (for example, skilled teaching) in the existing range of environmental conditions may increase the mean IQ in the population; but they will not affect the spread of individual differences in IQ.

Second, Layzer claims that Jensen's operational stance is a misapplication of the scientific method practiced by physical scientists. Measurement should stem from mathematically expressed theory as the tool of hypothetical observation or experiment; Jensen has reversed the usual process by trying to derive theory from quantified observations.

Jensen replies that Layzer has adopted the stance of "an extreme methodological bluenose" about Jensen's research whereas he relaxes these standards, significantly, in reviewing other research more favorable to his own ideological position.

Third, Layzer feels that the assumption that genetic and environmental contributions to IQ are additive and independent is highly suspect. This reduces the usefulness of the concept of heritability in the study of human intelligence. IQ does not measure a phenotypic trait on a continuous scale: it is a measure of the rank order of test scores in a given population. The appearance of uniformity between the multiplicity of different IQ tests can be obtained only by forcing the results of each test to conform to the Procrustean bed of a normal distribution. Two assumptions are made: that there is a unidimensional metric—intelligence—related to IQ in a one-to-one way; and that the values assumed by this metric are distributed normally. IQ scores, representing as they do a rank-order scale, are unsuitable for the kind of mathematical analysis required to calculate h^2.

Jensen concedes that IQ is not an absolute scale with a true zero point and that it can be regarded as an interval scale only if normal distribution of IQ is assumed. Nevertheless, since estimates of h^2 involve the calculation of squared differences from the mean (variance), an absolute scale is not essential. Jensen admits that the possibility of a multiplicative, nonadditive, gene-environment interaction cannot be ruled out; but he can find no statistical support for it. The simpler, additive (genetic + environmental) model, which is the basis of the formulas for derivation of h^2, has not been disproved and seems to explain the data adequately (Jensen 1973c).

Fourth, Layzer claims that Jensen has used medians, inappropriately, in calculating h^2 from data on the IQ correlations between different orders of sibship, data which were gathered from eight countries over a period of fifty years using different types of IQ test. The range in IQ correlations recorded covers a considerable span, introducing a large internal error factor. The data for separated MZ twins must be considered in the light of the fact that the environments in which they were reared were very similar. In fact, in those few cases where the environments were markedly disparate, considerable IQ differences were found between the twinship members.

In general, Jensen concedes Layzer's point about medians; however, when weighted means are employed, as Layzer recommends, it makes little difference to the statistics. The fact that markedly disparate environments cause moderate IQ differences in separated MZ twins is predictable and in no way alters the fact that nongenetic variance is relatively small.

Finally, Layzer says that "intelligence" is best defined in terms of information-processing skills. He suggests that genetic and nongenetic factors interact continuously in the production of these skills.[11] A child growing up in an environment providing opportunity and reward for acquiring verbal abilities will exploit the possibilities inherent in language in the solution of scholastic problems. In this case, the genetic contribution to verbal skills interacts constructively and nonadditively with the environment in the evolution of competencies fundamental to performance on IQ tests. Layzer proposes that cognitive development is cumulative and that people, regardless of class or race, should be regarded as having unlimited educability provided motivation and teaching strategies are optimized.

Jensen agrees with Layzer's definition of intelligence as information-processing competence and suggests that this is synonymous with the general intelligence factor, g, that underlies IQ. Jensen himself is pursuing studies in this area. Studies of h^2 can be regarded as a beginning; high h^2 indicates crude, global areas where the refined study of the primary, differential abilities involved in information-processing can be investigated in order to determine racial differences. According to Jensen, Layzer exaggerates the significance of gene-environment multiplicative interaction; the relative importance of this factor can be determined mathematically. It proves to be inconsiderable.

In my opinion, Jensen's *threshold hypothesis* warrants further examination. Black children are exposed to a caste-related environment that is *qualitatively* different from the mainstream white culture from which IQ tests are derived and that *quantitatively* lacks some of the experiences required to produce high performance on conventional tests of

11. Layzer (1974) suggests that *gene-environment correlation* is nearly always important in human populations; its absence is a necessary condition for the applicability of conventional heritability analyses. The uncontrollable, systematic errors in IQ scores, the systematic cultural differences between different human subpopulations, and an inescapable gene-environment correlation all indicate that the conventional calculation of h^2 is not reliable in human populations.

Chapter Two

competence. Black children develop a lifestyle that may conflict with, or even be antagonistic to, the requirements of conventional evaluation. In addition, they have been exposed *below a critical threshold* to experiences that foster an abstract, verbally mediated, "distanced" approach to problems. In other words the black boy's environment—that is, his parents, siblings, and peers—does not value or foster "g"; and he lacks the cognitive models in early life from whom "g" can be incorporated. Later, his peer group may even reject him for demonstrating "g". What does it take to make it on the ghetto streets, and what has this to do with "g"? This matter will be considered in more detail in chapters 3 and 7.

Above a certain level of stimulation, however, further increments make little difference, as is the case with middle- and upper-class children. Estimates of h^2, therefore, will be high for most whites. It is for this reason that preschool "enrichment" programs have produced little change in advantaged groups. Jensen's hierarchical learning abilities may have a similar explanation. Level 1 is based more on genetic potential than on environment. Level 2 is based to a larger extent on cultural experience in a threshold manner. Level 2 results partly from an extension of level 1 by the exploitation of the distancing possibilities inherent in language in the form of representational thought. Evidence for this key concept is discussed in chapters 3, 7, and 8; it is a central theme to which this book will repeatedly return.

EVIDENCE FROM AUSTRALIAN STUDIES

Additional evidence has recently become available from studies of Australian Aborigines. The relevance of such research to the Jensen controversy can be regarded as doubtful, however. There is no resemblance between Australian Aborigines and American blacks except sociologically: both have black skin, both are oppressed minority groups, both are disadvantaged in an educational and occupational sense, and both tend to have varying admixtures of allegedly superior Caucasian genes. To associate them in regard to innate potentials is a hazardous procedure, to say the least, but since both Jensen (1969b) and Eysenck (1971) do so, the argument should be followed through.

Jensen and Eysenck quote from an article by De Lemos (1969), who studied the development of conservation in two tribal Aboriginal groups. As a side issue in her study, she noted that in one Aboriginal group in central Australia there were a number of part-Aboriginal children with a small degree (no more than 15 percent) of European ancestry. There was no evidence of any difference between the Aboriginal and part-Aboriginal children in terms of social or environmental background. The part-Aborigines did better on all tests of conservation (of quantity, weight, volume, length, area, and number) to a significant degree. These results were regarded by Jensen as giving strong support to the genetic argument.[12] Dasen (1973) attempted to replicate these results four years later in the same Aboriginal settlement. This time, however, care was taken to select equal numbers of full- and part-Aboriginal subjects in each age group. When tests of conservation (quantity, weight, volume, length), seriation, ordering, and spatial skills were employed, differences between groups were found to be random. The genetic argument based on the De Lemos data was not supported.

McElwain and Kearney (1973) have applied the Queensland Test (a nonverbal, "culture-fair," evaluation instrument involving the manipulation of two-dimensional shapes) to over a thousand Aborigines with a wide range of contact with Europeans. They note that, overall, mean total scores for Aborigines are about one standard deviation below those for whites, but that the variance is about the same for both groups. Different Aboriginal groups test lower than Europeans in approximately the same degree they have lacked contact with Europeans. Kearney (1966) tested 120 Palm Island Aboriginal children with the Queensland Test and correlated test scores with proportion of Aboriginal ancestry (ascertained from records). The correlation of test scores with Aboriginality or European-ness was not significant.

Dasen's (1973) primary objective in central Australia was to compare three groups on Piagetian dimensions: (1) Aboriginal, brief contact; (2) Aboriginal, longer contact; and (3) European, middle class. The two Aboriginal groups, both from central Australia, were of full Aboriginal descent. He found that the order of development was the same for both races but much slower and asymptotic for Aborigines. By twelve years of age the proportion of children who had achieved conservation of quantity was as follows: (1) Aboriginal, brief contact: 20 percent; (2) Aboriginal, longer contact: 50 percent; (3) European, middle class: 100 percent. The difference was marked on all logical-mathematical tests but was not found on perceptual-spatial tests. Dasen ascribes this finding to the ecological demands of the traditional Aboriginal environment—to the need for hunters to develop spatial rather than numerical skills.

De Lacey (1970, 1971) studied classificatory ability in Aboriginal and European children of four groups: (1) high-socioeconomic white; (2) low-socioeconomic white; (3) high-contact Aboriginal; (4) low-contact Aboriginal. He found significant differences between (3) and (4) but no significant difference between low-socioeconomic Europeans and high-

---

12. Piaget's tests of conservation and classification are highly correlated with g and with standard IQ tests (Vernon 1969).

contact Aborigines. The original study was confounded by the fact that high-contact Aboriginal was associated with more European genetic admixture. Later he tested 63 full-descent Aborigines who had had a high degree of contact and found them equivalent in test scores to the high-contact part-Aborigines (and thus to low-SES whites) in his first sample.

Finally, a fortuitous natural experiment was discovered and its outcome assessed (Dasen, de Lacey, and Seagrim 1973). Thirty-five Aboriginal children who had been adopted (some younger and some older than eighteen months) into European families were found in Adelaide. Twenty-two were assessed on a variety of tests of conservation and on spatial, seriation, classification, and verbal skills. Their scores on all tests apart from conservation of quantity and weight were comparable with European controls. In regard to the conservation tests their results were well above a tribal Aboriginal comparison group but intermediate between it and the European children. These results were obtained despite the fact that some of the children were adopted quite late, many as foundlings after exposure to serious environmental hazards and neglect, and that all had had to struggle with the social problems of growing up as an Aborigine in a European environment. Many were already showing symptoms of psychological disturbance. The results of this study are all the more persuasive when these facts are kept in mind.

IMPLICIT ISSUES

Other important matters are involved in this controversy, matters which have to do with the nature of intelligence and which have been discussed in chapter 1. It is no longer acceptable to define intelligence operationally (that is, in terms of IQ score), to refer to studies showing the factorial loading of IQ scores with a hypothesized general intellectual capacity (g), and then to translate the relevance of such studies to other cultures. Vernon (1969), after an extensive study of English, Scottish Hebridean, Eskimo, Canadian Indian, Ugandan, and Jamaican boys, noted considerable differences in the factorial structures of each group's test scores following the administration of a battery of twenty-three diverse tests. The traditional first-order factor, g, was extracted but the tests that correlated highly with g and the degree of the correlation varied in different cultures. The first factor loaded heavily on tests of abstraction and matrix solution for Canadian Indians, for example, but the same tests were also heavily loaded on verbal-educational and spatial factors. The Jamaican g factor correlated with initiative, home support for education, family educational level, planful family environment, and male dominance. Hebrideans and Ugandans failed to show a clear g factor. The factor structure of the Jamaican sample did not replicate that of the English boys. The g factor in Jamaicans did not load widely, whereas a verbal-educational factor did so. Vernon's work offers limited support to the notion of hierarchical structuralization of mental abilities; however, it demonstrates that the structuralization is not the same for different cultural groups. This finding emphasizes that crude cross-cultural comparisons are unacceptable. Furthermore, the gap from IQ score to judgments about innate ability becomes wider as the great complexity of intervening variables is clarified.

Standard IQ tests are not based on theories of the development and functioning of intelligence. The items which make up these tests are selected pragmatically to predict scholastic performance. Where they are validated at all, they are validated against school performance. A distressing circularity creeps in. Tests were designed by middle-class whites with the modest primary purpose of predicting which children are likely to be unsuccessful in a conventional school setting. From this utilitarian statistic several further steps may be taken. Tests designed for, and valid for, middle-class whites are applied to a different subculture, and the results do, indeed, predict school success or failure quite well. The test scores are then related to a theoretical basic and comprehensive general competence which is further confused with, or collapsed into, an innate ability. From that point, dubious inferences about differential genetic endowment can be made.

Hebb (1949) and Cattell (1963) were aware of this problem in their distinction between two types of intelligence. Irvine (1969a) questions the concept of intelligence implicit in the usual tests applied cross-culturally. The factors regularly identified as important are closely related to Western educational skills. Cognitive skills valued in and fostered in non-Western cultures are discounted or, more usually, go unnoticed. Western psychological theories have artificially separated personality, affect, and intelligence in a way that renders the concept of intelligence increasingly disembodied and unmeaningful, even in Western society. The exportation of this scientifically unsatisfactory concept to other cultures is yet another aspect of educational neocolonialism.

SCIENCE AND SOCIAL RESPONSIBILITY

Jensen is no racist. He advocates a plural educational system, not a segregation on the basis of race. His conclusions about educational policy are somewhat similar to those recommended in this book (see chapters 4 and 6), although he and I have reached those conclusions by different routes. There can be no question that Jensen has a genuine concern for minority groups. He believes that if there is a racially determined difference in potential, a different policy may aid those who are at present disadvantaged by inappropriately designed school curricula.

Nevertheless, those with other axes to grind have made use of Jensen's conclusions. A Southern politician in the United States had Jensen's *Harvard Educational Review* article read into the *Congressional Record*. William Shockley, an eminent physicist, considers blacks to be genetically inferior and proposes a "bonus sterilization plan" for the intellectually unfit. Herrnstein (1971), writing in the influential *Atlantic Monthly*, accepts Jensen's theory *in toto*, and worries about the future, suggesting that our current egalitarian goals will produce a social caste system with a bright elite and dullards at the bottom. One can picture the nodding of heads as long-unvoiced suspicions were confirmed: the hewers of wood and drawers of water were born to it. Jensen, doggedly following the dictates of his logic, has inadvertently articulated the suspicions of the multitude. He must have known it would happen. Should he, therefore, have spoken out?

The question is no less important than that which faced atomic scientists in World War II. Should they lend support to the manufacture of the bomb or should they keep the information out of the hands of politicians? Educational policies based inappropriately on a premise of racially determined difference in intelligence could adversely affect a whole generation of children, like the fallout from a bomb; for once a system is committed to a policy, it is difficult to turn the juggernaut in a different direction.

My own belief is that Jensen was right to raise the question. I would criticize the degree to which he supports the hereditarian position from the equivocal evidence available. I think he was wrong to start his key article, sensationally, by asserting that compensatory education has failed.[13] It has scarcely begun. Moreover, I think there are serious fundamental questions about his premises and large gaps in his evidence. The question itself of differences in "intelligence" recedes like a mirage in the light of cross-cultural experience.

It is possible, indeed likely, that different selection pressures, social isolation, and genetic drift have produced differences in behavioral *potentials* in different ethnic groups. Such differences would be much more likely to produce different emphases in the spectrum of competencies rather than a crude deficiency of competence (such as "less *g*" or an "inability to think abstractly"). Given roughly equivalent environments,

---

13. Jensen did not have available the range of information about preschool programs presented in chapters 4 and 6 of this book. His conclusions about the inefficacy of compensatory programs appear to be premature; but in any case it is doubtful whether the success of these programs would be germane to Jensen's main argument.

whatever genetic differences there are appear to even out (de Lacey 1971). Cultural evolution is more rapid than genetic. The individual child who responds to a school curriculum incorporates, in seven years, thousands of years of cultural and genetic evolution. Given appropriate teaching and satisfactory motivation, the hypothesized genetic differences may not hamper acquisition. We just do not know. The original question appears to dwindle into a theoretical possibility which is of some scientific interest but which is difficult to answer with certainty without grotesque experimentation (for example, adopting blacks into white families and vice versa, precisely defining the environmental influences, and measuring differences with tests designed to cover the competency spectrum). This sort of experiment would be incredibly difficult to design, aside from its obviously unethical character. It is apparent, also, that the IQ tests now in use are inadequate and that we still await the design of instruments which will validly tap the spectrum and profile of base competencies. Such tests will not be designed until we know more about the competencies that constitute the spectrum and how they interact.

The genetic question could easily become an intellectual cul-de-sac. A medical analogy may help to make this point. It is apparent that the contraction of tuberculosis is related to a genetic factor. Twenty years ago practically everyone was exposed to, and infected by, the ubiquitous TB bacillus. But only some developed severe primary or secondary tuberculosis (of lung, intestinal tract, meninges, bone). Further infiltration from the initial primary infection was determined by a complex interaction of factors including polygenic inheritance, general physical health, and duration of exposure. Exposure factors are likely to compound genetic predisposition. Children of tuberculous parents, for example, are at great risk. Progress in the control of tuberculosis has come, however, not from eugenic measures but through advances in public health and chemotherapy. A unilateral diversion of research effort into the genetic question would have been counterproductive.

No, Jensen was right to ask the question. The vilification to which he has been subjected by some elements in the academic community is unacceptable. There *may* be genetic differences in potential between races. At this time the question is not answerable. My own belief is that, whatever the differences are, they are likely to be less major than Jensen hypothesizes and are probably related to profile differences in the competency spectrum potential compounded by differences in the realization and expression of those competencies.

I believe that, in the long run, good will come of the Jensenist heresy. A theory that directly attacked the prevailing ideological orthodoxy will have forced geneticists and cognitive psychologists to reexamine

CHAPTER TWO

the definition of fundamental issues—leading to a revision that will enable us to unload such excess baggage as the notion of "intelligence" in its contemporary protean forms. Fundamentally, the scientific question is not about a choice between "environment" and "heredity" but, rather, concerns the proportionate involvement and interaction of genetic and nongenetic factors in each of the multiplicity of primary and superordinate competencies required for human adaptation in diverse ecological situations. Jensen has generated a dialectic with potentially useful scientific consequences. "Intelligence," scholastic achievement, and whatever it is that IQ tests measure all involve the ability to apply the possibilities inherent in language to the solution of problems associated with abstract, "distanced" thinking. This ability is evolved from (1) genetic inheritance, (2) environmental influences that promote verbal competence and its application to problems illuminated by symbolic, hierarchical thought, and (3) influences that have caused children to be cued by such problems to express their competence in an appropriate way (in other words, *task orientation*). These appear to be the main factors operating in an environment which is not biologically suppressive as a result of disease or subnutrition. The problem that Jensen poses is to tease out the relative contribution of these factors in recognizable subpopulations and, ultimately, in individuals. The problem for educational psychologists is to determine the degree to which and the means by which factors (2) and (3) can be influenced by teaching programs in subpopulations for whom the factors of inheritance and biological suppression are, as yet, unknown.

The great debate has had another, unanticipated result. It has challenged the academic world to consider, anew, the questions of scientific freedom, social responsibility, ideological heterodoxy, and intramural censorship. Scientific ideas, properly expressed, must be debated in open forum. The muzzling of those who assert the unpalatable cannot be tolerated; but those who fly in the face of orthodoxy have a responsibility to present both sides of the argument as fully as possible and to be properly cautious where the evidence is equivocal or absent.

SUMMARY

This chapter has described the change from a rejecting attitude toward "primitive" people to concepts of cultural relativism and equipotentialism. The latter position was recently questioned by Jensen, who postulates genetically determined racial differences in the potential to develop *g*, produces evidence to support the hypothesis, and suggests means by which the hypothesis could and should be tested.

For the purpose of his argument, Jensen accepts an operational definition of intelligence: IQ score. He discusses in detail statistical evidence which strongly supports the finding that, in Euro-American white populations, the IQ score variance is determined by a hereditary factor which is four times as high as an environmental factor. Jensen considers it likely that similar figures apply to American blacks, although satisfactory data are not available. Those who postulate a predominantly environmental determination of IQ have failed to be specific about the operative factors.

Jensen considers that, on the basis of different gene frequency distributions, American blacks can be considered a separate race. Comparative studies have repeatedly showed IQ differences between Euro- and Afro-Americans of about 15 IQ points, or one standard deviation, in favor of whites. Even when socioeconomic factors are controlled, white superiority remains. American Indians, though even more depressed in socioeconomic status, score higher than blacks. It may be that the differences in potential between races are realized as different patterns of competencies, g-type thinking being one kind of competence. Jensen's own research suggests that IQ tests amalgamate two forms of thinking which are hierarchically related but which have become differentially distributed in the population according to SES: level 1 and level 2, associative learning and abstract thinking (g), respectively. Blacks do as well as whites on tests of associative learning, but they fall behind on abstract thinking. The education system should attend to this discrepancy and devise a more pluralistic approach. The current system puts minority groups at a marked disadvantage, since it overemphasizes g-type thinking.

From the hail of criticism that greeted Jensen's work, a number of cogent issues can be extracted. Jensen has examined and found wanting some recent studies about relevant environmental variables. He skirts around the serious problems involved in the crude application of IQ tests across cultures or subcultures. Jensen's own formula for the calculation of heritability has been questioned. It may appear he has implied that heritability relates to the extent a trait has been determined by genetic factors. This is not so; heritability refers to the variance of a trait in a given population. All heritability estimates of any reliability have been carried out on Euro-American white samples. The results cannot validly be applied to Afro-Americans. Even if it were proved that the heritability of IQ in the black population is high, this would not clinch the argument that interracial IQ differences are caused by differences in innate potential. In the absence of unequivocal empirical evidence, Jensen must rely upon the lack of inconsistency between a mathematical genetic model and the data available. More recent work in Australia and the United States, meanwhile, has given some support to the importance of environment in the process of realization of competence.

CHAPTER TWO

There is a circularity about much of the argument in this field. Middle-class people design tests and education systems. Tests are arranged to correlate highly with school activities. The statistical analysis of test results reveals factors that are associated with school and with middle-class cognitive styles. These are labeled "intelligence." There is a strong temptation to hurdle from such evaluation data to innate potential across the thorny hedges of assessment, competence, and realization.

Whatever the moral rights and wrongs of Jensen's argument, he has generated a reappraisal of fundamental issues, a dialectic that may lead not only to the setting aside of the confused and outmoded concept "intelligence" but also to a less ethnocentric examination of the nature and origin of the spectrum and profile of competencies in different cultures. He has made it clear, also, that we can no longer be satisfied with a simplistic choice between a "genetic" or an "environmental" model.

CHAPTER 3
DEPRIVATION, DISADVANTAGE, OR DIFFERENCE?

Books is stuffed with white man lies.
A black mother from Mississippi

Your slanders against our race are moral lies, told to throw all the blame for our troubles on to us.
Aboriginal Manifesto

THE EVOLUTION OF THE NOTION OF DEPRIVATION

Against the opposition of reactionary forces and the apathy of many in power, progressive educators have struggled to improve schools for those on the fringe of the cultural mainstream. To do so, they face the hard-bitten attitude that "If they're any good they'll make it under their own steam; those that haven't don't deserve to"—an attitude opposed by the idealistic notion that "All a nation's citizens have a right to equal opportunities." The moral issue is made more compelling by the fact that Russia and China appear to be less confused than the Western democracies about the principle of equality of opportunity, and more effective in actualizing it.

There is no doubt that, as a whole, educational opportunities have expanded in Australia and the United States. Nevertheless, the Coleman (1966) and the Jencks (1972) reports assert that the quality of the school's resources has not played much part in the final achievement of its pupils; income in adulthood is more closely related to educational level reached and to home environment. The contention that interracial differences in IQ can be put down to inequality of schools cannot be supported (Jensen 1973c). According to Jencks, the following variables, proportionately, determine adult status:

Chapter Three

> Cognitive potential: 5 to 10 percent
> Influence of home on cognitive competence: 10 to 20 percent
> Final educational attainment: 40 to 50 percent
> School resources: insignificant
> Uncertain: 20 to 45 percent

Whatever the merits or otherwise of expressing, in this way, the relative importance of the factors involved, it appears that above a minimum level the IQ score in adulthood is not a good predictor of income status, although it does correlate with type of occupation.

The conclusion that the improvement in school resources has been ineffective is terribly disheartening. In recent years the Australian government has provided generous financial support to keep Aboriginal children in secondary school and to send them to a university. It has been exceedingly difficult to find any candidates. Despite the manifest good intention of policy makers, by 1973 fewer than ten Aborigines had graduated from a university in Australia.

It is from observations such as this that the notion of *cultural deprivation* arose. The persuasive writings of Eels, Davis, and Havighurst (1951), Hunt (1961), and Bloom (1964) gave the concept impetus. Children of lower socioeconomic status were described as unable to benefit fully from school because they lacked certain crucial experiences required to prepare them for it. Middle-class children have already had these experiences at the time of entering school—the so-called *hidden curriculum* of the middle-class home (Strodtbeck 1964). The roots of cognitive competence are formed, predominantly, before the age of school entry. Minority-group children were seen to start school, therefore, at a serious disadvantage, and their cognitive deficits, in comparison to middle-class children, were seen to increase cumulatively throughout childhood and adolescence. The cumulative deficits[1] were demonstrated, for example, in the contentious IQ score differences between blacks and whites, and in the relatively inferior scholastic and occupational achievement of children from lower socioeconomic backgrounds.

The deprivation theory proved very attractive. It suggested potentially useful research into what a child needs to realize potential, and it hinted at the possibility of developing educational techniques to make good early deficiencies. It revived the flagging spirits of progressive educators and culminated in the great social experiment of Project Head Start (see chapter 4). This chapter deals with those observations and theories about cultural deprivation and difference that have been most influential in the past decade.

---

1. Jensen (1973c) criticizes the cumulative-deficit theory. He contends that the black-white achievement differential is consistent with a one-standard-deviation difference in intelligence at all ages, although the absolute difference will, of course, increase with age.

DEPRIVATION, DISADVANTAGE, OR DIFFERENCE?

The word *deprivation* refers to a dispossession or loss. In the fields of psychiatry and social psychology, during the 1960s, writers began to apply it to a situation in which an individual, family, or identifiable social group is undernourished, is exposed to disease or physical trauma, or lacks the wherewithal for full participation in mainstream culture. After a time, it was replaced by a less pejorative term—*cultural disadvantage*—but essentially the same meaning was retained. Three types of deprivation were described by Caplan (1964): physical deprivation, psychosocial deprivation, and sociocultural deprivation. Physical deprivation refers to subnutrition or excessive exposure to disease and trauma. Psychosocial deprivation refers to insufficiency of or disruption in early attachment due to parental loss, rejection, or unavailability. Sociocultural deprivation refers to a failure of the primary social group (the family or subcultural group) to transmit to the individual the values and skills required for participation in mainstream culture, or to a situation in which a dominant group discriminatingly bars another group from entry into the socioeconomic mainstream. Several forms of deprivation may coexist. Psychosocial deprivation, for example, is most likely to occur after family disruption or in unwanted children, situations that occur relatively frequently in lower-SES groups. Among the very poor, physical and sociocultural deprivation tend to coexist. Up to the present time, the following areas of deprivation have been subject to most investigation: health and nutrition; personality and motivation; and cognitive factors.

HEALTH AND NUTRITION

The brain may be exposed to traumata and privations that block or delay maturation before or after birth. There is an association between the following phenomena in Western society: low socioeconomic status, poor prenatal care, poor nutrition, spontaneous abortion, preeclamptic toxemia, renal infection, hypertension, antepartum hemorrhage, placental insufficiency, prematurity, low birthweight, high neonatal mortality, postnatal development delay, and cerebral palsy and behavior and learning disorders in childhood. The association is sufficiently clear to have been described by Pasamanick (1956) as the "continuum of reproductive casualty." These associated problems require more investigation, particularly in non-Western societies. In northern Australia, a recent study of Aboriginal birthweights and of the psychophysical development of children up to the age of two years demonstrated that there was a significant minority who had low birthweight and who were both physically and psychologically stunted (Duffy and Nurcombe 1969).[2] Similar

---

2. Physically stunted according to head circumference and bodily dimensions; psychologically stunted according to the Griffiths Developmental Scale (Griffiths 1954).

Chapter Three

findings have been noted in a longitudinal study of part-Aboriginal children in Bourke, New South Wales (Duffy 1973).

It is probable that medical concern with difficult birth (resulting, theoretically, in fetal anoxia) has exaggerated the importance of mechanical brain damage as a cause of reduction in cognitive capacity. It appears that certain babies are already vulnerable, prior to birth, and that minor difficulties during delivery may exaggerate the problem or be merely a rationalization for damage that occurred before birth. Postnatal insults such as head injury, infection, and lead poisoning may interrupt maturation but are of isolated importance. By far the most important factor appears to be nutritional.

Approximately half the population of the world have survived a period of starvation during childhood. As emerging countries industrialize, breast-feeding declines and malnutrition occurs at earlier and earlier ages. Although some of these children die, the majority survive. Some remain physically and intellectually stunted, unable to provide improved conditions for their own children. This is a complex scientific problem. The results of relevant animal experiments and clinical research have been summarized by Winick (1969). Three questions are posed: Does malnutrition cause significant brain changes? If so, are these changes associated with functional impairment? And is there a time during development when the brain is most susceptible to malnutrition?

Animal studies have demonstrated different critical periods during which the brain is vulnerable to lack of protein. Structural damage can be measured by DNA content, brain weight, and myelin content, all of which correlate with histological evidence of brain damage. (Deoxyribonucleic acid [DNA] is a constituent of cell nuclei. Myelin is the fatty covering of the conductive fibers of brain cells, rather like the insulation around an electric cable, which is important for rapid conduction. The process by which the nerve-fiber sheaths are laid down is called *myelination*.) The studies suggest that a critical period of brain growth can be defined in terms of cell division and myelination. Different parts of the brain reach their final number of cells at different times, but brain growth slows long before body growth.

Clinical studies suggest that, in man, the total number of brain cells increases in a linear fashion after birth and then more slowly until six months of age, after which there is little, if any, change. The most rapid myelination of nerve sheaths appears to be at birth, although myelin synthesis is still occurring after two years. Adequate nutrition is necessary for these processes to proceed normally. Starvation causes an interruption of cell division and myelination, resulting in permanent abnormality of the brain that is measurable biochemically and observable histologically.

There is also evidence suggesting that prenatal subnutrition renders the brain more vulnerable to later nutritional insults.

Are these structural changes reflected in functional deficits? The evidence is inconclusive but, according to Winick, strongly circumstantial. Malnutrition in animals has been associated with electroencephalographic and neurological abnormalities, reduced exploratory behavior, and poor maze-learning; but the problem of measurement and of adequate norms is a major one in studies of function in nonhuman species. Prospective and retrospective studies of malnourished children (in Serbia, the United States, Central America, South America, and South Africa)[3] suggest an association between physical retardation (for example, in head circumference, height, and weight) and intellectual stunting; but there are major problems of control since most of these children come from disintegrated, deprived backgrounds. It appears that the earlier the malnutrition, the more profound the psychological retardation. Children malnourished after six months of age recover fully if they are properly fed. The weakest aspect of the animal experimentation is the correlation between structural damage and functional deficit. The weakest links in the clinical studies are in proof of structural change following malnutrition and in the uncertainty that later psychological retardation is not due to lack of environmental stimulation rather than to earlier protein-calorie subnutrition.

Unresolved details remain: How much undernutrition? What kind? When is the brain no longer susceptible? How severe is the retardation? What cognitive and general adaptive competencies does the subnutrition predominantly affect? Despite these questions, a number of conclusions can be drawn: The problem is self-perpetuating from generation to generation. Time is critical—the earlier the maturation, the more severe the effect. The first public health goal in developing countries, therefore, should be to eliminate prenatal and postnatal starvation by improving the nutrition of pregnant and lactating mothers and encouraging breast-feeding.

Cheek, Holt, and Mellits (1973) point out that Winick's data and more recent evidence must be interpreted with caution. The effect of subnutrition on different animals varies considerably. There are major problems involved in generalizing from rat, pig, or monkey to humans. More recent work has failed to replicate Winick's studies concerning the association between reduced brain-cell population and subnutrition. Developmental follow-up studies have suffered from lack of control of environmental stimulus variables which appear to be of major importance

3. See: Harrell, Woodyard, and Gates (1955); Graham (1972); Scrimshaw and Gordon (1968); Cravioto and Robles (1965); Cabak and Najdanvic (1965); Garrow and Pike (1967); Stoch and Smythe (1963).

in animal as well as human studies. It is not a scientifically proved fact that if malnutrition exists for the first six months of life, "brain damage" will occur. The condition is better described as *growth arrest*. Cheek et al. conclude, tentatively, that most children subject to early protein restriction can be completely restored if the adverse, hostile, or desolate environment is enriched and if normal food requirements are offered. Until current longitudinal studies have come to fruition, the connection between malnutrition and IQ depression must be regarded as unproved.

Although the details of this major world problem are unclear, it seems probable that starvation and its frequent accompaniments (lack of material and language stimulation; infection of the eye, skin, ear, brain, respiratory system, and intestinal tract; intestinal infestation) can affect both physical and cognitive development, producing a serious overall stunting. It is apparent that this is the predicament of a significant proportion of the world's population. It is open to question whether subnutrition, to the degree required to cause growth arrest, affects a significant number of low-SES children in the United States or other developed countries. Jensen (1973c) considers that this factor should not be overrated.

PERSONALITY AND MOTIVATION

Most of the work in the field of personality and motivation has been impressionistic. There has been a tendency for authors to quote each other in circular fashion so that an enormous literature has accumulated, much of which has a fragile empirical base. As Jessor and Richardson (1968) point out, the very term *deprivation* is misleading since it emphasizes negative factors and ignores the many positive factors in such an environment. The insufficiency of an attribute may have quite different implications depending upon the overall pattern of attributes present. The experience of belonging to an impoverished family depends upon which ethnic or local group the family defines itself as allied with and whether the group is discriminated against by a dominant majority. The different histories of the American black and the American Indian, for example, are positive issues with distinctive implications for the contemporary social situations of the two groups. There are enormous variations between and within groups labeled as "disadvantaged." One should keep in mind, therefore, that to some extent the need to characterize others as "deprived" is a function of middle-class ethnocentrism and a tendency to divide society into *us* (the haves) and *them* (the have-nots).

To consider this matter further, it would be convenient to limit discussion of personality factors to one example: the North American urban black. The impressions advanced in this section do not necessarily apply to groups other than the urban black in the United States. It should also be kept in mind that most of these studies have a rather clinical, white ethnocentric bias; the subjects in question are scrutinized, as it were, f[rom outside, and observati]ons recorded are probably, to some extent, an [artifact of this scruti]ny.

[Much has bee]n written about (1) *distal* environmental [and social conditi]on such as race, socioeconomic status, [and family stru]cture in relation to (2) such distal variables [as school failure, a]ddiction, and delinquency. Much less has [received attent]ion between the *distal* variables and more [*proximal* ones: (3) p]arental child-rearing techniques, patterns [of parent and p]eer-models, (4) beliefs, values, attitudes, [level of social ab]ility and the need for achievement. This [includes more prox]imal personality factors.

Jessor and Richardson (1968) define self-esteem as the individual's attitude toward himself—his self-evaluation according to the extent that his attainment approaches his expectation in matters he values highly. Black schoolchildren are described as characteristically low in self-esteem. They are likely to have had repeated experiences of failure in school. They may deny their low self-esteem by devaluing education, but this is a defensive reaction likely to be aggravated by the explicit or implicit transmission to them of their white teachers' expectation that they will not succeed (Coleman et al. 1966; Rosenthal and Jacobsen 1968).
In a family, self-esteem is developed when parents accept the child, set clearly defined limits, transmit consistent values, and allow the child latitude within those limits. In an overcrowded home, with a mother who is often overwhelmed by economic, health, and emotional problems, all too often in the absence of a male parent, these prerequisites are unlikely to be available. Parental acceptance of the child may be inconsistent; limits may vary with parental moods; and it is likely that there are no achieving role-models. In short, environmental circumstances prevent such children from realizing their social potential in directions favorable to good school adjustment.
Moynihan (1965, 1969) has described how the historical background of slavery, which disrupted the African family, has affected the structure of contemporary black society. Serial common-law marriage, with large families on welfare, is common. The men, barred from property ownership or adequate participation in mainstream economy, are geographically mobile, passing from wife to wife. Families are necessarily

57

CHAPTER THREE

strongly matrifocal, and women convey to their sons a self-fulfilling prophecy: men are unreliable and bound to fail. The picture of the steel-hard black woman dominating and disparaging her men is portrayed by Eldridge Cleaver in *Soul on Ice* (1967). Boys carry their resentment toward women into the school, where they are liable to reject the female achievement models offered to them.

The black boy is propelled early into a peer culture in which admired older males convey values that deviate from those offered by the school. The boy who does well in school may find himself out of step with his peers or even rejected as one who curries favor with white authority. The particularly difficult identity crisis of the adolescent black male may explain why he is outstripped by the girl who does better in school, reaches a higher level of education, is more stable occupationally, and does better on IQ tests by 3 or 4 points (Shuey 1966). The consequences of low self-esteem are lack of confidence, withdrawal, the rejection of personal perceptions, and high levels of psychosomatic distress, manifest in tension symptoms and a tendency to "act out" impulsively when under pressure.

STIGMA

Stigma refers to any attribute of a person or group—skin color, for example—that discredits them in some way and puts them at a disadvantage in relation to others. Other people react to the stigmatized person or group with uneasiness, lack of acceptance, outright rejection, or defensiveness. The stigmatized group may become stereotyped and act out the stereotype, a phenomenon illustrated by Cleaver (1967) and Fanon (1965). Note, by the way, the traditional black stereotype: on the one hand, fun-loving, childlike, rhythmical; on the other, impulsive, dangerous, and sexually prodigious.

LACK OF BASIC TRUST

Marans and Lourie (1967) describe a fundamental uncertainty in poor children that their dependency needs will be satisfied. The mother is often overwhelmed by her own needs and inconsistent in her perception of the child's. She may rely, too much, on physical rather than verbal methods of comforting her child. Multiple mothering, the early assignment to the child of household responsibilities (especially child care, in the case of the black girl), exposure to overstimulation (such as frightening adult quarrels or premature sexual arousal), the tendency to use physical punishment rather than praise to control behavior, a lack of patience with the child's exploratory behavior—all these factors affect personality development at a fundamental level. The child is likely to develop a precocious pseudomaturity that defends against unsatisfied needs and propels the boy, early, into the absorbing world of the teenage gang.

IMPULSIVENESS

Compared to the middle-class child, Marans and Lourie assert, the black lives in an environment in which adults speak less with children (an assertion challenged by Horner and Gussow [1972]). This leads to a less verbally mediated control of action and a tendency for emotions to be expressed through the body rather than in words. The child may have difficulty in sitting still in the classroom, in attending to new material, and in tolerating frustration. Magical, preoperational thinking tends to dominate cognition in the form of action images, at the expense of the abstract representational thought that is necessary for scholastic attainment. In short, the child tends to be impulsive rather than reflective and to rely on a physical rather than a verbal expression of feeling.

ASPIRATIONS AND VALUES

Symbolic reward for postponement of gratification plays little part in the motivation of black children. Their goals tend to be immediate and utilitarian. The differences between the black girl and the middle-class girl are not so much in her values as in the circumstances in which those values are called into play (Gordon 1970). The black boy shares with his more privileged fellow a desire for possessions and status and a concern for in-group morality; but the black is less likely to express these through the acquisition of formal scholastic knowledge in the conventional competitive setting. The middle-class child is more likely to have been exposed to consistent expectations of competitive success and to have developed a desire for individual scholastic achievement. Children of low socioeconomic status tend to have low scholastic and occupational aspirations, the latter being surely an accurate reflection of the real situation. There is evidence that a newfound sense of positive identity and political power may change the traditionally passive and inadequate self-concept of the black (Coles 1963). The presence of black adults who have been successful will also be beneficial.

COGNITION

It is artificial to think of knowing stripped of feeling. Zigler (1966) has suggested that educational policies have failed to the extent that they have emphasized the cognitive to the exclusion of the motivational; yet the bulk of research work in this field has dealt with cognitive deficits and differences (in disadvantaged children from different ethnic groups), and in this section they will be reviewed separately.

CHAPTER THREE

One of the more serious theoretical problems concerns causation. Almost all the research available is correlative; it is impossible to be sure whether the cognitive characteristics described are causally or noncausally associated with the environmental factors described. The evidence of causal connection is, therefore, largely of circumstantial nature. Wolf (1963), for example, was able to associate a number of environmental variables with measured IQ in disadvantaged Chicago schoolchildren. He found that parental socioeconomic status correlated at a .40 level with the child's IQ; however, IQ correlated at a much higher (.76) level with certain definable characteristics of the home environment. Wolf classified the following factors as relevant to the development of IQ:

1. Press for achievement motivation
    (*a*) Nature of intellectual expectations of the child
    (*b*) Nature of intellectual aspirations for the child
    (*c*) Amount of information about the child's intellectual development
    (*d*) Nature of rewards for intellectual development

2. Press for language development
    (*a*) Emphasis on use of language
    (*b*) Opportunities to enlarge vocabulary
    (*c*) Emphasis on correctness of language usage
    (*d*) Quality of language models available

3. Provision for general learning
    (*a*) Opportunity for learning in the home
    (*b*) Opportunity for learning outside the home
    (*c*) Availability of learning supplies
    (*d*) Availability of books and magazines
    (*e*) Nature and amount of assistance provided to facilitate learning

These findings were replicated by Dave (1963) in regard to educational achievement rather than IQ. In the United Kingdom, Wiseman (1964) found that the important influences on children's school attainment were not economic so much as morale versus social disintegration of the neighborhood; standards of maternal care; and the characteristics of the school. But the crucial factors appeared to be parental intelligence and parental attitudes to education. Genetic and environmental factors are thus inevitably intertwined and mutually confounding.

Partly as a result of the influence of Hunt's (1961) book, *Intelligence and Experience*, the theory of sensory deprivation was promoted. It had been found in a number of important animal experiments that severe restriction of visual or kinesthetic stimulation in early childhood could result in developmental arrest and neurological abnormality. Perhaps the disadvantaged child lacked sensory stimulation at a critical time. This theory had little to recommend it, as Bereiter and Engelmann (1966) have pointed out. The amount of deprivation described in the animal experiments is extreme and in no way comparable to the early experience of the underprivileged child. In a free environment, organisms will seek out their optimum level of stimulation. It is not common to find developmental arrest in the first two years; if anything, Afro-American children are developmentally advanced at that age (Bayley 1965). What the deprived child lacks is not quantity of stimulation but a particular quality: certain *patterns* of input that are important in promoting the cognitive competencies required for primary school.

Schoggen (1969), Smilansky (1968), and Eiferman (1968) describe how disadvantaged children are less likely to be guided in the acquisition of cognitive strategies by reinforcement from their parents. Klaus and Gray (1968) consider that confused background noise may interrupt the discrimination of figure and ground. Zigler and Butterfield (1968) suggest that the child may be unused to accepting verbal rather than material (for example, food) rewards. The child thus develops relative deficiencies in the use of verbal abstractions (Blank and Solomon 1968), in speaking about an object in the absence of the object (Deutsch 1963), and in orienting himself to three- and, especially, two-dimensional representations of concrete objects (Sigel 1968b). Lack of verbal and eye-hand stimulation leads to a depression of IQ test scores and scholastic achievement. The basis for these deficits is laid already before school entry, since 80 percent of the variance in IQ is thought to be determined by the end of early childhood (Bloom 1964).

Cazden (1968) and Sigelman (1972) have reviewed the voluminous research on language competence in disadvantaged children. Loban (1963) has described the cognitive impoverishment of the disadvantaged who use fewer of the structural resources of language, for example in categorization skills, syntax, and nominals. Already by eighteen months of age, higher-SES children are developmentally more advanced in phonology than are lower-SES children (Irwin 1948). Numerous studies (for example: Lesser, Fifer, and Clark 1965) have shown that higher-SES children have a larger vocabulary and that low in contrast to high SES seems to have a more adverse effect on verbal and other abilities in the black child. Templin (1957) has found that the mean length of utterance (MLR)—an index that he claims corresponds with grammatical complexity—is greater for high-SES children.

Cazden classifies the possible mediating variables as follows:

Chapter Three

1. Context of language acquisition
   (a) Affective quality: Language acquisition may be fostered in a warm interpersonal climate.
   (b) Adults versus children: The peer group may offer the predominant language models for disadvantaged children.
   (c) Contextual variety: Variety in family activities may foster language development.
   (d) Signal-to-noise ratio: A high noise level in the disadvantaged home may induce a habitual inattention.
2. Stimulation of the child
   (a) Conformity to standard English: This may be less important than the extent of verbal interaction among family members.
   (b) Linguistic variety: The variety of words and syntactic forms to which the child is exposed may affect language acquisition.
   (c) Sequence: It has been suggested that the disadvantaged child may be exposed to a less well ordered sequence of language stimulation.
   (d) Quantity: The frequency of exposure to language stimulation may function as a threshold effect.
3. Response to the child's speech
   (a) Reinforcement: It is still an open question whether reinforcement, in Skinner's (1957) terms, affects language acquisition. Cazden suggests that, in a broad sense, a subcultural emphasis on verbalization, as in the Jewish community, does promote verbal abilities.
   (b) Corrective feedback: This is particularly likely in the form of expansion, the child's utterance (*Mommy come*) being fed back in extended form (*Yes, Mommy is coming*). Echoing may have a similar effect. Corrections, except in the case of mistaken reference (*No, that's not a cow, it's a horse*), seem to be less important.

John (1963) describes three major levels of language behavior: labeling, relating, and categorizing. *Labeling* is akin to a morphological analysis of the relationship between word and referent. *Relating* is equivalent to syntactic analysis. *Categorizing* involves covert, internal language function. By the fifth grade, in primary school, middle-SES children are superior in labeling ability, expressive vocabulary, nonverbal IQ, and classificatory skills. The middle-class child therefore has a more precise, abstract, and integrative language competence. John and Goldstein (1964) suggest that the crucial difference is in the use of language in lower- and middle-class homes, the lower-class child experiencing less feedback correction, and expansion—particularly when the relationship between word and referent is indirect or abstract. In the middle-class home, the verbal mediation of adult-child interaction aids the child in the search for word-referent invariances.

An extreme version of the language deprivation theory has been propounded by Bereiter and Engelmann (1966) in their rationale for the development of a direct language-instruction, preschool program (described in chapters 4 and 6 of this book). They consider that language is a convenience but not a necessity for the young child whose needs are predominantly social; it becomes essential in a context in which knowledge is to be transmitted and concepts manipulated. Deliberate teaching is not characteristic of the underprivileged home; the poor boy first experiences a world of explicit meanings when he goes to school. He is not without a culture but, rather, deprived of that part of culture which can only be acquired by direct, verbal communication. Consequently, when he arrives at school a disadvantaged child has a language development characteristic of a younger middle-class child. Bereiter and Engelmann describe how he often tends to run words and phrases together to form "giant word units," failing to break a sentence up into its constituent sequential parts: *That is a red truck*, for example, becomes *Da're'truh*. Grammar is drastically reduced; inflections and structure words such as prepositions and conjunctions are particularly affected. The point at issue is not the degree to which the dialect used is technically competent to convey information but the extent to which the underprivileged child actually makes use of language to convey explicit information and to carry on those internal dialogues required by conceptual thought. Bereiter and Engelmann base the objectives of their program on these considerations.

RESTRICTED AND ELABORATED CODES

The British sociologist Bernstein (1961) has attempted to correlate social class, linguistic environment, language codes, and psychosocial characteristics. He has been very influential. Bernstein was the first to propose a theory about social class, child-rearing, language development, and scholastic competence that relates these factors in an empirically testable way. He thus goes beyond the rather naïve and essentially ethnocentric theories of "deprivation" and "deficit" to examine the positive aspects of SES groups in the same culture and the qualitative differences between them.

Chapter Three

Bernstein has cataloged the scholastic problems of the English working-class child as follows: depressed verbal scores on ability tests; poor reading skills; verbal and written expression dominated by concrete action; syntax limited; thinking rigid due to dislocation of propositions and difficulty in generalizing operations; and lack of understanding of arithmetical processes.

Bernstein distinguishes two types of language code. One, the *restricted code*, is characterized by a rigid use of syntax and a restriction of the formal possibilities of verbal organization. Thus sentences in this form tend to be short, grammatically simple, stressing the active voice, with limited and repetitive use of conjunctions, little use of subordinate clauses, limited use of adjectives, and infrequent use of impersonal pronouns as subjects of conditional clauses. Restricted-code users have difficulty in sustaining a formal subject through a speech sequence, characteristically confuse reason and conclusion,[4] and rely upon idiomatic colloquial stereotypies in a predictable way. The restricted code is a language of implicit meaning in which feelings are differentiated by idioms that are the result of shared experience. The restricted code relies upon contextual cues for comprehension. It becomes predominant in an environment in which the mother places little pressure on the child to verbalize experience, and in which spoken language is not perceived as a major vehicle for conveying inner states. The restricted code symbolizes the normative aspects of the group and reinforces the existing pattern of social relationships. It deals with direct, immediate, unspecifically descriptive aspects of the environment. It supports a particular kind of authority in which social power is quickly revealed, in a setting which stresses group solidarity and loyalty.

The following extract—from one of Bernstein's (1961) transcripts of a tape-recorded discussion with a sixteen-year-old youth of average intelligence—illustrates the stereotypies, the narrative, active style, and the implied meaning and concreteness of the restricted code: "It's all according like these youths and that if they get into these gangs and that they most have a bit of a nark around and say it goes wrong and that and they probably knock someone off I mean think they just do it to be big getting publicity here and there."

Bernstein contrasts the restricted with an *elaborated code* more characteristic of middle-class speakers. The elaborated code has a much less predictable grammar and phraseology. Precise and accurate syntax is employed. Logical modifications and stress are mediated through a grammatically complex sentence construction, for example by the use of

---

4. For example: Q. *Why can't I go out to play?* A. *Because I said so!*

a range of conjunctions and subordinate clauses. Prepositions are frequently used, to indicate logical relationships as well as temporal and spatial contiguity. The first personal pronoun is frequently used. There is a wide range of adjectives and adverbs. Individual qualifications are mediated through the structure and internal relationships within and between sentences. It is a language form which develops the possibilities inherent in a complex conceptual hierarchy for the organization of experience, stressing universal rather than context-dependent meanings.

The restricted code stresses group solidarity, consensus, and the authority structure in that group. The elaborated code stresses individuality and individual responsibility. The working-class child is likely to be limited to one code, whereas the middle-class child can switch from a private to a public code in accordance with environmental circumstances and individual needs.

The concept of *code-switching*, the ability to shift at will from a restricted to a more elaborate form of speech, has stimulated useful research. The middle-class child is thought to be more facile in the ability to switch and thus better able to benefit from school. Lawton (1964, 1968), in England, did in fact find a cumulative difference between lower- and upper-SES children in this respect, although lower-SES adolescents were not unable to switch codes if necessary. The difference was one of degree. When Williams and Naremore (1969), in the United States, compared black and white schoolchildren who were matched for age, sex, and SES, they noted status differences in length of utterance and syntactic complexity. The low-SES child, regardless of race, sex, or age, tended to speak more in the first person and to be more concrete and particular (a detail not in accord with Bernstein's observations in Great Britain).

The work of Fries (1940) and of Shatzman and Strauss (1955), which antedated Bernstein's, is consistent with the latter's theory. Analyzing letters to an army authority and oral descriptions of a tornado, respectively, from lower- and middle-class subjects, they noted: dialect differences; a greater concern for precision on the part of the middle class (MC), as shown by the use of prepositions, conjunctions, and compound nouns; a more egocentric perspective in the working class (WC) associated with less qualification and elaboration, the tendency to rely upon "sympathetic circularities"[5] (for example: *and stuff like that . . . you know*), and a straight narrative approach; and a tendency for the middle class to adopt a more general and relative perspective with a more organized marshaling of facts.

---

5. Bernstein's term, referring to idiomatic stereotypies employed usually to evoke consensus.

CHAPTER THREE

Bernstein (1962a, 1962b), in England, found that, in a discussion of capital punishment, lower working class (LWC) subjects, compared to MC subjects matched for intelligence and age (sixteen years), used shorter words, a longer mean phrase length, and less frequent pauses. The last phenomenon was related by Bernstein to a relative lack of verbal planning, the LWC adolescent relying more on precoded verbal stereotypies (for example: *and that ... you know ... isn't it*). Lawton (1968) replicated this study and found, in addition, that the middle class used deeper clause-imbedding and more abstract and categorial examples. Lawton's conclusions as to code-switching have already been mentioned.

Henderson (1970), working with five-year-old English children, described a tendency for MC children to change syntax and lexis more than LWC, when switching from a narrative to a descriptive oral style. Hawkins (1969) found similar characteristics in LWC narratives and descriptions: fewer pronoun referents, fewer epithets at the head of sentences, and fewer adjectival modifiers, ordinatives, intensifiers, and rank-shifted head clauses. Two recent investigations in the United States, by Shriner and Miner (1968) and by LaCivita, Kean, and Yamamoto (1966), could find no class differences in the application of syntactic rules to nonsense syllables and in the use of grammatical cues to identify parts of speech; but these two studies have been severely criticized by Robinson (1973) on the basis of inadequate sampling and matching.

From the use of written material and the *cloze procedure* (subjects have to guess randomized deletions from a corpus of speech or writing), Robinson found class differences in twelve-year-old English children in lexis, variety and type of response, and verbal conformity and predictability, in accord with Bernstein's theory. Deutsch et al. (1967), in the United States, found that whereas MC and WC children were equally accurate in guessing gaps in WC speech, MC children were more effective than WC in regard to MC speech. Similar observations applied to a black-white comparison: blacks had more trouble with white speech than the reverse.

The technical problems and issues involved in this research have been reviewed by Robinson (1973). Generally speaking, Bernstein's theory that WC speech and MC speech differ in syntax and lexis appears to have been supported. But what of the broader issue? Does the middle class *use* language for purposes foreign to the working class? In all the studies cited, MC and WC language expression appear to diverge when referential function is stressed, the WC having a less efficient syntax and lexis for the transmission and reception of descriptive and general—rather than narrative and particular—messages. But much more work needs to be done before the association between the structure and functions of language in different social classes can be regarded as defined.

DEPRIVATION, DISADVANTAGE, OR DIFFERENCE?

Hess and Shipman (1965), following Bernstein's theory, postulated that the child's cognitive style is related to his mother's linguistic system and to her style of limitation and control. They compared four different groups of black mother-child pairs, ranging from college-educated to welfare-dependent, by observing the pairs directly as they were involved in tasks requiring interaction. All findings were in the directions predicted. Relative to the upper-SES group, lower-SES mothers spoke less with their children, used less elaborated language, and tended to use controls that were "status-oriented" (*Stop that; because I say so*) rather than "person-oriented" (*Stop that; because you will get hurt*). Middle-class mothers used more descriptive and categorial concepts whereas welfare mothers concentrated more on relational concepts;[6] and the comparative emphasis on categorization correlated with the level of the child's concept development. In teaching their children a task, middle-class mothers revealed a wider range of interactional styles and a more reflective and verbal approach. This study represented a milestone since it depended on a controlled and systematic observation of what goes on between parent and child, rather than a static assessment of one or the other and a purely theoretical attempt to intercorrelate the two. Robinson and Rackstraw (1972) have reported corroborative findings from a more static interview study of English mothers and their children.

CULTURE AND DIALECT

Recently, theories of sociocultural deprivation have been criticized by a group of linguists (Baratz 1967, 1969b; Labov 1970a, 1970b; Stewart 1964). These workers assert that the language-deficit interpretation is a misconception. Black children speak a dialect that differs in its grammatical rules from standard English. Black English is a fully developed language and should be properly understood before intervention programs are begun. The scholastic problems of black children are due not to language deficits but to the fact that they are not naturally bidialectal: in other words, they are not naturally proficient in standard English as an alternative to their primary nonstandard dialect. Osser, Wang, and Zaid (1969), for example, found that black children had difficulty comprehending and imitating constructions in standard English (SE), whereas Baratz (1969b) found that white children had difficulty in comprehending and imitating nonstandard English (NSE). Labov has suggested that the marked opposition between school and peer influences in regard to values is more important than the language

6. A descriptive concept employs form or color. A relational concept involves use. A categorial concept comes from inferential, superordinate, verbal categorization. A saucepan and a frying pan may be associated on the basis of form (both round), color (both silver), use (both used for cooking), or categorial inference (both utensils).

Chapter Three

environment in early childhood in determining lack of scholastic success; he also suggests that there is no justification for the conclusion that NSE is inferior to SE as a medium for communication or thinking.

Labov's (1970b) lively article on the logic of nonstandard English has been very influential. For that reason it deserves to be reviewed in some detail. He begins by selecting comments from Bereiter and Engelmann (1966) on language deficits in lower-SES children to represent the cultural deprivation theory. He criticizes the argument that black children have "no language at all" by presenting samples of speech from eight-year-old black children who were first interviewed and then allowed to interact in a less formal, natural setting. In the latter context the children were more communicative though, on the evidence offered, scarcely as fluent as Labov suggests. His conclusion is that formal testing and conventional school situations do not allow children to express their full competence. Labov then offers examples of how NSE can be flexible, colorful, and logical whereas a speaker of SE may be dull, confused, and illogical. He points out that NSE operates by grammatical rules (unrecognized by Bereiter and Engelmann) that are no less complex than— only different from—SE. The English of NSE speakers differs from that of SE speakers in surface structure only; the logic of the deep structures is equivalent. Language programs based on an inappropriate verbal deprivation theory are damaging not only because they support the ethnocentric prejudices of middle-class teachers but also because they are bound to fail since they are based on a false premise—giving further support to those who propound theories of innate racial differences.

Labov's paper is a healthy corrective to oversimplified notions of language deprivation; but in his resounding attack he goes far beyond the data available. Bereiter and Engelmann represent an extreme viewpoint; Labov caricatures it. Bereiter and Engelmann refer to four-year-old children; Labov draws his refuting evidence from anecdotes about children twice to four times as old. The issue at stake is not whether a selected black boy can be induced to be more fluent verbally, or even whether he can apply NSE to a logical problem, but whether blacks as a group can and do express their language competence in this way. The problem will not be solved by appeals to linguistic orthodoxy, gratuitous presumptions about other workers,[7] the demolition of straw men, or the substitution of anecdotes for properly controlled empirical research.

Cole and Bruner (1973) develop the cultural difference theory further. Linguists assert that all languages are equivalent, functionally, in their communicative capacity. The apparent deficits in the conceptual

---

7. Labov (1970b: 156) describes Bernstein's views as "filtered through a strong bias against all forms of working-class behavior."

thinking of culturally different children may be due to their inability or unwillingness to express basic competencies in a formal test situation, especially if the tester speaks SE and the subject NSE. "Cultural deprivation" represents a special form of cultural difference that arises when a person is faced with the demand to perform in a manner inconsistent with past experience.

It is useful at this point to examine the arguments in the light of the definitions provided in chapter 1. The two approaches will be labeled *cultural deprivation* and *cultural difference*. Cultural deprivation theorists implicitly agree with the cultural difference group in their assertion that different races have equivalent potential. The difficulty comes with realization. Culturally deprived children are described as not realizing their competencies in the same way or to the same degree as the nondeprived. In particular, the basic competencies—cognitive and motivational—required to make progress in formal schooling are poorly realized. It is assumed that the key deficit is in language, although the causal interaction between language and intellectual process is unclear. Deprived children have not been exposed to a rich language environment and thus lack the vocabulary, the concepts, and the flexible, precise syntax required for the operational thinking of primary school. There are subsidiary and related problems: the self-image of a group stigmatized by skin color; impulsivity; social expectations of failure; lack of a need for achievement; lack of experience of verbal (rather than material) rewards; poor educational facilities; and subnutrition. But the central issue, stressed by all workers, is the degree to which language is exploited in the service of decentered thought. It is hypothesized, with some empirical evidence (Hess and Shipman 1965), that the inadequate realization of potential is related to the fact that the parents of deprived children interact less intensively (than middle-class parents) with them, verbally, regarding phenomena that are either immediate and concrete or remote and abstract.

Cultural difference theorists place more weight upon differences in the *expression* of competencies. Minority-group children are described as having more competence than unimaginative psychometricians have detected. They do not express their competence in formal test situations, partly because of social inhibition and partly because of their poor comprehension of both tester and test. NSE dialect has the capacity—that is, the child has the competence—to express the same range of ideas as SE; but ethnocentric evaluators fail to maximize the child's performance by recognizing and drawing out the child's full competence.

Do Labov, Baratz, and Cole and Bruner believe that the culturally different child has the same range and depth, the same spectrum

Chapter Three

and profile, of competencies as the middle-class child? If so, one logical solution would be to change the educational system and arrange a segregated streaming of children according to language code. This is, in effect, a conclusion akin to that which Jensen (1969a) has reached. Black children would be taught by black teachers, or at least by white teachers who speak NSE, using educational materials based on NSE. Baratz and Shuy (1969) and Labov have proposed that reading should be taught initially from NSE materials and that SE syntax should be gradually introduced. Labov asks for a "healthy eclecticism" and concedes that some speakers of NSE may fail to exploit the possibilities inherent in the dialect. We should determine which SE speech patterns facilitate learning and then try to make black children bidialectal in these terms. How can we provide each child with motivation to exploit the language he already has? Educators should not attempt to eliminate NSE.

Cole and Bruner also retreat, somewhat, from their initial stance. They wonder whether black children can use language of a decentered type, out of immediate context and in a hypothetical way. If not, they may become locked into the life of their own cultural group and their migration into other groups will become difficult. Cole and Bruner point out that we do not know the nature of the social situations that permit the control and utilization of the resources of a culture by one of its members; nor do we understand the cognitive skills that would be demanded of one who would use these resources. What are the rules for applying cognitive skills? We have yet to define them.

Cultural difference theorists do not rule out the possibility of competency differences derived from developmental experiences that have not fully stimulated the realization of potentials important for school achievement. They concede that there may be differences in competency profile. Cole and Bruner point, also, to the need to learn the rules of expression of cognitive competencies. The black child may lack a knowledge of some of the context-related rules that transform deep competency structures into performance (see chapter 7).

Bernstein (1972) has recently expressed criticism of the notion of cultural deprivation and counsels against a simple equation of restricted code with language deficit. The term *deprivation* has a pejorative aspect; it shifts attention from school to home by labeling parents as "inadequate" and children as "deficit systems." It drives a wedge between school and home when what is required is to bring the two closer together and, by planning not only for preschool but for the entire educational period, to adapt our rather inflexible schools to suit a culturally diverse community.

Nevertheless, Bernstein goes on to say, the communicative competence associated with an elaborated code puts the middle-class child in touch with *universal meanings*, in contrast to the more context-related semantic space of a restricted code. The middle-class child may have access to deep interpretive rules that regulate linguistic response in the formal context of the school, a consequence of an explicit elaboration of those rules in the middle-class home. The working-class child is more oriented toward *particular meanings* which do not transcend the context.

The school is concerned with the transmission of explicit, universal meanings by elaborating universal principles and operations as these apply to people and things. Middle-class children are already oriented to this approach when they get to school; whereas working-class children are more familiar with particular, implicit meaning. In Bernstein's terms, the school attempts to transmit public, explicit knowledge through various metalanguages of control and innovation that may not be part of the poorer child's prior experience. But there is no basis for the description of a restricted code as "deprived." There is nothing in a dialect form per se that prevents a child from learning universal meanings—provided he has the necessary vocabulary and the interpretive rules for their reception and expression. Teachers should begin, therefore, with what the child has to offer. This is not compensatory education; it is education.

Leacock (1972), like Bernstein, criticizes the way that tentative linguistic and psychosocial theories have become dogmatized and applied in a grossly distorted way. A case in point is the widely accepted class difference in the ability to think abstractly and the dichotomy between abstract and concrete speech. Abstract speculation, necessarily, grows from and returns to concrete observation if it is to be fruitful. Black speakers, for example, make extensive use of metaphor in conveying the general, essential intangible qualities of people and things, although this is not usually thought of as abstraction; take for example the phrases *He hangs cool* and *He sustains his calmness*. Group differences in styles of speech and thought are associated not with a crude absence or presence of abstract thinking but with different contexts of application and different styles of elaboration. The predominant differences are therefore in the strategies, tactics, and contexts of expression rather than in underlying competence.

According to Kochman (1972) the new culturally relative approach will transform education in three ways: it will cause teachers to acknowledge the legitimacy of native dialect, language, and culture; it will make clear the need to learn more about native language and culture; and it will lead to a decentralization of educational administration and an acceptance of—and planning for—cultural diversity.

CHAPTER THREE

Hymes (1972) affirms that there is no basis for assuming that different language or dialect groups have different underlying communicative competencies. But some children are, indeed, at a disadvantage if the contexts that permit the expression of their competence are absent at school or if their manner of expressing competence is punished by the teacher. Hymes has introduced the important notion of *communicative repertoire* to augment the abstract and formalized ideas of competence and performance proposed by Noam Chomsky (see chapter 7). Repertoire has a threefold meaning here: the set of means, and the meanings attached to those means, that make up communicative competence; the contexts in which the particular means may be expressed; and the strategies of expression of the means in those contexts. The second and third aspects of repertoire greatly enrich the idea of linguistic performance, a concept that had been relegated to a position of relative unimportance by Chomsky. Those who share a communicative repertoire can be regarded as belonging to the same *speech community*. Speakers of the same language may not belong to the same speech community: a university professor, for example, may be at a loss in a group of professional football players. One person may belong to a number of speech communities— another way of saying that such a person has an ability to switch language codes in Bernstein's sense. When the issue is put in these terms, its educational relevance is clear: if the child is to participate in the community of the school then the teacher must participate in the community of the child.

The growth of linguistic knowledge about minority groups heralds a much greater awareness of the positive features of their competencies. The deprivation theory served a purpose, initially, in alerting educators to a potentially ameliorable "problem."[8] The emergence of the notion of cultural pluralism, and an awareness of the potentially damaging aspects of the puritan ethic and the ethnocentrism associated with it, have given rise to the notion of cultural difference. Educational approaches based on deficit theory alone may fail to exploit and build upon the strengths already exhibited by the child. More work needs to be done: (1) to determine the spectrum of competencies manifested by different cultural and subcultural groups and the relative development— the profile—of the individual competencies in each group (see chapter 7); (2) to elucidate the personality and motivational factors associated with the expression of those competencies (Cole et al. 1971); (3) to elicit the natural cognitive styles of those groups (Witkin 1967) and the sensory modalities favored by them in learning (Wober 1966; Marsella and Higgenbottham 1973); and (4) to design educational objectives consonant

8. Although the growth of a passive attitude has been noted (Winschel 1970)—some teachers have given up on the basis that deprivation has rendered the child ineducable.

with the group's lifestyle as well as instructional strategies that complement rather than violate their cultural norms.

THE CENTRAL FUNCTION OF LANGUAGE

The reader will have noted the way in which language has been stressed in these studies of cultural disadvantage and difference. The precise function of language in the realization and expression of cognitive competence is in some dispute (see chapter 7), but most writers see it as a cornerstone on which other cognitive skills are built. It is for this reason that the development of language competence is a central objective in most preschool compensatory programs. The work of Sigel and his colleagues (Sigel and McBane 1967; Sigel 1968a, 1968b; Sigel and Olmstead 1970a, 1970b) is germane to this issue and forms a useful introduction to the next chapter, on preschool programs.

Sigel has paid particular attention to the development of representational thought and classification. He sees both issues as interwoven and both, in turn, as affected by the culture in which they develop. Things or events may be represented in the form of internalized actions (think of a tennis backhand), images (think of a Christian cross), or words (which are quite arbitrary representations of the things or events to which they refer). Classification is the organization of instances on the basis of one or more observable or inferred criteria, such as color, form, or utility.

Sigel found that lower-SES preschool children have a relative difficulty in classifying two-dimensional pictorial representations of objects. Lower-class children are more likely to classify on the basis of color whereas middle-class children use form and color. A high variability was found among the "deprived" group, suggesting that it is heterogeneous (a fact obscured by such collective terms as "deprived," "disadvantaged," or—to a lesser extent—"different"). Preschool programs contribute, potentially, to a stabilization of the idea of objects and of word-referent associations. Sigel suggests that intervention programs should attempt to help the child switch from an action-oriented, sensorimotor form of thought to a representational one. In subsequent studies, he has tried to promote the ability to classify concrete objects and two-dimensional representations of things by comparing a variety of teaching techniques.

Sigel considers that when children are in transition between cognitive stages, a more flexible language may provide the impetus to propel them onward. Cognition is reinforced by the syntactic structures of language. A less flexible and extensive syntax may be associated with difficulties in representational classification and logical-mathematical problems. Sigel notes that the underprivileged child's play is highly motoric and both less reflective and less well ordered than that of the middle class. The upper-SES parent is more likely to inject structure into the child's play, to integrate it with language, and to provide demonstrations, cautions, and explanations.

Sigel asserts that we transform our perceptual world by creating representations of it and then reimposing them on the world. Western technological societies stress the development of verbal, categorial symbols which represent superordinate conceptual systems and which constitute both the rationale of the categorization as well as the content of the category. The word *transformation*, for example, describes both a kind of process and the condition of having undergone that process. Piaget suggests that representation extends adaptation in space and time. Representations can be external (as in a picture) or internal (as in a mental image). They are *distal* from the perceptual world. Sigel considers language to be a system of signs that can function to evoke representations. The acquisition of representations is hypothesized to be a function of life experiences which create temporal, spatial, or psychological *distance* between self and object and which separate idea from action. Distance may be in terms of time (past–present–future), space (here–not here), or reality (observable–inferential). Middle-class homes foster distance in representation by providing a relatively structured and sequential environment; a linguistic environment with a high frequency of words denoting distance between referent and reality; and role-models who demonstrate the relevance and pragmatic value of distancing.

SUMMARY

In the 1960s the concepts of cultural deprivation and disadvantage became influential. The underprivileged child was described as lacking in certain crucial experiences, prior to school entry, that were important for adaptation to school. The deprivation–deficit theory evolved in an attempt to explain why improvement in elementary and high school facilities had not had a more significant effect upon the scholastic attainment of minority-group children. Deprivation was described as affecting physical, personality, and cognitive development.

Physical deprivation involves protein-calorie subnutrition and exposure to disease and other dangers. It is of particular importance in developing countries in which the incidence of breast-feeding is declining and infant feeding is of poor quality. There is some evidence of a critical period in brain development before, and about six months after, birth. Protein restriction at that time may lead to an irreversible growth arrest with permanent reduction of brain-cell population. The effects of starvation occurring later can be reversed by restoration of normal diet.

Lower-SES children may be at a disadvantage in school because of personality factors. The black child has been described as lacking in self-esteem as a result of adverse home and school experiences, stigmatized, lacking in basic trust, apt to be impulsive rather than reflective, and liable to express feelings physically rather than in words. The validity of these impressions is probably reduced by the clinical, ethnocentric bias of many of the observers who formed them.

The cognitive deficits due to cultural disadvantage have been related to a lack of pressure at home for achievement, a relatively meager language environment, and poor provision for general learning. Language deficits have been described repeatedly: especially immature phonology, restricted vocabulary, a less extensive and flexible syntax, and a relative difficulty in the use of abstractions.

Bernstein describes two language codes: the restricted and the elaborated. The restricted code is context-bound, simpler in syntax, and characteristic of status-oriented working-class groups. The elaborated code is more precise and complex in syntax, more abstract, and more characteristic of formal thought in middle-class groups. The lower-SES child has difficulty switching from a familiar, restricted code to the public, elaborated, written and spoken code of school.

Recently a group of linguists has challenged the theory of cultural deprivation and language deficit. The black child is said to speak a dialect —black, nonstandard English—that operates by syntactic rules different from those of standard English. The finding of cognitive deficits may be—at least partly—a result of the failure of observers to appreciate the cultural differences manifest in differences in the structure and expression of SE and NSE. Moreover, the characteristically lower test results of people culturally different from the white middle class may be due in part to a failure of testers to mobilize the cognitive competencies of those tested, since the structure and content of the tests are alien to, or violate, the norms of the subculture in which they are applied.

Despite these observations, there is universal attention to the function of language in the development of representational thought. Some cultures, more than others, exploit the possibilities inherent in language to foster symbolic, verbal, categorial, abstract thought. By this means, *distance* is fostered between self and object and between idea and action. The middle-class home appears to offer a particularly favorable environment for such distance to develop.

The points of contention can be represented by the angles of a triangle. At one point are Bernstein, Sigel, and the cultural disadvantage

Chapter Three

theorists: Underprivileged children are handicapped at school, predominantly by the lack of a distanced, more general and relative, language and language-based approach to problems; and this is an outcome of a lack of exposure to certain patterns of stimulation in early life. At the second point is Jensen: The deficit in verbal-abstract thinking has a primarily genetic origin. At the third point are Labov and Cole et al., who oppose both Bernstein and Jensen. These writers, they claim, have failed to detect the full competence of disadvantaged children. The underprivileged child is culturally different, speaks a different dialect of English, and has different rules for the expression of competence. The adherents of each of these views make corrections to modify the extremities of their positions vis-à-vis the others; but the polarized triangle suggested here is a useful representation of the main views in the current controversy.

CHAPTER 4
EARLY CHILDHOOD EDUCATION: SUCCESS OR FAILURE?

Mankind is one and all men are alike in that which concerns their creation and all natural things, and no one is born enlightened.
Bartolome de Las Casas

Teachers have been assigned the task of saving the human race by educating a superior new generation who will rectify the evils created by past generations or at least not succumb to them. But the same humanistic ethos that tells them what qualities the next generation should have also tells them that they have no right to manipulate other people or impose their goals upon them.
Carl Bereiter

Compensatory education has been tried and it apparently has failed.
Arthur Jensen

HISTORICAL BACKGROUND

In Australia and North America, the impetus for the development of preschools gathered after World War I. Many forces contributed to the educational philosophy associated with this movement; Froebel, Pestalozzi, Freud, Montessori, and Dewey were prominent influences. As a consequence of the movement, the child's development was viewed as a whole and broad social, emotional, and psychomotor goals were advocated. The importance of play as a rehearsal for life was affirmed and the child's independence, peer relations, exploratory curiosity, and creativity were defined as central issues.

CHAPTER FOUR

Although in Australia and the United Kingdom there were sporadic attempts to provide preschool and day-care centers in poor inner city areas, for the most part these facilities were available only for middle-class suburban children in communities cohesive and affluent enough to organize and support them. A typical contemporary Australian preschool, for example, offers a half- or full-day program, with a teacher/pupil ratio of about 1 to 20 for three- to five-year-old children. It functions in a one-story building, in spacious grounds, and offers a wide variety of attractive toys, manipulative objects, and play equipment. Although there is a definite regularity in the preschool day, within this framework the child is encouraged to explore spontaneously, at his own pace, in an accepting environment. In effect, what has evolved is a system well designed to supplement the already enriched but often restrictive and overdirected environment of the middle-class child.

In the early 1960s, in the United States, the growth of the concept of cultural deprivation led to the promotion of preschool education as an antidote to the cumulative cognitive deficits described in disadvantaged children. Piaget, for example, had proposed that logical ("operational") intellectual competencies arise from sensorimotor skills in early childhood; for this reason, the long-neglected perceptual training techniques of Maria Montessori were rediscovered and advocated. The concepts of critical early periods for learning, and of the malleability of the young child, suggested that a little enrichment in "the magic years" might have far-reaching later effects. Early childhood education, which had been languishing in the United States, was promoted as the means of enabling disadvantaged children to benefit from the formal educational system, a system that had become increasingly discredited because of its manifest incompetence to educate a large proportion of the country's youth. For the first time, cognitive rather than social and emotional preschool goals were stressed. The children in question, compared to the white middle class, were described as having deficiencies in intellectual and language development. Educational technology and strategies would be brought to bear on these target areas. But which technology? What strategies? And how would they be evaluated?

The scope and importance of the idea attracted the dedicated support and involvement of a large number of skilled people. The buoyancy of the Kennedy era, and of President Johnson's War on Poverty, spawned Project Head Start in 1965. With hasty preparation and rather vague goals a large number of preschools were established for minority-group and other disadvantaged children. A thousand different flowers bloomed in a unique and historic venture.

Early Childhood Education

THE WESTINGHOUSE EVALUATION

In 1969 came the reckoning. The task of evaluating the impact of Head Start was contracted out to the Westinghouse Learning Corporation, which was asked to answer the following questions: Does Head Start have a measurable impact on the early school performance and adjustment of the children who have experienced it? If so, how much? What is the benefit of summer Head Start (six to eight weeks) compared with the full-year program? If there are benefits, are they durable?

From almost 13,000 Head Start programs, a sample of 104 was drawn for evaluation: 75 summer and 29 full-year. Although a "before, after, and follow-up" evaluation would have been preferable, time exigencies made this impossible. The evaluators, therefore, compared ex-Head Start children in the first three grades of school with others who had not been to preschool and who were matched for grade, area of residence, previous eligibility for Head Start, race, and sex.[1] The total sample was of approximately 2,000 Head Start and 2,000 control children.

The evaluation instruments employed were aimed at cognitive, affective, and environmental areas. The first-grade children were given a learning readiness test (the Metropolitan Readiness Test) and the second- and third-grade children a standard achievement test of scholastic progress. (the Stanford Achievement Test). All children were tested as to language development with the Illinois Test of Psycholinguistic Abilities. Tests of self-concept, classroom behavior, and attitudes were also designed, although these were regarded as of uncertain validity. The third set of tests comprised questionnaires about social background, parental aspirations for the child, and the school environment.

White (1970) has described the many controversial features of the evaluation. Could and should a definitive study have been done while Head Start goals and strategies were still unclarified? Were the evaluation methodology and instruments acceptable? Should summer and full-year programs be lumped together?[2] Which type of statistical analysis should be employed? At the same time, a political contest was brewing: on the one side congressional forces that wished to continue poverty programs, including Head Start; on the other, the new Nixon administration which sought to change them. There was severe pressure on the evaluators to get out a report, a preliminary form of which appeared in April 1969.

In summary, the Westinghouse evaluation revealed that the

---

1. The appropriateness of this matching procedure has been severely criticized by Campbell and Erlebacher (1970).
2. Eventually, they were evaluated separately.

CHAPTER FOUR

summer Head Start programs, generally and locally, did not produce measurable gains in those aspects of the cognitive and affective domains tested; and this was true in each grade. The full-year programs produced positive effects in the first two grades. (The number of children in the third grade was too small for meaningful comparison.) Head Start children were superior on the first-grade learning readiness test, and elsewhere there were scattered results favoring Head Start. There was a suggestion that Head Start produced its most favorable results in the southeast and with blacks. There were no differences in affective status between Head Start and control children. Thus marginal positive results in cognitive areas were all that could be pointed to.

The evaluation was directed to whether Head Start had made a national impact. It did not answer whether it might do so in the future or which programs in particular did, or were likely to, produce results. It was not designed to find out what had prevented better results from being manifest. The conclusion drawn by many—that Head Start had been an expensive failure—was premature. Nevertheless, clearly the time had come for taking stock.

One of the major deficiencies of the question to which Westinghouse directed itself is its very comprehensiveness. If one were to ask a health service whether surgery were effective, nationally, one would surely expect the evaluators to ask: What kind of surgery? By which surgeons? With what kind of patient? With what aim? Appendectomy performed upon cardiac patients by trainee operators for the purpose of curing duodenal ulcer would certainly not be expected to produce useful results. One can push the medical analogy too far, of course, but it does have the advantage of emphasizing the imprecise nature of some educational ventures. Into the statistical hopper of the Westinghouse analysis were fed all shapes and sizes of program: from custodial to systematic. A rough evaluation, aimed to guide the government in budget allocation,[3] became a stick to beat a fledgling movement. The opinion gained currency: Head Start was a failure.

This chapter aims to show that such a conclusion is premature, but that much better planning will be required in the future if preschool programs are to be effective and if their assessment is to be valid. Finally, the broader educational, social, and ethical issues of preschool intervention will be considered. Elementary school programs, though clearly continuous with the preschool, will not be discussed; instead, the reader is referred to Maccoby and Zellner (1970), Evans (1971), and Bissell (1973).

3. By 1969, $350 million a year was being spent on Head Start.

HOW TO DESCRIBE AND ASSESS A PRESCHOOL PROGRAM

The issues to be addressed in this section are relevant to the reader who wishes to understand a specific program, to the formal evaluator who must analyze its nature and effects, and to the educator who is planning to establish a preschool. For these purposes a number of questions must be asked:

1. What is the educational philosophy underlying the program?
2. What is the balance aimed at between child-centered and teacher-directed learning?
3. Has there been systematic planning in terms of stated objectives?
4. Are the teaching strategies and learning experiences clearly described and are they congruent with the objectives and philosophy of the preschool? Are the learning experiences designed in such a way as to draw upon and extend the children's natural experiences in their everyday environment?
5. Do the teachers attempt to evaluate the effects of their program and to modify it progressively in the light of these effects? In an experimental program, is a pretest–posttest –follow-up design employed? Is the study adequately controlled? Is care taken to choose tests that are valid? Is care taken to ensure that the program is not merely teaching the tests? If gains have been derived, do they last after the program terminates and do they predict better school performance? Has the terminal testing been carried out by evaluators independent of the project and, preferably, by testers who are unaware of which child is a control and which child is from the program?
6. What are the qualifications, motivations, and cohesion of the staff? What part does it play in initial and progressive planning? Is there provision for staff supervision? What is the staff/pupil ratio?
7. What is the age of the children?
8. What is the nature of the building, plant, and equipment? How do these express the philosophy of the program?
9. Are parents involved in the program? If so, how? Have teachers or teaching aides come from the children's social

CHAPTER FOUR

> group? Is there any home-school liaison or home-teaching program?
> 10. Does the preschool collaborate with the local elementary schools? Is there provision for a follow-through program?
> 11. Does the staff seek independent, external criticism of its program?

In fact, very few elementary schools, high schools, or colleges could face such a barrage of questions with equanimity. It is time that they did.

A number of these issues will now be discussed. Others will be considered in chapter 6.

EDUCATIONAL PHILOSOPHY

Weikart (1972) has described how preschool programs vary along two dimensions (see Figure 4.1): whether the child and whether the teacher is initiative or responsive. Following this paradigm, programs may be classified in four types: programmed or structured; semi-structured; child-centered; and custodial.

In a *programmed* or *structured* preschool the teacher takes the initiative and the child responds. A good example of this strategy is the Bereiter-Engelmann (1966) or DISTAR approach (see chapter 6). Educational goals are clearly stated and the steps required to reach the goals are articulated in sequence. The goals are framed in relation to the

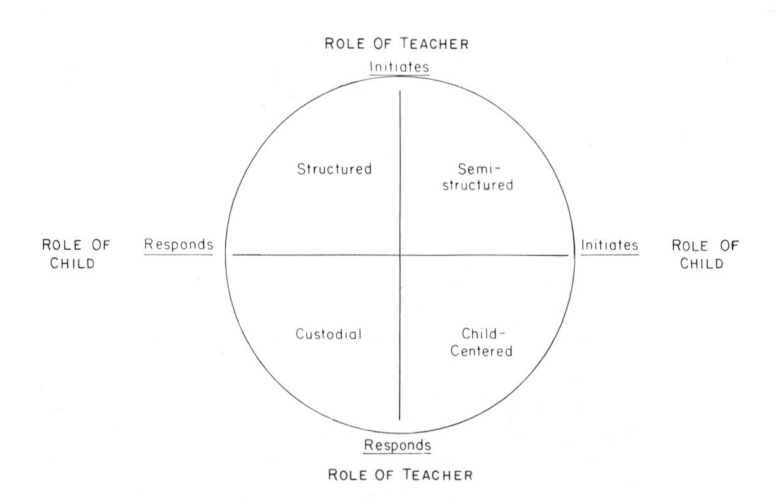

FIGURE 4.1 Types of preschool program

skills required by the child to adapt to formal primary school. So far as possible the educational strategies to be implemented by the teacher are clearly prescribed. The emphasis is on language pattern drill, defined structure, and convergent thinking.[4] The program derives from two major educational philosophies: the systematic planning associated with Ralph Mager and Robert Tyler and, to some extent, the reinforcement behaviorism of B. F. Skinner. Learning is described as requiring extrinsic reward, initially, to "stamp in" a pattern or sequence.

An example of *semistructured* teaching is the cognitively oriented program of Weikart (1967, 1972). Here the teacher and the child are initiators. The teacher, working from stated goals, creates the curriculum and designs learning experiences which will stimulate the children to engage in interaction with her and each other over sensorimotor materials, for example, as in block play. One strategy is to help the child to develop and apply the possibilities inherent in language to objects and activities, interest in which has been fostered by the design of the curriculum. Education is seen, essentially, as a transaction. It is considered that advanced learning cannot be negotiated until rudimentary intellectual structures have stabilized. Following Piaget, therefore, the teacher ensures that the sensorimotor basis of intellect is fully established before more complex language-based tasks are attempted. The child is seen as naturally curious; learning has intrinsic reward.

Most "traditional" programs are *child-centered*. The child initiates and the teacher waits and responds. The child is considered to be unable to develop intellectually on a solid basis unless in an atmosphere of trust and security. Thus the whole child is stressed: social, emotional, motor, and intellectual development are seen as intertwined. The environment is open; the emphasis is on free, spontaneous play, fantasy, role play, individualized handling, peer relations, and the gradual fostering of independence from adults. There has been some resistance in these programs to the imposition of overly precise objectives upon children who are seen as needing to define and pursue their own goals, creatively. Child-centered programs have been influenced by a variety of philosophies and theories, particularly those of Froebel, Dewey, Freud, Erikson, and Montessori. Nimnicht (quoted in Maccoby and Zellner 1970), for example, favors the child's involvement in freely chosen, self-rewarding activities in an environment that responds to the child when he is ready to learn and provides immediate feedback on his problem-solving efforts.

4. *Convergent thinking* refers to the application of competence to the solution of a problem by finding the "correct" answer. *Divergent thinking* refers to the elaboration of new from given information; the aim is the generation of a variety of problem solutions.

Chapter Four

The *custodial* type of program is mentioned only to be dismissed. This is what other programs become if the staff is unskilled, overburdened with too many children, or low in morale. There are no objectives, no planned activities, no educational transaction. Children and staff are isolated from each other. Learning is random and mostly between peers. This type of program has no educational philosophy.

OBJECTIVES

Without objectives a teacher is rudderless. Without objectives there is no way of knowing whether a program has been successful. Without objectives a program is likely to become flaccid and custodial. The question is: How should objectives be expressed? Objectives may be broad—"to promote a positive self-concept"—or highly specific: "The child will be able to identify the following colors from concrete objects and two-dimensional representations: red, yellow, green, blue, black, white, brown, gray, and orange." They may be expressed in terms of the teacher's activity—"to promote creativity and independence"—or in terms of what the children will be able to do when they have reached the end of the planned learning experiences: "The child will be able to use an *if–then* construction when asked to make deductions from blackboard color–shape–size categorization problems." The latter are called *behavioral objectives*. Behavioral objectives may be general—"The child will demonstrate mastery of basic number concepts"—or specific: "The child will be able to count aloud to twenty, with or without concrete objects." The advantages of specified behavioral objectives are these: they indicate clearly the terminus of the teaching-learning transaction; they may offer guidelines as to the most appropriate learning experiences; and they indicate the most relevant techniques of evaluation of outcome.

One of the commonest objections to the writing of behavioral objectives is that trivial cognitive aims (for example, of recall nature) are the easiest to write and, therefore, the most likely to be written.[5] In answer to this criticism, it can be pointed out that the publication of goals allows the reader to be aware of triviality—or distended rhetoric, for that matter—and to reject the unimportant as unworthy of effort. Behavioral objectives are sometimes criticized as undemocratic and dehumanizing, being associated with a fragmentary approach to complex integrative behavior. The whole is indeed more than an articulation of its parts; but the holistic approach may become a defense against clarity of thought and purpose, and a willingness to take criticism. Again, it is

---

5. The pros and cons of objective writing are discussed by Popham (1970).

doubtful to what degree the teacher-pupil relationship can be fully democratic; the older, the wiser, or the more skillful usually exercise an influence on the younger and less sagacious if the two share common goals. And even the sharing of goals may be the result of the identification of the pupil with the teacher. The question may also be expressed as: To what degree and in what way is the teacher prepared to accept responsibility for teaching directly? There is no single answer to that question. It derives from each teacher's philosophical stance and personality. But whatever the educational philosophy of the planners and teachers, the objectification of goals implies accountability. Objectives clearly indicate to teachers what they are expected to help their pupils attain; not the means of arriving at those ends. Different teachers and different students will find different teaching strategies more efficient, satisfying, and congenial.

SYSTEMATIC PLANNING

The writing of objectives is part of systematic planning (see Figure 4.2). Objectives are derived from needs—from an assessment of what the learners most require and what it is feasible to help them attain. The basic philosophy of the planners is expressed through their assessment of

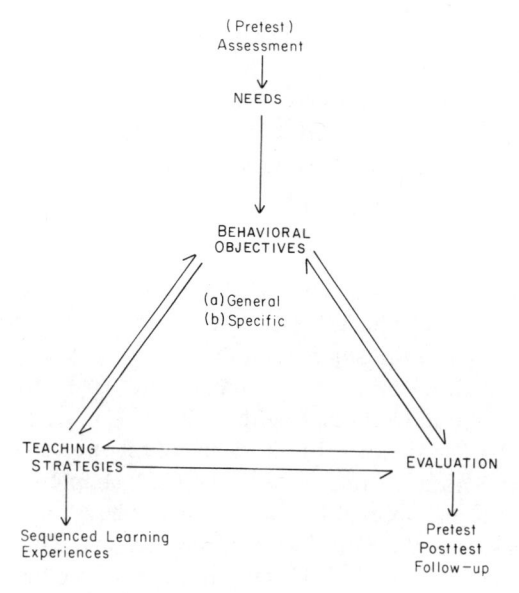

FIGURE 4.2 Systematic planning

needs, for this implies a speculation about what directions the learners are likely to take in the future.

Behavioral objectives lead to the design of a sequence of *learning activities* to help the learners reach the objectives. Different children prefer different kinds of learning experience. A sophisticated design takes this fact into account. Different teachers prefer different teaching strategies, each of which also expresses a basic philosophy.

Evaluation helps planners to find out whether objectives have been reached. If not, they must review their objectives (Are they realistic or feasible?) and their strategies (Have they been ineffective? Why?) in order to replan. This process is known as *summative evaluation*. It may be formal (involving standardized psychological tests) or less standardized (as in a classroom test designed by the teacher). An evaluation should be carried out in the following sequence: pretest at the beginning of instruction; posttest at the end of instruction; and follow-up to determine whether the gains have been durable. Evaluation is also potentially available during the learning process as a guide to the teacher and as feedback for the learner so that both may check on their progress. This process is known as *formative evaluation*.

Objectives, strategies, and evaluation are reciprocally linked in systematic planning (see Figure 4.2). The planning–teaching–learning process in dynamic. Objectives may need to be rewritten in the light of evaluation findings. New alternative learning sequences may be required. The techniques of evaluation may need to be improved. New ideas about needs may have to be incorporated. Above all, the explicitness of the planning exposes the program to critics; for without criticism innovation can fossilize into dogma, objectives inflate into rhetorical slogans, and self-evaluation dissolve in self-congratulation.

THE STAFF

The teachers involved in the new preschool movement have varied considerably. Most have been young; for this teaching requires energy, flexibility, and optimism. Some have been highly qualified; some have had basic qualifications; others have come from the children's social group itself and have trained on the job.

The staff/student ratio is important. Most successful programs have operated on a ratio of one to five, although chapter 6 describes a program that has been successful with a ratio of one to eleven. In some experimental programs the ratio has been one to one. This may be rewarding from a theoretical point of view; but eventually the problem of replicability must be considered. A program requiring a one-to-one ratio, teachers at the doctoral candidate level, and highly specific training is impossible to implement widely.

It is important to know the extent to which the teachers take part in initial and continued planning. If objectives or strategies are imposed on them, against their better judgment, failure is almost certain. To what degree do the teachers plan their daily work together, sharing problems and helping each other with solutions? How much support do they get (and feel they get) from their supervisors? Do they welcome external observation and criticism?

Underlying all is the teacher's motivation for becoming involved in this field. There is no doubt that an uncommon commitment is required. The origins of this commitment are varied; but least appropriate is a missionary approach to children that is based on self-doubt or guilt, an approach expressed in a need to change others into a facsimile of oneself. All too often the inevitable failure to do so results in pessimistic rejection of the recalcitrants. Children recognize those who have a personal axe to grind.

THE CHILDREN

From which sociocultural group do the children come? How have they been selected to enter the preschool? What are the criteria for eligibility—both positive and negative? How do the teachers define and manage difficult behavior, and what is their rationale for doing so? Are children ever suspended from the preschool? Have any of the children showed disturbance as a result of the teaching program and, if so, how would the staff ascertain and deal with this problem?

Most preschools admit children between four and five years of age. Some start at three and a few have attempted to work with even younger children. How long is the preschool day? It may vary from two to eight hours. (An eight-hour preschool day is most likely in a day-care center for the children of working mothers.) Does the preschool make provision for health, dental, and nutritional care? Is there a casework service for parents and an affiliation with local social and health agencies?

How long does the instruction last? It is doubtful whether programs lasting less than between six and twelve months will be effective unless the goals are very limited and specific.

THE PARENTS

It has become increasingly apparent that parental attitudes toward education, parental aspirations for the child, and parental provision for the child to learn in the home are more important than school resources or teaching techniques in ultimate scholastic attainment. The

CHAPTER FOUR

gains that accrue from a preschool program may be short-lived unless the parents support them thereafter. Education for preschool children—and indeed for all children—is the result of an implicit contract between family and educators. Such a contract cannot be negotiated unless each of the parties understands the strengths, the needs, and the aims of the other. This factor may be the key that explains the failure of conventional education to reach all members of a diverse community.

What attempt has the preschool staff made to understand and come to terms with the aims of the parents? What influence have the parents had on the framing of objectives and teaching strategies? What part do teachers from the child's sociocultural group play in the program? Do parents sit in on the classes? Are fathers involved in the school in some way? Is there a home-school liaison? (See chapter 6 for a description of such a program.)

THE PRIMARY SCHOOL

The teaching techniques of conventional schools have been inadequate to the task of aiding a significant proportion of the country's youth to learn. This is how the concept of cultural disadvantage arose in the first place. Teachers and parents were no longer prepared to allow the education system to hide behind excuses. Now we are faced with an extension of this problem. A number of preschool programs have produced major gains in their pupils; but elementary schools have been inadequate to sustain them.

It is clear that the preschool must open communication with the elementary school staff and aid them to introduce new, alternative programs. Cultural pluralism demands educational flexibility—but it is arguable that there are core skills which all members of a plural technological society require.[6] It is time we defined them. When we do so, the new preschool movement will be—and will have been—a spur in the side of the educational colossus in the direction of constructive planning. Along with an awareness of the need for parental involvement, this may eventually be the most productive contribution of the preschool movement.

EXPERIMENTAL PROGRAMS THAT WORK

A considerable number of experimental programs have produced significant changes in disadvantaged children. They have been reviewed by Evans (1971) and Clough (1972) and in Stanley (1972, 1973). In this section the most important examples will be briefly described. All the

---

6. An attempt at such a definition, in terms of a *repertoire* of linguistic, attentional, sensorimotor, and motivational competence, can be found in Staats (1968).

experiments to be discussed have been controlled and meet reasonable scientific standards. (A more detailed account of alternative methodological designs can be found in chapter 6.)

INFANT EDUCATION PROGRAMS

Programs have been designed for young children from about eighteen to forty-eight months of age. They may be divided into day-care programs and home-teaching programs.

Day-care Programs McConnell, Horton, and Smith (1969) worked in a day-care setting using a structured program involving perceptual training and language development. On a variety of language, intelligence, and perceptual tests, they demonstrated major gains after one year compared to unschooled controls. Palmer (1969) worked with two-year-olds, on a one-to-one basis, two hours per week for eight months. Two programs were compared: direct concept training and discovery training, each with the same language, concept, and percept objectives. The children in both programs achieved similar large gains, compared to controls, on IQ (Stanford-Binet) testing, language comprehension and expression, perception, motor control, and other relevant tasks. Other promising programs have been described by Caldwell and Richmond (1968), Robinson (1968), and Provence (1969).

Sigel, Secrist, and Forman (1973) have described the results of an infant stimulation project carried out with children from impoverished, black, inner-city families. Their aims were to foster "distance" in terms of conceptual and symbolic behavior and also a sense of personal competence. The two-year-old children, who were participating in a nursery school program, were taught individually with a game format. The teacher indirectly stimulated the child to think about things that were not present, to consider alternative solutions to problems, and to account for the different properties of objects and their temporal and physical relationships. A battery of tests was employed of language, imitation, perception, classification, memory, and number skills. Despite some control problems —the experimental children initially tested lower than black controls— significant improvements were demonstrated, especially in imitation and seriation performance. (Seriation is the ordering of objects along a dimension such as *big, bigger, biggest.*) Important sex differences in cognitive and affective behavior were described. The authors stress the need for more conceptual model-building to integrate discrepant data and to provoke hypotheses.

Home-teaching Programs Painter (1969) and Schaefer (1969) used teachers in the children's homes. Schaefer's subjects commenced at fifteen months of age and continued in the program for twenty-one months. The teaching involved verbal stimulation in a context of varied designed experiences. At the end of the program the experimental group had made major gains on IQ (Stanford-Binet) testing. Painter employed a structured infant-stimulation home program with children eight to twenty-four months old. Language, conceptual, and sensorimotor training were used. After twelve months, the experimental group was significantly superior to controls in intelligence (Stanford-Binet) and other conceptual tasks.

I. J. Gordon (1969) and Karnes et al. (1968, 1970b) have attempted to work through the child's parents. Gordon used "parent educators," mothers who had graduated from high school. After in-service training, he had them instruct the experimental mothers on how to interact with their children using sensorimotor experiences, perceptual stimulation, and verbal exchange in a game format. After twelve months the experimental group made major gains in IQ, verbal reception and expression, muscular coordination, and social adaptation. Karnes et al. trained mothers, directly, to carry out a teaching program over a fifteen-month period. The focus was on language development and perceptual-motor skills. The experimental group made significant gains in IQ (Stanford-Binet) and in language development. The control subjects tended to regress in IQ score and language age during the experimental period.

PRESCHOOL PROGRAMS

The majority of experimental studies have involved preschool settings with children between four and five years of age (or, in some instances, as young as three years). The most successful programs will be described according to methodology as *structured*, *semistructured*, or *child-centered*; or, in those studies in which a variety of programs were compared, as *multiple*.

Structured Programs The prototype of the structured program is that developed by Bereiter and Engelmann (1966) and later formalized by Becker and Engelmann in the DISTAR method. Bereiter and Engelmann have clearly described the rationale of their strategies. The culturally deprived child is considered to be lacking in basic language skills, particularly in standard English syntax.[7] Vocabulary, verbal comprehension and expression, and the application of syntax to classification problems, for example, are to be developed by techniques derived from the teaching of English as a foreign language. Bereiter and Engelmann

---

7. This contention is criticized particularly by the linguists who emphasize cultural difference rather than language deficit.

advocate the building of language structures from a basic identity statement (*This is a pencil*) to more complex structures (*This is not a piano. This pencil is under the table. This pencil is long and thin and red*). In addition to language skills, the program also promotes basic mathematical and prereading skills.

Working with a group of five children, the teacher asks for individual and group responses to her questions, changing rhythmically from one to the other and rewarding the child who tries with verbal praise (or, initially, with candy or dried fruit). Incorrect responses are immediately corrected; but the child is always rewarded for trying. Shouting responses are reinforced, and there is much repetition—pattern drill—of basic language structures such as identity statements, attribution, interrogatives, negatives, polar opposites, comparatives and superlatives, *and* and *or* constructions, prepositions, and *if–then* constructions. The general atmosphere is one of excitement, demand, noise, and involvement such that the inhibited child is carried along by the spirit of the group and the teacher, through her request for individual responses, always knows how each child is functioning.

The advantages of the techniques are fivefold: the deliberate building in the child of a need for and a pleasure in mastery; the clear objectives and the well-designed steps for reaching them; the built-in feedback system for the teacher associated with the individual responses; the absence of competitive pressure between children; and the highly economic use of time in that the teaching technique ensures the maximum, intense teacher-child contact.

Teachers who are used to the more gentle and individual approach of traditional preschools often find the wham-bang, pressure-cooker atmosphere of a twenty-minute Bereiter-Engelmann class quite distasteful. There are a number of criticisms of the technique: the teaching method is exhausting for the teacher and too demanding of the child; the language gains may be restricted to a school environment and not applied outside it; and Bereiter and Engelmann's rationale assumes, incorrectly, that the children are deficient in language skills. (This assumption is criticized as an artefact of the testing situation; black children, it is pointed out, speak a fully developed language that differs from standard English in an important and regular way. Moreover, the reinforcement techniques involved are artificial and not congruent with normal processes of language acquisition.) These criticisms, already introduced in chapter 3, will be discussed further in chapters 5, 6, and 7. A cogent criticism which emanates particularly from Piagetians is that the structured program does not evolve from a coherent theory of child development. The concentrated language stimulation is not based on a prior consolidation of sensorimotor structures as in natural development. As a consequence, a lack of synchronic and diachronic transfer of skills is likely; whatever gains accrue are likely to be restricted to the classroom and to erode rapidly without continued artificial reinforcement.

Bereiter (1968) has reported on the progress of two waves of children exposed to this teaching approach. One wave, which was uncontrolled, made a 10-point IQ (Stanford-Binet) gain over a two-year period. By the second year of grade school they were above grade norms in arithmetic and just below them in spelling and reading. The second wave was compared with four control groups: a group exposed to an open-framework, educational games technique (C_1); a group from traditional child-centered preschool classes (C_2); a middle-class group receiving a Bereiter-Engelmann program (C_3); and a middle-class group receiving a Montessori program (C_4). The experimental and the first two control groups were matched on IQ, race, and SES. No tests of significance were reported, but the experimental group was superior to all groups except C_3 in educational achievement by the second year of elementary school. Over the twelve-month period of the teaching, the experimental group gained 17 points of IQ. Bereiter, however, is skeptical of IQ tests in this context and doubts their validity.

Engelmann (1970) analyzed the results of this experiment in more detail, after further follow-up. After two years of instruction, the mean IQ of the experimental group was 121, a net gain of 26 points. The group in the traditional, child-centered program, after gaining 8 points in year one, dropped down to a mean IQ of 99.6 at the end of year two for a net gain of 4.6 points. The IQ gains of the experimental group correlated with achievement in reading, spelling, and arithmetic. The IQ performance of the structured-class higher-SES children, after one year, was only about 2 points higher than that of the disadvantaged structured-class subjects after two years of instruction. The reading performance of the disadvantaged children was attained after a duration of ninety-six hours of instruction, about one-fifth of that to which children in conventional elementary school are exposed. Engelmann draws the obvious conclusion about the marked inefficiency of conventional teaching techniques for early reading skills. He also discusses the marked improvement in social adjustment of the disadvantaged children, a side effect of their newfound pleasure in mastery.

Erickson et al. (1969) compared the effects of a Bereiter-Engelmann program with a no-treatment control group in a crossover design. Significant effects were shown on IQ score (Stanford-Binet).

Blank and Solomon (1968) have reported on a direct one-to-one instructional program aimed to develop an abstract attitude—in particular: selective attention, categorical exclusion (draw something that is *not* a circle), imagery for future events, inner verbalization, separation of word from referent, cause-and-effect reasoning, ability to categorize, the active use of language, sustained sequential thinking, and concepts of number, speed, direction, temperature, and emotions. Twenty-two disadvantaged children were divided into four groups: experimental, receiving twenty minutes instruction per day for five days per week (E_1); experimental, receiving twenty minutes instruction per day for three days per week (E_2); control, receiving daily sessions with a warm, responsive teacher who did not interact with the child over cognitive materials (C_1); and control, receiving a conventional preschool program without additional attention (C_2). The mean IQ (Stanford-Binet) increases were:

E_1 : 14.5 points
E_2 : 7.0 points
C_1 : 2.0 points
C_2 : 1.3 points

The increases in the tutored groups were significantly superior to those of the untutored groups; but the difference between the two tutored groups, E_1 and E_2, did not reach a significant level. Marked behavioral improvements were noted in the tutored groups.

The importance of time is illustrated in a study of Dickie (1968), who compared the effects of structured and child-centered approaches to language instruction in preschool. No significant differences were found; but the language instruction was limited to a brief duration and only twenty minutes per day in an otherwise traditional curriculum.

Van De Reit and Van De Reit (1968) implemented a program (E) based on structured, sequentially presented curiosity games and compared its effects with a child-centered preschool (C_1) and a no-preschool control group (C_2) over a twelve-month period. At the end of the teaching period mean IQs (Stanford-Binet) were:

E : 104
C_1 : 90
C_2 : 83

E was significantly greater than C_1 and C_2; this superiority was lost when, after one year in grade school, the IQ scores were:

E : 101
C_1 : 89
C_2 : 84

Karnes et al. (1968) compared a traditional child-centered program with the ameliorative program, a direct structured technique of their own design. In the ameliorative program, the teacher/pupil ratio

CHAPTER FOUR

was one to five. There were three 20-minute structured sessions per day involving language, reading readiness skills, social studies, science, and basic mathematical concepts in the five-day-a-week, full-year program. An attempt was made to present the material in game format. The general aim of the traditional program was to promote personal, social, and motor development. The goals of the ameliorative program were more precise and in the areas of vocabulary, classification, perceptual attention and discrimination, body awareness, self-concept, geometric shapes, matching and equivalence, dimensions, seriation, counting, basic addition and subtraction, two-dimensional representations, and left-to-right page progression. After one year, the traditional group had made an 8.1-point gain in IQ (Stanford-Binet), a 6.5-month gain in total language age (Illinois Test of Psycholinguistic Abilities), and an 8.4-point gain in perceptual quotient (Frostig Test); the comparative figures for the structured program were: 14.3 points IQ, 16.5 months language age, and 18.4 points perceptual quotient. Both programs had had success; but the structured program was clearly superior. The ameliorative program was later employed with disadvantaged three-year-olds who were compared with no-treatment controls (Karnes et al. 1970b). Over one year, the experimental group gained 16.9 IQ points and 16.8 language age months whereas the control group lost 2.8 IQ points and gained 7.7 language age months. The difference between the groups was significant.

Semistructured Programs One of the earliest studies in this field was that by Dawe (1942), who worked, using a language program, with institutionalized children. The techniques involved were semistructured and employed excursions, discussions, stories, and concept-development tasks. Over an eight-month period, the experimental group made a 14-point IQ gain on Stanford-Binet whereas a group in a conventional program (probably mainly custodial) lost 2 points of IQ. It should be pointed out that these children, like those described by Skeels (1966), were grossly stimulus-deprived in a way not strictly comparable to the alleged cultural deprivation of the minority-group child (see chapter 3).

Smilansky and Smilansky (1970) have reviewed thirteen years of work in Israel, much of it with culturally different Jewish immigrant children from Africa and Asia. They employ language interaction, sociodramatic play, and mixed-age groups in their program and have demonstrated major IQ gains compared to Israeli preschool programs without this specific emphasis.

Martin Deutsch (1967) and his group in New York have produced a large volume of research on the nature of cumulative deficit. Their objectives have been in language, conceptualization, self-concept, and self-motivation. Their programs have covered a five-year span (two years preschool, three years grade school) and have demonstrated sustained and major IQ gains as well as higher achievement scores in comparison with controls.

Ball and Bogatz (1973) have produced evidence that *Sesame Street*, a television program aimed at developing the preacademic competencies of disadvantaged children, has been effective. In terms of a battery of tests of verbal, number, associational, prereading, representational, and categorizing skills, frequent viewers significantly outpaced infrequent viewers from both disadvantaged and middle-class homes.

Gray and Klaus (1968, 1970) compared groups with three or two 10-week summer group programs and one to two year's regular home instruction by visiting teachers, comparing them with control groups from local and from distant areas. The teaching program utilized the systematic manipulation of puzzles, paints, rhythm, interaction, and language and concept enrichment. Initially the experimental group demonstrated a major IQ gain (9 points, Stanford-Binet) whereas the controls lost ground (3 and 6 points of IQ, respectively). By the fourth grade, the IQ differences, though still favoring the experimental group, were small and there were no significant differences in scholastic achievement. Differences between experimental and control groups were restricted to cognition, an observation due possibly to the crudity of psychological testing in the affective domain.

Child-centered Programs McAfee (1972) has described a child-centered program—based on the Moore (1964) and the Nimnicht et al. (1969) "autotelic responsive environment" model—that was employed with disadvantaged Chicano, Chicano-Indian, black, and Anglo children in Denver. The objectives of the program were in perceptual acuity, language, conceptualization, problem-solving, and self-concept. No pretesting was carried out, but by the end of a year's program there were major IQ differences (Stanford-Binet) from a control group. These differences, together with differences in scholastic achievement, were sustained three years after the end of the program.

Multiple Programs Di Lorenzo and Salter (1968) have described a study comparing, over two years, more than a thousand four-year-old children and controls exposed to each of a variety of educational experiences: reading readiness, Bereiter-Engelmann, semistructured, child-centered, teaching machine, and Montessori programs. The six programs shared the same general cognitive, language, psychomotor, and affective objectives. The reading readiness and Bereiter-Engelmann classes yielded by far the most impressive results, as measured by Stanford-Binet IQ, Peabody Picture Vocabulary Test, Illinois Test of Psycholinguistic Abilities, and scholastic achievement tests. The teaching machines were ineffective, as were the traditional programs and those that merely mixed middle-class with disadvantaged children. The preschool experience appeared to be more advantageous, overall, for disadvantaged nonwhites. After one year in primary school the significant difference between children who had been to preschool and those who had not was sustained but not increased on scholastic attainment tests. This result was due entirely to the attainment of nonwhite females which was apparently sustained, though not improved, in grade school. Other children tended not to be different from controls on scholastic tests one year after the preschool program had terminated.

Miller and Dyer (1971) compared the effects of Bereiter-Engelmann, semistructured, Montessori, and child-centered traditional programs on 200 four-year-old children. Testing was carried out blind and was counterbalanced to eliminate the effects of tester differences. The structured and semistructured approaches stimulated roughly similar gains and were markedly superior to the other two techniques over a one-year period.

Bissell (1973) has described the results of an extensive study of the implementation and effects of eight preschool models ranging from child-centered, open-classroom, semistructured-Piagetian, cognitive-discovery, and parent-education projects to preacademic and behaviorally structured programs. The levels of success of the implementation of the programs were documented together with outcomes in terms of the child's scholastic achievement, cognitive development and response style, and the quality of parent-child interaction and parental involvement. It appeared that the more structured, programmed models promoted a more faithful implementation (in terms of the strategies originally designed), a consequence that was due perhaps to their less ambiguous, more "cut-and-dried" character. In all children—those from model as well as control Head Start classes—mean scholastic and cognitive gains were noted in advance of those to be expected from maturation alone. Children in the model classes achieved gains significantly greater than those in the control classes. The largest gains appeared in structured preacademic and cognitive-discovery classes. All children developed more mature motor control and inhibition of impulsive responses in a school situation. The greatest improvements in parent-child interaction were noted in structured and cognitive-discovery classes. In general, therefore, those programs with clear general and specific objectives yielded most improvement in relation to the orientation of the program, particularly in measures of achievement, cognitive function, and response style.

The final studies to be discussed, by Karnes et al. (1970a) and by Weikart (1967, 1972), are distinguished by their unusually detailed and prospective approach. Karnes and colleagues compared the effect over one year, on four-year-old disadvantaged children, of the following programs: traditional child-centered; traditional programs that deliberately mixed disadvantaged with middle-class children; Montessori; Karnes ameliorative; and Bereiter-Engelmann. The gains in IQ (Stanford-Binet) at the end of twelve months were:

>Traditional: 8.2 points
>Integrated: 5.1 points
>Montessori: 6.4 points
>Ameliorative: 13.8 points
>Bereiter-Engelmann: 13.0 points

In language development, the traditional and Montessori groups had made little progress; the integrated group had made modest gains; and the Bereiter-Engelmann group appeared to be superior to the ameliorative.

During the second year of this experiment the first three groups were enrolled in public school without supplementary programs. The ameliorative group had public school plus a one-hour-per-day supplementary structured program. The Bereiter-Engelmann group remained in their specialized teaching program. In the following year, grade one, all children were reviewed.[8] For the end of the first and second years of public school, the mean IQ scores are shown in Table 4.1. Similar findings were noted for language development and scholastic achievement. By the end of the third grade the Karnes ameliorative group was at grade level for achievement and ahead of the Bereiter-Engelmann and traditional groups, who were slightly below grade level.[9] Both Bereiter-Engelmann and traditional groups had stabilized at IQ 100, the ameliorative group

TABLE 4.1 Mean IQ Scores of Children in Five Programs at Beginning and End of Preschool and at the End of the First Two Years of Primary School (Karnes et al. 1970a)

Program	Pretest	Posttest	Year 1	Year 2	Year 4
Traditional	94.4	102.6	99.5	100.0	100.0
Integrated	93.3	98.4	99.0	NA	NA
Montessori	93.4	99.8	100.0	NA	NA
Ameliorative	96.2	110.0	108.5	105.0	103.5
Bereiter-Engelmann	94.6	107.6	113.0	110.0	100.0

8. The usual American and Australian sequence is preschool, transition or kindergarten class, grade one—corresponding roughly with four, five, and six years of age.
9. The interpretation of these results is uncertain since there was a large attrition rate in the Bereiter-Engelmann class.

at 103.5. One thing at least is clear: An erosion of gains begins when the child is transferred from a focused, objective teaching environment to the less differentiated environment of public school.

Karnes (1973) points out that a comparison of the later attitudes of the children in the ameliorative and traditional classes did not support predictions that the highly structured program would adversely affect the children's acceptance of school and social adaptation; on the contrary, both programs had a beneficial affect on general adjustment. In a separate experiment the ameliorative program was effective, also, with children whose mean initial IQ was 66.4, raising it to 87.5 after one year. Karnes has, further, successfully trained mothers to implement programs in the home and indigenous paraprofessionals to work in the classroom.

Weikart (1972) has reported comprehensively about research carried out with disadvantaged preschool children in Ypsilanti, Michigan. This work is of particular importance because of its careful control, comparison, and follow-up. Three programs were investigated: child-centered, semistructured,[10] and Bereiter-Engelmann. All treatment groups were balanced by IQ, sex, and age. All classes were taught five days per week for half a day. In each of the children's homes a ninety-minute teaching session was carried out every two weeks. Teacher/pupil ratio was low, about one to four. At the end of the first year of the program, intelligence testing revealed the results shown in Tables 4.2 and 4.3. The three-year-olds made almost identical large gains whereas the four-year-olds in the child-centered program were slightly below the other two; but all groups made large gains. Equivalent posttests were noted on the Leiter International Performance Scale and on the Peabody Picture Vocabulary Test for the three programs in both age groups.

At the end of the second year these results were replicated. By the third year of the project the child-centered approach was not matching its former large gains whereas the children in the other programs continued to show major gains. Weikart, candidly, puts this down to poor staff supervision. In follow-up studies it was noted that children who had been to preschool, compared to controls, had significantly higher IQ scores up to but not beyond grade three, as well as better scholastic achievement, academic ratings, and social adjustment up to that time.

DISCUSSION

Weikart (1972) concluded from his studies that structured, semistructured, and child-centered approaches can produce similar excellent

---

10. The Piaget-based Cognitively Oriented Curriculum designed by Sonquist and Kamii (1968).

TABLE 4.2 Results on Stanford-Binet IQ Test of Three Treatment Groups of Four-Year-Old Children (Weikart 1967)

	Mean IQ		
Program	Pretest	Posttest	Gain
Child-centered	76.4	94.1	17.7
Semistructured	75.3	98.6	23.3
Bereiter-Engelmann	73.9	98.2	24.4
Contrast group	80.8	84.1	3.3

TABLE 4.3 Results on Stanford-Binet IQ Test of Three Treatment Groups of Three-Year-Old Children (Weikart 1967)

	Mean IQ		
Program	Pretest	Posttest	Gain
Child-centered	73.6	101.1	27.5
Semistructured	82.7	110.7	28.0
Bereiter-Engelmann	84.4	114.6	30.2
Contrast group	80.8	81.2	0.4

results provided the teachers have a clear curriculum, are involved in daily planning toward intermediate and terminal objectives, and are well supervised. Curricula are for teachers, to aid in organization and planning. It should be pointed out, however, that *all* three groups in his study also had home teaching, which thus confounds his results and his conclusions about the equivalent efficacy of the three methods he employed.

Bereiter (1972a) has pointed out the difficulty of generalizing from a variety of outcome-evaluation studies when there are such major problems of experimental control. Nevertheless, he concludes that the Bereiter-Engelmann approach is clearly superior to the traditional child-centered approach, though not necessarily superior to other structured or semistructured programs with a strong instructional emphasis. He points out that there is a common body of content in those programs with a impact; whereas, in the traditional approach, the teacher is not held accountable for seeing that the objectives (if indeed they have been stated) have been reached. Montessori programs do not appear to have been effective in terms of the evaluation techniques (IQ and language tests) employed. This may, however, be an unfair criticism since Montessori considered that her sensorimotor training was the basis of later conceptualization; in other words the testing may have been premature. Bereiter makes a plea for more direct observation of what goes on between teacher and children in different programs—similar rhetoric may cover quite different activities. He concludes that the long-term results of effective preschool programs are about as good as expected; no preschool program by itself can have a permanent effect. The next step is to combine preschool and elementary school research and to plan for continuity. What do we need to teach a four-year-old that can be built on in elementary school? And how should we build on it?

Beilin (1972) has discussed the unreliability of IQ tests in evaluation, the fact that pretests underestimate competence, and that there may be a Hawthorne effect.[11] He suggests that the impact of the school day is unlikely to overcome the influence of larger social experience or genetic defect (although 20 to 25 percent of children do seem to benefit to a large extent from these programs) and that it will take more than one generation for educational innovations to create major social changes.

CONCLUSIONS

The fanfare is over. The confetti of the Great Society has been swept up. A visionary educational movement, after premature birth, has faltered and is in danger of being jettisoned in the wake of national retrenchment, a victim of oversell and overhaste.

We have learned that there is no educational magic in the early years and that effective teaching, at any age, is a matter of skilled planning and implementation. We have learned that one year in a preschool, by itself, is unlikely to change the lifeways of a people. To find out these things preschool workers have examined their efforts with professional, unbiased evaluation techniques superior to any previously employed in education. It is doubtful whether other educational ventures at any level could stand up as well to such scrutiny. In this, once again, those in the preschool movement are leaders. The benefit of the self-criticism is that we are now in a position to make some statements with assurance.

First, there are few clear examples in the literature of a purely child-centered program in which major cognitive gains were achieved. Unless the traditional child-centered program is shaped by clear instruc-

---

11. The Hawthorne effect is a phenomenon in which the subjects of an experiment are swept up by the enthusiasm of the experimenters and produce inflated performances. Actually, it is difficult to see how this effect could be operative with disadvantaged preschoolers who are unlikely to comprehend the experimental significance of the program or the relevance of the tests to that program. A validity problem in which the teachers inadvertently teach aspects of the evaluation instrument is a far more serious issue.

tional objectives it is unlikely to be effective in the cognitive domain. Current evaluation techniques are inadequate to assess objectives in the affective domain and need further development.

Second, the most effective programs have been either structured or semistructured with clear, stated objectives; strategies appropriate to the objectives; planned, sequenced learning experiences; continuous feedback evaluation; and an intensive staff model.

Third, the teacher/pupil ratio is important. A ratio of over one to five makes it difficult for the teacher to keep track of each child's progress.

Fourth, anything less than a one-year program for five half-days per week is probably inadequate. A great deal of time in preschool, necessarily, is spent in other than teacher-pupil interaction. The child needs time to absorb and apply knowledge; but at least one hour per day of intensive interaction is required.

Fifth, the programs that have been successful (in their own terms) have focused on objectives in the areas of language, conceptual problem-solving, basic logical-mathematical competence, body image, spatial ability, and self-concept. The derived sense of mastery and achievement contributes very positively to psychological health.

And sixth, gains made in even the most successful programs are unlikely to last beyond the third grade without specific modifications in elementary school teaching to support those gains.

PREDICTIONS

Training programs for preschool and infant teachers will offer a wider variety of instruction than they do at present. The teaching of culturally different children will become a diverse specialty. Adequate teaching will require a much clearer understanding of the culture of the people involved in the program. This includes a knowledge of the indigenous language or dialect.

As Sigel (1973) has pointed out, the realization of potential in the form of competence is more than a linear adding of skills. Different competencies interact to form superordinate competencies which then, reciprocally, affect the process of further realization. Evaluation techniques will be developed to account for this interaction and will replace the rather crude and static instruments now in use (with an emphasis on criterion-referenced rather than norm-referenced test instruments [Carver 1970]). Evaluation techniques will also be developed to predict more accurately the child's competence to deal with elementary schooling. We will seek and promote those cornerstone competencies that generate a multiplicity of subordinate skills. We will also define the existing competencies of the children involved and find ways of exploiting them to facilitate the realization of the competencies objectified.

More adults from the indigenous group will be involved in teaching at all levels. The ultimate aim, when appropriate, will be to have the people, working through trained professionals from that culture, control their own educational system. A period of transition and training will be required.

Involvement of parents and adults will have the effect of opening up education and creating a unity between home and school, rather than the dichotomized compartmented systems of today. A revolution of these dimensions will not be won in one generation. Numerous false starts and major readjustments will be experienced.

Preschool programs are but one element in a complex system. Adequate attention to housing, health, and community development must continue in parallel. People of any culture must feel they have control over their collective destiny before they will be able to be involved in continuing education.[12]

Preschool and elementary school programs will aim not to erase the culture of those they help. On the contrary, they will affirm the cultural identity of their pupils and try to offer them the additional skills required to adapt to a technological world—provided that the people as a whole and the individual families involved concur with this aim. Education is a transaction between family and educators; it cannot be successful unless both agree about goals and teaching methods. The transaction requires initial and continuing negotiation between the parties involved. Only in this way can ethical questions about intervention be answered.

The content and strategies of the preschools of the future will probably involve a judicious amalgamation of the developmental principles of Piaget and the detailed sequencing of the behaviorists, together with the development of mastery and self-esteem in a setting that emphasizes integration with the community. There will be a shift from abstract, rhetorical aims and overly concrete, fragmentary objectives to something else: cornerstone competency processes that have been found to generate, in continuity, the general and specific skills required for adult life. No single educational strategy is appropriate for all children; a plural culture will demand educational diversity.

12. The Australian Aboriginal Family Education Center movement, under the auspices of the Van Leer Foundation and the directorship of A. Grey, aims to promote the involvement of Aboriginal families in education by stimulating them to build, equip, and staff their own preschools.

CHAPTER 5
CULTURAL DISADVANTAGE IN AUSTRALIA

It's not so bad that the whitefeller came, but it spoiled the people. It made 'em ashamed to talk their own lingo and marry wrong. They don't learn from the old people. ... They were better off in the old days camped on their own, working on stations. ... They knew who their aunties and cousins were.

Old Aboriginal man

Our life is wasted. There's no hope for us now. All we've got to live for now is to bring up the kiddies and see them educated. ... They'll find what to do with it when they get it.

Aboriginal mother

But I'll drink and roam till the cows come home,
If it will give my poor heart ease,
I don't care who knows, I work for my dough
And I'll spend it as I please.

Dougie Young, Aboriginal song

ABORIGINAL SOCIAL GROUPS

Prior to the coming of the white man the Aborigines of Australia lived in nomadic hunting groups. They functioned in harmony with nature, perceiving themselves as kin to the flora and fauna upon which they depended for survival. The introduction of the first metal axe disrupted their intricate economy and produced an era of chaos and disintegration which continues to this day.

Before the eighteenth century was out, whites and blacks were in competition for land, food, and women. The whites varied their

Chapter Five

policies, from seeking negotiation and harmony to unofficially—or officially—sanctioned genocide. By the middle of the nineteenth century the disintegration of Aboriginal culture was advanced. Many tribes of the coast and inland plains had been wiped out or forced off their traditional lands. Those whom gun, dog, or poison had failed to eliminate were finished off by disease and alcohol. The remnants, living on the outskirts of bush townships and pastoral properties, intermarried and interbred with Caucasians and Asians. Traditional tribal groups remained in the arid center and the jungles of the tropical north on land which the white man did not, yet, want.

Outright genocide was too much for the lawmakers of the end of the nineteenth century. The Aborigine was seen as a Darwinian relic, like the platypus, who had developed, in isolation, in a cultural backwater. Destined to extinction as he was, his terminal throes should not be aggravated needlessly. The dominant culture would provide a "death pillow" in the form of separate reservations in which nature would eventually take its course. After World War II, the "dying race" policy was gradually displaced by assimilation: through education and intermarriage, Aborigines would eventually be absorbed (and disappear) into the mainstream of Australian society (Rowley 1970; Cawte 1972).

Since about 1950 it has become apparent that the "dying race" theory is outmoded. Taking root in apparently unfavorable soil, both traditional and fringe-dwelling groups so began to increase in numbers that their birthrate and infant mortality have been elevated to among the highest in the world. In 1970, the total Aboriginal population of the Northern Territory was 10,000, of whom 50 percent were aged less than fifteen years and 20 percent less than five. Mortality rates in the first year of life, since 1963, have varied from 135 to 166 per 1,000 live births—seven to eight times that of Australia as a whole (Kirke 1972). The major causes of morbidity are gastroenteritis, bronchiolitis, bronchiectasis, suppurative otitis media, skin and gut infestations, skin infections, and malnutrition. The malnutrition is of the "total calorie deficiency" type; kwashiorkor is rare, as is florid vitamin deficiency. The population has an average daily income per head of $0.50 and an annual birthrate of about 50 per 1,000 per year.

Similar though less extreme observations have been made of fringe-dwelling part-Aborigines (Coolican 1973). Part-Aborigines, compared to rural whites, have larger families and higher birthrates, lower occupational status, higher deathrates, substandard housing and diet, and a higher incidence of chronic anemia, parasitic disease, venereal disease, alcoholism, eye, ear, skin, and chest disorders, gastroenteritis, and antenatal kidney infection, toxemia, and abortion.

The research to be described in chapter 6 was carried out in a bush town in the outback of New South Wales. A preliminary description of the historical background and social organization of the black and white people of this district will illustrate the complexity of the factors obscured by such generalizations as "disadvantage" or "difference." It will demonstrate, also, that the contemporary society, values, and cognitive competencies of a people cannot be understood except as interlinked derivations of their unique history and perception of the collective and personal future. While anthropological generalizations such as the "culture of poverty" (Lewis 1966) have pertinence, they should not be allowed to obscure the differences between "disadvantaged" groups.[1] The contemporary attempt to equate urban ghetto black Americans and part-Aboriginal Australians is a case in point. Nor should these generalizations be allowed to blur the great range of individual differences within minority groups.

THE HISTORICAL BACKGROUND OF BOURKE[2]

Before one considers the environment of Bourke Aborigines, it is essential to understand something of the history of this district. Spreading westward from the coastal Great Dividing Range are the plains of western New South Wales. The rainfall decreases from forty to less than ten inches per year as the interior is approached, and the vegetation changes from rich wooded savanna grassland to desert saltbush, spinifex, and low, sparse scrub. Through this huge flat country meanders the Darling River system, from northeast to southwest, until the main stream joins the Murray River and empties into the Great Australian Bight. About 500 miles northwest of Sydney, on the Darling and at the transition between the more fertile plans and arid center, is the old river port of Bourke. The natural climatic variations of good years and bad years of drought, flood, and dust are reflected in the history of this town and its surrounding district.

The early explorers Charles Sturt and Thomas Mitchell reached the area in 1829 and 1835, the latter building a stockade for protection against "marauding blacks" who appear, in this area, to have been more numerous and belligerent and relatively less nomadic than most Australian tribes. Following the explorers came pioneer "squatters," cattle or sheep ranchers who settled on virgin land beyond the limits of previous settlement, anticipating official validation of ownership or leasehold. But

---

1. For some cogent criticisms of Lewis' culture of poverty theory, the reader is referred to Leacock (1971).
2. This section has been derived, largely, from Coolican (1973) and Cameron (1968).

the hostility of the Aborigines closed the area for settlement until after 1858. Cattle were displaced by sheep as the transport of wool to coastal markets was developed. Bourke soon became a miniature Kansas City, since it was a natural crossroads for camel caravans from the interior, bullock teams carting wool from the surrounding district, sheep- and cattle-droving routes along the great river system, and paddle-wheel wool-transport steamers that plied up and down the Darling and Murray. By the 1880s a telegraph line and railway had been pushed through and the town entered a brief period of remarkable expansion. In 1890 there were two hundred businesses, nineteen pubs, and a population of over 5,000 in the district. Land in the main street changed hands for $20,000 per foot of frontage.

In the early 1890s the whole of Australia was plunged into a disastrous depression. This reversal was particularly severe in Bourke. The effects of a devastating drought were accentuated by the overstocking of land. The price of wool fell. Rabbits, introduced from England in 1859, spread and infested the land. Industrial tensions between shearers and and pastoralists exploded in open violence. The town and district went into a long decline, accentuated by the depression of the 1930s and the superseding of river transport by the extension of the railways.

Gradually, following World War II, scientific land management, the conservation of water, improvement of sheep and cattle productivity, and the elimination of rabbits by the introduction of myxomatosis[3] have led to a recovery of the Bourke district. A temporary setback, due to a drop in the wool price in the 1960s, has been largely overcome by pastoral diversification and by the introduction of irrigated cotton. Bourke has learned to roll with the economic and climatic punches. Boom and despair have been replaced by a tempered optimism.

The history of the Aboriginal people is in stark counterpoint to the struggles of the hard-bitten bush whites. In the beginning, along the Darling River, lived the Bagundji (literally, "river people"). Further to the south were the Ngjemba and to the southwest the Bulali. Other large tribal groups, culturally related to the powerful Bagundji, dwelt in the far west, while to the north were tribes more closely associated with those of southwest Queensland. Unlike surrounding tribes, the Bagundji did not practice initiatory circumcision or subincision but, rather, hair depilation and piercing of the nasal septum. They lived on game (kangaroo, emu, goanna, duck, fish) and native vegetables, and they traded extensively with neighboring tribes. They dwelt in thatched huts, in larger groups than have been described elsewhere in Aboriginal Australia,

---

3. This viral disease, lethal to rabbits, was deliberately introduced in 1956 after experimentation by the Commonwealth Scientific and Industrial Research Organization.

and had an extensive artistic life involving cave painting and the sculpture of stone cyclons, large round or cigar-shaped stone artifacts the significance of which has been lost. In a remarkably brief period, between 1860 and 1890, violence, disease, and social disintegration reduced the Bagundji from about 3,000 to no more than 80 people, paupers on the fringe of white society. Many interbred and intermarried with Europeans and Asians in the local district, and the full-descent Aboriginal population disappeared. In 1970 there were 655 people in Bourke who identified themselves as Aborigines. Of these more than 200 lived on a "reserve" on the outskirts of town, about 200 lived in the town itself, and the rest were elsewhere on the fringes of Bourke or in the adjoining district.

Beckett (1958) has described how, initially, the part-Aborigine adapted well to the nomadic life of the bush stockman or shearer and was an important part of the work force; but the breaking up of the large pastoral properties and the great depression reduced the need for casual labor. Aborigines, who originally camped around homesteads, moved to the fringes of townships or were settled on government-controlled stations, where they have evolved a way of life characterized as "intelligent parasitism" and are described by their white neighbors as "no-hopers," "Abos," or "Darkies."

CLASS, STATUS, AND SOCIAL ORGANIZATION IN PART-ABORIGINAL COMMUNITIES[4]

Much of the old culture has disappeared and that which remains has been modified by the partial identification of Aborigines with the white, rural, laboring class. Aside from isolated words and phrases, few people under fifty years of age remember the traditional languages. Most are ashamed or confused when Aboriginal phrases are used in front of whites. The traditional chants are forgotten by the young men, who now prefer drinking songs or melancholy guitar ballads in hillbilly style. They interpret recent history, accurately, as the robbing of their lands by whites and their hounding by the government ("the Welfare"). They look back to a golden age lost to them through the trickery and injustice of Europeans. They are aware of the tighter controls and sanctions of tribal life and they contrast it to the disorganization and insecurity of the present. Beneath the surface a belief in sorcery remains, more often of malevolent than of healing character, a factor that may be associated with the attraction of revivalist religious sects in some areas.

Today the Aborigines retain a strong attachment to their own "country," which is usually delineated by place of birth and presence of

4. This section has been derived, largely, from the anthropological work of Reay (1949), Reay and Sitlington (1948), Fink (1957), and Beckett (1958, 1964a, 1964b, 1965).

CHAPTER FIVE

close kin. Commonly each has a "beat," a familiar route along which young and old people travel to visit their kinfolk. By this means, some degree of exogamy (marriage outside the clan group) is consciously maintained. In contrast to traditional times, the mobility of Aboriginal men and the frequency of serial common-law marriages have rendered the family strongly matrifocal: the mother, and often a dominant maternal grandmother, are the emotional fulcrum of family life. A characteristic reserve picture is of the grandmother's shack which is near the dwellings of her daughters, their menfolk, and the grandchildren, and the home to which her sons periodically return. Thus, while some old beliefs and customs remain, shorn of their ritual significance, Aboriginal society has lost autonomy and organization and is oriented, dependently, toward the dominant white group, which rejects it as a whole. This marginal position has produced characteristic attitudes and stratifications within the fringe group that increase its disequilibrium and the tensions between it and surrounding society. Reflecting the erstwhile policies of official administration, the Aborigine sees the only way out of poverty as the rejection of the reciprocity of kin relationships and an identification with the individuality, the collection of possessions, and social mores of whites. In short, the price of an uncertain assimilation appears to be the rejection of Aboriginality.

Thus, within the part-Aboriginal population of each country town, there has evolved a two-class system that is defined, predominantly, by the attitudes of each subgroup to the European community. Between the two classes are individuals and families in transition from one to the other, a transition emphasized by the quality and locality of housing. The "higher" class lives in permanent dwellings in the town with fences, yards, and furniture of European style. The "lower" class lives, usually some distance out of town, on a reserve, in galvanized-iron shacks with dirt floors, little furniture, outside cooking arrangements, and no electricity or running water. Many of those who do so say they prefer the "free and easy" ways of the reserve to the social demands of conventional life within the town. In short, the higher-class group values *independence* (from reliance on white charity) whereas the lower-class group prefers *freedom* (from the pressures and demands of living with Europeans). The move from lower to higher group is called "going the white man's way," and those who have done so are often referred to, derogatively, as "flash." The higher group, on the other hand, resists the moving of a lower family into their housing area, unless that family is prepared to conform to the more conventional standards of their neighbors. The higher Aboriginal group regards the reserve and its inhabitants as a disgrace to the town and to themselves. The aim of the higher group is acceptance by and maintenance of status in the white community; to be outcast as "black" is the final ignominy.

Higher-class Aborigines tend to marry within their own subgroup and to maintain distance from the lower class in sport and gambling activities, considering themselves "a cut above the others" and closer to the white community. Lower-class Aborigines are described in terms adopted from whites as "dirty," "irresponsible," "immoral," and "uncivilized." The attainment and maintenance of higher status is determined, largely, by the ambition and struggle of women. Ultimately, it is the matriarch who determines the degree of class consciousness of the group; it is she who spurs her husband and children to "make good" in education and later work.

The higher-class husband is expected to be faithful to his wife. The lower-class woman knows that men seek new faces and is likely to live with a series of husbands in common-law marriage. Sexual attractiveness and masculine virility are emphasized by the lower group, in contrast to romantic love and fidelity by women in the higher. Women of both classes fear and disapprove of drunkenness in their men; among women, only a female prostitute would consistently drink heavily.

Earlier policies that sought to prevent the sale of liquor to Aborigines have given drink an important status. Hard drinking, especially the ability to hold one's liquor, is of great social significance among European men in country towns. In fact, the man who cannot hold his liquor is derided as a "two-pot screamer." For Aboriginal men, the purchase, sharing, and consumption of liquor has become a ritual, drunkenness being periodically sought and flaunted to the dismay and fear of women and to the disgust of whites. Alcohol offers recreation, immediate gratification, and the opportunity to gain status through sharing in a social outgroup, a pattern derived originally from the seminomadic, masculine, white, pastoral tradition of the nineteenth century.

> The people in town just run us down;
> They say we live on wine and beer.
> But if they'd stop and think, if we didn't drink
> There'd be no fun around here.[5]

The man who happens to be "flush" (to have money) "turns on the grog for young and old." Men are judged by their ability to get and share liquor. Alchohol thus becomes the means by which adolescents, impotent otherwise to demonstrate achievement, assert their maturity.

The higher social group emphasizes thrift and the accumulation

---

5. From an Aboriginal popular song by Dougie Young, quoted by Beckett (1964b). Going on a drinking spree is called "cutting a rug," "breaking out," or "letting off steam."

and care of possessions. Those of the lower group do not save or value material goods in this way but spend, enjoy, and share what they have. When they are in need they depend on relatives or neighbors and on child endowment, a regular government subsidy to parents determined by the number of children in the family. Those of the higher class have smaller families and are more likely to use contraception. They wean their children earlier, place more emphasis on cleanliness, "good" behavior, regular school attendance, and scholastic progress, and encourage ambition while being realistic about color prejudice. Lower-class parents knowingly compensate their children for later disadvantage by indulging them as much as possible when they are young and by avoiding pressure. Physical discipline is rarely used, and then inconsistently. Upper-class girls are protected from sexual encounters during adolescence whereas the lower-class girl commences regular sexual intercourse at that time, usually with a boy of her choice who may come to live with her family and contribute to it economically.

The Aboriginal woman is the key in determining to which class her family will aspire. White women, on the other hand, are dominant forces in determining the racial prejudice of their menfolk and children toward all Aborigines. Both white and upper-class black women see life as a struggle to maintain self-imposed standards against the intrusion of disorder and poverty. Both are preoccupied with the symbolic significance of *dirt* in this struggle.

Eckermann (1971, 1973), in a recent study of a larger town, has questioned the solidarity and reciprocity of part-Aborigines. She describes the group as much more identified with European values, and more individualistic, than anticipated. Her findings possibly reflect the beginning of assimilation of geographically dispersed Aborigines into the urban working-class community. Berry (1973a) has described a new phenomenon in a coastal part-Aboriginal community: a tendency to reaffirm Aboriginal identity despite a high level of acculturation to European society. The high acculturation level was associated with (1) a marginal status in terms of insecurity, aggressive defensiveness, suspicion, and lack of solidarity vis-à-vis the white group, (2) deviant social behavior, and (3) psychological stress symptoms. If the individual sets aside Aboriginal identification and sees himself as an "Australian," stress symptoms appear to be reduced. Berry concludes with an awkward question: Is it possible for a minority group to retain a sense of identity and to share in the economy of the total society without conflict, stress, and alienation? The answer to this question, surely, depends largely on the future attitude of white Australians to the aspirations of Aborigines. At the present time, as Sommerlad and Berry (1970) point out, those who describe themselves as "Aborigines" favor integration, with the retention of Aboriginal separate identity, and reject assimilation; whereas those Aborigines who identify as "Australians" favor assimilation and conclude that Aborigines can become successful only by dissociating themselves from others of their own ethnic group and becoming absorbed into white Australia.

THE CULTURE OF POVERTY: AUSTRALIAN VERSION

The term *culture of poverty* (more correctly, "subculture of poverty") was introduced in 1959 by Oscar Lewis, the American anthropologist. In a series of brilliant biographical and analytic studies of poor families in different countries, Lewis (1959, 1961, 1964, 1966) found cross-cultural regularities that suggested a new conceptual model. He saw the culture of poverty as having its own structure and rationale, passed down from generation to generation, a positive issue that is not merely a matter of deprivation or deficit.

According to Lewis the subculture of poverty flourishes when the following conditions coexist: (1) cash economy, wage labor, and production for profit; (2) high rates of unemployment for unskilled labor; (3) low wages; (4) failure to provide social, political, and economic organization for the low-income group; (5) a bilateral rather than a unilateral kinship system;[6] and (6) the existence of a set of values in the dominant class that stresses the accumulation of wealth and upward mobility and throws opprobrium upon those who do not succeed in individual competition. In rural Australia there is little doubt that the first, fourth, and sixth factors apply. Aborigines form a marginal part of the cash economy; they are almost totally dependent politically and economically on the dominant group; and they are rejected *en bloc* as "no-hopers" by the whites. Rates of unemployment vary considerably, depending on the prevailing economic conditions in white rural Australia; but Aborigines tend to be on the bottom of the wage scale for unskilled labor and to be the first to lose their jobs during a recession. In regard to the fifth factor—bilateral kinship—part-Aboriginal society, like that of working-class whites, can be described as stressing neither matrilineal nor patrilineal descent, despite the matrifocal organization of the family.

To some extent, the culture of poverty can be regarded as an adaptation of the poor to their marginal position in a class-stratified capitalistic society. The extension of ingroup social credit, for example, compensates for the inability to obtain loans or credit from businesses

---

6. Unilateral descent groups trace their lineage back to a common female (matrilineal) or male (patrilineal) ancestor. Unlike bilateral descent groups, unilineal clans may act in collective or corporate fashion, for example to enact vengeance or to accumulate property.

CHAPTER FIVE

and banks. Lewis suggests, however, that the values of the culture of poverty are more than an adaptation, that they are positive factors transmitted, explicitly and implicitly, from parents to children. The most likely candidates for the culture of poverty are those who come from the lowest strata of a rapidly changing society and who are already partly alienated from it. The dispossessed, detribalized, and socially rejected part-Aboriginal people of Australia fit this characterization very well.

Lewis has studied the culture of poverty from the following points of view: the relationship between the subculture and the larger society; the social organization of the slum community; family structure and function; individual attitudes, values, and personality. The relevance of Lewis' views for Australian fringe-dwelling part-Aborigines will now be discussed.

RELATIONSHIP TO LARGER SOCIETY

The members of a poverty subculture are described as being effectively blocked from social, political, and economic integration in the larger society. This situation results, in marginal part-Aboriginal communities, from color discrimination, a de facto (and partly voluntary) segregation of habitation, mutual fear and suspicion, a lack of economic resources, and the "inertia" of both groups in regard to social change.

Their inadequate management of economic resources prevents the poor from owning property, saving money, or accumulating food and possessions. These difficulties are counterbalanced and perpetuated by a tendency toward social reciprocity in groups of kindred. The denial of reciprocity, as described previously, is required if a family or individuals are to migrate from black poverty and assimilate into white Australian society.

Lewis describes the poor as having a low level of education, harboring a distrust of labor unions, political parties, welfare agencies, and police, and making little use of banks or cultural facilities. This description is true for Aborigines, although they may utilize the local hospital provided the country general practitioner is sympathetic to them. Their high latent potential for protest has scarcely been realized, in Australia, despite the recent importation of radical black politics from North America through newspapers and films, and the return from overseas of those who organize or stimulate protest.

In contrast to middle-class society, formal marriage is uncommon in culture-of-poverty unions. Serial consensual unions are more adapted to a situation in which marriage ceremonies and divorce are expensive, men have no property or job security, and women, like men, value the freedom to discard unsatisfactory spouses. This is as true for Australia as it is in the Caribbean or Mexico City.

SOCIAL ORGANIZATION

As Lewis describes of the culture of poverty, Aboriginal slum communities are characterized by poor housing, overcrowding, lack of privacy, and little organization beyond the level of the nuclear and extended family. This situation is in marked contrast to the complexity of tribal society. There may be a degree of communal spirit among the poor; but it is difficult for a leader to mobilize this spirit toward a goal of community development.

THE FAMILY

As Lewis describes of the culture of poverty, the Aboriginal family is characterized by consensual marriage, early initiation into sex, a high incidence of abandonment of families by men, a matrifocal basis, authoritarianism, and a verbal emphasis on family solidarity that is rarely achieved because of sibling rivalry and competition. Lewis also mentions the absence of childhood as a specially protected phase. This does not appear to be the case in Aboriginal families except when parents are overwhelmed by large numbers of children; Aboriginal mothers often cling to their children and may see the commencement of primary school as an excessive expectation of an immature child. Separation anxiety is therefore often pronounced in Aboriginal children. Adolescents, on the other hand, are much less likely to be supervised and protected than in middle-class society.

THE INDIVIDUAL

In Australia, a sense of marginality, helplessness, dependence, and inferiority is accentuated by racial discrimination. Lewis also describes other personality characteristics—orality, weak ego structure, poor impulse control, strong present-time orientation, fatalism—that need further study in Australia. In addition, he mentions a spontaneity, vitality, sensuality, and ability to indulge impulse that the more constricted middle-class white often envies and a sense of mutual involvement and warmth that is foreign to the highly individuated.

The observation of marginal Aboriginal communities supports Lewis' generalized propositions about the culture of poverty in most respects; but the peculiar characteristics of Australian part-Aboriginal subculture are determined by its historical background of attempted genocide, dispossession, and discrimination, by its mixed racial ancestry

CHAPTER FIVE

and partial identification with the ethos of the nomadic white rural laboring class of the nineteenth century, and by its present dependence upon the rural pastoral economy and government aid. Its lack of effective political solidarity is accentuated by a division into two social classes—one aspiring to and one rejecting assimilation. The culture of poverty, despite its positive features, is impoverished in a historical sense, since its history and traditions have either been lost, in the main, or adopted and modified from the larger society within the last four or five generations.

CULTURAL DIFFERENCE AND SCHOLASTIC ADJUSTMENT

Less than 10 percent of Aboriginal children in New South Wales progress beyond the second year of high school. Fifty-five percent are classed as "slow learners" (Duncan 1973). Despite recent economic support and encouragement to stay at school, it is obvious that pitifully few Aborigines today have the motivation and competence to benefit from formal education. The reason for this must be sought in an understanding of their history, social background, and aspirations.

Watts (1973), in a comparison of high-achieving and low-achieving adolescent Aboriginal girls, found that achievers had higher aspirations and were less content with themselves, more likely to see humanity's relation to nature as one of mastery (rather than harmony or subjection), and more individualistic. Aborigines, as a whole, compared to whites, saw school success as less important. Aborigines were dominated by a need to maintain affiliation with their own social group, rather than to stand out as successful in individual performance. Aboriginal girls like to please adults, however, and are responsive to appreciation and praise. Cawte (1972) has described the vulnerability of Aborigines to ridicule and their great resentment of the sarcastic criticism sometimes used as a spur by white teachers. Aboriginal boys, especially, may define scholastic success as an attempt to ingratiate white authority and thus reject those who pursue it.

A considerable amount of work has been done in Australia on the formal cognitive and language competence of Aboriginal children. Teasdale and Katz (1968) studied the verbal abilities of lower-SES whites, Aborigines, and middle-class whites in a New South Wales rural town, using the Peabody Picture Vocabulary Test (PPVT) (Dunn 1965) and the Illinois Test of Psycholinguistic Abilities (ITPA) (Kirk, McCarthy, and Kirk 1968). They found that there were no significant differences between lower-SES whites and Aborigines in PPVT scores, but that both were significantly below middle-class whites. The same observations applied to the results of the ITPA survey. From this study it appeared that part-Aborigines functioned at a level equivalent to that of working-class rural whites in language performance. The two lower groups had deficits particularly in the areas of aural decoding of phrases, forming associations between words, oral expression, and standard English syntax.

The work of Bruce, Hengereld, and Radford (1971) in Victoria, the Van Leer Foundation in Queensland (Hart 1973), and data from Bourke have all corroborated the observation of marked language deficits in rural, part-Aboriginal children. In 1969 we tested all children in Bourke aged between thirty-six and forty-eight months. The comparative results on the PPVT (a test of verbal reception and recognition of two-dimensional pictorial representations) are shown in Table 5.1 (Nurcombe and Moffitt 1970). The surprise was the low performance of the Europeans.

TABLE 5.1 PPVT Scores of Aboriginal and White Preschool Children in Bourke, 1969

	n	PPVT IQ Mean	SD	t	p
Aborigines	22	67.4	10.9	2.8	.005
Europeans	35	79.5	17.9		

TABLE 5.2 Mean Difference Scores between Chronological and Language Ages on ITPA of Aboriginal and White Preschool Children in Bourke, 1969

	Deficit in Language Age (Months)	
ITPA Subtest	Aboriginal	White
Auditory reception	−15.9	− 8.4
Visual reception	−16.6	− 8.0
Auditory association	−18.4	− 8.2
Visual association	−16.9	− 9.0
Verbal expression	−16.2	−10.6
Manual expression	−19.1	− 7.7
Grammatic closure	−20.8	− 2.2
Visual closure	− 6.3	− 3.4
Auditory sequential memory	+ 1.4	+ 4.5
Visual sequential memory	−13.5	− 2.4

CHAPTER FIVE

Further analysis in terms of the ITPA (a test of different facets of language ability) revealed marked deficits. When these were expressed in terms of the mean language age, in months, that each group was below the norm, the pattern shown in Table 5.2 emerged. It can be seen that Aborigines have marked global deficits—apart from in auditory memory—and that they have a particular deficit in the grammatic closure subtest; that is, in the use of standard English syntax.

De Lacey (1971) compared the PPVT scores of a variety of Australian children who ranged in age from five to twelve years (see Table 5.3). He found that fringe-dwelling part-Aborigines tested lowest of all his groups. Full-descent Aborigines from the north and center of Australia retain their own language and are bilingual. Part-Aboriginal groups, as in Bourke, have almost completely lost the old languages and speak English exclusively. The English used in the far north of Queensland has retained some features of the traditional language, particularly in phonology and contextual characteristics. Farther to the south, as in Bourke, colloquial speech merges with that of the working-class rural white society. Flint (1970) has described the linguistic characteristics of Aboriginal English in different communities. Where the traditional language is in disuse, a small corpus of single vernacular words remains and is integrated with English (for example: in Bourke, *gaba* means white person and *mari*, Aborigine). There are important differences, grammatically, from standard English (SE). For example:

1. Noun plural markers (/s/ or /z/) are sometimes used, sometimes not.
2. Possessives are signaled by word order or by use of phrase /balong ta/: *Where gun balong to Eddy?*
3. Third person singular pronoun feminine is sometimes /ʃi:/ (*she*), sometimes /i:/ (*'e*).

TABLE 5.3 Mean PPVT IQ Scores of Different Groups of Australian Children (de Lacey 1971)

Sample	n	Mean PPVT IQ
Bourke, part-Aboriginal living on reserve	11	55.9
Northern Territory, full-descent Aboriginal	63	66.4
Bourke, part-Aboriginal living in town	13	69.3
Bourke, lower-SES white	22	86.9
Northern Territory, lower-SES white	25	91.3
Sydney, higher-SES white	30	110.3

4. Distinctive possessive pronoun forms are absent except /ja/ (*yours*) and /mai/ (*my*).
5. Future tense is signaled by auxiliary /gona/ (*going to*), never by *shall* or *will*.
6. Continuous tense is signaled by bound morpheme /an/ without auxiliary.
7. Simple and coordinate clauses predominate; complex sentences with subordinate clauses are rare.
8. Constituent clauses of coordinate sentences are sometimes linked by /an/; but arrangements with pause separations are characteristic.
9. Use of direct speech in narration is usual, with the sentence marker /ei/ (*eh?*) serving to punctuate or invite confirmation.
10. The phonological system is different from SE, which may impair intelligibility.

The grammar seems to vary with context—for example, in conversation with the linguist it more closely approximated SE. Flint concluded that a *diglossia* is operating: a mixed dialect of English is in familiar daily use; but there is a stylistic continuum, between dialect and SE, depending on topic, situation, and person addressed. There are also individual variations within the Aboriginal community, different people being able to adjust to different degrees along the continuum, depending predominantly upon education.

The Van Leer Foundation in Queensland (Hart 1973) has analyzed the patterns of the naturally occurring speech of Aborigines and working-class whites between two and five years of age. Two hours of utterances were recorded from each child in the natural environment by using a specially designed microphone. The transcribed tapes were analyzed by computer in terms of the relative frequency of single words, the relative frequency of word sequences forming developmental language units, and the relative frequency of sentence transformations. The results showed that four-year-old Aboriginal children used single words and phrases with frequencies different from that of whites. The most common Aboriginal words were function terms (*look, there, la, one, hey, he, got*) whereas whites made more use of articles, copula,[7] conjunctions, and prepositions. The interpretation was that Aboriginal four-year-old speech resembled white two-year-old speech and could be meaningfully related to a *pivot grammar* (Braine 1963), which is characteristic of the stage in

---

7. A copula is a verb that links complement to subject; usually it is a variation of the verb *to be*, as in *He is a good boy*.

CHAPTER FIVE

TABLE 5.4 Index of Frequencies of Different Transformations in Either Standard or Aboriginal English Used by White and Aboriginal Four-Year-Old Children (Hart 1973)

Transformation	White Index	Aboriginal Index
Contraction (e.g.: *He'll*)	375	35
Negation (e.g.: ...*not*...)	166	45
Interrogative (e.g.: *You going, eh?*)	164	10.5
Got verb (e.g.: *I got a*...)	96	142
Causal clauses (e.g.: ...*because*)	14	0
So clauses	14	0
If clauses	9	0

speech development when children begin to form two- and three-word phrases (*look here, Billy car, Hey look, That a..., Here la, He name*).[8] An index of the frequency of transformations was calculated by determining the frequencies with which the particular word or phrase was used in the ethnic groups at particular age levels and then multiplying this figure by the ratio

$$\frac{\text{Number of speakers using the word or phrase}}{\text{Total number of possible speakers}}$$

Some extracts from this index are presented in Table 5.4.

There is strong evidence from these two linguistic studies that Aboriginal English is a distinct dialect and that idiolectal variation depends on context and the educational level of the speaker. Flint's description of a diglossia is appropriate, with Aboriginal English merging along a continuum into standard English. Thus the assertions of Labov and Baratz are supported (see chapter 3). It is likely that an important reason for the finding of Aboriginal language deficits cited earlier is that such tests as the PPVT and the ITPA assess performance in standard English. The children probably had difficulty in understanding the instructions, and some of their responses, though correct in Aboriginal English, would be marked incorrect by the assessor. But this is not the whole story. The Van Leer Foundation analysis shows that, aside from diglossia, the Aboriginal child is markedly behind the European child in the frequency and range of his use of transformations in either NSE or

---

8. An alternative hypothesis, suggested by Mark Lester, is that the Aborigines are speaking a *creole*. Creoles are characteristically less complex than standard forms. Thus a briefer or less complex surface structure in creole might be derived from a deep-structure equivalent to that of a more complex standard surface structure.

SE grammatical forms. The speech of four-year-old Aborigines closely resembles the pivot language characteristic of white two-year-olds.

It would therefore appear that—in Australia—both the cultural deprivation and the cultural difference hypotheses apply to part-Aboriginal children. Chapter 3 described how cultural deprivation theorists pointed to an improverishment of language, in terms of syntax and vocabulary, as the basis of scholastic underachievement in disadvantaged groups. This approach has recently been attacked by a group of linguists who contend that the apparent language impoverishment is a reflection of two facts: that minority groups may speak a dialect of English which differs in grammar from standard English; and that minority groups are prevented, by unfamiliarity with the test or school situation, from fully expressing their competence. What is the Australian evidence in regard to this controversy? Although it is by no means conclusive, the evidence suggests that both approaches are correct. Aborigines speak a dialect and operate in a diglossia that has rules which are on a continuum with standard English. At the age of four years, however, before entering elementary school their vocabulary and syntax, in nonstandard English terms, are less well developed than in their white age mates. Part-Aboriginal children do have relative deficiencies in language competence, produced by different realization experience. Their syntactic development may be relatively lower. Their language competencies differ also in expression compared to whites, in both context and strategy. The evaluation of language and cognitive performance is therefore affected by qualitative and quantitative differences in both competence and expression in the part-Aboriginal child at the crucial age of school entry.

SUMMARY AND CONCLUSIONS

The traditional, nomadic, tribal basis of Aboriginal life rapidly disappeared, after the colonization of Australia by Europeans, as a result of the combined depredations of genocide, disease, and the social disintegration engendered by traumatic contact with the steamroller of white culture. In the southeast and southwest of Australia, most of the remaining groups are part-Aboriginal, living on the fringes of white rural townships or gradually merging with the urban laboring classes. Here they are stigmatized by the adjoining white communities, have substandard housing and health, and have evolved a loose social organization, largely dependent on the whites, that is a variant of the culture of poverty.

In these part-Aboriginal communities kinship relations are close, the mother or maternal grandmother typically being a matriarchal figure. Remnants of traditional beliefs remain, shorn of their ritual significance, but the mobility and relative economic exclusion of Aboriginal men ensure that the values of the community are, in many ways, similar to those of the seminomadic, pastoral white workers of the nineteenth century.

Within the fringe groups two social classes have evolved: one is characterized by poorer housing, less interest in the collection and care of possessions, more adherence to traditional reciprocity, and less pressure on their children to achieve in school and work; the other aspires to the standards of the white community in housing, possessions, and education. There is tension between the two classes, the upper consciously maintaining social distance from the lower. The upper class seeks "independence" from white charity; the lower class prefers "freedom" from the social and economic pressures of European society. Progress from lower to upper class demands that the family deny the reciprocity of kin relationships, become more individualistic, and withstand the derogation of the fringe group. Even so, the likelihood is that only an imperfect assimilation into white society will be possible. There is some evidence that those groups who have become most acculturated, having experienced the color bar of white society, have begun to reaffirm their Aboriginality and that their reaffirmation may be associated with a high level of psychosomatic tension.

Generalization obscures exceptions, but it is apparent that children of fringe Aboriginal groups do poorly in formal school and attain only marginal employment. Tests of intelligence, scholastic attainment, language development, and perceptual-motor skills show them to be behind rural whites who, in turn, have lower mean scores than city whites.

Adequate linguistic surveys have not been carried out, but there is evidence of the existence of a nonstandard dialect, Aboriginal English, that varies in characteristics in different parts of Aboriginal Australia. For the individual, a diglossia is operating: different speakers are able to move to different extents along a continuum from nonstandard to standard English.

Circumstantial evidence supports the contention that, compared to their white peers, Aborigines have both relative deficits in certain cognitive competencies and different rules—for example, of syntactic nature—for the expression of those competencies. The evidence also indicates that Aboriginal children do poorly in school because they lack the competencies required to adapt to the Western educational system. These competencies are in the areas of cognition, language, perception, spatial skills, and also, initially, in the ability to sustain separation anxiety, to concentrate and attend to formal school tasks, and to derive pleasure from achievement. Repeated experiences of failure, lack of educational support and aspirations in the home, and an adolescent peer culture explicitly antagonistic to the school all lead to cumulative deficits in scholastic attainment. The dominant motives of Aboriginal people are group-oriented rather than individualistic; they concern a need for affiliation and acceptance rather than achievement and competitive success. Hard work and attainment in school may be defined by the outgroup as an attempt to ingratiate alien white authority. Scholastic effort may be the first step in the difficult route toward an uncertain assimilation; but the Aboriginal people have begun to question whether assimilation is an appropriate future for them.

CHAPTER 6
AN AUSTRALIAN PRESCHOOL

There is a point when one must regard the consequences of ignorance as sinful, and that point was reached for the advocates of nurture when they expected that the core of blackishness would quickly change; and it was reached by the advocates of nature when they concluded that the overall failure of compensatory programs demonstrated the significance of genetic factors on which new programs should be based. With friends like that, the blacks need not waste time worrying about enemies, a lesson Jews learned well over the centuries.

Seymour Sarason

HISTORY

THE ECOLOGY OF THE ARID ZONE

In 1966, Brian Ross, a social psychologist, began to work out of Bourke on an ecological survey of the upper Darling region of New South Wales. He was supervised in this project by John Cawte of the University of New South Wales, and he collaborated with Ted Coolican, a medical practitioner, who completed during this time a twelve-month survey of his practice that was later published under the title *Australian Rural Practice* (Coolican 1973).

Ross's aim was to discover prior and current social factors associated with adjustment, personal contentment, and work efficiency. To do so he gathered, by interview, data from a randomized sample of 600 black and white people in the region concerning such matters as age, sex, occupational level, marital status, length of residence, geographical mobility, and political sophistication, in order to derive indices of *cultural exclusion* (from mainstream white Australian society) and *economic advantage*. These factors were related to interview measures of anxiety, psychosomatic distress, authoritarianism, and history of psychiatric illness.

In summary, Ross found that social factors influenced adjustment more than geography or climate did. Aborigines were at a marked disadvantage and since almost all whites considered that their disadvantage had an innate racial basis, the problem was compounded. The incidence of Aboriginal illiteracy was high, educational levels were low, and few had permanent employment. Aboriginal children grew up in an environment that was detrimental to educational success—a self-perpetuating problem. The absence of attainable goals was associated with a hedonistic, unplanned approach to life and a feeling of powerlessness.

In 1970, Coolican found that almost 50 percent of the total Aboriginal population of Bourke was under sixteen years of age. More than 200 people lived on the Bourke Reserve, about 200 lived in newly built Housing Commission homes, and the remainder were on the outskirts in poor circumstances. The 200 Reserve Aborigines today live two miles out of town in dilapidated tin shacks with dirt floors, no electricity, open cooking fires, and little furniture. Sanitation is primitive and overcrowding severe, up to fifteen people sleeping in one room at times. Diet is often poor, personal hygiene difficult to maintain, and the prevalence of respiratory, skin, eye, and intestinal infection and parasitic disease alarmingly high. The climate is fiercely hot in summer and bitterly cold in winter; the houses are scoured by dust and infested with bushflies. Rainfall is sparse and drought seasons common, yet the township suffers from recurrent floods.

Almost all Aboriginal workers are unskilled. Families are large and common-law marriage usual. There is a relatively high incidence of complications of pregnancy and childbirth and of illness in early childhood. Aborigines are less likely than whites to go to a doctor with overt psychiatric disorder; but the incidence of alcoholism, personality deviation, delinquency, and family disintegration is high.

The initial medical and sociological findings of the Arid Zone Survey, coordinated by John Cawte, confirmed and extended our understanding of fringe-dwelling society: a particular version of the culture of poverty molded by its peculiar history and ecological-economic setting. The second phase moved into intervention.

Dr. Max Kamien, psychiatrist and research fellow of the New South Wales Institute of Psychiatry, was appointed in 1971 to foster community development and improve health standards in the Aboriginal group. Shortly prior to that, in late 1969, a preschool was established. This chapter deals with its design, function, and results.

EARLY RATIONALE AND ESTABLISHMENT

The original aim of those who designed the preschool—Barry Nurcombe and Paul Moffitt—was to provide a resource center for Aborigines. Encouraged by the early results of compensatory education overseas, we sought to enlist the support of the Aboriginal community in developing a "language stimulation" program that would prepare their children for primary school. While we applied for funds to build the school, we explored possibilities with white and Aboriginal leaders.

We avoided any suggestion that our aim was to "change" Aborigines. An unfortunate Sydney newspaper article stating, among other things, that we planned to improve hygiene produced considerable resentment. Fortunately, as it happened, we had something to offer that Aborigines appreciated—a chance of helping their children's education. Almost universally, the parents valued this offer and perceived education as a means of economic improvement that had been denied them.

It became apparent that a preschool of the type we envisaged could not be established without white support. A committee of white and Aboriginal community leaders was thus established to further the plan. Consultation with the committee revealed something that caused a change in our thinking: neither ethnic group wanted a segregated preschool. Aborigines wished to help their children mix with whites; Europeans considered that *their* children needed, and should not be denied, preschool experience. The eventually integrated preschool has been a positive factor in promoting better relations in the town, at a time when a degree of "backlash" has occurred among economically hard-pressed rural whites in Australia as a result of increased Commonwealth expenditure for Aboriginal welfare. In fact our preliminary 1969 survey (see Tables 5.1 and 5.2) revealed that white children, on the whole, also had serious language "deficits" potentially ameliorable by the kind of program we had in mind.

With the help of the local shire council we obtained and renovated an old house. In view of the fact that our first year was to compare a traditional, child-centered with a direct, structured teaching program, the house was divided: on one side we built two enclosed rooms for the structured classes; on the other we built a larger, more open room for a child-centered program. A large veranda and grounds for outdoor play, a spacious kitchen, an office, toilets, and laundry completed the building. The kitchen, which directly overlooks the larger playroom, was to become a popular meeting place for parents, staff, and visitors.

The issue of "experimentation" has required explanation on a number of occasions. Parents are sensitive to the suggestion that their children will be treated as guinea pigs. They have been assured that we would not use teaching techniques we thought dangerous, that we were seeking the methods which worked best for outback children, and that our findings would probably have relevance for all children living far from the big cities of the coast.

By the end of 1969 preparations were complete and our first teacher, Megan Passmore, was appointed. We started with a child-centered program for eleven children. In 1970 a second teacher, Ann McMillan, joined us and three more classes—one traditional and two structured—began. In the first year there was considerable separation anxiety in the Aboriginal parents and children. Our original plan—to have mothers remain in the preschool initially—was altered; the children settled more quickly when their parents left. Mothers were scheduled to help with food preparation and cleaning; we found that the Aborigines preferred to work with others from their own group. Monthly meetings of all parents were begun and have continued. There are no tuition fees, but the parents purchase, organize, and prepare the morning and afternoon snacks. We had no precedent as there had been no previous similar venture in Australia. We were helped, in the establishment of the traditional program, by the Kindergarten Teachers' Union, Sydney, who gave us access to useful literature and allowed our infant-school-trained teacher to observe preschool classes in operation. For the structured classes we drew upon, and modified, a program from Bereiter and Engelmann's *Teaching Disadvantaged Children in the Preschool* (1966). The exceptionally clear rationale and techniques in this book were very helpful. To those who have criticized the first year of our program on the basis that the traditional preschool classes were not taught by trained preschool teachers,[1] we can only answer that we began with open minds—one of our teachers frankly preferred the child-centered approach—and that we did our best to recreate typical, conventional preschool classes.[2]

It will be noted that, every year, we have attempted to compare the effectiveness of teaching programs contrasted in terms of degree of structure, teacher- or child-centeredness, and precision of sequence. In 1970, we contrasted a highly structured with a relatively unstructured program. In subsequent years—1971, 1972, 1973, 1974—we have compared structured with semistructured teaching techniques. Putting it another way, we have contrasted an analytic, programmed, non-

---

1. Both teachers were infant-school-trained in 1970. Since 1971, at least one of our teachers has been preschool-trained.
2. Except that our teacher/pupil ratio was one to eleven whereas in a typical suburban preschool it is one to twenty or more.

theoretical, structured technique with more integrative, global techniques evolved from theoretical concepts of the natural course of cognitive, affective, and psychomotor development.

ACTION RESEARCH: DESIGN

OBJECTIVES

Each year the program has been designed to promote specified terminal objectives. Apart from minor clarifications, these aims have remained the same over the four years of operation (1970–1973), except insofar as we refined the specific psychomotor objectives in 1971 as a result of our 1970 results.

Affective objectives. In this area we specify that the children will be able to:

1. Tolerate separation from their parents for the length of a school day
2. Relate to and cooperate with peers, with enjoyment
3. Relate to adults in play and in formal learning
4. Respond favorably to verbal praise
5. Assimilate and adapt to the regularity of an organized school day
6. Demonstrate effort and show pleasure in achievement
7. Answer orally, as individuals, when asked to do so by a teacher
8. Sense their separate identities and demonstrate this by the ability to describe their experiences and feelings in the first person and to give their own names

Moreover, we specify that the parents will demonstrate their involvement in the child's education by supporting the preschool through participation at scheduled meetings and by intensifying their communication with the child at home.

Perceptual-motor objectives. In this area we specify that the children will be able to:

1. Demonstrate body-image knowledge by naming parts of their own bodies and by drawing a pictorial representation of a human being of a quality commensurate with chronological age
2. Orient themselves to and recognize two-dimensional pictorial representations of common objects
3. Discriminate between geometric shapes (square, triangle,

rectangle, circle) and colors (blue, green, red, yellow, orange, brown, black, white) from concrete objects or two-dimensional pictorial representations (for example, a red triangle drawn on a blackboard)
4. Demonstrate age-appropriate perceptual-motor skills in tracing, coloring in, and copying with pencil and paper; threading beads; cutting and pasting paper shapes; manipulating three-dimensional blocks; and solving jigsaw puzzles

Language and cognitive objectives. In this area we specify that the children will be able to:

1. Use affirmative and *not* statements in response to question and command
2. Use appropriate polar-opposite terms (*fast–slow*) in relation to objects or events
3. Use prepositions (*on, in, over, under, between*) in relation to concrete objects or actions
4. Quote positive and negative instances of at least four categorical classes (tools, clothes, furniture, food, vehicles)
5. Use simple *if–then* constructions to solve logical problems related to two-dimensional, abstract, blackboard representations involving shape, color, and size
6. Use *not, and,* and *or* in simple deductions
7. Count objects to 10, aloud to 20, and to 100 with help at decade points
8. Describe a concrete object, using *and*, from three separate dimensions
9. Use the following terms appropriately in relation to concrete objects: *only, all, some, more than, less than*
10. Use personal pronouns correctly
11. Use comparatives and superlatives in relation to concrete objects
12. Distinguish between and express the singular and plural forms of common nouns.

These objectives have been written as an outcome of four factors: our judgment of how the children most needed help to adapt to elementary school; how the parents could be constructively involved in the education of their children; what the parents most wanted for their children; and what we thought we had to offer. The objectives are therefore the outcome of judgment, negotiation, and deliberation.

Chapter Six

SELECTION

Yearly, all children in Bourke who would be eligible to commence preschool in January of the following year are tested with the Peabody Picture Vocabulary Test (PPVT) (Dunn 1965)—a test of receptive vocabulary in which the child is required to point to the correct one of four alternative two-dimensional pictures in response to a stimulus word (*Put your finger on...nest*). The popularity of the preschool is such that, each year, all eligible children have come voluntarily for selection. From the total number of children tested (between 50 and 73), the forty-four (1970, 1971, 1972) or forty-eight (1973, 1974) who test lowest in terms of PPVT IQ are chosen. The parents of children excluded on this basis are informed that their children are progressing well and have no need of our special program. (All these children have been white. All the Aboriginal children in town have been selected every year.) From 1974, a separate classroom, teacher, and child-centered program will be arranged for these excluded children.

Using the PPVT IQ as criterion, the children selected are divided into four classes of eleven or twelve children. In 1970, it was arranged that all four classes had approximately the same IQ and ethnic mix. Experience showed that this method of selection created a wide IQ range and caused difficulties for the teacher because of marked intragroup variations in learning rate and baseline. Since then, two upper and two lower classes have been selected and matched, one against the other, for IQ and ethnic admixture. Two classes, one upper and one lower, are exposed to one comparative teaching technique under investigation and two to the other. In 1973, for example, one upper and one lower class experienced a structured Bereiter-Engelmann technique; they were compared with one upper and one lower class who experienced a semistructured Piaget-based program. Since each teacher teaches each program (one in the morning and the other in the afternoon), one teacher in 1973, for example, taught an upper structured and a lower semistructured class while the other taught a lower structured and an upper semistructured class.

ATTENDANCE

Each class attends during the Australian school year, from February until early December, for two hours per day.[3] There are, there-

---

3. We do not contend that this is the ideal duration. A two-hour day was a compromise dictated by the number of children presented and our resources in staff, space, and equipment. It is possible, indeed likely, that in a longer day, structured and less structured approaches could be beneficially combined. A core of instructional teaching could be embedded in semistructured activities that are more congruent with the child's natural experience and development.

TABLE 6.1 Experimental Methodology of Comparison between Teaching Techniques

Group	Time 1	Time 2	Preschool	Time 3	Kindergarten	Time 4
E_1	Selection	Pretest	Program 1	Posttest	8 months	Follow-up test
E_2	Selection	Pretest	Program 2	Posttest	8 months	Follow-up test
C						Follow-up test

fore, two classes in the morning and two in the afternoon. Every second Friday no classes are held because the teachers are involved in planning. During the year, afternoon and morning classes are switched several times. The children from the reserve are picked up and returned daily in the preschool's station wagon. Total attendance has been very good (in 1970, for example, it was over 80 percent).

METHODOLOGY

The experimental methodology for comparison between the teaching techniques used each year is summarized in Table 6.1. The two experimental groups, E_1 and E_2, are matched for age (all are between four and five), for PPVT IQ, and (roughly) for ethnic mix on the basis of the selection test in the previous year. In the beginning of the preschool year E_1 and E_2 are administered the battery of pretests to be described in the section on evaluation. It has been found (Taylor, de Lacey, and Nurcombe 1972) that the PPVT in Bourke has a test-retest reliability coefficient of .68 at four years of age, over a period of two weeks. It has been found, also, that previous matching on PPVT IQ ensures satisfactory matching on the pretest PPVT and on the other language, cognitive, and perceptual tests in the pretest battery.

During the preschool year E_1 and E_2 (each divided into matched E_1 upper, E_2 upper and E_1 lower, E_2 lower) experience the teaching programs to be compared. After nine months E_1 and E_2 are administered the posttest battery to determine the degree and characteristics of change during the preschool year. After eight months in the kindergarten class of elementary school, all the children are retested at follow-up. For comparative purposes we have administered the same follow-up test battery to a group of children (C) who were in kindergarten in 1970 and thus had had no preschool experience. It is our intention to carry out long-term yearly follow-up studies in primary school.

The problems involved in experimental and quasi-experimental research have been discussed by Campbell and Stanley 1973, who describe sixteen types of design. The methodology used in our studies is a modification of their fourth design:

Chapter Six

	Time →		
R_1	O_1	X	O_2
R_2	O_3		O_4

In this pretest-posttest control group arrangement, two samples are randomized (at R_1 and R_2) and pretested (at O_1 and O_3), one is exposed to an experimental treatment (X), and both are posttested (at O_2 and O_4). The advantages of our design are:

1. It controls for *historical effects* preceding the experiment; that is, the children have been exposed to the same range of environments in the same town before they enter preschool.
2. It controls for the possible *practice effect* of testing on comparative scores; that is, the tendency of practice on pretest to inflate posttest scores artificially.
3. It controls for the effects of normal *maturation* on posttest scores.
4. Since E_1 and E_2 experience their programs simultaneously, over nine months, the possibility of *extraneous environmental influences* affecting one group preferentially is reduced.
5. *Instrumentation* is controlled to this extent: posttesting has always been carried out by psychologists hired for that purpose from outside the project. All posttests are blind; that is, the testers are unaware of which children experienced which experimental program. In 1973, pretesting was performed by the same external psychologists who completed the posttesting.
6. *Regression*, the tendency for extreme scores to revert closer to the mean (such as PPVT IQ, 100) statistically, is controlled.[4] Both E_1 and E_2 could be expected to demonstrate this effect to the same extent. This is an important issue since there are so many low scorers in this program.
7. The *selection* problem is reduced since the children represent the entire Aboriginal population of the town and most whites in the appropriate age group. They have been assigned, randomly, to E_1 and E_2 by starting with the child who has the lowest PPVT IQ and working up from there until forty-

---

4. Except to the extent that in the white group a small number of higher-IQ children have been excluded in 1970, 1972, and 1973; this would tend to cause a greater regression artefact in the scores of the whites included.

four or forty-eight children have been chosen. E_1 and E_2 therefore represent matched groups, which are first matched and then randomized, from the appropriate (in age and performance) population available, in every year of the preschool's operation.

8. Since staffing, equipment, and building are designed to be representative for Australia, the results can be regarded as having *external validity*. They could be replicated, potentially, without extraordinary effort and can thus be regarded as applicable to appropriate classes elsewhere.[5]

9. The replication of results in Bourke, over a number of years, supports their *internal validity*. Is Bourke, however, representative of other outback Australian towns with part-Aboriginal and white populations? We have no reason to believe it is exceptional.

All designs, however, are a compromise and can be criticized. In Bourke, the exigencies of action research created certain imperfections in our design. We did not feel justified in including a simultaneous no-treatment control group,[6] for two reasons: our numbers would have been too greatly reduced and our relations with the townspeople would have suffered as a consequence. In each year, therefore, the changes found in E_1 and E_2 could conceivably be due to something outside the preschool. In 1972, for example, children in the contrasting structured and semi-structured classes made large gains. How can we be sure that something else—the pretest for example—was not the operative variable? We cannot; but other considerations suggest that it is unlikely.

In 1970 we found that children who had experienced a structured program made very large performance gains, whereas those in a child-centered, unstructured program did not. Ex post facto, we take the unstructured program to have been a placebo. In other words, the factors of mere pretesting, attendance, teacher enthusiasm, unspecific attention, nutrition, or desire to please (the so-called Hawthorne effect) have been controlled and excluded. There was something specific to the structured program that produced the results. We contend that the results gained in succeeding years were also due to something specific to the programs employed. We are supported in this by the finding of Harries (1971), in another Australian country town, that Aboriginal children made no

---

5. Extraordinary, that is, in the degree of sophistication of staff, lavishness of equipment, size of class, and so forth.
6. Aside, that is, from group C, the non-preschooled kindergarten group of 1970 who have served as follow-up controls.

Chapter Six

language or cognitive performance gains after one year in a traditional preschool.[7]

Other related problems will be considered in the section entitled "Action Research: Discussion". Despite the difficulties and unavoidable compromises involved, we decided at the outset that an experimental approach was mandatory if we were to generalize from our experience with any validity. In this decision we are bolstered by the fact that this has been no one-shot study but a continuing and evolving project—a project in which the objectives, strategies, and evaluation involved each year have been designed in the light of previous findings.

TEACHING STRATEGIES

Each year a group of children passes through the preschool and on into elementary school like a wave through the sea. For this reason the classes (and their preschool year) are called Waves I (1970), II (1971), III (1972), and IV (1973). The teaching techniques used with each wave will now be described.

Wave I. In 1970 we set out to compare two teaching strategies—*traditional unstructured* and *structured direct*—in terms of their relative promotion of the terminal objectives and later elementary school progress. We thus sought to polarize our comparison, the two strategies being almost diametrically opposed in educational philosophy. The polarization affected our two teachers: one felt that the direct, Bereiter-Engelmann approach was too demanding of the children; the other appreciated its clear directions and rational sequencing. This is of interest in view of the eventual results.

The characteristics of an unstructured technique have been described in chapter 4. Ours was designed to resemble as closely as possible a suburban Australian preschool except that class size was comparatively low (eleven children). After morning assembly and free play there were periods of singing and rhythm, art and craft, outdoor play, nature study, conversation (involving finger play, poetry, and group games), storytelling, snack, and music. The teachers emphasized creativity, experience with a wide variety of objects and play media, sensorimotor development, and peer relations. The teacher was required to respond to individual children when they requested it or she felt they would not be interrupted by it. Despite the individual freedom allowed, the unstructured program

---

7. In fact, the Head Start experience in the United States has shown how very *difficult* it is to attain measurable changes in cognitive or language development with culturally different children. Despite the expertise, goodwill, and enthusiasm of the teachers involved in Head Start, few centers appear to have been successful in these terms. This matter is discussed in detail in chapter 4 and later in this chapter.

had considerable organization and regularity. In particular, we wished to expose the children to a rich language environment—through story, music, verbal games, and conversational play. In this respect the unstructured resembled the structured program; but in the latter the language and cognitive-development objectives were fostered in a more precisely sequenced manner.

The Bereiter-Engelmann structured program has already been discussed in chapter 4. Bereiter and Engelmann (1966) argue that since disadvantaged children are already at least one year behind the middle class at four years of age, time is at a premium. Admirable though the traditional goals of individual development and creativity may be, other objectives must take priority and must be directly taught for. Cultural deprivation is defined, basically, as *language deprivation*. Disadvantaged children have not been deprived of stimulation; rather, they have lacked exposure to certain *patterns* of stimulation—especially language stimulation—required for adaptation to formal schooling. The teaching technique they have designed aims to accelerate the development of vocabulary and syntax and to help the children apply their language competence to reasoning, planning, and clear communication.

In contrast to Bereiter and Engelmann's smaller classes, we used a teacher/pupil ratio of one to eleven. The two-hour day included three 20-minute periods of intensive, direct-instructional, group work. The balance of the school day was spent in free play, snack time, and general preparation. Finding that her structured class contained children with a wide range of abilities, one teacher divided it into two subgroups, allowing one to advance faster and spending more time on fundamental work with the other. The other teacher did not split her structured class of eleven in this way. Neither of the two unstructured classes was split.

In our adaptation of Bereiter and Engelmann's original program, we placed more emphasis on the language component than on prereading and prenumber skills. Beginning from identity statements (*This is an apple. These are apples. This is not a bike*) and second-order statements (*This apple is red. These apples are red. These apples are not green*), the teacher helps the child to build up polar concepts (*A worm is slow; a plane is fast*) and nonpolar concepts (*This horse is a big one*) and to use prepositions (*This block is on the floor*) and conjunctions (*This pencil is long and red*) appropriately. She teaches, in the more advanced phase, the basis of categorization reasoning (*If something can take you somewhere, it must be a vehicle*) by using conjunctions; *only*, *all*, *some*, and *if–then* constructions; verb expansions of tense and number (*These babies were crying*); sense verbs (*sound, taste, smell, feel*); pronouns; and comparatives and superlatives.

Chapter Six

The basic strategy employed has been adapted from techniques of teaching English as a foreign language; it is called *pattern drill*. The teacher presents material verbally, referring to concrete objects and two-dimensional representations of objects or abstract forms (square, rectangle, triangle, circle). She follows this with questions directed to individual children or to the group as a whole. The atmosphere is one of demand, excitement, and rapid interchange from individual to unison responses. The basic rhythms and structures of speech are accentuated and repeated over and over; the child is given verbal reward for effort; competition is avoided except, playfully, between child and teacher (*Now, children, I'm going to trick you*); and wrong answers are immediately corrected. The expectation of the level of the child's response begins with pointing, progresses to a *yes-no* answer, through a *yes-no* repetition (*No, this box is not a piano*), to the identification of criterial attributes or conceptual relations (Q. *Tell me about this box.* A. *This box is big and red. It is on the floor*).

As Evans (1971) describes, the distinctive principles of learning and instruction in this approach are the use of *behavioral objectives*; the grouping of children in *homogeneous small classes*; intensive *active oral involvement* of the child; immediate *feedback*; a carefully designed *graduated sequence*; a strategy that aims to facilitate *vertical transfer* of cornerstone competencies to the formal school setting; and *criterion-referenced testing*—evaluation that aims to determine whether the child has or has not attained the minimum competencies objectified. In comparison with the semistructured program to be described later, there is much less emphasis on sensorimotor experience as a basis of later logical-mathematical operations.

Wave II. In view of the relative success of the structured program in 1970 (to be described), all children in the 1971 wave were exposed to the modified Bereiter-Engelmann Program (BEP). The 1970 results indicated that neither the unstructured nor the structured technique had produced gains in those aspects of the psychomotor domain evaluated. We reasoned, therefore, that in addition to attempting to replicate the impressive gains of the Wave I structured classes in language, we should also teach, specifically, in the psychomotor domain during 1971.

Two classes, grouped as upper and lower in terms of mean PPVT IQ, were exposed to a perceptual-motor program designed by Frostig and Horne (1964)—the Frostig Program (FP). Two classes, one upper and one lower (in terms of PPVT IQ), were matched with the FP classes and exposed to a perceptual-motor stimulation program of our own design—the Bourke Perceptual-Motor Program (BPMP). The two upper classes had a mean PPVT IQ of 87.29 and the two lower classes a mean IQ of 72.18. The FP and BPMP were each taught for one 20-minute period per day each day.[8]

Marianne Frostig defines perception as the capacity to recognize stimuli. It involves the reception and interpretation of sensation and its integration with past experience. She considers that the age of most rapid perceptual development is from three to eight years. Adequate development during this period is a necessary, but not a sufficient, prerequisite for higher-order cognitive competence, particularly in reading and writing. The five specific perceptual subfunctions described by Frostig are eye-hand coordination, figure-ground perception, form constancy, position in space, and spatial relations. She has designed tests of these functions and has also prepared perceptual-motor stimulation exercises that are aimed to promote development in all five areas. We did not use Frostig's tests since we wished to avoid criterion contamination (invalidating experimental test results by teaching the content or form of the criterion test during the experimental treatment); but we used the teaching program included in "Pictures and Patterns Part I" (Frostig and Horne 1964). The FP is structured and graduated in sequence to an extent similar to the BEP: the child is provided with a workbook and prepared, sequenced materials to develop competence in the five aspects of perception described.

The Bourke Perceptual-Motor Program was designed to contrast with the Frostig Program. In this approach we provided play materials similar to those of conventional preschools and allowed the children more latitude in exploration and construction, the teacher intervening only when the child appeared to be having difficulty manipulating the materials or comprehending the task. The following materials and techniques were derived from traditional preschool practice:

1. Block-building: free play to encourage eye-hand manipulation by the fitting and balancing of block components of different shapes. When appropriate, the teacher asks questions of the child in this and the other twelve techniques (for example: *How do you make it go up? Which is the tallest ... the shortest ... the longest?*).
2. Cutting and pasting: a variety of materials, including colored paper, cloth, straw, string, wool, bottle tops, and

---

8. The schedule for each two-hour day therefore consisted of three 20-minute structured classes, one 20-minute perceptual-motor class (FP or BPMP), one 20-minute period of free play, and one period for snack and other preparation.

match boxes, are cut out with scissors and fixed to paper backing with brush and paste to form abstract shapes, representations of objects (house, ball, car), and collages.
3. Tearing and pasting: the free tearing of paper; tearing and pasting strips and large and small pieces on the outside and inside of cardboard boxes.
4. Cutting: free cutting with scissors; directed cutting out along lines and abstract and representational shapes.
5. Coloring: free coloring using large sheets of paper and large crayons and finer work with pencils and felt pens. Directed coloring in of large and small abstract and representational shapes.
6. Threading of large and small colored beads in free and directed sequences with thread and string of different color and thickness.
7. Jigsaws: wooden puzzles of different size, complexity, and abstractness.
8. Picture-matching.
9. Painting on paper, boxes, cardboard cartons, with finger or brushes, using different media and colors.
10. Cooking: pouring and stirring large, small, and divided amounts and noting transformation after cooking in oven.
11. Sand play: transporting, stirring, pouring, and molding dry and wet sand.
12. Dough play: free manipulative play with colored dough, followed by cutting and molding with dough cutter, knife, fork, and mold and roller.
13. Sorting of different objects with different form, size, and color.

Wave III. In 1972, in view of the relative success of both the perceptual programs, the FP and the BPMP were retained, each with one upper and one lower class. This year we decided to contrast the Bereiter-Engelmann Program with a semistructured program of our own design based on Piagetian principles. We called it the Extended Experience Program (EEP).

The EEP sought to draw upon the child's experience, to foster the preschool objectives, in five dimensions: (1) by stimulating the use of language in his spontaneous or guided activities, especially sociodramatic play; (2) by organizing more activity in the natural environment by means, for example, of excursions and nature study; (3) by fostering more divergent thinking in contrast to the convergent processes heavily emphasized in the structured program; (4) by stimulating the sense of individual identity and fostering a positive self-concept through the experience of success; (5) by arranging greater parental involvement in the educational process through the provision of homework requiring parental assistance.

The teaching techniques were less formal, less direct, and less structured than in the BEP. More emphasis was placed on helping the child to develop a sensorimotor basis for the intellectual development and language skills to be fostered. The syllabus was as follows:

> *Term I:* Orientation, free play, constructional games, naming objects, self-identity games (using mirror), and the gradual introduction through designed play experiences of concepts based on alternatives (*or*), negatives (*not*), comparatives, superlatives (*big, bigger, biggest*), prepositions (*on, in, under, over, between*), and polar opposites (*fast–slow*).
>
> *Term II:* Consolidation of term I experience and extension of experience to outside the classroom. Stimulation of divergent thinking by posing problems and employing make-believe games. Colors, shapes, sizes, counting, and pictorial or model representation.
>
> *Term III:* Manipulation of three-dimensional objects, classification, categorial exclusion (*This pencil is not an animal.* Q. *Why not?* A. *Because it doesn't breathe*), seriation (for example, with bead play), and conservation. Continued emphasis on self-concept and personal competence.

The Extended Experience Program (see the appendix for details) makes considerable use of sociodramatic play to enhance the personal relevance of the learning experience. An example from the third term will illustrate this technique. The teacher reads her class the story of the three little pigs. She then asks them questions (*What happened next?*) to determine whether the children have remembered the sequence of the tale. The class then moves out to the playground where with straw, wood, bricks, and mortar they build three playhouses, the teacher and her assistant engaging them continually in conversation about their activity. After the buildings are completed, the cast is chosen: the wolf and the three pigs. The story is enacted. Other children reenact the drama if they wish. After the play the teacher asks questions about physical properties and causality (*Why didn't the brick house blow down?*) and stimulates divergent thinking (*What else can you build a house with? Tell me all the things you can do with a brick*).

In summary, the EEP contrasts with the BEP in the following ways. The EEP is based upon the Piagetian principle of the need to consolidate sensorimotor experience before operational thinking whereas the BEP is relatively nontheoretical. The EEP utilizes natural individual experience as the starting point for teaching whereas the BEP is based on contrived classroom experiences. Although there is a graduated sequence of activities and tasks in the EEP, these are less precise than in the BEP and there is more opportunity for individual children to proceed at different rates. In the EEP there is more opportunity for children to explore their own interests (though less so than in an unstructured program). The EEP deals with global experience and helps the child to understand its components whereas the BEP tends to emphasize molecular aspects of a total experience and to help the child integrate them. In the EEP the teacher and her assistant must exercise more initiative and imagination than in the BEP, particularly in the way they engage the individual child at his level of knowledge and interest. In the EEP there is a less systematic emphasis on reinforcement for effort; achievement, mastery, and the exercise of ability are considered to have intrinsic reward. The EEP calls for more parental involvement by the provision of homework in a game format to be completed by the child with the parents' assistance. And, finally, the EEP places more emphasis on divergent thinking: the production of more than one solution or answer when alternatives are appropriate (*Tell me some of the things you can do with string*). The BEP tends to reinforce convergent thought: the production of "correct" answers.

The EEP and the BEP are similar in the following ways. Both are taught to homogeneously grouped classes of eleven children, for two hours per day during the school year, by a teacher and teaching assistant. Both aim to foster the same terminal objectives. In both, each day's work is planned in detail at the fortnightly teacher's conference in accordance with the graduated curriculum. In both, each teacher and her assistant teach. Both were programs married to a perceptual-motor program—the former to the FP and the latter to the BPMP. The BEP + FP and the EEP + BPMP represent contrasting amalgamations of the structured and the semistructured elements of our total program for 1972.

We considered that we were ethically justified in testing the EEP since, although the BEP had proved successful, we had reservations about the convergent nature of the teaching techniques in it. Research in the United States had already demonstrated the effectiveness of semistructured programs (see chapter 4); we were not shooting in the dark.

Wave IV. In 1973, in view of the relative success of both EEP and BEP, both were retained. The BPMP was dropped since it produced results inferior to the FP. Thus both EEP and BEP were married to the FP which was taught, as before, for one 20-minute period per two-hour preschool day.

The most important change in 1973 was the addition, for all children, of a home-school liaison teaching program. For this purpose two teachers, one white and one Aboriginal, were appointed. (Our total staff in 1973 thus consisted of two preschool teachers, two Aboriginal teaching assistants, and one white and one Aboriginal liaison teacher.) This program was designed to operate in parallel with the BEP and EEP.

For thirty minutes each week one of the liaison teachers visits the home of each child. There, in the mother's presence, the teacher conducts with the child a planned lesson on a particular topic. If the lesson is on polar opposites, for example, the teacher offers illustrations of *big* and *small*, *tall* and *short*, *fat* and *thin*. The mother is invited to join the interchange. After the lesson the mother is given relevant material (scissors, colored paper, books, predesigned puzzles, written instructions, problems) to complete with the child before the scheduled meeting in the following week. Each week's lessons are designed, as far as possible, to complement, consolidate, and extend the new concepts introduced in the preschool that week.

EVALUATION

In this section the rationale and nature of the tests employed will be described. For Wave I we used Form B[9] of the PPVT (Dunn 1965) and the following subtests of the ITPA (Kirk, McCarthy, and Kirk 1968): auditory reception, visual reception, auditory association, visual association, verbal expression, manual expression, grammatic closure, visual closure, auditory memory, and visual memory.[10] We also used the geometric designs subtest of the Wechsler Preschool and Primary Scale of Intelligence (WPPSI) (Wechsler 1963).

In subsequent Waves II, III, and IV we employed the PPVT; the ITPA auditory association, visual association, and grammatic closure subtests; the WPPSI information, geometric designs, and vocabulary subtests; and the Draw-a-Person Test (DAP) (Harris 1963). In 1973 we added the Boehm Test of Basic Concepts (Boehm 1966).

In 1971 we used the following tests for follow-up of Wave I: the Nixon Test of Classification (Nixon 1967); the ITPA auditory association and grammatic closure subtests; the WPPSI vocabulary subtest; and the PPVT. In 1972 and 1973, for follow-up of Waves II and III, we added the ITPA visual association subtest to this list. Each of these tests will now be described in detail.

ITPA. The ITPA is a composite test of different aspects of psycholinguistic functioning, designed for children between two and ten

9. The alternative version of the PPVT, Form A, had been used in 1969 for preschool selection.
10. Two of the twelve subtests of the ITPA, auditory and visual blending, were not used.

Chapter Six

years of age. For each subtest, raw scores can be expressed as scaled scores by allowing for age. The total scaled score may be expressed as language age (in months) or as language quotient (in percentage form):

$$\text{language quotient} = \frac{\text{language age}}{\text{chronological age}} \times 100$$

The subtests cover a range of abilities involving auditory and visual reception, association, and memory; verbal and gestural expression; syntactic competence in standard English; and the ability to discriminate specific details in pictures. Thus the ITPA gets at five abilities: (1) to decode or analyze visual and auditory signals; (2) to encode or synthesize verbal and gestural signals; (3) to form associations between orally presented words and visually presented pictures of objects; (4) to remember and reproduce sequences presented visually and orally; and (5) to use standard English syntax and discriminate pictorial details. The respective tests involved are auditory and visual reception; verbal and manual expression; auditory and visual association; auditory and visual sequential memory; and grammatic and visual closure. The different subtests have been conceived as a matrix of three dimensions: communication channel (auditory and visual); psycholinguistic process (reception, organization, expression); and level of organization (automatic and representational). The results on the different subtests of the ITPA provide an individual or group psycholinguistic profile that can be compared either with the test norms or with itself in a pretest-posttest design.

PPVT. The PPVT tests the child's ability to identify, by pointing, the correct one of four two-dimensional pictorial representations in a graduated series of pictures in response to the examiner's spoken instruction (*Put your finger on the...*). It is simple to use and suitable for pre-school children—particularly inhibited ones—because it requires only a pointing response. The results can be expressed as a raw score, as verbal age in months in relation to age norms, or as an IQ. The PPVT IQ is an index of receptive verbal intelligence. It correlates well with other measures of verbal competence and is a fair predictor of school success, especially with older children.

WPPSI. This composite intelligence test has been designed for children aged between four and six years. It is divided into two scales: verbal and performance. In our study we have used selected subtests from both verbal and performance scales: vocabulary, information, and geometric designs. The vocabulary subtest measures the child's ability to give the correct meaning of a graduated series of words; information is a test of general knowledge appropriate to a child of this age; and in geometric designs the child is asked to copy a variety of geometric shapes of increasing difficulty. The WPPSI correlates with the Stanford-Binet Intelligence Test (1960) at a level of .75. Subtest reliability is said to be high—between .80 and .90.

DAP. In this test, the child is asked to draw, with pencil and paper, the representation of a person—a man or woman, mummy or daddy, boy or girl. The quality of the drawing can be scored and related to age norms (Harris 1963) to derive a drawing age (in months) or drawing quotient (DAP IQ). The DAP is therefore a simple test of visual-motor coordination and body-image knowledge.

Nixon Test. This test requires the subject to manipulate twenty wooden rods that vary in three attributes: five *colors*, two *heights*, and two *diameters*. Starting with two sets of four rods grouped according to one of the three attributes, the subject is asked to regroup the rods according to a new criterion defined by two rods placed apart before the subject by the examiner. To score an operationally correct response, the subject must both solve the reclassification and nominate the new criterion, which he can usually do with a single word (such as *red*, *tall*, or *fat*). For example, if the sets of four red and four blue rods (red or blue: tall fat; tall thin; short fat; short thin) are grouped separately before the subject, and the examiner places two examples before the subject—tall red fat and tall red thin—as a guide to reclassification, the correct and only possible solution is according to diameter. A response is scored 1 when it is considered to be operational according to these criteria.

In Australia, this test has been found to discriminate well between children aged from five to seven years from social backgrounds of different levels of enrichment (de Lacey 1970). It yields results in agreement with Piagetian tests of additive and multiple classification.

De Lacey (1971), de Lacey and Taylor (1972), and Taylor, de Lacey, and Nurcombe (1972)—in the process of testing (and supporting) the hypothesis that IQ tests and tests of operational thinking are likely to correlate more highly in children from culturally more advantaged backgrounds—found that PPVT and Nixon Test scores correlated at a .36 level for full-descent Aborigines and .50 for white children in the same outback school. Other correlations are shown in Table 6.2. Scores on the Nixon Test were found to have an insignificant correlation with measures of divergent thinking ability.

Boehm Test. This recently developed test has been reviewed by McCandless et al. (1972). It was inspired by Boehm's realization that many children beginning school do not comprehend basic concepts taken as "given" by their teachers and that such deficits are cumulative. The criterion-referenced test consists of fifty items, designed for preschool and early elementary school children, in the form of black line drawings. The

Chapter Six

Table 6.2 Correlations of Scores on Nixon Test with PPVT (from de Lacey 1971)

Group	Correlation
Bourke part-Aborigines	.12
Bourke LSE whites	.45
Wollongong[a] LSE whites	.49
Northern Territory Aborigines[b]	.52
Sydney HSE whites	.73

[a] A large coastal industrial city forty miles from Sydney.
[b] A selected group of high-achieving full-descent Aborigines attending secondary school.

items are answered by indicating which picture refers to the concept in question. Concepts are drawn from the following areas: space (location, direction, orientation, dimension), time, quantity (for example: *whole*, *some*, *every*), and miscellaneous. Reliability coefficients of .68 to .90 are quoted by Boehm (1966). The test has face validity only: it taps those concepts that Boehm considered to be fundamental to, but seldom taught in, the kindergarten and early school grades. Raw scores, in the form of the number of items correctly answered, were used in our 1973 evaluation.

SUMMARY

In summary, in 1970—for Wave I—we have the following pretest and posttest assessment data on language and information-processing:

> Overall language performance (ITPA)
> Ability to decode and analyze auditory speech and visual symbols (ITPA, PPVT)
> Ability to synthesize and express verbal and gestural messages (ITPA)
> Ability to form logical associations between orally presented words and visually presented pictures of objects (ITPA, PPVT)
> Memory for auditory and visual sequences (ITPA)
> Use of standard English syntax (ITPA)
> Vocabulary knowledge (WPPSI)
> General information (WPPSI)

Moreover, we have corresponding data on perceptual-motor skills:

> Ability to discriminate details from complex two-dimensional representations (ITPA)
> Ability to copy two-dimensional geometric shapes (WPPSI)
> Ability to demonstrate coordination and body knowledge through drawings of the human figure (DAP)

Follow-up data, for Wave I, are available for:

> Verbal receptive ability (PPVT)
> Vocabulary (WPPSI)
> Standard English syntax (ITPA)
> Auditory word association (ITPA)
> Ability to reclassify objects with three dimensions (Nixon Test)

In subsequent years we have reduced the total number of ITPA subtests and added other tests. In 1973, for example, data are available on pretest and posttest for:

> Receptive vocabulary (PPVT)
> Verbal association (ITPA)
> Visual association (ITPA)
> Syntax (ITPA)
> General information (WPPSI)
> Expressive vocabulary (WPPSI)
> Basic concepts (Boehm)
> Ability to reproduce geometric designs (WPPSI)
> Body knowledge and eye-hand coordination (DAP)

The areas of evaluation should be checked against the stated objectives of the preschool. It will be noted that although we have attained a reasonable coverage of the language, cognitive, and perceptual-motor objectives, we have not been able to find or design tests of the affective objectives with acceptable reliability or validity. So far as possible we have attempted to use standard tests that are suitable for Australian schoolchildren and have had adequate studies of reliability and validity. Those tests that are least satisfactory in this regard are the Piaget-Bruner tests and the DAP. We reject the idea that these are tests of potential; they are to be regarded as instruments for internal comparison that may predict later scholastic adjustment and achievement. This, of course, remains to be seen.

ACTION RESEARCH: RESULTS

Scores on all pretests, posttests, and follow-up tests were expressed as means and standard deviations for each teaching technique, each racial group, upper and lower classes, each teacher, for no-treatment controls (when available, on follow-up), and for various combinations of the above. We were particularly interested in comparisons of the results of Aboriginal structured and white structured with Aboriginal and white unstructured or semistructured classes. In 1971 and 1972, we were interested in a comparison between the FP and the BPMP. Whenever comparative gain scores were used for statistical analysis, care was taken

CHAPTER SIX

TABLE 6.3 Wave I: Mean Results on PPVT, WPPSI Vocabulary, and WPPSI Geometric Designs of Aborigines and Whites Combined, Unstructured Traditional and Structured BEP Classes Compared

Test	Program	n	First Test	SD	Second Test	SD	Difference	p
PPVT IQ	Traditional	17	68.94	22.55	74.18	17.54	5.24	NS
	Structured	18	67.67	23.54	92.67	21.80	25.00	.005
WPPSI scaled scores								
Vocabulary	Traditional	17	6.71	2.31	7.12	2.39	.41	NS
	Structured	18	6.35	2.76	10.70	3.20	4.34	.005
Geometric designs	Traditional	17	8.05	2.98	7.55	2.20	−.50	NS
	Structured	18	8.00	3.14	7.12	2.73	−.88	NS

to ensure that pretest scores were not significantly different; in fact, we ascertained that they were virtually equivalent. One-tailed t-tests of significance were performed on all comparisons. (The t-test is a statistical technique to determine the likelihood that the difference between two mean values could be caused by chance.) The salient detailed results for each year's program, and for the follow-up of each wave, will now be presented.

WAVE I, 1970

Results for the total group of children in the structured program are compared with those for the traditional unstructured program in Tables 6.3, 6.4, 6.5 and in Figures 6.1 and 6.2. In these and subsequent tables it will be noted that n falls short of the total of 44 or 48; for example, in 1970, n for the unstructured group on PPVT was 17 (instead of 22) and 18 (instead of 22) for the structured group. The full "experimental mortality" of nine cases was due to failure to respond to pretest (five cases), failure to respond to posttest (two cases), left district during 1970 (one case), and dropped out of school (one case).[11] In subsequent years, roughly similar reductions of n prevailed. The attrition due to failure of response to tests, emigration, or dropping out affected Aborigines more than whites—six of the nine cases lost in 1970 were Aboriginal, for example—but in no year have there been significantly more losses from one program than the other, from one teacher than the other, or from one class level (after 1970, in Waves II, III, IV) than the other.

Table 6.3 reveals that children in the structured classes achieved

---

11. Actually, some children respond on some pretests or some posttests and not on others. All results obtained were included in the analysis provided both pretests and posttests were available for the test or subtest in question.

TABLE 6.4 Wave I: Mean Results on Composite ITPA Scaled Scores, Aborigines and Whites Combined, Traditional and Structured BEP Classes Compared

Program	n	Test 1	SD	Test 2	SD	Difference	p
Traditional	16	30.22	4.08	32.84	3.74	2.62	.05
Structured BEP	17	31.41	4.30	39.30	5.22	7.89	.005
Difference		1.19		6.46			
p		NS		.005			

TABLE 6.5 Wave I: Mean Scaled Score Results on ITPA Subtests, Aborigines and Whites Combined, Unstructured Traditional and Structured BEP Classes Compared

Subtest	Program	n	Test 1	SD	Test 2	SD	Difference	p
Auditory reception	Traditional	14	28.14	3.16	33.50	3.16	5.36	.005
	Structured	17	31.17	6.16	40.47	6.36	9.30	.005
							p NS	
Visual reception	Traditional	16	30.81	5.89	34.19	6.53	3.38	NS
	Structured	17	31.35	8.36	41.70	5.52	10.35	.005
							p .005	
Auditory association	Traditional	16	27.19	5.89	32.75	5.73	5.56	.01
	Structured	17	29.00	7.42	43.35	4.81	14.35	.005
							p .005	
Visual association	Traditional	16	26.94	5.42	30.44	7.75	3.50	NS
	Structured	17	28.29	6.10	32.88	6.62	4.59	.025
							p NS	
Verbal expression	Traditional	16	27.87	3.91	33.81	6.53	5.94	.005
	Structured	17	30.12	4.24	46.06	8.06	15.94	.005
							p .005	
Manual expression	Traditional	16	30.87	6.49	33.12	6.59	2.25	NS
	Structured	17	28.76	5.02	37.23	7.39	8.47	.005
							p .005	
Grammatic closure	Traditional	16	30.81	7.39	29.75	6.56	−1.06	NS
	Structured	17	30.06	5.90	39.05	11.71	8.99	.005
							p .005	
Visual closure	Traditional	16	35.19	7.18	35.69	7.32	.50	NS
	Structured	17	32.29	6.54	38.18	8.16	5.89	.025
							p .05	
Auditory memory	Traditional	16	32.94	7.94	34.37	5.55	1.43	NS
	Structured	17	38.70	8.53	40.59	10.31	1.89	NS
							p NS	
Visual memory	Traditional	16	31.69	6.62	31.12	5.15	−.57	NS
	Structured	17	34.29	5.89	33.47	6.41	−.82	NS
							p NS	

Chapter Six

major gains in PPVT IQ and WPPSI vocabulary, compared with those in the unstructured classes. Similar observations apply to Table 6.4: major overall language gains on ITPA in the structured classes and only slight gains in the unstructured classes. It should be noted, from Table 6.3, that neither group made gains in WPPSI geometric designs, despite the provision of manipulative toys and drawing materials.

In Table 6.5 and Figures 6.1 and 6.2, the results of language testing are set out in detail. In the unstructured classes there were significant, though modest, gains in auditory reception, auditory association, and verbal expression. In the structured program there were larger significant gains in these three subtests and, in addition, impressive gains in visual reception, manual expression, and grammatic closure with smaller though still significant gains in visual association and visual closure. In the following posttests the structured group, as a whole, exceeded the norms (the average scaled score is 36): composite scaled score, auditory reception, auditory association, verbal expression, manual expression, grammatic closure, visual closure, and auditory memory.

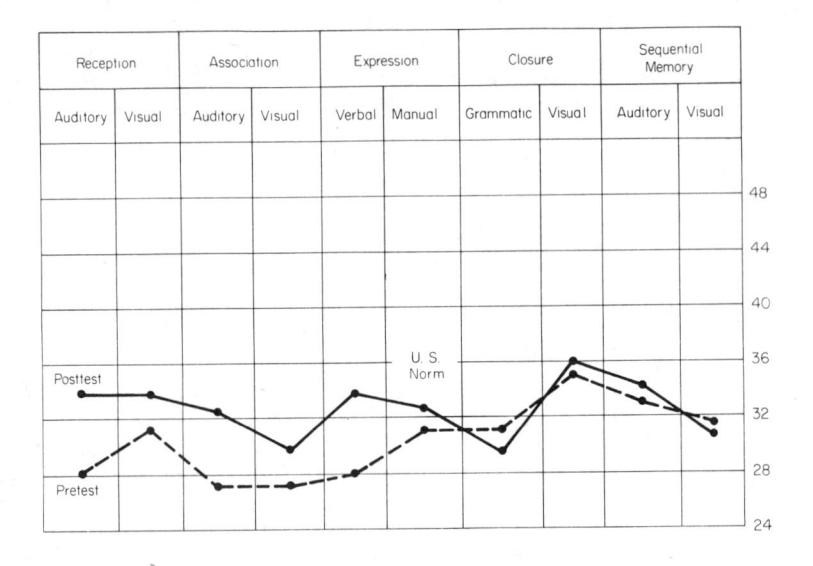

FIGURE 6.1   Wave I: IPTA profile means for unstructured traditional classes, Aborigines and whites combined

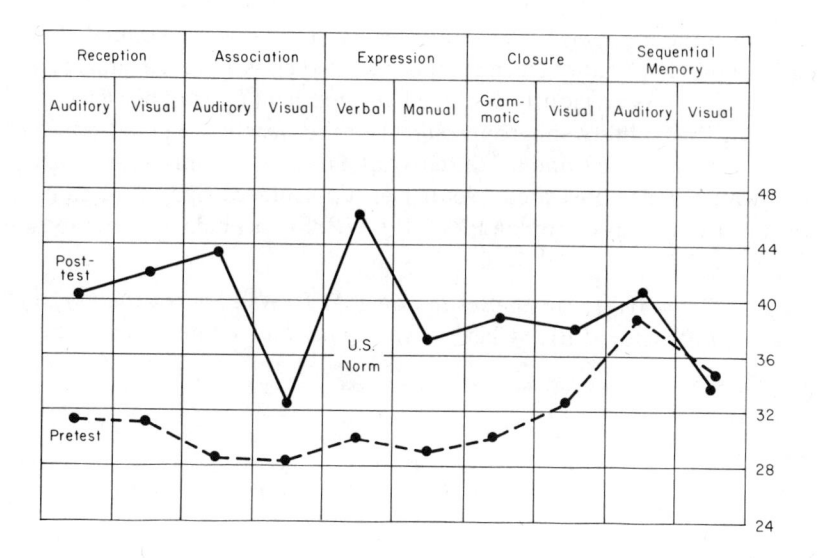

FIGURE 6.2 Wave I: profile means for structured BEP classes, Aborigines and whites combined

Figures 6.1 and 6.2 illustrate the comparative scope and magnitude of language performance changes.

The data can be analyzed in greater detail. In Tables 6.6 and 6.7 the results of the two ethnic groups in the unstructured and structured classes are compared. Table 6.8 demonstrates gain scores of white and

TABLE 6.6 Wave I: Mean Results on PPVT, WPPSI Vocabulary, and ITPA for Unstructured Traditional Classes, Aborigines and Whites Compared

Test	Group	n	Test 1	SD	Test 2	SD	Difference	p
PPVT IQ	White	10	74.30	23.14	82.40	12.47	8.10	NS
	Abor.	7	61.29	20.89	62.43	17.70	1.14	NS
WPPSI vocabulary[a]	White	10	7.80	1.81	8.10	1.85	.30	NS
	Abor.	7	5.14	2.12	5.71	2.49	.57	NS
ITPA composite[a]	White	9	32.25	3.21	34.30	2.86	2.05	NS
	Abor.	7	27.61	3.70	30.97	4.11	3.36	NS

[a] Expressed as scaled scores.

Chapter Six

Aboriginal children in the structured classes on PPVT, WPPSI vocabulary, and ITPA subtests; since the pretests for Aborigines and whites were so disparate, no statistical analysis of this comparison was attempted. In Table 6.9 the results gained by each teacher in the two structured classes are compared. (Neither teacher's unstructured class achieved gains of any significance.) As previously described, one teacher (T_2) split her structured class into two ability subgroups and the other teacher (T_1) did not.

In Tables 6.6 and 6.7 the effect of the two programs on Aborigines and whites is demonstrated. Neither group achieved significant gains in the unstructured program on PPVT IQ, WPPSI vocabulary, or composite

TABLE 6.7 Wave I: Mean Results on PPVT, WPPSI Vocabulary, and ITPA for Structured BEP Classes, Aborigines and Whites Compared

Test	Group	n	Test 1	SD	Test 2	SD	Difference	p
PPVT IQ	White	9	80.22	23.99	101.00	21.99	20.78	.05
	Abor.	9	55.11	15.72	84.33	19.24	29.22	.005
WPPSI vocabulary[a]	White	9	7.55	2.60	12.00	2.83	4.45	.005
	Abor.	8	5.00	2.39	9.25	3.10	4.25	.005
ITPA composite[a]	White	8	34.31	4.08	40.96	6.19	6.65	.025
	Abor.	9	28.82	2.54	37.90	4.04	9.08	.005

[a] Expressed as scaled scores.

TABLE 6.8 Wave I: Mean Gain Scores on PPVT, WPPSI Vocabulary, and ITPA of Whites and Aborigines in the Structured BEP Classes

	Whites			Aborigines		
	n	Mean Gain	SD	n	Mean Gain	SD
PPVT IQ	9	20.78	24.27	9	29.22	22.27
WPPSI vocabulary[a]	8	4.45	3.00	8	4.25	2.81
ITPA[a]						
Auditory reception	8	6.87	8.11	9	11.44	10.21
Visual reception	8	7.25	5.90	9	13.11	3.79
Auditory association	8	10.50	5.45	9	17.78	7.12
Visual association	8	4.25	7.02	9	4.89	5.21
Verbal expression	8	15.75	8.68	9	16.11	7.03
Manual expression	8	9.12	2.42	9	8.66	7.28
Grammatic closure	8	7.75	11.83	9	10.11	9.31
Visual closure	8	6.62	4.98	9	5.22	9.54
Auditory memory	8	.75	7.26	9	2.98	6.92
Visual memory	8	2.37	5.55	9	.55	11.50

[a] Expressed as scaled scores.

TABLE 6.9 Wave I: Mean Results on PPVT, WPSSI Vocabulary, and ITPA for Structured BEP Classes, Two Teachers T_1 and T_2 Compared

Test	Teacher[a]	n	Test 1	SD	Test 2	SD	Difference	p
PPVT IQ	T_1	10	72.50	20.52	83.50	17.61	11.00	NS
	T_2	8	61.62	27.00	104.12	22.03	42.50	.05
WPPSI	T_1	9	7.22	2.05	11.22	1.79	4.00	.05
vocabulary[b]	T_2	8	5.37	3.25	10.12	4.36	4.75	$.10 > p > .05$
ITPA	T_1	10	30.90	3.11	37.03	3.11	6.13	.05
composite[b]	T_2	7	32.1	5.81	42.64	6.08	10.51	$.10 > p > .05$

[a] T_1 class not split; T_2 class split into two ability groups.
[b] Expressed as scaled scores.

ITPA score. (The numbers were reduced, considerably, and this made it more difficult for the small gains registered to reach a significant level.) The whites achieved an 8.1-point PPVT gain, but the Aborigines remained practically static on this and the other tests. What meager gains were registered could well be explained by a test-practice effect. Significant—mostly highly significant—gains were recorded on the same tests by both white and Aboriginal children from the structured classes. Aborigines, for example, gained 29.22 points on PPVT, almost doubled their pretest score on WPPSI vocabulary, and gained 9.08 scaled score points on the ITPA, thereby exceeding the norm on posttest.

Table 6.8 illustrates in detail the gains of the two ethnic groups in the structured program. Both groups improved greatly in PPVT IQ, WPPSI vocabulary, and ITPA auditory reception, visual reception, auditory association, verbal expression, and grammatic closure. Since the Aborigines scored at a considerably lower level on all pretests (apart from ITPA auditory and visual memory), it would not be appropriate to compare the gain scores of the two ethnic groups.

Table 6.9 illustrates the effects of splitting and not splitting the structured classes into faster-learning and slower-learning subgroups. The gains were roughly equivalent in WPPSI vocabularly and ITPA, but were markedly superior in PPVT for the split class which gained, overall, 42.50 IQ points. It is also instructive to note that the teacher who split her class was the one who had the greater reservations about the Bereiter-Engelmann Program.

In summary, the traditional program produced modest gains in tests of the ability to comprehend standard English, to form associations to what is heard, and in the capacity for verbal expression. These gains occurred in both ethnic groups. The structured program produced bigger improvements in these areas, together with large gains in the comprehen-

CHAPTER SIX

sion of visual stimuli, the capacity to form associations to visual stimuli, to discriminate in figure-ground problems, to express ideas in gesture, and in receptive and expressive vocabulary. In general, these observations were true for both ethnic groups. There was some evidence, though inconclusive, that splitting the structured classes facilitated teaching. The teacher who did so found it much more efficient. Neither program produced changes in the test of perceptual-motor coordination; in fact the children in both programs lost ground in this domain.

From a social viewpoint, the preschool programs were a great success. Children who at the beginning were bewildered, inhibited, and mute were by the end of the school year mixing well and concentrating on problems for up to forty minutes at a time; moreover, they were able to answer questions directed to them, gain pleasure from achievement, and respond to praise. Superficial observation revealed no difference in this result between the structured and unstructured classes. Both white and Aboriginal mothers had been reasonably reliable in attending at their scheduled times; but we still felt that Aboriginal parents and adults should be more directly involved—a problem not really addressed until 1973.

WAVE II, 1971

As a result of our findings in 1970, we attempted to replicate the striking gains yielded by the structured program and to supplement it with a program aimed at the perceptual-motor domain. The following changes were made: all children were exposed to the BEP; the classes were divided into two upper and two lower on the basis of PPVT IQ; one upper and one lower class were exposed to the structured FP, and one upper and one lower to the BPMP.

The results are presented in Tables 6.10, 6.11, 6.12, and 6.13. Tables 6.10 and 6.11 set out the results for all, for white, and for Aboriginal children in intelligence, language, and perceptual-motor tests. Table 6.12 illustrates the mean results of all children in perceptual-motor performance, comparing the FP and the BPMP. Table 6.13 compares the results of Aborigines and whites on both perceptual-motor programs.

Table 6.10 reveals that large gains were achieved by all, by white, and by Aboriginal children on all tests of verbal ability except for Aboriginal children in standard English syntax (ITPA grammatic closure). None of these gains was as impressive as in the preceding year; for example, Aborigines gained 29.22 points on PPVT IQ in 1970 (see Table 6.8) compared with 16.76 points in 1971. In 1971, aside from in PPVT IQ, Aboriginal gains were less than white gains despite the fact that Aborigines, uniformly, had lower pretest scores (and could have been expected to show larger regression artefacts). Whites approached or exceeded the

TABLE 6.10 Wave II: Mean Results on Intelligence and Language Tests for All, for Aboriginal, and for White Subjects in the Structured BEP

Test	Group	n	Test 1	SD	Test 2	SD	Difference	p
PPVT IQ	All	41	79.56	17.89	89.58	16.75	10.02	.001
	White	25	87.23	14.91	95.77	10.25	8.54	.01
	Abor.	16	67.76	15.48	83.06	15.07	16.76	.01
WPPSI information[a]	All	34	7.26	2.54	9.76	2.45	2.50	.001
	White	22	8.08	2.38	10.68	2.34	2.60	.001
	Abor.	12	5.69	2.05	8.00	1.52	2.31	.001
ITPA auditory association[a]	All	36	29.65	6.31	36.03	7.42	6.38	.001
	White	24	30.84	6.52	37.92	7.61	7.08	.001
	Abor.	12	27.17	5.03	32.08	5.11	4.91	.01
Grammatic closure[a]	All	38	30.90	7.02	35.10	9.07	4.20	.001
	White	24	34.12	6.28	39.16	7.83	5.04	.01
	Abor.	14	25.14	3.89	27.86	6.16	2.72	NS

[a] Expressed as scaled scores.

TABLE 6.11 Wave II: Mean Results on Perceptual-Motor Tests for All, for Aboriginal, and for White Subjects

Test	Group	n	Test 1	SD	Test 2	SD	Difference	p
WPPSI geometric designs[a]	All	36	8.70	2.96	9.57	2.46	.87	$.10 > p > .05$
	White	22	9.74	2.52	10.35	2.28	.61	$.10 > p > .05$
	Abor.	14	7.29	2.68	8.29	2.19	1.00	$.10 > p > .05$
ITPA visual association[a]	All	37	29.97	5.57	30.95	6.99	.98	NS
	White	24	31.88	5.01	33.60	6.62	1.72	$.10 > p > .05$
	Abor.	14	26.57	4.85	26.21	4.78	−.36	NS
DAP IQ	All	38	88.72	18.84	102.44	15.65	13.72	.001
	White	24	94.89	19.73	106.19	15.71	11.30	.05
	Abor.	14	77.33	5.37	94.00	11.76	16.67	.01

[a] Expressed as scaled scores.

norms in all posttests; Aborigines remained well below the norms, still, on posttesting.

Table 6.11 shows the effect of both programs, FP and BPMP, on perceptual-motor functioning. Compared to 1970 (see Table 6.4), moderate improvements were attained, except in Aboriginal visual association. Large gains were recorded in DAP IQ. Whites exceeded the norms in WPPSI geometric designs and DAP IQ.

Table 6.12 reveals little difference between the effects of either the FP or the BPMP on perceptual-motor functioning. Aside from in

CHAPTER SIX

TABLE 6.12 Wave II: Mean Results on Perceptual-Motor Tests for All Children, FP and BPMP Compared

Test	Program	n	Test 1	SD	Test 2	SD	Difference	p
WPPSI geometric designs[a]	FP	20	8.76	2.81	9.67	2.66	.91	.05
	BPMP	20	8.63	3.12	9.44	2.15	.81	$.10 > p > .05$
ITPA visual association[a]	FP	20	30.09	4.98	31.00	7.37	.91	NS
	BPMP	18	29.82	6.24	30.00	6.46	.18	NS
DAP IQ	FP	20	86.57	21.05	101.52	19.37	15.05	.01
	BPMP	18	91.22	15.51	103.50	9.55	12.18	.01

[a] Expressed as scaled scores.

TABLE 6.13 Wave II: Mean Results on DAP IQ, for the FP and the BPMP, Aborigines and Whites Compared

Program	Group	n	Test 1	SD	Test 2[a]	SD	Difference	p
FP	White	11	91.79	23.88	107.36	19.16	15.57	.01
	Abor.	6	77.86	3.83	89.96	13.67	12.10	.05
BPMP	White	13	95.92	15.56	104.92	10.69	9.00	$.10 > p > .5$
	Abor.	8	77.60	5.89	99.80	3.54	22.20	.01

[a] The differences between Aboriginal FP and BPMP, and white FP and BPMP, posttest scores were not statistically significant.

DAP, neither program produced striking improvements. Table 6.13 suggests that, insofar as the DAP was concerned, the FP may have been slightly more successful for whites and the BPMP for Aborigines; but the posttest scores on which this observation is based were not significantly different.

In summary, we partly replicated the striking effects of the 1970 structured program, but there were some disturbing aspects to the results. Aborigines had not achieved significant gains in the key area of standard English syntax and, overall, their improvements were not as impressive as those of the white children. On the other hand, we had been successful in correcting a major deficiency in the 1970 program—the lack of improvement in perceptual-motor functioning; both the BPMP and the FP appeared to be promising in this regard.

At the end of 1970, one of our teachers had resigned. She was replaced by a young, recent graduate from a preschool teachers' college who found it difficult to adapt to the unfamiliar BEP. Both teachers found that the strain of teaching two structured classes per day was considerable; the resultant lack of variety in their work may have reduced their effectiveness.

WAVE III, 1972

This was the first year of comparison of the structured and semistructured programs, allied, respectively, to the FP and the BPMP. Upper and lower class divisions were used, as before.

The results are demonstrated in Tables 6.14 to 6.20. Table 6.14 shows the overall results on all tests. Table 6.15 shows the results of Aborigines and whites on both programs combined; Table 6.16 displays the results of both ethnic groups combined on each of the two programs. Tables 6.17 and 6.18 show the comparative effectiveness of each program for Aborigines and for whites. Tables 6.19 and 6.20 compare the gains achieved by the FP and the BPMP for Aborigines and for whites.

TABLE 6.14 Wave III: Mean Results on All Tests in Both Programs (BEP–FP and EEP–BPMP) for Total Group, Aborigines and Whites Combined

Test	n	Test 1	SD	Test 2	SD	Difference	p
PPVT IQ	37	70.84	23.15	78.89	19.90	8.05	.01
ITPA scaled scores							
Auditory association	38	28.11	7.17	35.60	8.40	7.49	.001
Visual association	38	27.13	5.16	31.29	6.82	3.16	.001
Grammatic closure	38	29.08	8.82	39.92	8.16	10.84	.001
WPPSI scaled scores							
Information	38	5.95	3.05	10.50	3.14	4.55	.001
Geometric designs	38	7.55	3.01	8.66	2.72	1.11	.05
Vocabulary	38	5.61	2.46	11.05	3.05	5.44	.001
DAP IQ	38	82.89	18.26	112.95	16.73	30.06	.001

Table 6.14 demonstrates that statistically significant gains were attained, overall, in all areas tested. Particularly noteworthy were large improvements in auditory association, grammatic closure, information, vocabulary, and drawing skill. Table 6.15 compares Aboriginal and white results. Aborigines achieved larger gains in PPVT and DAP but demonstrated improvements somewhat less impressive than those attained by whites in auditory association, grammatic closure, information, and vocabulary. Apart from in PPVT, none of these differences was statistically significant. It is noteworthy that whites have exceeded the test norms in auditory association, grammatic closure, information, geometric designs, vocabulary, and drawing. Aborigines did so only in drawing.

CHAPTER SIX

TABLE 6.15 Wave III: Mean Scores of Aborigines and Whites on All Tests in Both Programs (DEP-IP and EEP BPMP) Combined

Test	Group	n	Test 1	SD	Test 2	SD	Difference	p
PPVT IQ[a]	Abor.	15	51.80	10.7	68.13	16.46	16.33	.01
	White	22	87.18	17.77	91.26	16.26	4.08	NS
ITPA scaled scores								
Auditory association	Abor.	16	24.75	6.08	27.56	5.92	2.81	NS
	White	22	32.09	6.82	40.27	6.02	8.18	.001
Visual association	Abor.	16	23.50	2.67	27.19	5.83	3.69	.05
	White	22	29.77	4.92	34.32	5.93	4.55	.05
Grammatic closure	Abor.	16	22.88	1.83	32.69	4.48	9.81	.001
	White	22	33.59	9.14	45.18	5.89	11.59	.001
WPPSI scaled scores								
Information	Abor.	16	3.69	1.10	7.88	2.26	4.19	.001
	White	22	7.59	2.96	12.41	2.15	4.82	.001
Geometric designs	Abor.	16	5.63	2.15	6.81	1.70	1.18	NS
	White	22	8.95	2.75	10.00	2.52	1.05	NS
Vocabulary	Abor.	16	3.81	0.88	8.56	2.21	4.65	.001
	White	22	6.91	2.41	12.86	2.18	5.95	.001
DAP IQ	Abor.	16	74.38	7.23	106.63	13.15	32.25	.001
	White	22	89.09	21.14	117.59	17.61	28.50	.001

[a] t-test on difference between gain scores: $p < .05$, Abor. > whites. All other differences between gain scores: not significant.

In Table 6.16 a comparison of the effects of the structured and semistructured programs on combined ethnic groups shows roughly equivalent large effects in PPVT and DAP and in information and vocabulary. The structured program was significantly superior in its effect upon visual association and yielded a trend in that direction in auditory association and geometric design. These observations can be extended, in more detail, by extracting the comparative effects of the two programs for Aborigines and for whites.

Table 6.17 demonstrates that the gain scores of Aborigines in the two programs are not significantly different; however, trends were noticed for the structured program to yield superior improvements in PPVT IQ (20.62 compared to 11.29), DAP IQ (37.12 compared to 27.37), auditory association, visual association, and geometric designs. Roughly equivalent improvements were noted in grammatic closure, information, and vocabulary.

Table 6.18 compares the gain scores of white children in the two programs. The structured program produced a significantly greater improvement in visual association. Trends were noted for the semistructured program to be superior in PPVT and grammatic closure

TABLE 6.16 Wave III: Mean Scores of Aborigines and Whites Combined on All Tests, Structured BEP–FP and Semistructured EEP–BPMP Compared

Test	Program	n	Test 1	SD	Test 2	SD	Difference	p
PPVT IQ	Structured	20	77.50	23.6	86.05	17.90	8.55	.05
	Semistructured	17	67.47	21.52	77.00	20.99	9.53	.05
ITPA scaled scores								
Auditory association	Structured	20	28.45	7.64	37.55	8.27	9.10	.001
	Semistructured	18	27.17	6.61	33.70	7.78	6.53	.001
Visual association[a]	Structured	20	27.45	5.23	34.15	6.73	6.70	.001
	Semistructured	18	26.78	5.05	28.11	5.35	1.33	NS
Grammatic closure	Structured	20	31.05	10.89	40.70	9.03	9.65	.001
	Semistructured	18	26.89	4.85	39.06	5.74	12.17	.001
WPPSI scaled scores								
Information	Structured	20	6.00	3.16	10.60	2.69	4.60	.001
	Semistructured	18	5.89	2.92	10.39	3.56	4.50	.001
Geometric designs[a]	Structured	20	7.20	3.06	9.15	2.69	1.95	.01
	Semistructured	18	7.78	2.92	7.94	2.41	0.16	NS
Vocabulary	Structured	20	5.70	2.64	11.40	2.71	5.70	.001
	Semistructured	18	5.44	2.22	10.67	3.35	5.23	.001
DAP IQ	Structured	20	85.15	22.18	114.55	16.21	29.40	.001
	Semistructured	18	82.56	17.46	110.00	6.56	27.44	.001

[a] t-test on differences between scores: $p < .05$, BEP > EEP. All other differences between gain scores: not significant.

TABLE 6.17 Wave III: Mean Scores of Aborigines on All Tests, Structured BEP–FP and Semistructured EEP–BPMP Compared

Test	Program	n	Test 1	SD	Test 2	SD	Difference[a]	p
PPVT IQ	Structured	8	55.13	10.31	75.75	5.56	20.62	.01
	Semistructured	7	48.14	9.90	59.43	20.07	11.29	NS
ITPA scaled scores								
Auditory association	Structured	8	23.00	2.34	31.88	5.56	8.88	.01
	Semistructured	8	22.38	2.69	27.25	6.98	4.87	NS
Visual association	Structured	8	23.63	2.34	29.25	5.56	5.62	.05
	Semistructured	8	23.38	3.00	25.13	5.35	1.75	NS
Grammatic closure	Structured	8	25.75	2.17	33.25	4.89	7.50	.001
	Semistructured	8	23.00	1.41	32.13	3.96	9.13	.001
WPPSI scaled scores								
Information	Structured	8	3.88	1.17	8.38	1.73	4.50	.01
	Semistructured	8	3.50	1.00	7.38	2.60	3.88	.01
Geometric designs	Structured	8	5.13	2.17	7.38	1.80	2.25	.01
	Semistructured	8	6.13	2.67	6.25	1.39	.12	NS
Vocabulary	Structured	8	3.88	1.05	9.13	2.26	5.25	.001
	Semistructured	8	3.75	.66	8.00	2.00	4.25	.01
DAP IQ	Structured	8	72.88	4.43	110.00	11.74	37.12	.001
	Semistructured	8	75.88	.66	103.25	13.62	27.37	.01

[a] None of the t-tests on the difference (BEP vs. EEP) between gain scores for each test reached a significant level.

TABLE 6.18 Wave III: Mean Scores of Whites on All Tests, Structured BEP–FP and Semistructured EEP–BPMP Compared

Test	Program	n	Test 1	SD	Test 2	SD	Difference	p
PPVT IQ	Structured	12	92.25	17.27	92.91	19.89	.64	NS
	Semistructured	10	81.10	16.39	89.30	9.99	8.20	NS
ITPA scaled scores								
Auditory association	Structured	12	32.92	7.20	41.33	7.44	8.51	.01
	Semistructured	10	31.10	6.17	37.90	3.29	7.80	.01
Visual association	Structured	12	30.00	5.02	37.42	5.31	7.42[a]	.01
	Semistructured	10	29.50	4.72	30.50	3.98	1.00[a]	NS
Grammatic closure	Structured	12	36.58	10.84	46.50	7.41	9.92	.01
	Semistructured	10	30.00	4.36	43.36	2.42	13.36	.001
WPPSI scaled scores								
Information	Structured	12	7.42	3.48	12.08	2.14	4.66	.01
	Semistructured	10	7.80	2.52	12.50	2.11	4.70	.01
Geometric designs	Structured	12	8.83	3.02	10.58	2.63	1.70	NS
	Semistructured	10	9.10	2.39	9.30	2.10	.20	NS
Vocabulary	Structured	12	7.00	2.65	12.92	1.75	5.92	.001
	Semistructured	10	6.60	1.74	12.60	1.83	6.00	.001
DAP IQ	Structured	12	91.67	23.20	118.42	18.57	26.75	.001
	Semistructured	10	84.20	13.00	116.50	16.18	32.30	.001

[a] The differences between the gain scores are not significant except in the case of visual association ($p = .05$).

Chapter Six

(although, in both these tests, the semistructured group had rather lower pretests and the larger gains may be caused by regression artefacts). In all other tests the two programs produced roughly equivalent results.

TABLE 6.19 Wave III: Mean Gain Scores (SD in Parentheses) of Aborigines in Perceptual-Motor Tests, FP and BPMP Compared

Test	Program	n	Gain Score	p
ITPA visual association[a]	FP	8	5.63 (5.45)	NS
	BPMP	8	1.75 (5.99)	
WPPSI geometric designs[a]	FP	8	2.25 (1.30)	NS
	BPMP	8	.13 (2.67)	
DAP IQ	FP	8	37.13 (11.92)	NS
	BPMP	8	28.13 (11.88)	

[a] Expressed as scaled scores.

TABLE 6.20 Wave III: Mean Gain Scores (SD in Parentheses) of Whites in Perceptual-Motor Tests, FP and BPMP Compared

Test	Program	n	Gain Score	p
ITPA visual association[a]	FP	12	7.42 (6.68)	.05
	BPMP	10	1.00 (6.94)	
WPPSI geometric designs[a]	FP	12	1.75 (2.89)	NS
	BPMP	10	.20 (1.89)	
DAP IQ	FP	12	25.83 (21.82)	NS
	BPMP	10	32.90 (16.77)	

[a] Expressed as scaled scores.

Tables 6.19 and 6.20 deal with the comparative effects of the FP and BPMP on perceptual-motor tests in each ethnic group. They reveal one significant difference—in visual association, for whites, the FP is superior—and show trends for the FP to be either superior, or equivalent, to the BPMP in other tests.

In summary, the spectacular Aboriginal PPVT improvements of 1970 were partially replicated in the structured program of 1972; but the whites did not do as well as in Wave I. The EEP yielded promising results that were, perhaps, not as impressive as in the BEP. As the EEP was an innovatory program that had never been applied before, we considered that it should be polished and implemented again in 1973. The disturbing lack of significant improvement in grammatic closure noted in 1971 was reversed: the two 1972 programs appeared to produce roughly equivalent improvements in this domain. The BPMP did not appear to be as effective as the FP and was subsequently eliminated in 1973; thus all children were exposed to the FP in Wave IV.

Both teachers enjoyed teaching the new EEP and appreciated the greater initiative and less repetitive strategies involved in this technique. It offered a welcome contrast to and relief from the exhausting pattern drill of the BEP.

WAVE IV, 1973

In this year we attempted to replicate the 1972 results by comparing structured and semistructured programs. All classes were exposed, in addition, to the Frostig perceptual-motor program—the Bourke Perceptual-Motor Program having been dropped—and to home-school liaison teaching which commenced in 1973.

The results are demonstrated in Tables 6.21 to 6.25. Table 6.21 shows the overall results on all tests, for all children and for both programs combined. Table 6.22 compares the results of Aboriginal and white children in both programs combined. Table 6.23 compares the effects of each program on the two ethnic groups combined. Tables 6.24 and 6.25 compare the results of Aborigines and whites, respectively, in the structured and semistructured programs.

TABLE 6.21   Wave IV: Mean Results on All Tests in Both Programs for Total Group, Aborigines and Whites Combined

Test	n	Test 1	SD	Test 2	SD	Difference	p
PPVT IQ	35	75.74	21.93	80.89	22.06	5.14	$.10 > p > .05$
ITPA scaled scores							
Auditory association	37	28.78	5.81	31.51	7.40	2.73	.005
Visual association	37	28.19	5.68	29.38	6.12	1.19	NS
Grammatic closure	37	27.41	6.31	34.86	9.82	7.46	.001
WPPSI scaled scores							
Information	37	5.86	3.67	8.03	2.54	2.16	.001
Geometric designs	37	7.73	2.92	8.54	2.46	.81	$.10 > p > .05$
Vocabulary	37	5.97	3.93	7.27	2.30	1.30	.02
Concepts raw scores	34	9.35	5.52	26.18	6.44	16.82	.001

Table 6.21 demonstrates significant gains, overall, in all language and cognitive tests aside from the PPVT, in which a strong trend was apparent. There were no significant gains in perceptual-motor tests, although a strong trend was evident in geometric designs. The results were not as impressive as in 1972 (see Table 6.14). A comparison of the

CHAPTER SIX

gains in the two years in equivalent tests reveals superior results across the board in 1972 ($p = .02$, sign test, two-tailed):

	Overall Gains	
Test	1972	1973
PPVT IQ	8.05	5.14
Auditory association	7.49	2.73
Visual association	3.16	1.19
Grammatic closure	10.84	7.46
Information	4.55	2.16
Geometric designs	1.11	.81
Vocabulary	5.04	1.30

Note: All subtest scores are scaled.

Very large gains were demonstrated on the test of conceptualization. Similar large gains are obvious in all like comparisons made in 1973.

Table 6.22 reveals that Aborigines achieved significant gains in grammatic closure, information, geometric designs, vocabulary, and concept tests; whites, in contrast, did so in auditory association, gram-

TABLE 6.22 Wave IV: Mean Scores of Aborigines and Whites in Both Programs, Structured and Semistructured Combined

Test	Group	n	Test 1	SD	Test 2	SD	Difference	p
PPVT IQ	Abor.	17	63.00	19.72	67.29	18.24	4.29	NS
	White	18	87.78	16.73	93.72	17.35	5.94	NS
ITPA scaled scores								
Auditory association	Abor.	19	25.32	2.11	26.37	4.95	1.05	NS
	White	18	32.44	6.25	36.94	5.41	4.50	.002
Visual association	Abor.	19	26.11	5.70	27.21	6.42	1.11	NS
	White	18	30.39	4.90	31.67	4.99	1.28	NS
Grammatic closure	Abor.	19	23.79	5.77	28.89	6.31	5.11	.02
	White	18	31.22	4.37	41.17	8.95	9.95	.001
WPPSI scaled scores								
Information	Abor.	19	3.05	1.68	6.68	2.24	3.63	.001
	White	18	8.83	2.73	9.44	1.85	.61	NS
Geometric designs	Abor.	19	6.37	2.01	8.16	2.27	1.79	.02
	White	18	9.17	3.09	8.94	2.64	−.22	NS
Vocabulary	Abor.	19	4.26	1.85	5.89	1.66	1.63	.001
	White	18	7.78	4.73	8.72	1.99	.94	NS
Concepts raw scores	Abor.	16	7.12	3.67	23.12	5.63	16.00	.001
	White	18	11.33	6.20	28.89	6.01	17.55	.001

TABLE 6.23 Wave IV: Mean Scores of Aborigines and Whites Combined on All Tests, Structured and Semistructured Programs Compared

Test	Program	n	Test 1[a]	SD	Test 2[a]	SD	Difference	p
PPVT IQ	Structured	18	76.94	15.86	81.17	24.40	4.22	NS
	Semistructured	17	74.47	27.41	80.59	20.02	6.11	.10 > p > .05
ITPA scaled scores								
Auditory association	Structured	19	28.05	5.53	31.47	7.78	3.42	.02
	Semistructured	18	29.56	6.15	31.56	7.19	2.00	.10 > p > .05
Visual association	Structured	19	27.52	4.99	30.58	1.15	3.05	.05
	Semistructured	18	28.89	6.41	28.11	7.02	-.78	NS
Grammatic closure	Structured	19	26.79	7.46	35.84	11.44	9.05	.002
	Semistructured	18	28.06	4.96	33.83	7.96	5.78	.001
WPPSI scaled scores								
Information	Structured	20	5.58	3.42	7.95	2.32	2.37	.001
	Semistructured	18	6.17	4.00	8.11	2.86	1.94	.01
Geometric designs	Structured	19	7.89	3.51	8.58	2.54	.68	NS
	Semistructured	18	7.56	2.23	8.50	2.43	.94	NS
Vocabulary	Structured	19	5.79	3.82	7.26	2.37	1.47	.10 > p > .05
	Semistructured	18	6.16	4.14	7.28	2.29	1.11	.10 > p > .05
Concepts raw scores	Structured	17	9.41	6.36	24.82	7.07	15.41	.001
	Semistructured	17	9.29	4.72	27.52	5.63	18.24	.001

[a] Two-tailed t-tests on differences between all pairs of pretests and posttests: all nonsignificant.

Chapter Six

TABLE 6.24 Wave IV: Mean Scores of Aborigines on All Tests, Structured and Semistructured Programs Compared

Test	Program	n	Test 1[a]	SD	Test 2[a]	SD	Difference	p
PPVT IQ	Structured	9	69.00	16.53	68.00	20.21	−1.00	NS
	Semistructured	8	56.25	17.09	66.50	17.09	10.25	.02
ITPA scaled scores								
Auditory association	Structured	10	25.30	2.31	26.00	4.47	.07	NS
	Semistructured	9	25.33	2.00	26.78	5.67	1.44	NS
Visual association	Structured	10	25.40	3.13	28.90	5.66	3.50	$.10 > p > .05$
	Semistructured	9	26.89	7.80	25.33	7.00	−1.56	NS
Grammatic closure	Structured	10	23.20	7.72	27.60	7.14	4.40	NS
	Semistructured	9	24.44	2.60	30.33	5.29	5.89	.01
WPPSI scaled scores								
Information	Structured	10	3.10	1.37	6.50	2.01	3.40	.001
	Semistructured	9	3.00	2.06	6.89	2.89	3.89	.002
Geometric designs	Structured	10	6.40	1.89	7.80	2.53	1.40	$.10 > p > .05$
	Semistructured	9	6.33	2.37	8.55	2.01	2.22	$.10 > p > .05$
Vocabulary	Structured	10	4.50	1.78	6.10	1.79	1.60	.01
	Semistructured	9	4.00	2.00	5.67	1.58	1.67	.025
Concepts raw scores	Structured	8	7.87	4.51	21.62	7.01	13.75	.001
	Semistructured	8	6.37	2.67	24.62	3.70	18.25	.001

[a] Two-tailed t-tests on differences between all pairs of pretests and posttests: all nonsignificant.

AN AUSTRALIAN PRESCHOOL

TABLE 6.25 Wave IV: Mean Scores of Whites on All Tests, Structured and Semistructured Programs Compared

Test	Program	n	Test 1[a]	SD	Test 2[a]	SD	Difference	p
PPVT IQ	Structured	9	84.88	10.93	94.33	21.62	9.44	.10 > p > .05
	Semistructured	9	90.66	21.38	93.11	13.10	2.44	NS
ITPA scaled scores								
Auditory association	Structured	9	31.11	6.54	37.55	5.89	6.44	.01
	Semistructured	9	33.78	6.02	36.33	5.15	2.56	.10 > p > .05
Visual association	Structured	9	29.89	5.75	32.44	3.68	2.55	NS
	Semistructured	9	30.89	4.17	30.89	6.17	.00	NS
Grammatic closure	Structured	9	30.78	4.89	45.00	7.59	14.22	.001
	Semistructured	9	31.67	4.03	37.33	8.90	5.67	.05
WPPSI scaled scores								
Information	Structured	9	8.33	2.82	9.55	1.42	1.22	.10 > p > .05
	Semistructured	9	9.33	2.69	9.33	2.69	.00	NS
Geometric designs	Structured	9	9.55	4.21	9.44	2.40	−.11	NS
	Semistructured	9	8.78	1.48	8.44	2.92	−.33	NS
Vocabulary	Structured	9	7.22	4.50	8.55	2.35	1.33	NS
	Semistructured	9	8.33	4.69	8.89	1.69	.56	NS
Concepts raw scores	Structured	9	10.77	7.66	27.67	6.14	16.89	.001
	Semistructured	9	11.89	4.73	30.11	5.97	18.22	.001

[a] Two-tailed t-tests on differences between all pairs of pretests and posttests: all nonsignificant.

matic closure, and concept tests. Neither group, as a whole, improved significantly in PPVT or visual association. A comparison of these results with those of 1972 reveals that the latter were superior in eleven out of fourteen tests ($p = .06$, sign test, two-tailed).

Table 6.23 demonstrates that when Aborigines and whites are combined, the structured program produced significant changes in auditory association, visual association, grammatic closure, information, and concepts; a near-significant trend in vocabulary; and insignificant changes in PPVT and geometric designs. The semistructured program yielded significant changes in grammatic closure, information, and concepts; trends in PPVT, auditory association, and vocabulary; and insignificant change in visual association and geometric designs.

Table 6.24 shows that Aborigines in the structured program made significant gains in information, vocabulary, and concept tests; near-significant gains in visual association and geometric designs; and insignificant gains in PPVT, auditory association, and grammatic closure. Those in the semistructured program demonstrated significant gains in PPVT, grammatic closure, information, vocabulary, and concept tests; a near-significant gain in geometric designs; and insignificant changes in auditory and visual association. In all eight tests, the semistructured program produced the superior gain score ($p = .02$, sign test, two-tailed);[12] whereas superiority was randomly distributed between the two programs in 1972 (see Table 6.17).

A comparison of Tables 6.17 and 6.24 reveals that for Aborigines in structured classes, the 1972 program produced superior gains in all seven comparable tests ($p = .02$, sign test, two-tailed).[13] Superiority was randomly distributed between 1972 and 1973 tests in regard to the Aboriginal semistructured program. Combining semistructured and structured gain superiorities, the ratio is 11:3 in favor of 1972 ($p = .06$, sign test, two-tailed).

Table 6.25 reveals that for white children, the structured program produced significant gains in auditory association, grammatic closure, and concepts; trends in PPVT and information; and insignificant changes in visual association, geometric designs, and vocabulary. The semistructured program yielded significant changes in grammatic closure and concepts; insignificant changes in PPVT, visual association, information, geometric designs, and vocabulary; and a trend in auditory association.

12. That this rough measure of significance is reliable is supported by the facts that in no pretest pair comparison in 1973 was the difference statistically significant and that the structured program pretest was superior in only five out of eight instances.
13. The 1973 pretests were superior to those of 1972 in six out of seven comparable instances ($p = .12$, NS, sign test, two-tailed).

The structured program produced superior gains in seven out of eight comparisons ($p = .07$, NS, sign test, two-tailed); in 1972 a similar comparison reveals random differences in superiority (see Table 6.18).

A comparison of Tables 6.18 and 6.25 reveals that, in regard to white structured classes, the 1972 program yielded superior gains in six out of seven comparable tests ($p = .12$, NS, sign test, two-tailed). The 1972 semistructured program produced superior gains in all seven tests ($p = .02$, sign test, two-tailed). Combining structured and semistructured gain superiorities, the 1972 program yielded gains for whites superior to those of 1973 in thirteen out of fourteen tests ($p = .002$, sign test, two-tailed). (Pretest superiority was randomly [8:6] distributed.)

In summary, despite gratifying gains in grammatic closure and conceptualization, the 1973 programs appear to have been less successful than those of 1972. In particular, the white structured and semistructured and the Aboriginal structured programs appear to have been superior in 1972. The 1972 and 1973 semistructured programs for Aborigines appear to have been comparable. In 1972 there was no evidence that either of the programs was superior; in 1973 the semistructured program appeared to produce superior results in Aborigines and there was inclusive evidence that the structured program was more effective for white children.

The reason for the difference between the 1972 and 1973 results is unclear. It may be due to a change of staff: the new teacher, who found the structured program very difficult to adjust to, was much more comfortable with the semistructured approach.

FOLLOW-UP

In Tables 6.26 to 6.31 children from Waves I and II who were tested (in 1971 and 1972) in the middle of their first year in elementary school are compared with a control group of children from the Bourke elementary kindergarten who had never been to preschool and who were tested in mid-1970. Also, in 1972, a control group of thirty-six children who were in the first year of elementary school and who had not been to preschool were matched for age, sex, and race with fifteen Aborigines and

TABLE 6.26 Mean Ages of All Preschool and Non-Preschool Samples in 1970, 1971, and 1972

	White Boys	White Girls	Aboriginal Boys	Aboriginal Girls
Preschool	5:6	5:6	5:6	5:6
Non-preschool	5:5	5:6	5:6	5:8

CHAPTER SIX

twenty-one whites from Wave II and compared on a number of measures.

Table 6.26 demonstrates that satisfactory matching for age was attained. In Table 6.27 the follow-up comparison of 1970 controls, of Wave I, and of Wave II is illustrated. Aborigines who had been to preschool scored significantly more highly than controls in PPVT IQ and showed a trend in this direction in Nixon Test scores, whereas preschool whites showed a superior trend in PPVT IQ and a significant difference in Nixon Test score.

TABLE 6.27 Follow-up Comparison of Mean Scores of Unmatched 1970 Non-Preschool, 1971 Wave I Preschool, and 1972 Wave II Preschool Children on PPVT and Nixon Test

	Non-preschool Mid-1970			Preschool Mid-1971			Preschool Mid-1972		
Test	n	Mean	SD	n	Mean	SD	n	Mean	SD
PPVT IQ									
Aboriginal	11	63.2[a]	13.1	15	75.3[a]	15.1	15	73.4	11.3
White	12	86.9[b]	11.4	15	90.6[b]	15.8	21	91.7	12.2
Nixon Test[e]									
Aboriginal	11	17.4[c]	75.2	15	27.3[c]	15.5	15	26.0	21.8
White	12	31.1[d]	19.7	15	53.3[d]	23.7	21	57.5	22.2

[a] $.05 > p > .025$
[b] $p = NS$
[c] $.10 > p > .05$
[d] $p = .005$
[e] Percentage of items answered operationally.

TABLE 6.28 Follow-up Comparison of Mean Scores of 36 Non-Preschool and 36 Matched Preschool Children from Wave II on PPVT, ITPA, and Nixon Test in Mid-1972

	Non-preschool			Preschool			
Test	n	Mean	SD	n	Mean	SD	p
PPVT IQ	36	80.67	14.75	36	87.47	14.20	.05
ITPA scaled scores							
Auditory association	36	28.1	9.29	36	33.41	5.53	.01
Visual association	36	27.13	6.81	36	29.80	9.25	NS
Grammatic closure	36	30.47	8.78	36	33.11	6.90	NS
Nixon (raw)	36	2.44	1.83	36	2.83	1.72	NS

TABLE 6.29 Follow-up Comparison of Mean Scores of 15 Aboriginal Non-Preschool and 15 Matched Aboriginal Preschool Children from Wave II on PPVT, ITPA, and Nixon Test in Mid-1972

| | Non-preschool ||| Preschool ||||
Test	n	Mean	SD	n	Mean	SD	p
PPVT IQ	15	70.53	10.36	15	76.20	11.46	NS
ITPA scaled scores							
Auditory association	15	21.60	9.58	15	30.80	4.99	.01
Visual association	15	24.00	4.97	15	25.60	7.87	NS
Grammatic closure	15	24.06	6.27	15	28.13	3.99	.01
Nixon (raw)	15	1.20	1.11	15	1.80	1.42	NS

TABLE 6.30 Follow-up Comparison of Mean Scores of 21 White Non-Preschool and 21 Matched White Preschool Children from Wave II on PPVT, ITPA, and Nixon Test in Mid-1972

| | Non-preschool ||| Preschool ||||
Test	n	Mean	SD	n	Mean	SD	p
PPVT IQ	21	87.90	13.10	21	95.53	9.83	.05
ITPA scaled scores							
Auditory association	21	32.81	15.48	21	35.27	5.13	NS
Visual association	21	29.38	7.11	21	33.29	8.15	NS
Grammatic closure	21	35.05	7.33	21	36.67	6.33	NS
Nixon (raw)	21	3.33	1.64	21	3.57	1.53	NS

TABLE 6.31 Follow-up Comparison of Mean Scores of 15 Aboriginal and 21 White Preschool Children from Wave II on PPVT, ITPA, and Nixon Test in Mid-1972

| | Aboriginal ||| White ||||
Test	n	Mean	SD	n	Mean	SD	p
PPVT IQ	15	76.20	11.46	21	95.52	9.83	.01
ITPA scaled scores							
Auditory association	15	30.80	4.99	21	35.29	5.13	.01
Visual association	15	25.60	7.87	21	33.29	8.15	.01
Grammatic closure	15	28.13	3.98	21	36.67	6.33	.01
Nixon (raw)	15	1.80	1.51	21	3.57	1.53	.01

CHAPTER SIX

Table 6.28 compares Wave II preschool children with matched non-preschool children in mid-1972, eight months after the termination of the preschool year. Preschool children were superior on all tests—PPVT, ITPA, and Nixon Test—although this finding reached a level of statistical significance only in PPVT and auditory association. These observations can be examined in more detail, for each ethnic group, in Tables 6.29 and 6.30. Wave II Aborigines were superior to controls in all tests—significantly so in auditory association and grammatical closure. Wave II whites were also superior in all tests, and significantly so in PPVT. Table 6.31 demonstrates that Wave II whites were still superior to Wave II Aborigines in all tests at follow-up in 1972.

It is instructive to examine the graphic representation of Wave I results and follow-up in Figures 6.3, 6.4, 6.5, and 6.6 in the following tests:

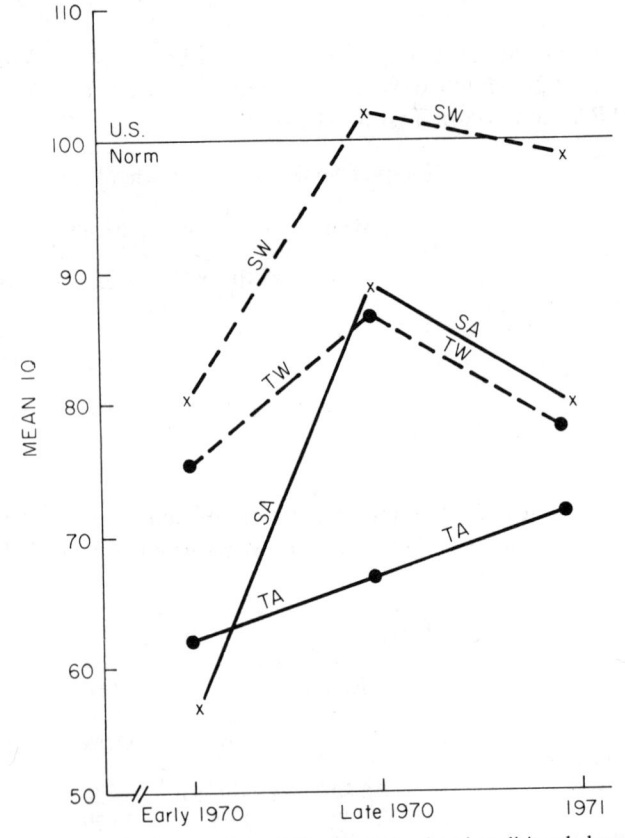

FIGURE 6.3 Wave I: follow-up into 1971 of structured and traditional classes on PPVT IQ. · ———— · Traditional Aboriginal ($n = 7$); · ———— · Traditional white ($n = 7$); × ———— × Structured Aboriginal ($n = 8$); × ———— × Structured white ($n = 8$)

168

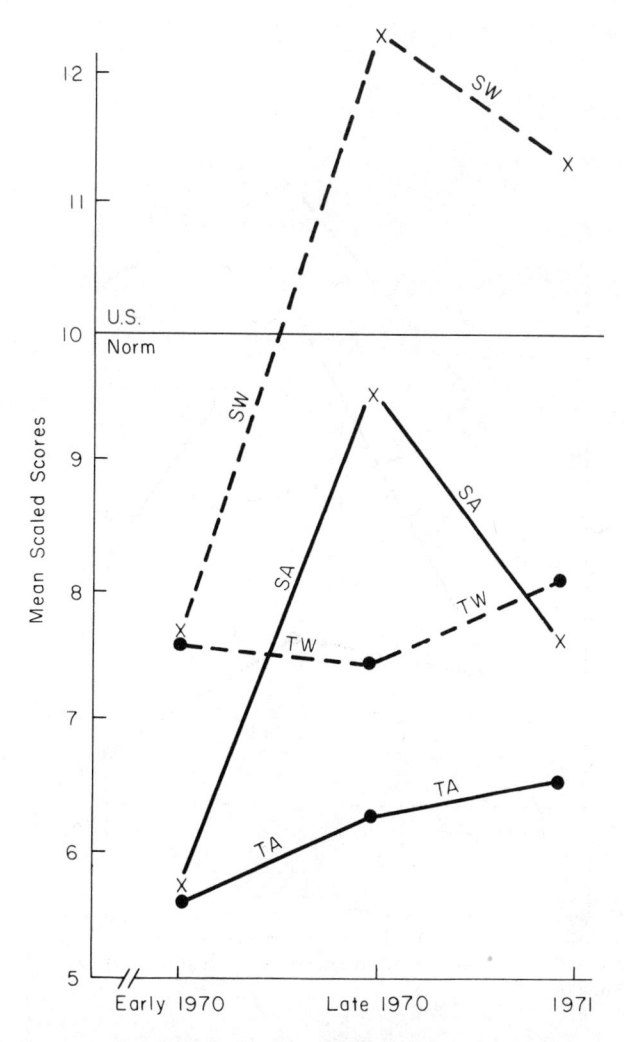

FIGURE 6.4 Wave I: follow-up into 1971 of structured and traditional classes on WPPSI vocabulary. ·————— · Traditional Aboriginal ($n = 5$); · —————— · Traditional white ($n = 7$); × ————— × Structured Aboriginal ($n = 7$); × —————— × Structured White ($n = 8$)

PPVT, WPPSI vocabulary, and ITPA grammatic closure and auditory association. The results in each test run parallel: whites and Aborigines were separated by wide margins at pretest and follow-up but were closer at posttest; whites and Aborigines in unstructured classes showed little change during the eighteen-month period; whites and Aborigines in the structured classes showed parallel large gains at posttest; Aborigines in

CHAPTER SIX

FIGURE 6.5 Wave I: follow-up into 1971 of structured and traditional classes on ITPA grammatic closure. ·————· Traditional Aboriginal (*n* = 6); ·——————· Traditional White (*n* = 7); ×————× Structured Aboriginal (*n* = 7); ×——————× Structured White (*n* = 7)

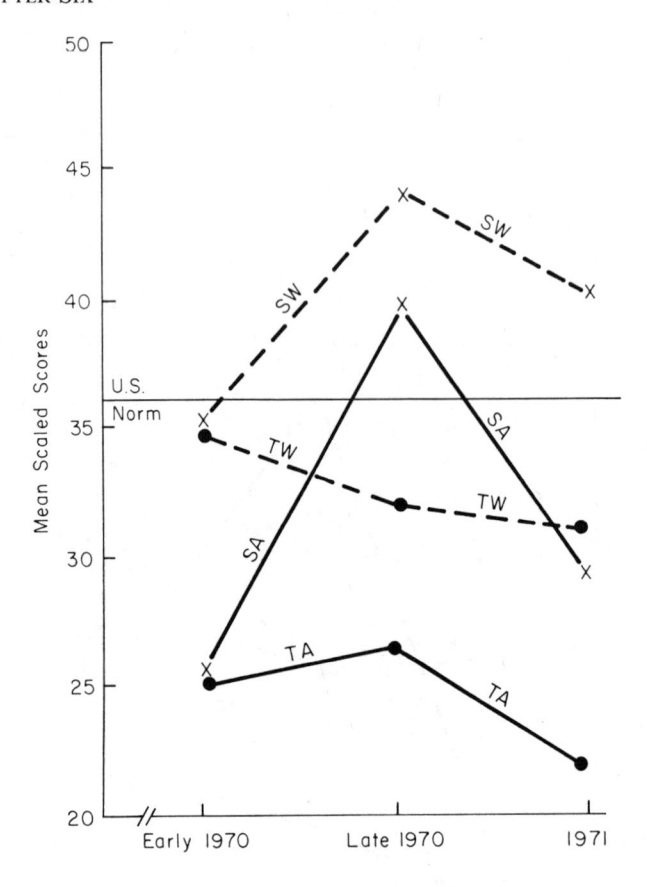

the structured classes suffered an erosion of posttest gains at follow-up of between 30 and 85 percent whereas whites from structured classes tended to sustain their gains, with insignificant loss, at follow-up. It should be pointed out, however, that we discovered three of the eight Aborigines from the Wave I structured class had not attended elementary school in 1971, due to an unfortunate oversight (all three had lost all their gains); whereas all the other children from Wave I had done so. Thus the tendency for erosion of posttest gains was greatly exaggerated.

FIGURE 6.6 Wave I: follow-up into 1971 of structured and traditional classes on ITPA auditory association. ———— Traditional Aboriginal ($n = 6$); ·————————· Traditional White ($n = 7$); ×————× Structured Aboriginal ($n = 7$); ×————————× Structured White ($n = 7$)

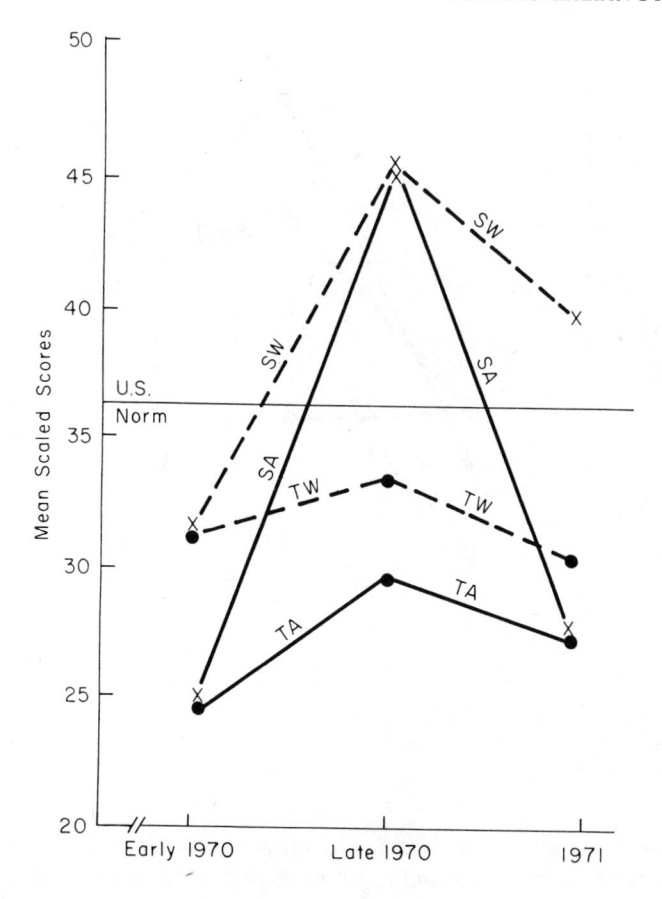

Figures 6.7, 6.8, and 6.9 compare pretest, posttest and follow-up results of Aboriginal children who were exposed to structured programs in Waves I, II, III, and IV in PPVT, auditory association, and grammatic closure. The gains and erosions of Wave I scores appear to have been the greatest, whereas those of Wave III were intermediate in scale between Waves I and II.

In summary, eight months after they left preschool our children compare favorably with control children who have not been to preschool.

Chapter Six

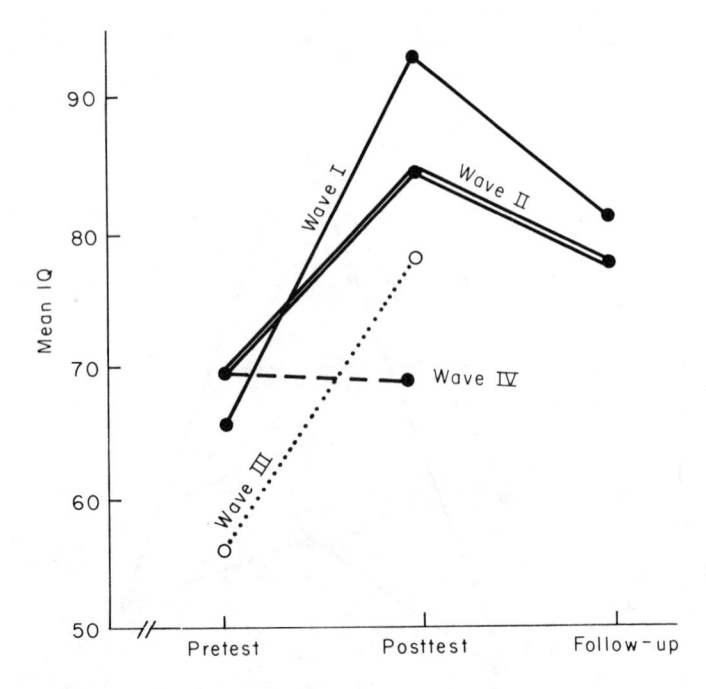

FIGURE 6.7 Waves I, II, III, IV: mean results of Aboriginal children on PPVT, Bereiter-Engelmann technique

This observation applies to Aboriginal and white children in a variety of language performance tests and a test of classificatory ability. Nevertheless, a serious erosion of posttest gains has been demonstrated, and this appears to affect Aborigines more markedly than whites.

SUMMARY OF RESULTS

A structured language-stimulation program, borrowed from the United States and modified to suit Australian conditions, has been implemented with success on four successive years, producing considerable gains in the language performance areas objectified. It proved to be markedly superior to a traditional, unstructured program in the first year of operation. Neither the structured nor the unstructured program was effective in improving perceptual-motor functioning. Accordingly, in the second and third years of the preschool's operation, two perceptual-motor

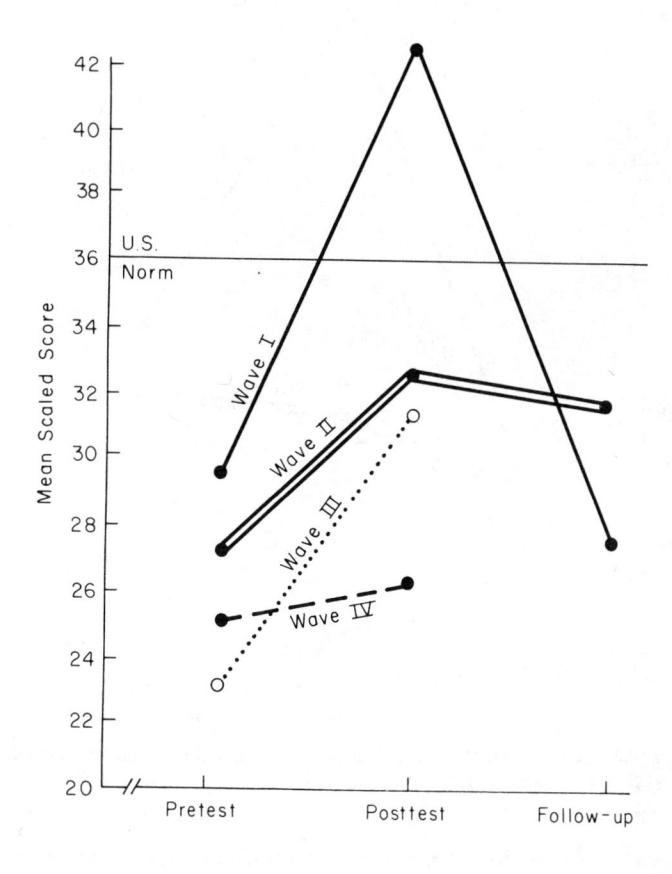

FIGURE 6.8 Waves I, II, III, IV: mean results of Aboriginal children on ITPA auditory association, Bereiter-Engelmann technique

stimulation programs were amalgamated with the language programs and compared. The more structured perceptual program proved more successful and was retained, alone, in the fourth year of the preschool. In the third and fourth years of the preschool, the structured language program was compared with a semistructured program of our own design. Both techniques produced promising results and have been retained for further development and comparison. Follow-up of the preschool children into elementary school has revealed them to be superior, in general, to controls on tests of language and classificatory performance.

CHAPTER SIX

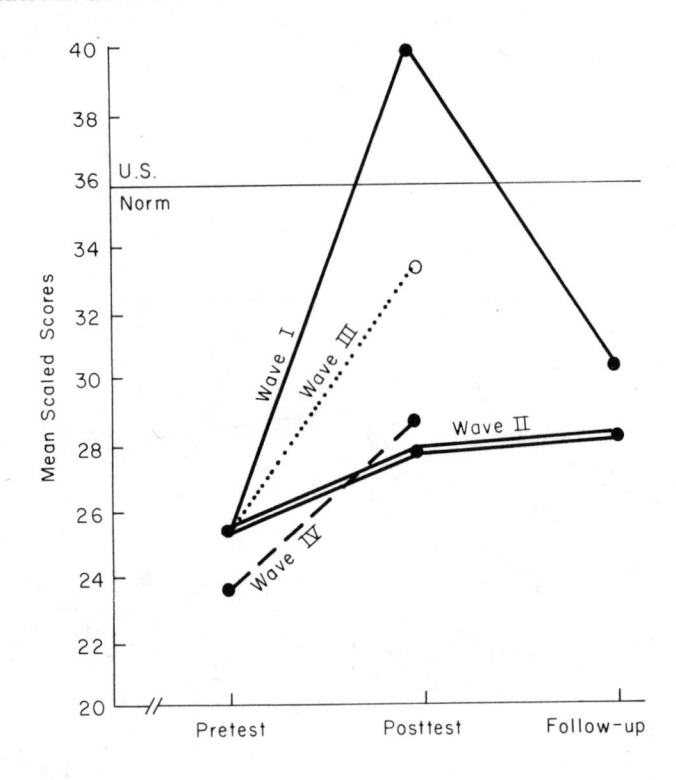

FIGURE 6.9 Waves I, II, III, IV: mean results of Aboriginal children on ITPA grammatic closure, Bereiter-Engelmann technique

A tendency toward erosion of the improvements in language performance has been noticed in Aboriginal children eight months after the cessation of the preschool program; white children, on the other hand, appear to have sustained their gains.

ACTION RESEARCH: DISCUSSION

THE STAFF AND OBSERVERS

We have found that the chief requirements of our preschool teachers are youth, flexibility, a willingness to try new techniques, and a lack of preconception about "the right way." Experience is less essential than the former attributes, though useful up to a point. Long experience, on the other hand, may be associated with rigid preconceptions and difficulty in either adapting to the directness and pace of the structured technique or developing the initiative, flexibility, and imaginative perception demanded by the semistructured program.

Essentially, our teachers have trained on the job with early supervision from the administrative staff. They meet regularly to plan each week's activities ahead of time and, since 1973, to coordinate preschool teaching and home-school liaison. The more experienced director of the preschool is the leader of the planning group and is encouraged to use her initiative within the framework provided by the objectives and the curriculum that outlines each program.

Observers are generally welcome, regardless of their origin, provided their visits have been arranged beforehand. As a result we have had a wide variety of comments ranging from openly antagonistic to highly encouraging. The noisy pattern drill of the Bereiter-Engelmann Program often disturbs those who are used to gentler, less direct teaching and obscures the greater subtleties of the EEP. Others have been openly hostile on the basis that we are destroying Aboriginal identity, wasting our time on irrelevancies when the most important problems are otherwise (medical, legal, housing and so forth), imposing discredited middle-class white aspirations upon an alien group, or focusing excessively on language without adequate sensorimotor foundation. We have accepted the criticisms and, when we thought it feasible and advisable, modified the program progressively. The very clarity of the objectives and the comparative basis of the methodology lend themselves to criticism from outside, and constructive evolution from inside, the project.

What conclusions and recommendations we have made have been both substantiated by our experimental results and properly qualified. The Aboriginal people of Bourke are not representative of the entire Aboriginal population of Australia. We contend that our findings in Bourke are applicable to fringe-dwelling and transitional rural part-Aborigines and also to some white children in small outback townships. We have never claimed that the teaching techniques employed in Bourke are necessarily the best or the only techniques appropriate. Our observations have caused us to draw some conclusions about what is not effective in this setting; we are beginning to understand the kind of programs that are likely to be fruitful.

THE PARENTS

In the first two years of the Bourke project our preoccupation with establishing the school, developing curricula, and teaching ourselves

CHAPTER SIX

the new strategies—together with a shortage of staff and other resources—prevented us from doing much more than having good intentions about parental involvement. Criticism from outside and our own growing realization of the discontinuities between home, preschool, and elementary school have caused us to devote more time to the parents of our children.

Both European and Aboriginal parents respected the preschool, rather from afar, and looked to it to prepare their children scholastically. They were most interested in improvements in articulateness, general knowledge, vocabulary, and pencil and paper skills. Aboriginal parents were also concerned that their children should be able to mix better, hold their own with whites, and speak up when the teacher asked them questions—social competencies that they, themselves, well remember having lacked. Some mothers, in our first year, hesitated about letting the child go ("He's too young. Next year's soon enough"); but this reluctance disappeared as the reputation of "The Pre" grew. Now all mothers with eligible children voluntarily present their children for entry into preschool at the end of the preceding year. The initial emphasis of our programs on preacademic skills—in part a response to the expressed wishes of the Aboriginal people—was influential; parents saw their children learning and were proud.

It is difficult to tap the critical feelings of Aboriginal parents. We know too little of their reservations about the school. The only adverse comments we have been able to evoke are: "She's got a bit cheeky since she started at pre" (heard once; a reflection, possibly, of greater verbal fluency and curiosity); and "He doesn't seem to have learned as much as his sister did last year" (occasional).

The initiation of the home-school liaison program in 1973 has created a new level of relationship with the Aboriginal people. Parents have been enthusiastic about their weekly visits and lessons and are pleased that they can support the preschool by their efforts at home. Regular parent meetings have been well attended and the nature of our teaching techniques further explained. Mothers sit in on classes and act as aides during the school day. The successful development of the Aboriginal Advancement Association, the seeds for which were sown by Dr. Kamien, has increased cohesion in the Aboriginal community and a number of meetings have been held under their auspices. At one of these gatherings we were directly criticized by a militant young Aboriginal man: according to him, we were just a bunch of university people experimenting with Aboriginal children in order to get figures for books for our own advancement. The criticism stung; for it was not without an element of truth. But the preschool is now solidly enough established to withstand attacks of this nature; or it would not be so vigorously supported and defended by Aboriginal and white parents. The young man's challenge enabled us to explain further the purpose of our tests, the urgent need to develop, for outback children, teaching techniques that are of proved effectiveness, and the importance of the Bourke experiment for Aboriginal children elsewhere in Australia.

THE CHILDREN

At the outset, in 1970, we were most concerned about the possible adverse side effects of the structured program. Aboriginal children who had never experienced anything similar were now expected to concentrate on problems, answer questions directed to them from adults, and try their hardest. We were warned and continue to be warned that the children would be overstressed. It is indeed true that Aboriginal children have had little experience of direct, individual expectation of performance and of praise for achievement before they commence school; thus one objective of the preschool is to promote a pleasure in achievement. Liberal praise is offered for effort, even if the child is incorrect. (Mistakes are corrected at once; effort is always rewarded.)

In four years of operation we have had only two children who were upset by the structured program. Both were white and from homes in which parental expectations were very high; both children already had tension symptoms. In the first week of the Bereiter-Engelmann Program both developed headaches and complained at home of the noise in class. Both children were transferred to a less structured class.

In fact the demanding, intense, and noisy atmosphere of the Bereiter-Engelmann Program is balanced by individual support and attention. The Aboriginal girl who characteristically withdraws from a difficult task into reverie—eyes glazed and thumb in mouth—is deterred from doing so by the excitement of the group responses and by the effort of the teacher to keep her involved. As she begins to understand and master new problems—problems that are presented in carefully graduated sequence—a marked change can be seen. Formerly shy, withdrawn, and almost mute, she becomes eager, responsive, and lively. The program fosters a whole new motivational set associated with individuality, mastery, and self-esteem. Thus positive adjustment can stem from the effect of cognitive development on self-concept. We have been accustomed to viewing psychological disorder in the reverse: emotional disturbance and poor self-concept disrupting cognitive development and producing learning disorder. This may be a result of the prevailing Western tendency to split cognition and motivation and to think of each of them as emanating from separate compartments (ego and id, for example, a matter considered further in chapter 7) and interacting only secondarily.

We acknowledge in all our programs the importance of praise and the need to promote a sense of competence, a pleasure in exercising skills, and a desire to master new problems. It may be that the main purpose of a preschool program is not so much to develop these motivational forces *de novo* but to harness what is already present and to help the child apply it to problems that are relevant to later scholastic learning. In other words: The preschool induces the children to redefine the context-related rules of expression as well as promoting the realization of their potential. (This matter is treated in chapters 3 and 7.)

In the four years of operation we have suspended only one child, a hyperactive white boy who was psychologically very disturbed following abandonment by his mother. His attacks on other children were too difficult for us to manage in the classroom and he was referred elsewhere for psychiatric help. The usual range of naughtiness, inattention, and separation anxiety usually settles quickly in response to familiarity, a pleasure in learning, and classroom management.[14]

INTEGRATION

As the Commonwealth Government has spent more money on Aboriginal welfare, a discernible backlash has developed among whites, particularly in view of recent droughts and fluctuations in the rural economy. The development of the Aboriginal Advancement Association has provoked considerable opposition from those who resent its increasingly vocal presence. Yet, as bush towns go, Bourke is regarded as freer of racial prejudice than most. There is no segregation in public facilities —swimming pool, hospital, hotels, schools, or sport, for example—but there are clubs in town with no Aboriginal members and Aboriginal and white families seldom mix socially.

In the meantime, white and Aboriginal men labor side by side and drink together after work as they have always done. The greatest distance is between the women. There are really only two places where mothers from the two ethnic groups can meet: in church and at the preschool. Our project has been a positive force in promoting cooperation between the two groups at a time of unrest. The very existence of the preschool implies that, whatever their separate goals and values may be, and whatever the conflicts that arise on that account, Aborigines and whites are interdependent.

---

14. Some very useful techniques of management are described in Bereiter and Engelmann's *Teaching Disadvantaged Children in the Preschool.*

Aware of the racial undercurrents, we were concerned to detect reflections of adult attitudes in the children. At first there were very few remarks: odd comments passed in the group—"Blackfellows drink dirty water" and "Don't go near him; he's a dirty fellow"—no more. In the last year we have noticed a tendency for white and black children to play in separate groups; but these groups are not exclusive. We do not know whether this is a result of the prevailing adult tensions, of parental admonition, or of the propensity for children with similar interests and dialect to group together.[15] Our programs contain no material directly related to race relations, although we deliberately employ white and black staff and use books and stories depicting the races mixing and working together.

VALIDITY

Technical problems abound in the interpretation of our results. An important question concerns the validity of the improvements measured by posttests and follow-up: Do they have any predictive value in terms of later school adjustment? Are they merely methodological artefacts?

Could it be that the posttest gains are due to the fact that the children have become more sophisticated about tests as a result of the teaching program? Have they made gains chiefly because the pretest was a gross underestimate of competence due to their unfamiliarity with test procedure? Could the gains be explained by a mere practice effect? Undoubtedly, these factors are involved to some extent; but it should be noted that in 1970 little improvement was noted in the children exposed to an enthusiastically taught unstructured program—children who had as much practice on tests as those who did better in the contrasting structured program. We conclude that something in the structure of BEP produced the main effect.

The same argument applies to another question: Are our results due to a Hawthorne effect? Were the children inspired to do well at posttest because of our enthusiasm rather than because of the teaching programs per se? If so, the hypothetical artefact seems to have bypassed the children in the unstructured program in Wave I. For a Hawthorne effect to operate in this situation, it would be necessary for four-year-old culturally different children to discern the nature of the experiment and the relationship between complicated tests and the assessment of programs. This stretches the bounds of credibility to breaking point. It is,

---

15. This possibility is supported by Brislin (1971), who found that friendship choice in a heterogeneous group was determined by similarity of belief and language.

however, possible that our enthusiasm infected the parents (a consummation for which we devoutly wished) and that they, and not the teaching programs, stimulated the improvements. If so, the general esprit bypassed half the parents and preferentially inspired the rest despite the fact that, in 1970, we had no home-school liaison program.

A much more serious criticism concerns criterion contamination. Are the improvements measured due to our inadvertent teaching of the contents and procedures of the tests? If so, any improvements measured would have no generality beyond the test situation. This is a difficult problem to escape—language objectives demand language strategies and evaluation instruments based on language. So far as possible, however, we have tried to avoid this. We do not teach the contents of the WPPSI or PPVT, although some test procedures are similar to those in our programs. We do not teach the procedures of the ITPA, but there is undoubtedly an overlap in content, especially with the BEP. Similarly, our attempts to promote a more distancing, classificatory approach, and our training of the children to describe multiple attributes of objects, correlate with the content and format of the Nixon Test, but imperfectly. Follow-up testing will eventually decide whether *criterion-referenced* testing invalidates the results obtained.

Carver (1970) has pointed out that most standard tests are *norm-referenced*, that is, designed to measure differences between individuals and groups rather than change in individuals and groups. They therefore have limitations as test instruments in experimental research. In particular, their construction is such as, potentially, to underestimate change. This is a serious problem in relation to the tests used in Bourke.

DURABILITY AND FOLLOW-THROUGH

How lasting will the gains be? We do not know. Research in the United States (see chapter 4) and our preliminary assessments indicate the probability of serious erosion of gains among Aborigines. It is too much to expect a single year of preschool to have effects that last indefinitely without increased parental stimulation at home and without a continuity of teaching into elementary school. At the present time primary schools in rural Australia have not used teaching programs suitable for part-Aboriginal children, although the Van Leer Foundation of Queensland has developed curriculum materials specifically designed for Queensland Aborigines on the basis of a detailed study of their dialect and psycholinguistic needs.

In Bourke, we have begun to collaborate with the public school to develop a follow-through program that will consolidate the work of the preschool. This program is a development of the EEP. It builds upon the child's experiences and stimulates him to reflect on, describe, and reason from them. In addition, more specific and direct small-group teaching in language, number, and reading skills is attempted, although this is difficult when classes are large.

TRANSFER

We have no evidence on the important question of *horizontal transfer*. Do the children apply what they have learned in preschool beyond the classroom? Parents report increased articulateness and school games at home; but there is a danger that the new knowledge will be "compartmented." In view of the highly artificial nature of the direct structured program, it is possible that this problem applies particularly in this case. Research in the Northern Territory with neotribal Aborigines (Williams 1971) has demonstrated the cogency of this concern. Intellectual structures developed in the artificial situation of a classroom may dissipate if they are otherwise irrelevant, if they cannot be consolidated by expression in the world outside.

A related problem is that of *vertical transfer*. The aim of the preschool is to foster cornerstone skills that can be applied to the work of elementary school and enhanced in later years. We have some evidence of improvements in classificatory performance; but it remains to be seen whether this and other skills can be transferred, applied, and extended.

ACTION RESEARCH: THE FUTURE

The objectives of the preschool will be retained. In the immediate future we plan to extend the home-school liaison program and hire more Aboriginal teachers. The structured program will be retained. The Extended Experience Program will continue, with progressive modifications: to it we will add the distancing games introduced by Sigel (1973). A detailed follow-through program remains to be designed. To our evaluation instruments we will add tests of classification, seriation, conservation, and concept formation.

Ultimately we must find or design tests of social adjustment and self-esteem. The affective domain has been neglected in our evaluation, though not in our objectives and strategies. We need to know, in more detail, also the manner in which the various abilities we engender and measure interact, and whether they are in fact the cornerstone competencies we seek.

We need to know more about the social environment, kinship relations, values, and child-rearing techniques of Bourke Aborigines.

Chapter Six

Until we do so, we have only speculation upon which to erect our objectives and strategies. It is imperative, for example, to determine whether the teaching techniques used in school so violate the cultural norms of Aborigines that they are rejected. If so, how can they be modified to complement rather than deter the expressive strategies of the group in question?

We need to know much more about the communicative competence of Bourke's Aborigines. What is their nonstandard syntax and the contextual rules for its expression? Until we know more of this, our language programs are inappropriately, though not necessarily ineffectively, based upon the distorted and inadequate theories of deprivation and deficit.

Australia awaits its Oscar Lewis and William Labov.

THE RATIONALE AND ETHICS OF INTERVENTION

Before the European invasion, the Australian Aborigines lived, self-sufficiently, in delicate balance with the environment. It is true that Macassarmen had some influence in the north; but this was more a matter of local contact and trade, a cooperation resulting in mutual enrichment, the evidence of which can be detected even today in Arnhem Land.

Spreading over a dry continent, the Aboriginal people evolved a seminomadic society of interrelated descent groups cohering by means of a complex culture, a culture both highly spiritual and profoundly earthy. Spirit, serpent, rainbow, snake, and rainy season were not different entities but different aspects of a central idea, inseparable as the facets of a gem and radically different from the dichotomies and linearity of Western thought. Executive power was invested in the fully initiated men, the gerontocracy, who guarded sacred objects, preserved religious secrets from women and children, and determined the time of the ceremonies by which clan members affirmed their solidarity and continuities.

In the space of one hundred years the European destroyed it all. Moving inward from the coastal strips he competed with the Aborigine for territory, women, and food. Finding the indigenes incomprehensible, he saw them as part of an essentially hostile environment that had to be overcome. Sometimes he hunted them down; usually he dispersed them and watched them disintegrate. By the end of the nineteenth century the takeover was almost complete and the outcome historically inevitable (Rowley 1970).

Whole peoples were displaced from their traditional territories and, by mass migration, settled with the remnants of other groups on the fringes of country towns. Others, remaining closer to their former country, lived on the handouts of pastoralists. Many interbred with Asians and Europeans. Some have graduated to larger cities where they are slowly merging with the urban proletariat. Today there are roughly four Aboriginal ways of life: the traditional; the neotraditional on reserve or mission; the fringe-dwelling; and the urban. The races are increasingly mixed from the first to the fourth. Traditional customs are retained less and less until they finally merge with those of the European working class. Male dominance and the gerontocracy dissolve. Matriduxy—often based on the stability of a maternal grandmother—supersedes them. The men drift, economically impotent and unable to acquire property. A few, led perhaps by an unusually gifted father, migrate successfully to the cities. Others are forced to follow, often unsuccessfully, as the pastoral industry contracts.

We know most of all about the social organization of the traditional groups that remain in the north and center of Australia. This is the result of brilliant anthropological research—from Spencer and Gillen, Roth, Radcliffe-Brown, Warner, Elkin, Tindale, and the Berndts to Meggitt and Hiatt. Much of the work has been of reconstructive nature, necessarily; but some recent studies have concentrated upon the dynamic changes and equilibria of contemporary traditional Aboriginal society (Hiatt 1965).

It is clear that the contrast of Aboriginal culture with European is marked. Western industrial society is specialized, highly technical, and based on differential rewards in a market economy. Values are transmitted in a nuclear family and later in formal education. The emphasis is on individuation and competitive striving. Traditional Aboriginal culture on the other hand was seminomadic, improvisational, and dependent upon the immediate environment. As a consequence, to ensure the survival of the group, individual striving was subordinated to the need for social cooperation and sharing. The wider clan transcended the immediate family as a source of values; and individual demands were kept in check by a complex medico-legal system (Cawte 1974). Ultimately, the Aborigines saw themselves in continuity with, not opposed to, the nature upon which they depended. Their technological goals were, of necessity, short-term, whereas their capacity for long-term projection was shown in the ritual and kinship system. How jarring, therefore, their initial contact with a powerful culture that preaches mastery of the environment and the desirability of foresight, leadership, and individual effort—a culture that had a need to eliminate or evangelize the primitives and convert them to a belief in the dignity of labor.

In east Arnhem Land, for example, the language, the marriage system, and many of the ancient ceremonies remain. The older men who

Chapter Six

control them struggle hard against the intrusion of Western education, coca-cola values, cowboy guitar, and twist. The European adolescent fashions of yesteryear live on in strange and sometimes defiant forms, while the old men mutter ominously about the dangers of tribal incest. The young people are not so much marginal to one culture as caught between two cultures, between Christian and ancestral, individual and group-centered, technological and improvisational. They resent and fear the power of the older men; they reject and envy the whites. They may try to escape the dilemma on the hallucinatory fumes of petrol if alcohol is unavailable (Nurcombe et al. 1970). The closer industry comes, the more acute the conflict and the greater the confusion of identity.

We know but little of the culture of fringe-dwellers, the marginal people of mixed descent who live on the outskirts of country towns, who cook over open fires, sleep in one-room huts with earth floors, and seek escape in cheap wine or gambling. Their health situation, at least, is apparent: the incidence of prematurity, infant mortality, malnutrition, infestation with intestinal parasites, anemia, respiratory tract infestion, and eye and ear disease is disturbingly high. Their uncontrolled birthrate is at least twice that of the surrounding European population and so the relative proportion of races in these country towns is changing. In fact, the lack of basic biological supplies and protection amounts to a severe physical deprivation. On the other hand, we know so little about the child-rearing practices, and the values and skills explicitly and implicitly transmitted to children in the marginal situation, that we are prone to describe it too in terms of deprivation—a sociocultural deprivation (Nurcombe 1970b).

In ethnocentric comparison with the middle-class environment, the fringe-dweller's home is deprived. It functions by few rules or routines. It is virtually uncarpentered. There are no books, no pictures, few toys. Families are large—beyond the coping capacity of mothers—and there is much rivalry between the younger children for the limited supply of material goods. Verbal communication patterns are comparatively horizontal, between adult and adult or child and child, rather than vertical, from adult to child or the reverse. The distressed child is comforted with body contact or food, not words. The annoying child is cuffed or commanded, not argued or reasoned with (Grey 1969).

By middle childhood the children form their major allegiance with the peer group. As in the neotraditional setting, these large bands of age mates bring each other up, so to speak, engendering attitudes inimical to Aboriginal and European authority. By the time they reach primary school, fringe children are about one year behind their rural white counterparts in language development and about two years behind the city whites.

Using tests based on standard English, they are especially retarded in syntax, the ability to discriminate between words, the capacity to form associations between words, and the ability to express themselves (Nurcombe and Moffitt 1970). In fact they speak a dialect of English that operates by grammatical rules different from standard English, has different social conventions, and varies according to the district involved and the degree of acculturation. When they commence school they are utterly bewildered by the new environment, experience severe and sustained separation anxiety, and soon have reason to see themselves as failures. By the middle of primary school they have dropped out, effectively, although they are advanced from class to class until secondary school.

Why is this so? Are they constitutionally inferior as their white neighbors suggest? It is almost certain that they have a large admixture of allegedly superior European genes. Is their brain damaged by early protein subnutrition? Possibly, in some cases, but probably not in the majority although this conclusion must be modified in different areas. Are they sensorily deprived? Have they been exposed to a dull, sterile environment bereft of meaningful stimuli? If anything, the reverse is the case: their environment is rich, psychologically self-sufficient, full of people and events. Their experiences, however, are not *patterned* in such a way as to produce in them those structures which form the very basis of operational thought in Piaget's sense. Hypothetical abstract thinking, which Piaget holds up as the pinnacle, is not for the fringe-dweller (de Lacey 1970).

Thus, blinded by our ethnic spectacles, we see Aborigines in terms of deficit. Only recently have we begun to inquire about the nature of their dialect, their aspirations, and their self-image (Berry 1973a). We know little about their social system, about the apparently matrifocal system by which their families are organized, about the effect of this system on the relationship between marginal man and woman. We can only guess how hard it must be for them to leave a world that to the outsider is harsh but that binds its members with the ties of kinship (Beckett 1965).

It is an article of linguistic faith that no single language or dialect is more competent than another to generate word combinations in the service of communication. Theoretically, therefore, Aboriginal English is no less competent than standard English. More recent investigations have shown, however, that Aboriginal children do not use the range of syntactic transformations in dialect that the European working-class child employs in standard English (Hart 1973). Similar findings have been reported for black ghetto children in America (see chapter 3). The dialect user may have the abstract competence to express a particular sentence or phrase form but, in fact, this may seldom occur and the expression, if artificially produced, is rejected as unfamiliar or eccentric.

Chapter Six

This is an important theoretical and practical issue. What right do we have to intervene in what we perceive as cultural deprivation? What right do we have to foster transition in the traditional setting? What are the psychological and ethical implications, for example, of preschool language enrichment programs for fringe-dwelling children or bilingual tribal groups? If standard English has no linguistic advantage over dialect, why attempt to impose one upon the other?

Many white country people would reject intervention. Aborigines, they say, are hopelessly shiftless; those families that are worthwhile will improve themselves; meanwhile we should keep our hands off the rest and act as though they do not exist, except to move them on or apprehend them when they infringe the law. Many Aborigines agree in part. They reject the European and attempt to reaffirm traditional values in a search for identity.

But how can we ignore each other? By doing nothing we do something. Inevitably, the races will continue to interact and intermingle. The question of intervention can be expressed thus: How can we help the people in question to reduce the trauma of cultural impact from the majority society? How can we help them to decide, acquire, and use what they want of our culture? How can we help them attain a position where choice is possible? A position where they can pursue their own goals? Can our own society become sufficiently enlightened and diverse to contain a variety of people who have different customs but share a sense of community, however much they choose to separate? Is Australia capable of sustaining a cultural pluralism?

But the fringe child today has, and will have, no choice. Trapped by fatalism and low self-esteem, stigmatized by skin and background, drained by malnutrition and infection and bound by kinship ties, he can do little else than become what his parents were and what his white teachers and neighbors expect him to be.

Language is not only an academic problem but a central issue. Language is at the heart of cultural identity; yet without a flexible syntax and an adequate vocabulary the speaker is limited to an essentially concrete sphere of action. The aim of education should be to build on what is presented, not to replace it with what is regarded as better. Aboriginal English serves the speaker well as a restricted code (Bernstein 1961) in his family and intimate cultural group. If he wishes to acquire technical skills, however, he must have the capacity to switch into standard English as well. In doing so, he evolves the capacity for choice, a linguistic and social choice possessed in some degree by the rest of the Australian community; for all of us retain our own restricted codes but also have the capacity to switch into an elaborated, formal English when required.

If it is decided that an educational approach which stresses language is desirable, the question arises: When should it be introduced? Is it possible, for example, to build upon the dialect to begin with and then, gradually, expose the fringe child to more complex standard phrase forms? The problem is even more complex in the traditional, bilingual setting where English is a foreign language and should be introduced with care. Much more research is required on these points. The danger is that the technical language—standard English—will become not an alternative code but, rather, rejected along with the white, school authority structure; that it will become compartmented and relegated to a back shelf where it will atrophy from disuse (Williams 1971).

In the long run all these questions are academic unless the aim is for the Aboriginal people to contribute to education of their own children. In the past a great deal has been done *to* the Aborigines. Over the years a little has been done *for* them. Few have attempted to work *with* them; to help them determine their own goals. Once their opportunity for choice has developed and once they can take responsibility for their own continuing education, this kind of discussion will be an anachronism.

The Bourke preschool aims to find the most effective means of promoting the affective, language, cognitive, and perceptual-motor skills required for school adjustment. Our objectives have evolved from deliberation and negotiation with the people involved. We have found that merely exposing the child to a warm, supportive environment rich in perceptual stimulation and language models is inadequate to foster the skills required. The teaching program must be designed in such a way as to relate closely to specified objectives.

The structured program aims to foster cognitive and language competence by the direct, carefully graduated teaching of syntactic skills in standard English and by aiding the child through reinforcement and practice to apply the possibilities inherent in language to causality, classification, and logical-mathematical problems. We claim that the sense of competence derived from increasing mastery will have beneficial secondary effects in the affective domain.

The semistructured program aims to build upon the child's sensorimotor structures the language and cognitive competencies required to adapt to school. It does so by utilizing both naturally occurring and contrived experiences in a more integrative and divergent fashion than in the structured program. As in the structured program, it is assumed that an increase in self-esteem will follow a sense of mastery and achievement.

Both programs have been allied with a perceptual-motor stimulation program and complementary home-school liaison teaching that progresses along with the teaching in the preschool. An elementary school

Chapter Six

follow-through program aims to consolidate and extend the changes generated by the preschool.

The existence of the preschool is justified, fundamentally, by the fact that the Aboriginal people wanted it, have helped to frame its objectives, support the teaching techniques involved, and provide a large proportion of the staff. It is justified further by the fact that our efforts do not focus exclusively upon the child but on the family as a whole, particularly on the mother's interaction with her children. Finally, it is justified because it is not for Aborigines alone but serves the white community as well. The two ethnic groups in Bourke are interdependent, something of which both are aware. It remains to be seen to what degree Aboriginal children will wish to assimilate, to separate, or to integrate. The preschool aims to help them make that choice.

CHAPTER 7
POTENTIAL, COMPETENCE, AND PERFORMANCE— A CONCEPTUAL FRAMEWORK

Our brains are a cemetery of words. There is no way except with inner vision to explain how you feel. Thoughtless. Be careful or you will think with words. That's why I can do ballet. I can't write, I can't even spell. I am made in silence. As soon as I start speaking I stop seeing.

George Balanchine

FROM OBSERVATION TO THEORY

This chapter introduces a change of topic: from a consideration of empirical research findings to the elaboration of a conceptual model. In the words of Noam Chomsky (1968:63):

> Psychology conceived as behavioral science has been concerned with behavior and acquisition or control of behavior. It has no concept corresponding to "competence" in the sense in which competence is characterized by a generative grammar. The theory of learning has limited itself to a narrow and surely inadequate concept of what is learned—namely a system of stimulus-response connections, a network of associations, a repertoire of behavioral items, a habit hierarchy, or a system of dispositions to respond in a particular way under specifiable stimulus conditions....
> What is necessary, in addition to the concept of behavior and learning, is a concept of what is learned—a notion of competence—that lies beyond the conceptual limits of behaviorist psychological theory.

CHAPTER SEVEN

Elsewhere Chomsky (1967:397) elaborates:

> It is quite obvious that ... a person with command of a language has in some way internalized the system of rules that determine both the phonetic shape of the sentence and its intrinsic semantic content—that he has developed ... *linguistic competence*. However, it is equally clear that the actual observed use of language—actual *performance*—does not simply reflect the intrinsic sound-meaning connections established by the system of rules.... Extra-linguistic beliefs concerning the speaker and the situation play a fundamental role in determining how speech is produced, identified, and understood.

These generative comments will be taken as the basis from which a theory of human competence is derived. The elements of such a theory have already been propounded, piecemeal, by a number of people. In this chapter an attempt will be made to show how their work can be integrated to form a broad conceptual framework.

Just as a nation's policies are more likely to be effective—or, at least, internally less disruptive—if based on communally shared principles and values, so technical innovations in the field of education, for example, are more likely to be effective, generative, and replicable if they are based on a communicable conceptual framework. Systematic application of theory has the potential for broadening it, for confirming, sharpening, or contraverting a conceptual framework, and for associating the emotional, the interpersonal, and the cognitive in a way that is all too often avoided in contemporary system-building.

The conceptual framework outlined in this chapter was introduced at the end of chapter 1 in the form of a set of terms and definitions that have been employed in later sections of the book. These terms form the basis of the sequential organization of this chapter:

1. Potential
2. Realization
3. Competence
4. Expression and performance
5. Assessment and evaluation

The reader is asked to view this essay as a schematic road map of the competing and complementary theories in the field of the development and expression of cognitive competence, a road map that is concerned, particularly, with the relationship of language to thought.

POTENTIAL

THE BIOLOGICAL RUDIMENTS OF COGNITION

We have evolved as bipedal, binocular, manually dexterous, terrestrial, omnivorous primates who live in small cooperative groups.

We form strong pair-bonds and live collectively in such a way as to offer protection to our children, who are expelled from the uterus in a state of marked immaturity. Selective evolution has determined that we, beyond all other animals, should have developed, to a high degree, the ability to use tools and to communicate with our own species. It is no coincidence that the areas of the brain for dominant hand and expressive speech are approximated and lateralized in the human brain.

We have thus evolved biologically based, universal, species-specific, genetically determined potentials in the areas of tool use and communication (see Figure 7.1). Provided we are born and remain physically intact, and provided an average expectable environment furnishes us with timely and appropriate stimulation, these potentials will develop.

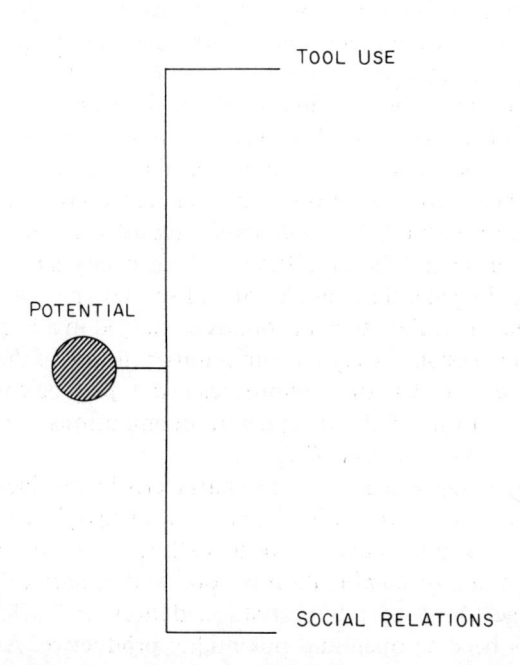

FIGURE 7.1 Potential: tool use and social relations

The potential for communication involves the reception and expression of gestural and other extralinguistic phenomena. It includes the potential for language, which has come to serve as a flexible and sophisticated vehicle for communication with others of the species. Language can also be exploited to facilitate thought, an internalized speech that tags cognitive processes and frees us from reliance on the immediately perceptual world. How is this so?

Chapter Seven

We share with other primates a complex social organization. We are distinguished from them firstly by the extent to which we have developed language to foster communication and bequeath our culture to our children and secondly by the extent to which we have augmented our physical resources by the carriage, use, and manufacture of tools and weapons. Hockett (1960) and Hockett and Ascher (1964) have discussed the phyletic origins of human speech and the peculiar features that distinguish it from the communication of other primates and animals, such as bees, fish, and birds. Among these features the following may be mentioned: semanticity, arbitrariness, displacement, productivity, transmission by tradition, and duality. *Semanticity* refers to the relatively fixed relation between a word (for example, *salt*) and its referent (a white granular substance). *Arbitrariness* refers to the fact that the word *salt*, for example, is itself nongranular and the word-referent tie has no apparent logical basis. Semanticity and arbitrariness apply to the call signals of other primates, but we are unique in our extraordinary capacity for *displacement*, for speaking or thinking about things that are remote in space or time. Human speech is also essentially *productive*; anyone can invent from a finite stock of words a comprehensible sentence the like of which has never been uttered before. The detailed conventions of a specific language are learned, by *traditional transmission*, in an interpersonal context during childhood, although the capacity and tendency to acquire language in general are universal and species-specific. Finally, the phonemes—the particular stock of sounds employed in a language— are restricted but the morphemes or meaning-units built out of the sounds are enormously extensive. The three phonemes *c*, *a*, *t*, may be combined, meaningfully, in the form of the morphemic permutations *cat*, *act*, or *tack*. This attribute is known as *duality*.

Hockett has suggested that the characteristic productivity of human language derived, originally, from a *blending* of call signals. Chimpanzees, for example, have separate calls for "food" and for "danger." The blending or combination of food and danger calls could convey the message "food here but situation dangerous." Closed call signals would thus become open and potentially productive. At a later stage, perhaps, the facial and gestural mimesis of hominoids could be supplemented by the explicit social utterances of hominid speech. Speech would then serve both near and distant communication.

Hockett proposes that the displacement function of language was intimately linked with the evolution of tools. Other animals have been observed to use tools—the chimpanzee, for example, will make a wad of leaves to soak up drinking water (van Lawick-Goodall 1971). Only humans, however, will carry tools, or make tools to make tools and weapons, or combine two disparate tools to make a third. A man will carry a hand axe to make a spear or combine a stick and an axe-head to increase the arc and power of his blows. To do so he must assume a distance from the perceptual object and make, retain, and apply an abstract plan that will govern his later actions.

The intimate association between tools, communication, and language is illustrated in Figures 7.1, 7.2, and 7.3. We have evolved universal, species-specific propensities for tool use and social relations (Figure 7.1). Figure 7.2 shows how language has greatly facilitated both functions. Language extends the range, precision, and complexity of face-to-face communication. It has also rendered enormously flexible the processes underlying tool manufacture and use, since it enables the user to maintain distance from the immediately perceptible object and to construct and store cognitive plans that can be recovered and applied to new contingencies. These plans, maps, or schemata can be modified, combined, superordinated, or subdivided to meet new problems. The distinctive function of language is this: to facilitate the elaboration, combination, superordination, and subordination of hierarchical schemata.

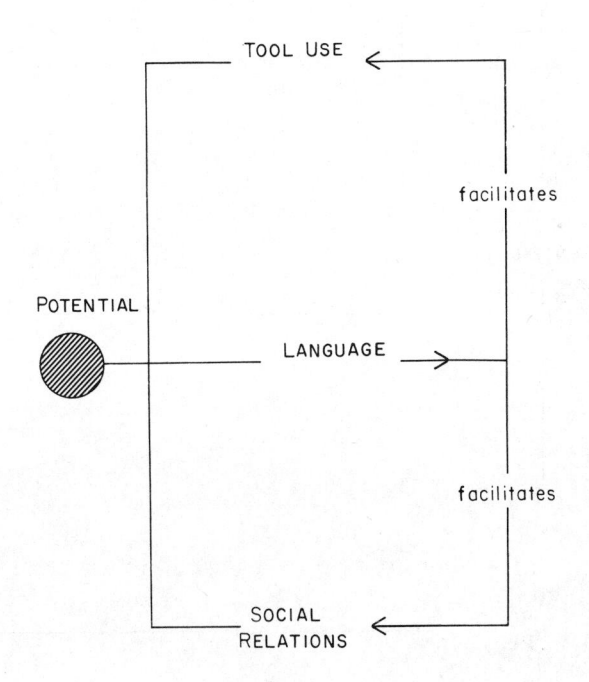

FIGURE 7.2 Basic schema: language, tool use, and social relations

CHAPTER SEVEN

    The means by which language facilitates tool manufacture and use is shown in Figure 7.3. Tool use evolves from biological rudiments, the behavioral manifestations of which are observable in early childhood. The infant's ability to interpret sensation, to blend and integrate percepts from different sensory channels, to control movement, and to orient in space begin to develop out of primordial schemata that operate from

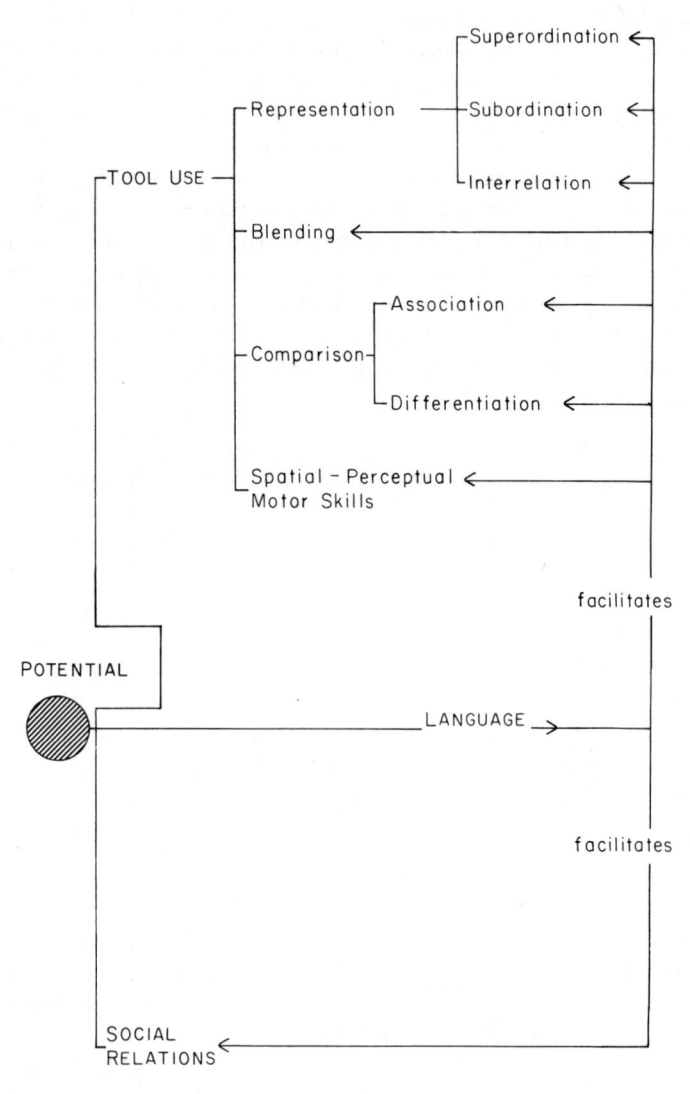

FIGURE 7.3 Extended schema: language, tool use, and social relations

194

birth. These schemata form the *sensorimotor intelligence* that Piaget describes as dominant in the first eighteen months of life. The use of tools requires such skills together with the ability to develop complex internal cognitive maps of an area of operation.

We are also born with a tendency to compare perceptions— with a comparator, as it were. We can thus establish whether perceptual objects are identical, alike, or different by *association* and *differentiation*, processes that can be rendered greatly more powerful by the labeling and attributive functions of language (Lenneberg 1967). Piaget describes differentiation as *recognitory assimilation*, the means by which the actor discriminates between objects and between actions-on-objects. Allied with this, as though on the other side of a coin, is *generalizing assimilation*, the means by which the actor establishes the identity and similarity of action objects. The infant, also, develops the capacity to blend perceptions from different modalities and to articulate and integrate his actions in the service of greater mastery of the perceptual world.

At the end of the sensorimotor stage, in the second year, children develop the potential to re-present the world to themselves, to picture things and events and, to some extent, follow them through. At first, representation is tied to perceptible objects but, gradually, children distance themselves until they can think about objects, events, or actions-on-objects in the absence of these phenomena. Out of association, differentiation, and representation grow interrelation (reciprocal assimilation), classification, and categorial thinking. Children develop *symbols* that are distinguished from their referents. They are able to *transform* representations, to manipulate, superordinate, and subdivide their associations and, gradually, to discover and learn the invariances of objects, time, space, and causality.

These potentials—perception, spatial skill, motor control, differentiation, association, blending, representation, and interrelation—used in combination, are fundamental to the discovery, choice, manufacture, and use of tools and weapons. Language, which tends to tag functions rather than perceptible features, has become the distinctive facilitant of these processes. One can picture an early hunter representing to himself, partly in imagery and partly in words, his need of a thing-to-cut-wood-or-attack-enemies. To that end, with the representation fixed, perhaps, by a function word (*axe*), he searches until he discriminates the most suitable large stone for this purpose and chips away a cutting surface on one side. Words may help him to maintain the correct sequence of motor movements in this operation. Eventually, his perceptual-spatial experience makes him aware that the wider the arc in which the axe-head is swung, the more powerful the blow. The hafted axe is discovered;

blade and handle are interrelated. Could it be that the emphasis of language on function (*What can I find to do the job? How can I improve it?*) is the key to such an invention? That language was shaped by creative function and, in turn, directed function and fixed it for later retrieval?

Thus description of the child's potentials inevitably leads to a description of his competence. Competence is the outcome of a spiral interaction between innate tendency, environmental stimulation, and learning.

THE DEVELOPMENT AND FUNCTION OF LANGUAGE

Pavlovian, Hullian, or Skinnerian concepts of learning cannot account for the rapid unfolding of innate abilities in the first five years. The acquisition of language remains a particular mystery.[1] Between the age of eighteen months and five years children develop the capacity to generate an infinite number of sentences according to the rules of grammar. It appears that they create their own grammar, spontaneously, in this sensitive period (Lenneberg 1967) by passing the corpus of utterances to which they are exposed through what McNeill (1966) calls a *language acquisition device*. Children form "hypotheses" on the basis of their scanning of the coherent organization of input and then "test" these hypotheses by the effect of their language productions on the environment. The system of transformations they learn is a highly economic, essentially abstract, method of dealing with representations. McNeill suggests that language and cognitive systems developed phylogenetically out of distinct primordial nuclei but, at some point of evolution, were brought into alignment by making language abstract at those points where cognition is abstract. Some controversy has arisen over the degree to which language structures are innate (Sinclair-De-Zwart 1969), but it is clear that Skinnerian S-R theory (Skinner 1957) is not able to cope with the problem of acquisition of competence (Chomsky 1959). Both Piaget and Chomsky emphasize the creative aspect of speech, but Piagetians (Sinclair-De-Zwart 1969) tie language, initially, to sensorimotor experience and consider that the coordination of sensorimotor schemata is a precondition for language acquisition. Thus language is described as growing out of thought rather than the reverse.

Whatever its origins, language is a potential powerhouse (Sapir 1921) that may—or may not—be intensively exploited by a culture in

[1]. Reinforcement theory is more applicable to what Chomsky calls performance. The speaker learns, by social reinforcement, the conventional strategies for expressing competence in different contexts; when, and to whom, for example, it is appropriate to say *Hi, Hullo, Good day,* or *'Morning*.

the service of various kinds of conceptual thought. Western technological cultures place a high value on this capacity. How is it manifest?

Language may play a part in higher-level spatial abilities. The man who exercises a complex skill may talk to himself to facilitate the following of a detailed sequence. The airplane pilot, for example, checks aloud his instruments before takeoff. The navigator conceptualizes and transforms the intricate details of time, tide, wind, speed, and geographical detail in the form of mathematical symbols and two-dimensional representational maps. More perceptually tied sensorimotor skills, on the other hand, are probably largely independent of language—driving a car, for example.

Words are important in the process of differentiation and association. Lenneberg (1967) considers that these cognitive processes are biologically fundamental and that language grows out of and facilitates them. The perception and production of language can be thought of as an especially efficient kind of categorization process, one that includes the subsuming of narrow categories under more comprehensive ones and the subdivision of comprehensive categories into more specific ones. The child learns, for example, that the four-legged objects that people sit on are called *chairs*, and that chairs can be made of wood or plastic and can be big or small, hard or soft. Language tags the categorization process. *Naming* is dynamic; it is both a method and a process.

Sometime in the second year the child develops the capacity to switch from sensorimotor to representational thought. This ability is expressed by the growth of symbolization, of which language is one example. The integral functioning of language in this process is in dispute. Sigel (1968b) adopts an intermediate position. He considers representation to be a kind of distancing—of subjective from objective, of self from others, and of ideas from actions. Technological societies place great emphasis on distancing and on different codes of representation. Sigel suggests that they do so by providing, during the socialization of their children, relatively ordered, structured environments; a linguistic input containing a high frequency of words denoting space, distance, and time past, present, and future; and achieving role-models who demonstrate the relevance and pragmatic value of distancing.

As children abstract themselves from the perceptible world (while, at the same time, operating upon it), they form interrelationships between representations. They note that distinct objects have common properties (redness, bigness, hardness) or common functions (things-to-eat). Categories may also be interrelated, in terms of time, space, or causality, by morphemes that have no function but to indicate such

Chapter Seven

abstract relationships (such as: *-ed, on, because*), semantic markers that are in themselves the expression of categorization processes (Lenneberg 1967).

To what degree is language the mere expression of, or the essential vehicle of, thought? Early workers like Sapir (1921) saw language and thought as virtually synonymous. Among contemporary psychologists, Bruner (Bruner, Olver, and Greenfield 1966) represents one theoretical pole: Language is integral to thought. Piaget (1970) and Furth (1970) adopt another, not completely polarized, position: Language grows out of, is associated with, but is not fundamental to, thinking.

Bruner (Bruner et al. 1966) proposes that representation be considered in terms of strategy and objective. The three strategies of representation are enactive, iconic, and symbolic; the three respective objectives are doing (action), sensing (description), and symbolizing (the derivation of abstract relations).

Enactive representations originate in sensorimotor activity. They are guided initially by specific action-schemata that are irreversible. The baby in the high chair who drops a ball and then goes through the motions of dropping it again and again shows a kind of perceptual representation that is fused with the action itself.

The *iconic* mode frees image from action by means of concrete internal imagery; but the utility of the imagery is limited because it is rigid, inextricable from the particular context to which it applies, egocentric, and susceptible to distortion by affect. It is both inflexible and excessively mobile, characteristics illustrated by psychoanalytic descriptions of the *primary process*, which is manifest, for example, in dreaming.

The *symbolic* mode, according to Bruner, is virtually synonymous with the use of language. Language revolutionizes cognition because it is flexible, manipulable, and inferential. It achieves a major reduction in cognitive load because of the possibility of superordinate generalization and because of the generative power of superordinate concepts. Language-based categorization chops up information into simpler forms, connects it with the rules of grouping already structured, and maximizes the possibility of combinatorial operations. Bruner traces analogies between the categories and hierarchies of syntax and the superordination of symbolic thought. Symbols are characterized by their semantic nature, arbitrariness, productivity, discreteness, distance from the objects or events represented, and their categoriality. The potential of words and syntax for thought is not fully harnessed until after the age of six years, when children become fully operational and apply the rules of syntax to the world as they have learned to do to language. Bruner points out, however, that not all cultures exploit the possibilities of language to the same degree. The culture may emphasize modes of representation that are predominantly iconic and concrete. Thus, in order to harness language fully as an instrument of thought, children must bring their experience under the control of structural principles that are, in some way, related to the structural principles of syntax. To do so they may need the support of the special training offered by formal education. The organization of experience must first develop to include, and to align with, the logical relations that the deep structures and transformational rules of language convey. This argument is of great relevance to the current controversy about cultural disadvantage, dialect differences, and language deficits which has already been discussed in chapter 4.

Bruner describes *evolution by prosthesis*. Homo sapiens has developed *implement systems* of three types: (1) amplifiers of motor capacity (such as tools and weapons); (2) amplifiers of sensory capacity (such as telescopes and radios); and (3) amplifiers of ratiocinative capacity (such as language and computers). We depend for survival on the transmission of acquired characteristics from the culture pool as well as inheritance from the gene pool. The methods of transmitting culture, therefore, are of crucial importance.

Herriot (1970) suggests that the stages of operational thinking described by Piaget and Bruner may be related to short-term memory and its gradual increase with age. The retention of the necessary criteria for problem-solving, and the functioning of semantic and syntactic systems, are affected by memory. The hierarchical organization of the memory-retrieval system represents a major gain in efficiency; and language, at that point, would be a highly useful mode of representation.

The views of Bruner have some similarity to Russian concepts of language and cognition (Pavlov 1927). In Pavlovian theory, language is a "second-signal system" in contrast to the "first-signal system"—all the physical stimuli to which animals and man respond. In humans the symbolic second-order system is highly developed. The laws of classical conditioning do not apply to the second system since words can control behavior without intermediate conditioning. Vygotsky (1962) considered that thought and speech have different origins but at a certain point intersect, speech becoming rational and thought verbal. Thought is a kind of speech which is highly abbreviated and consists mostly of predicates. This *egocentric speech* has the function of self-guidance. With development, egocentric speech becomes completely internalized—an inner speech—whereas at first it is not completely differentiated from socialized speech. Luria (1959) considers that language has a directive function. The verbal second-order signal system acts as an intention that programs motor acts. It has four functions: communicative, nominative (direct reference), semantic (conceptual), and regulating (directing sequences of behavior). When fully developed, it makes possible the production of novel behavior sequences without prior practice or conditioning. At first, speech is an impulsive regulator of behavior; but, later, discriminatory semantic control is evident.

Piaget (1968, 1970)[2] does not think language has a primary place in the development of cognition. Intellectual operations involve acting upon—manipulating—things and transforming them in such a way as to construct, internally, stable principles about the physical world, for example in the form of categorization and conservation. This "decentering," or moving away from the egocentric, allows the operator to think in a more relative and reversible way. For example: If A is bigger than B, and B is bigger than C, then C is smaller than A.) The genetic roots of operative thinking are not in language but emerge in the preverbal sensorimotor period. The development of representational thought—the ability to think about an object in its absence—is coincident with the emergence of language but the relationship is noncausal; both are correlates of a more general symbolic process that evolves in the second year. Thought is rooted in action, not language. Language is a symptom of—not a cause of—representation and later operativity.

Piaget uses the terms *signal*, *symbol*, and *sign* in an idiosyncratic way. In the earliest stages signals are external stimuli to which the individual has been conditioned to respond. This process involves no representation, since the signal and the response are fused and the signal, so to speak, is inseparable from the physical stimulus itself. After representational thought has evolved, it is served by two types of signifier: symbols and signs. *Symbols* are personal and often—but not necessarily—idiosyncratic internal representations that have a configurative link with the object or event signified. The use of the cross to symbolize Christ is an example of a socially validated symbol; whereas the German chemist Kekulé's fantastic creative imagery about the configuration of the benzene molecule—a snake eating its own tail—is an example of a personal symbol. *Signs* refer to words that are socially validated but purely arbitrary signifiers. There is no figurative connection between the word *cat* and the animal itself; the sign *cat* signifies the physical object, and the user clearly distinguishes sign from significate, word from referent.

Piaget considers that signs and symbols have meaning only insofar as they are rooted in deeper operative structures. He has noted certain similarities between his own structural theory and that of Chomsky. Piaget sees intellectual development as moving in three interlocked

---

2. See also Furth (1970) and Sinclair-De-Zwart (1969).

directions: (1) from concrete and particular to general and abstract; (2) from ego-centered to objective and relative; and (3) from static to dynamic and reversible. In the more mature *decentered* state the subject can maintain a distance between objective reality and his or her own perception of and affective involvement in that reality. Piaget thus reflects the high value placed on a disembodiment of intellectual functioning characteristic of Western psychological thinking (Irvine 1969a), of a nature that may be at odds with the kind of thinking valued in other cultures (Turner 1973). At the heart of the theory is the postulate of *structures*: relatively enduring operative dispositions to comprehend and deal with the world—self-regulating, dynamic systems of reversible transformations which form totalities and which are themselves capable of superordinate interrelation or subordinate specification. Structures consist of internal reversible dispositions to operate that are based on principles of invariance and conservation. These principles fixate the immutable aspects of a reversible relationship. For example, the child who, it can be inferred, has developed an operational structure to do with conservation of quantity is aware that: if a volume of water is poured from a short, wide glass into a tall narrow glass, although its perceptible qualities alter, the volume remains unchanged.

According to Piaget, language is not a sufficient condition for the development of operational structures, either concrete or formal. Structures are "constructed" out of interaction with—operation on—the environment. *Construction* is the result of an adaptive interaction between preexistent structures or schemata (primitive, irreversible, sensorimotor organizations) and the objective world. The internal system, seeking equilibrium, must accommodate to the demands of the environment and incorporate these accommodations into its structure in order to meet future contingencies. The organism attempts to assimilate new objects, new events, according to its preexistent structures. If it cannot do so, the structures must change and accommodate to the novelty. *Assimilation* tries to bring the environment in line with preexistent structure; *accommodation* alters structure in accordance with novel environmental demands. The aim is to find *equilibrium*. If there is a mismatch between internal structure and objective reality, equilibration activates accommodation.[3]

Experiments with the deaf (Furth 1970) have shown that children without a developed language are capable of learning logic and conser-

---

3. Provided the discrepancy is not such as to provoke a fear reaction, as in the phenomenon of stranger anxiety in the second half of the first year of life (Kagan 1971). In this phenomenon the discrepancy between the face of a stranger and that of a familiar person evokes distress.

vation. Sinclair-De-Zwart (1969) noted that children who had already learned to conserve quantity tended to use comparative and coordinated dimensional terms (*This glass is taller and thinner than that glass*). Nonconservers, on the other hand, used absolute, one-dimensional polarities (*This glass is big; that glass is small*). An attempt to teach nonconservers to use comparatives and coordinated dimensional words did not result in a significant increase in the number who learned to conserve. The conclusions drawn from this research are complex. It appears that operational thinking and linguistic development parallel each other. Appropriate lexical items are learned in the preoperational period. Coordinated syntactic forms are understood earlier but are employed only after operational thinking has begun. Verbal training may aid the already operational child to direct his attention to pertinent aspects of the perceptual array and of the problem as a whole, but it will not, ipso facto, lead to the acquisition of operations. Language therefore is not the source of logic; logic structures language.

Piaget elaborates the concepts of assimilation and accommodation further by linking them with two ways of knowing the world: figurative and operative. When operational thought has developed, one can speak of the subject as knowing an object in two ways. A girl may perceive the configuration of a ball and recognize it. One cannot, however, infer the level of her knowledge of the ball unless one knows to what operational structure her figurative identification is assimilated. At an advanced level of representation, in parallel with her use of a consensually validated sign (the word *ball*), she may identify a two-dimensional stereotyped symbol as *ball* and solve problems about balls that are presented to her in purely representational terms (what are the physical principles underlying the swerve of a spun baseball?). In Furth's terms, the meaning of a symbol or a sign resides in the underlying operative structures of which the symbol or sign is an expression at that point of time. The meaning of my use of *ball* will vary with the operational processes I am using at any moment. Representation, strictly speaking, is figurative knowing and becomes symbolic only through assimilation to operational structures. Operative and figurative knowing are therefore linked in the same way as accommodation and assimilation.

What, then, is the function of language in cognition? Is it no more than an expression of, rather than a facilitant or *progenitor* of, logical thought? Piaget's answer is ambiguous, if not ambivalent. Language and thought are different faces of a coin; their distinction is a conceptual artefact. The representative aspect of language is figurative; the meaning of language involves operational thought. The crucial question, therefore, concerns the interrelation of language and operative structures. The development of operative thought, in one sense, depends upon *overcoming* language. Language may actually hinder thought. Is it possible, on the other hand, that once operational structures have developed (independent of—or even in spite of—language), language could "challenge" thought and facilitate the evolution of logical operations? Piaget concedes this possibility, but he reiterates that language, although it may stimulate intellectual growth, is not the primary source of that growth. He points out that the implicit knowledge of syntactic rules achieved by four to five years is attained long before formal logical operations. (Formal, logical operative thinking, involving induction, deduction, and the consideration of the merely possible in hypothetical form, is not attained until after eleven years of age, if at all.) Only after formal, abstract, logical operations have been attained does language appear to come into its own as the tool of propositional, hypothetical thought. Bruner, in contrast, points to language as the cornerstone of thought in the earlier period of concrete operations.

SUMMARY

Homo sapiens has evolved innate, genetically determined, biologically based potentials. The potentials that distinguish us most particularly are in the areas of social relations, language, and the use of tools. Underlying the use of tools are sensorimotor potentials and the tendency to differentiate, associate, and blend objects and events; to re-present these objects to the self even in their absence; and to conceive of interrelations, subordinations, and superordinations between the representations. Language can be exploited, firstly, to facilitate social relations and, secondly, in the service of the functions that underlie the use of tools. The degree to which language is the progenitor, the facilitant, or the mere expression of operational and representational thought is controversial; but its relevance at least for formal, abstract logic is undisputed. It has become the distinctive facilitant of hierarchical thinking, a particularly economic and powerful way of organizing knowledge and of orienting toward technological problems.

REALIZATION

How are the potentials realized? Three major factors influence realization: maturation, equilibration, environment. Realization results from an interaction between biological tendencies toward maturation and equilibration, on the one hand, and the pressure of the environment on the other. Figure 7.4 illustrates how internal schemata develop into more stable structures diachronically—over time. They do so as a result

CHAPTER SEVEN

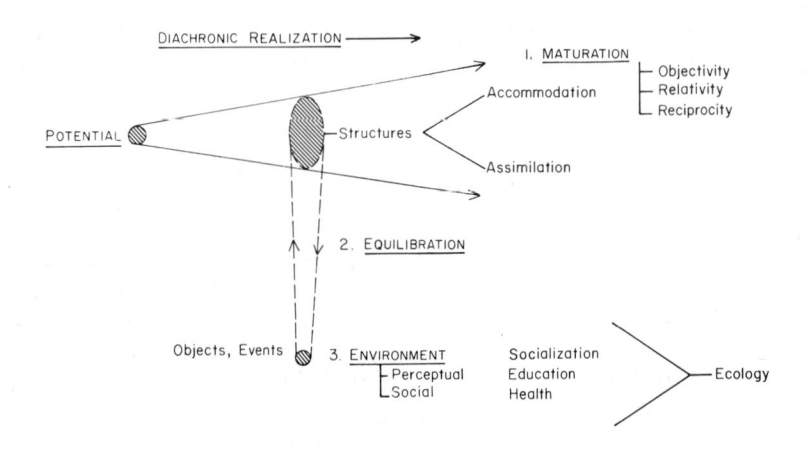

FIGURE 7.4   Realization

of maturation and of an equilibrated interaction with environmental objects and events, provided the developing organism is protected from the damaging effects of disease, trauma, or subnutrition (as discussed in chapter 3). The environment furnishes objects and social events appropriate to the child's level of development. In response to long-prevailing ecological pressures, the society educates children by fostering in them skills which are adaptive in that social and physical environment. Diachronic maturation and equilibration—through accommodation to and assimilation of objects and events in the perceptual and social environment—proceed in the direction of increasing objectivity, relativity, and interpersonal reciprocity. Children thus gain intellectual distance from the world, become aware of the graduations between polarities, and appreciate the point of view of those with whom they interact.

MATURATION

The physically intact organism has a genetically determined tendency to interact with the environment and mature. In the case of the central nervous system, maturation involves (1) the multiplication of nerve cells, which probably ceases during the first year after birth if not earlier (Cheek, Holts, and Mellits 1973; Winick 1969); (2) the proliferation of dendritic connections and synapses between neurons; (3) the proliferation of neuroglia (nervous connective tissue); and (4) the myelination of the sheaths of neuronal axons.

Physical and neurological maturation are paralleled by cognitive growth. Piaget, for example, describes cognitive development as passing through invariant stages: sensorimotor (0–2 years), preconceptual (2–4 years), intuitive (4–7 years), concrete operational (7–11 years), and formal operational. It appears that the sequence of stages is invariant, although the time at which each stage is reached may vary between individuals or cultures, while in some cultures the terminal stage of formal operations may not be reached (Dasen 1973). The latter observation strongly suggests that some cultures, in comparison to others, "push" development more in the direction of abstract thinking (Cole et al. 1971) although there could be no culture in which abstract thought is absent.

Maturation moves in the direction of greater *decentration*: that is, toward objectivity, relativity, and reciprocity. The individual becomes able to distinguish between subject and object, self and others, action and object, fantasy and action, signifier and significate. He can then take a relative stance toward phenomena previously interpreted absolutely and, in a kind of social reversibility, put himself in another's shoes, so to speak, in order to understand a different viewpoint from his own.

EQUILIBRATION

The fundamental cognitive process that underlies maturation is called *equilibration*. External stimuli are assimilated to the deep structures or schemata that form the basis of knowing. If the deep structures or schemata cannot accommodate to the new input, then disequilibrium arises and the system attempts to reequilibrate. The whole system of processes is called *adaptation*. Structures accommodate by association, differentiation, and interrelation. If preexistent structures cannot accommodate the novel stimulus—if there is a mismatch between input and structure—new structures will form and interrelate. Superordinate and subordinate structures are elaborated. These internal processes underlie the differentiation, grouping, discovery of new relations, categorization, and operational thinking manifest in behavior and discussed in the previous section.

It is important to realize that the system propounded by Piaget is not homeostatic. The organism actively seeks input (*aliment*) and attempts to accommodate novelties into its structures, provided they are not too discrepant or fearsome. If the structures can accommodate them (for example, if the baby can throw a golf ball or a ping-pong ball), or if reequilibration allows comprehension of the input at a new level, the individual will experience functional pleasure. Assimilation and accommodation, arousal and tension-reduction, are seen as in dynamic balance, within certain limits.

ENVIRONMENT

The environment provides the objects that the individual, guided by his structures, acts upon: the stimuli that activate equilibration and cognitive growth. This, in turn, provides the fuel for maturation. The stimuli with which the individual interacts are inanimate and perceptual (the balls, blocks, toys, and household objects that fascinate small children); animate, nonhuman (cats, dogs); linguistic (the speech utterances to which the child is exposed); and social (the significant people in the child's environment). These categories are not exclusive. The child may interact with a loving parent over an object through the medium of speech, thus combining inanimate, linguistic, and social perceptions. It is likely that learning takes place more readily in the setting of such a relationship. Cultures vary, however, in the degree to which socialization learning is made explicit.

Bruner (Bruner, Olver, and Greenfield 1966) and Cole et al. (1971) suggest that in Kpelle and Bushman societies, technological learning is largely implicit. The children learn (*in situ*) by direct association with, and imitation of, the significant adults with whom they live. There is little explicit, self-conscious teaching. Children vigorously interact. Much information is transmitted via play in the peer group; but, in general, learning is an extralinguistic matter, making it difficult for those of the tribe to describe their skills. Verbal representation may not consistently support tool use as suggested in the previous section on potential, unless the culture emphasizes explicit, verbal teaching during socialization.

The child exposed to a variety of geometric forms in a carpentered world may have an advantage over a child who has not been so exposed, in regard to the development of logical-mathematical structures. The child whose interaction with significant adults includes a rich verbal stimulation, particularly about objects or events at a distance from the events or in the absence of the objects, is likely to develop a more complex, precise, and flexible syntax. This, in turn, may form a basis for—or at least facilitate—operational thought (Hess and Shipman 1965). Formal education in the Western mode places high value on language skills; hence the very important role of the verbal-educational factor in cross-cultural analyses of scholastic and cognitive abilities (Vernon 1969). In any culture, some socializing, educational practices are implicit and others explicit. The degree of explicitness and the nature of that which is made explicit will vary between cultures. Those matters which a culture implicitly or explicitly transmits to the young depend, ultimately, on the ecological pressures upon that society. Berry (1971) describes this approach as one of *ecological functionalism*. The individual interacts with his environment, using technology to transform his physical surroundings. Culture, particularly language and technology, is defined as the group's general mode of adaptation to prevailing ecological pressures. It can also function as a filter of ecological stimuli. Socialization, particularly in subsistence societies, plays a dominant role in shaping behavior adaptive to ecological pressure.

In a four-culture comparison study, Berry predicted that hunting people, in contrast to agricultural people, would have the following characteristics: highly developed visual discrimination and spatial skills; language containing a high number of spatial concepts; shared, rather than specialized, arts and crafts; and socialization practices emphasizing independence rather than obedience. He then compared four societies, one hunting, one agricultural, and two intermediate. All hypotheses were supported. Berry's conclusion was that the relationships between ecological factors, on the one hand, and perceptual, linguistic, technological, and socialization variables on the other, seem to covary in a systematic way. Witkin (1967) and Dawson (1967) have also discussed the interrelation between socialization practice and adult cognitive style. Cultures that emphasize strictness and obedience in child-rearing produce adults who are more field-dependent, that is, more prone to respond to the perceptual field as a whole. This tendency is in contrast to independence-fostering cultures which tend to produce field-independent adults who respond to the perceptual field in a more analytic, discriminatory way. It was Berry, however, who introduced the concept of ecological pressure as the integrating factor that ties together child-rearing practice and dominant cognitive style. Agricultural societies, characterized by high food accumulation, emphasize responsibility and obedience; hunting societies, characterized by low food accumulation, emphasize independence and achievement (Barry, Child, and Bacon 1959).

Piaget (Flavell 1963) describes the influence of affect on behavior as a energetic force and, like intellectual life, a continued adaptation. Feelings express the interest and value given to actions, of which intelligence provides the structure. Affective schemata involve actions toward persons and their associated feeling-tones. Affect and cognition are inseparable in real life. Thus, in accord with representation and decentration, affective structures become separable from their immediate interpersonal-action connotation and superordinate structures evolve that concern values, attitudes, and aspirations.

Chapter Seven

Within the same culture, the affective structures of individuals may vary. In Western society, the middle class tends to transmit strong needs to achieve. Thus cognitive performance, particularly that related to competitive success in school, is highly valued and carries connotations of pleasing and receiving praise. Some children incorporate these values and go on to express them in the form of a persistently high achievement drive toward scholastic success (or toward physical competition in sports or artistic success, to take examples from other fields of endeavor). Other children resist parental pressures that are perceived as excessive, unfair, or based not on love but on the need for the child to fulfill something the parents themselves have lacked. Such a child may develop persistent opposition toward authority figures who are perceived as demanding, unreasonable, and intrusive.

Just as the intellectual structures of earlier stages of development may never be completely superseded and may underlie or replace more mature thinking in times of stress (*regression*), so the less rational, highly personal, iconic affective schemata of early life may revive to dominate regressive mental life in dreams or during psychological disorder. The affects of anxiety, depression, or despair, which may be rooted in earlier or current psychic threats to attachment schemata (Bowlby 1968), characteristically invade and disrupt the function of operational structures, producing a drop-off in school performance, poor concentration, and erratic classroom behavior.

It is a fair criticism of Piaget to point out that, in his preoccupation with epistemology, he has neglected the influence of figurative thought and affect on everyday human behavior. Even Einstein functioned at a formal operational level only for limited periods; controlled regression with visual imagery illuminated his problems and contributed to his creativity (see Ghiselin 1955).

Wolff (1960) suggests that there is a potential link between Erikson's concept of *organ* or *zonal* modes and Piaget's congenital schemata. The zonal modes can be considered as aprioristic, patterned sensorimotor schemata concerned with the discharge or building-up of tension in relation to drive states. The whole issue of the interrelation between psychoanalytic and Piagetian developmental theory is potentially fruitful for further study.

MODAL CULTURAL THEMES AND SOCIALIZATION

Although the concept of *modal personality* has fallen into some disrepute, it is still possible to point to motivating forces that differ in their emphasis between different cultures. In a projective test study[4] of a northern Australian tribal group, for example, I could find no evidence of themes relating to a need for achievement: that is, for individual competitive success following striving. On the other hand there were repeated and almost universal references to the fear of ridicule and being shamed in front of the group, and the fear of loss of loved ones by death or separation. Themes of being left alone, lost, hungry, physically ill, and of being sad or crying as a result of separation, death, or illness of kin were predominant, even among adolescent boys who might have been expected to be more circumspect about expressing such emotions. These projective themes are in accord with the anthropological description of Aboriginal society as organized on collateral rather than hierarchical or individual lines. The need to foster and sustain affiliative ties to clan members has a clear survival value for both individual and group in a nomadic, hunting, subsistence society.

The socialization practices of a culture—particularly the interaction between parent and child and, later, between peers—will indicate the kinds of cognitive behavior that are valued: for example, a sense of rhythm, the knowledge of ritual, visual-perceptual acuity, rapid reaction time, knowledge of traditional agricultural practice, artistic skill, or logical-mathematical reasoning. The culture will also convey the dominant motives and affective states that accompany the learning or exercise of each cognitive skill. An Aboriginal boy may learn to dance well, for example, by identification with adults and out of a need to avoid the ridicule he gets if he is clumsy; but he may also do so in order to attract the admiration of the group for the masculine grace of a star performer.

It is clear that the formal operational logic, stripped of affect and contextual significance, that Piaget regards as the pinnacle of cognition is a disembodied abstraction of but incomplete relevance even in Western culture. It appears to be closely tied to formal education. This is not to say that other cultures do not reason abstractly; but it has become increasingly obvious that the exercise of a cognitive skill cannot be considered as occurring in a vacuum. Context and motivational set are integral to performance (Cole et al. 1971). The adolescent Aboriginal boy, called on by a white teacher to compete in school, may be in conflict if he also experiences affiliative ties to his classmates; particularly if his peers view scholastic success as an attempt to ingratiate white authority. Watts (1973), in a previously mentioned study of high-achieving versus low-

4. In this investigation (Nurcombe 1973), a modified version of the Thematic Apperception Test was used. A series of pictures illustrating tribal Aborigines in different situations was presented, and the subject was asked to tell a story about each picture. The responses were then analyzed to determine predominant affective and motivational themes.

CHAPTER SEVEN

achieving adolescent Aboriginal girls, found that high achievers had higher aspirations, were less content with themselves, were more likely to see our relation to nature as one of mastery rather than of harmony or subjection, and were more individually rather than collaterally or lineally oriented. Aborigines, compared to whites, saw school success as less important; whereas the need to please others was a dominant motive that might well have been utilized, early, by teachers. In Bourke we found (see Moffitt et al. 1971) that fringe-dwelling Aboriginal children, at the time of entry into the preschool enrichment program, had had little experience of verbal or other reward for effort. For this reason, a strategic feature of our preschool program is the provision of verbal praise when children do their best. No criticism is offered if children try but give a wrong answer; they are praised for effort and then told the correct answer.

SENSITIVE OR FAVORABLE PERIODS

A further issue should be introduced at this point. It is likely that there are especially favorable periods for the development of certain competencies. The acquisition of a new language, for example, is much more facile between the ages of eighteen months and twelve years. After that, it is laborious and incomplete. In a very different field of endeavor, it is becoming apparent to swimming coaches that their charges must be "molded into the water" before puberty if they are to become olympic champions (Carlisle 1973). Similar considerations probably apply to the acquisition of symbolic logical-mathematical structures. Without the kind of ground offered by formal schooling in childhood it may be difficult to teach such skills, *de novo*, in adolescence or later. Whether the favorable periods mentioned are an expression of neurobiological receptivity or socioaffective plasticity is unclear. Probably both factors are involved.

SUMMARY

The realization of potential is affected by three factors: maturation, equilibration, and environment. Maturation is biologically based and aims, by stages, in the direction of decentration toward objectivity, relativity, and reciprocity. Congenital schemata evolve, differentiate, and form superordinate structures as a result of an interaction with the environment. Equilibration is the functional process underlying a dynamic balance between accommodation and assimilation. Gradually, from more rigid, irreversible primitive schemata, superordinate, stable, reversible operational structures evolve. The same processes underlie the evolution of primitive affective interpersonal schemata into more stable structures associated with values, attitudes, and aspirations. It is in this way that ecological pressures, affecting socialization and educational practices, determine which of the potentials will be actualized, to what degree they will be developed, and in which perceptual and affective contexts the competencies will be utilized. Piaget inflates the importance of a disembodied formal abstract thinking at the expense of a more comprehensive approach to cognition, thus reflecting the artificial separation of affect, value, and intelligence current in Western science. The question of favorable ("sensitive") periods for the development of cognitive skills is another crucial issue. It is uncertain whether this phenomenon is related to neurobiological receptivity, or to early social plasticity, or to both.

COMPETENCE

SYNCHRONICITY

Competence is the outcome of the realization of potential. Realization must be considered *diachronically*: longitudinally through time. Competence must be conceptualized *synchronically*: as though longitudinal development were cross-sectioned and the cognito-affective structures already realized could be examined at that point of time. Competence, itself, cannot actually be examined; it can only be inferred from performance. Figure 7.5 illustrates the realization of a spectrum of competencies from basic potential, and provides examples of these competencies.

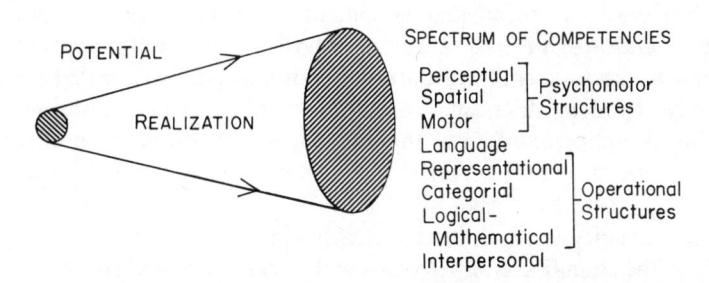

FIGURE 7.5 The spectrum of competencies

A SPECTRUM OF COMPETENCIES

To speak of competence in the singular is merely a convenient simplification. The synchronic configuration of competencies can be regarded as a large number of interrelated, superordinate, and subordinate cognitive structures or abilities in association with affecto-relational structures to do with feeling, value, attitudes, and motivational disposition. Cognitive and psychomotor structures never operate in pure

CHAPTER SEVEN

culture; they are activated, directed, and energized by associated motives which arise from significant personal relationships but which may become more generalized and abstracted. Thus a man may perform well in sport for a variety of reasons: to impress his girlfriend, because of the functional pleasure at exercising an internalized sense of style, out of pleasure in competition, from a desire to destroy the opposition, or simply because it is his livelihood. The competence is expressed in much the same physical way, but the context and affective connotation may differ widely.

What are the basic cognitive structures that underlie performance? They are not yet fully understood; but whatever they are, it is likely that they are shared by all cultures in different degrees. One culture will emphasize one set of competencies more than another, perhaps, but no culture will have huge gaps in the overall configuration (Cole et al. 1971). There is no culture that does not think abstractly in some situations, for example, although the intensive use of abstract, symbolic logic is largely a Western development. Other cultures, on the other hand, develop paralogical (Nurcombe 1970a) thought forms with an intensive use of iconic, figurative, metaphorical symbology—thought forms that are more influential in Western culture than Piaget has described. Lévi-Strauss has dealt extensively with them in *The Savage Mind* (1962) insofar as preliterate groups are concerned.

In addition to intercultural variation, there is an intracultural variation in abilities. If individuals are biologically intact, they will develop the basic competencies, but to differing degrees depending on genetic endowment and experience. All individuals share the basic repertoire, so to speak, but different competencies within that spectrum are developed to different extents. Not only is there variation in the profile of competencies, but the affective structures associated with the profile also vary. On the other hand, if two distinct racial groups—for example, Australian Aboriginal and Caucasian Australian—have had the opportunity to share even roughly similar environments,[5] then the variance of cognitive competencies within each race will be much greater than the variance between them (McElwain and Kearney 1973; de Lacey 1971). This suggests that all cultures share common potentials although none will realize all potentials to the same degree. All people who are biologically intact have the same fundamental competencies. Individuals and cultures vary not in the presence or absence of the actual competencies, but in their comparative *profile*. In societies which allow marked occupational specialization, population variance within the profile of the competency spectrum will be considerable.

5. For example: Aborigines who have integrated into a white township over at least one generation, and working-class whites in that town.

The list of competencies suggested in Figure 7.5 is undoubtedly incomplete, speculative, and uneven. What is needed is a spectrum outline in which each fundamental competence is at the same level of operational abstraction as the others. It is entirely speculative, for example, to assert that representational skills are at the same level as categorial. The base spectrum, so to speak, will not be properly understood until cross-cultural research has abstracted abilities that apply to a variety of cultures. Then, perhaps, empirical laws of cognition may be derived and operational definitions of the competencies framed. Until then, one can only speculate.

Some structures are built out of basic ones by superordinate integration. Other structures differentiate into a larger number of specific abilities. The ability to play a violin, for example, requires the operation of highly differentiated affective (interpretive, artistic), cognitive (reading musical notation), and psychomotor (finger dexterity) structures that are interrelated and harmoniously integrated. These integrated superordinate competencies stem from a fundamental, generic spectrum or repertoire that has yet to be delineated.

Representational skills which first emerged in childhood continue to develop. Iconic, figurative imagery lives on personally in fantasy and dream and socially in myth, ritual, and art. Such representations may illumine the creative process of the theoretician constructing new formal propositions or that of the researcher struggling for a clue to the solution of a formal problem. Turner (1973), in a review of Piaget's *Genetic Epistemology* (1970), suggests that Piaget's concept that maturation is in the direction of decentration is incomplete. The decentered individual voluntarily *recenters*, facilitating the mutual coordination of subject and object and the creation of a balance between assimilation and accommodation. Figurative thought imposes either a socially validated or quite personal form upon external reality, and it reconnects the individual with his own affective life and concrete reality. Decentering and recentering are complementary. Language is a major representational skill and may be involved in figurative skills such as poetry and song as well as in formal operations.

Operational structures (see Figure 7.5) have been extensively discussed by Piaget. They include *inter alia* the categorial skills of class inclusion, equivalence, superordination, seriation, and asymmetrical relationships; logical-mathematical structures involving groups, lattices, and combinatorial and probabilistic reasoning; the conservation of the physical properties of objects despite phenomenal change; and the hypothetical-deductive, propositional logic of the formal period.

Perceptual, spatial, and motor skills are part of the psychomotor domain (see Figure 7.5), as they frequently operate in coordination. The spearing of a fish from above requires keen perceptual acuity, correction for parallax error and foreshortening of depth, rapid reaction, the aiming of the spear by goal-corrected approximation ahead of the target, and a vigorous rhythmic movement of wrist, elbow, and shoulder. The skilled fisherman does all this with economy of effort, automatically. It can be inferred that the deep structures for this performance have been consolidated. Until then, he must practice more or less self-consciously until the structure has evolved.

The affecto-relational structures underlying the feeling states that emanate from vicissitudes in interpersonal relations, motives, values, and attitudes also form part of the spectrum of competencies and play an integral role in the exercise of interpersonal, operational, and psychomotor structures. This matter is elaborated later in the chapter. Many plans, for successful completion, involve the persuasion and cooperation of others. This constraint may force the person who wishes to promote collaboration to negotiate diplomatically and perceptively with interested parties. A cognitive plan—for example, for an amalgamation between two groups of warriors in order to repulse a powerful threat—would be useless if the negotiators did not have a highly developed interpersonal and social competency.

A MULTIDIMENSIONAL MODEL OF THE STRUCTURE OF COMPETENCE

Guilford (1967), basing his concepts on the taxonomic power of factor analysis, has proposed a multidimensional matrix model of competence that directly challenges the unidimensional, g-based model of Spearman and Burt. In Guilford's system, the parameters of intellect are termed *operation, content,* and *product.* Individual competencies are defined by the intersection of the different classes within each parameter. For example: one of the five defined operations is *cognition,* or information-decoding; one of four content classes is *semantic,* concerned with the meaning of representations; and one of the six product classes is *units,* relatively circumscribed items of information. The intersection of these three classes—*cognitive semantic units*—refers to the kind of primary ability conventionally measured by a vocabulary test. The $4 \times 5 \times 6$ matrix proposed by Guilford provides a total of 120 theoretical competencies, a large number of which have been described and for most of which primary ability tests have been devised.

Guilford's theory has been derived from the extensive testing of Western subjects. Only tentative attempts have been made to explore the competencies of non-Western people in a similar comprehensive way. Lesser, Fifer, and Clark (1965) and Stodolsky and Lesser (1967), working in New York City and Boston respectively, noted that in a study of four

POTENTIAL, COMPETENCE, AND PERFORMANCE

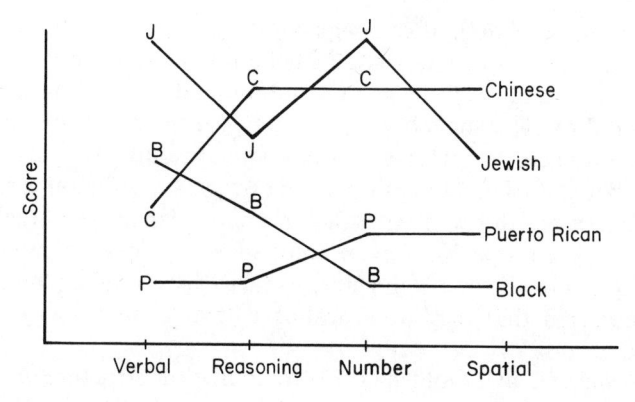

FIGURE 7.6 Profiles of primary abilities of four ethnic groups (modified from Stodolsky and Lesser 1967)

"primary" abilities (verbal, reasoning, number, spatial), Chinese, Jews, blacks, and Puerto Ricans have quite different profiles. These profiles were constant regardless of SES, although there was the expected class differential within the profile for each ethnic group (see Figure 7.6). It should be noted, however, that Irish Catholics in Boston showed neither a distinct pattern nor SES parallels, a finding that may be related to the greater social dispersion and cultural diffuseness of this older immigrant group.

Irvine (1969b) points out that the patterns of mental abilities represented theoretically by intertest correlations must be similar before one can infer ability differences between cultural groups from differences in mean scores. Unless this criterion is followed, test scores will not have the same meaning in different cultures. In an analysis of the incorrect answers given by Shona people to ability tests, Irvine extracted three orders of factor: the first concerned number and memory facilities; the second related to reasoning and short-term memory; and the third was associated with perceptual style. The adult cognitive style of these people encompasses modes of thought that may be incompatible with Western logical systems, modes of thought about which conventional test instruments provide little information. Irvine (1966:31) has written: "To conceive of intelligence as a statistical constraint with the same meaning in other cultures that impose rules of behavior only partly related to that of Western societies could mislead further efforts to clarify the roles of language, ecology and affect on cognition within and across cultures, if only because it would tend to inhibit the sampling of behavioral domains that are irrelevant in the construction of 'intelligence' tests in Western societies."

Chapter Seven

Guthrie (1963), after analyzing the structure of abilities among Philippine college students, extracted the following factors: numerical, verbal, rote memory, visualization, motor and perceptual speed, and ideational fluency. Vandenberg (1967) assessed the degree of congruence between the factor structures of Chinese and South American student samples based on Thurstone's tests. He extracted a common first-order g factor together with seven other factors: native language, verbal ability, memory, spatial visualization, perceptual speed, number ability, and reasoning. Guthrie's and Vandenberg's factors are similar; but it should be remembered that they were dealing with relatively highly educated subjects.

Marsella and Golden (1973) compared the structure of cognitive abilities in Americans of Japanese and European ancestry in Hawaii. The subjects were administered a battery of factor-pure tests and each group's scores were subjected to a factor analysis. The two groups showed a similar factorial structure—spatial relations, verbal fluency, symbolic facility, and divergent thinking—but the primary abilities comprising these factors differed for the two ethnic groups. It was noted that Japanese and Europeans sometimes employed different primary abilities to solve similar problems.

It is clear that this line of research is in its infancy. The possibility of determining a full, universal spectrum of primary abilities and of establishing the cultural and genetic bases of the spectrum (or matrix, as Guilford would have it) is a more promising prospect than the search for racial differences in the inheritance of an elusive g.

COMPETENCE AND PERFORMANCE IN GENERATIVE LINGUISTICS

Noam Chomsky (1957, 1965, 1968), in a series of brilliant contributions, has revolutionized thinking on the structure of language. He clearly draws the distinction between *competence* and *performance.* Competence is the set of principles—linguistic rules—required to generate understandable sentences. Performance is the translation of competence into action. Performance may fall short of perfection because of, for example, transient affects, short-term-memory deficiencies, or distractions. Chomsky's model of competence—the rules or structures of language—and its translation into performance is worthy of close attention. It may be a model for the construction of a theory about competencies in general and their application and expression.

The theoretical model of idealized language competence presented by Chomsky does not necessarily correspond to the actual psychological process of perception and production of speech; but any such process must somehow incorporate a system of grammatical rules. It is to the elucidation of this system and to the formulation of universal rules of syntax and phonology that Chomsky has applied his research. Language learning, for both the linguist and the child, appears to proceed by means of hypothesis formation and testing. Although the languages of the world are superficially diverse, there are deep similarities. Thus it appears that all tongues share certain phonological characteristics and that all languages include such structures as subject-predicate, verb-object, modifier–head noun, question form, and command form. The problem for Chomsky is therefore to describe a universal grammar: a universal phonetics, a universal syntax, and a universal semantics.

Performance is subject to various nonlinguistic limitations such as memory and attention. For this reason, Chomsky asserts, competence cannot be accurately inferred from performance. As Herriot (1970) points out, this argument reduces to an absurdity: competence is not inferable from performance, but performance cannot be examined without taking competence into account! According to Herriot, Chomsky's rules are in fact mathematical abstractions that are unlikely to correspond to descriptions of psychological processes; at most they are descriptions of a system that is part of what a process description must account for.

Be that as it may, Chomsky's theory does furnish a model from which hypotheses concerning the psychological processes of language perception and production can be framed for heuristic purposes. It may also furnish insights about the structuralization of competencies in general.

A detailed presentation of Chomsky's model is beyond the scope of this book. The reader is referred to Lyons (1970) for an introduction to his work. It is important to realize, however, that Chomsky's basic aim is to design a generative program, as it were, which will (1) describe a particular grammar and (2) can eventually be abstracted until it has a universal applicability. His work is still at the first level, although his basic model has been applied with success to languages other than English. It is also important to realize that Chomsky's ideas are evolving and that many aspects of his earlier theorizing have been discarded or modified and reincorporated in his later work.

In his current theory, Chomsky describes the terminal word strings of written or spoken language as being generated by three components: the syntactic, the semantic, and the phonological. The syntactic component provides the deep plan of the overall sentence and the rules by which the meaning-bearing elements of the *deep structure* (the abstract deep plan of the sentence) are transformed, by ordering, deletions, and additions, into the *surface structure* of the sentence. The semantic component operates upon the deep structure to insert meaningful constituents

CHAPTER SEVEN

into it prior to its syntactic transformation into surface structure. The phonological component operates upon surface structure to produce terminal word strings, the utterances of the speaker that represent his linguistic performance. In current theory, it is proposed that the abstract deep structure of the sentence already contains information as to whether the terminal string is to be in statement, question, command, passive, or whatever form. The deep structure is then acted upon by obligatory rules that transform it—through reordering, deletion, and addition—into surface structure. Take, for example, a deep structure in the nature of a simple statement with a passive marker:

Boy hit dog. (passive)

The deep abstract plan of noun phrase (NP) and verb phrase (VP) can be represented by the following branching diagram:

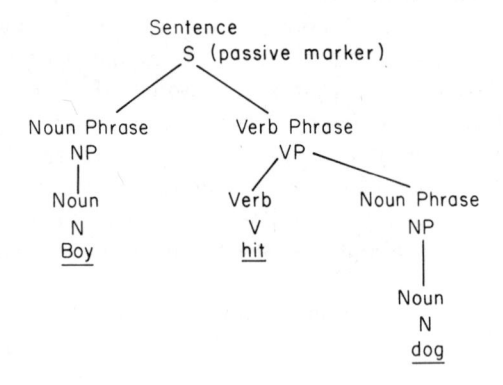

```
                    Sentence
                  S (passive marker)
                 /          \
          Noun Phrase     Verb Phrase
              NP              VP
              |              /    \
            Noun          Verb   Noun Phrase
              N             V        NP
             Boy           hit        |
                                    Noun
                                      N
                                     dog
```

Many simple active or attributive sentences are allied to deep structure, to a simple phrase-structure grammar. But, in the example given, the deep structure already contains information that the speaker wishes to emit a passive terminal string. Obligatory rules are applied to the deep-phrase structure and transform it:

Boy hit dog. (passive)

is transformed into

The dog is hit by the boy.

by what can be described as the *passive transformation rule*. Alternative rules can be described for question, command, conjunctive, imbedded clause, and other forms, the details of which are the domain of the transformational grammarian.

POTENTIAL, COMPETENCE, AND PERFORMANCE

The psychological reality of deep structure can be intuited by a consideration of ambiguous surface structures. Take:

The shooting of the hunters disturbs me.

This terminal string could refer either to my concern that somebody shot those hunters or to my concern at the racket they make as they go about their business. Are the hunters the subject or the object of the shooting? In other words an identical surface structure can be derived from different deep structures, as in this case:

Deep structure : *The hunters shoot.* + *Shooting disturbs me.*

becomes

Surface structure: *The shooting of the hunters disturbs me.*

Or, alternatively:

Deep structure : *(Somebody) shot the hunters.* + *The shooting disturbs me.*

becomes

Surface structure: *The shooting of the hunters disturbs me.*

Chomsky's major innovation was to distinguish between deep and surface structure. Prior to his work, grammarians tended to focus on the taxonomic analysis of surface structure. Differentiation between surface and deep allows for more economic, and more universally applicable, grammatical analysis.

Now take the sentence: *John is taller than Bill.* Intuition tells us that syntax has allowed us to delete quite a few words to produce this terminal string. From deep to surface structure the word combinations are roughly in this sequence:

Deep : *John be tall. Bill be tall.*

John be tall-er than Bill be tall.

Surface : *John is taller than Bill.*

Deep structure thus makes explicit a fact about the meaning that does not appear in the surface: both Bill and John have a degree of tallness which does not need spelling out since we can automatically derive the deep structure.

What experimental evidence is there to support the central concepts of Chomsky's theory? Has any correspondence been found between his idealized model of grammatical competence and psychological processes?[6] Herriot (1970) reviews the empirical evidence in three areas: (1) Do people actually use transformations in reception and production? (2) Are the semantic and syntactic components separable in function? (3) Is there any evidence for the existence of deep structure? The answers appear to be: (1) A qualified yes. Recall and sentence-matching experiments support the concept. However, semantic and contextual clues may be more important than syntactic rules in deriving deep structure. Thus (2) semantic and syntactic operations are probably separable only in artificial, experimental situations as in analyzing the nonsense sentence: *Colorless green ideas sleep furiously*. (3) In regard to the question of deep structure the evidence is quite strong. The analysis of sentences down to deep structure occurs if there are no pragmatic cues available. However, there are normally many such cues: context, intonation, facial expression, for example. Also, people need to have something to say before their grammatical competence is activated.

Herriot suggests how these scientifically rather isolated linguistic concepts may be allied with psychological theory, without falling back on S-R theory. To do so he applies the notions of strategy (plan) and schema (Lashley 1951; Miller, Galanter, and Pribram 1960; Lunzer 1968). *Schema* refers to structure, to the competence of the organism to behave in a regulated manner. *Strategy* corresponds to the actual operation of the organism, to mode of function. The terms correspond to *structure* and *expression* as used in this book. Strategies and schemata are hierarchical. They may overlap and articulate. They may be coordinated by superordinate strategies and schemata. Superstrategies may closely or freely determine the transitions from one strategy to the next.

The hierarchical organization of the constituents of a sentence suggests the operation of strategies. How can the deep structure of transformational grammar be described in this paradigm? Herriot suggests that deep-structure schemata mediate between nonlinguistic and linguistic domains. Deep structure is activated by nonlinguistic schemata and, in turn, activates grammatical schemata. Herriot goes on to account for acquisition, production, and the function of language in thought. Children are described as hearing language items uttered in temporal conjunction with behavior. They perceptually scan the scene to extract the criterial features of the situation. As a result, language items become stored, ready for release in the correct behavioral context. When appropriate behavioral schemata are activated, the mediating schemata that

---

6. Chomsky does not claim that his idealized model necessarily describes psychological reality. Nevertheless, it has been attractive enough to psycholinguists to have provoked considerable experimentation.

constitute deep structure are triggered. Deep-structure components have to be filtered through grammatical and phonological schemata before they can be expressed as terminal word strings. Deep structure is based in nonlinguistic storage banks that activate linguistic schemata. In regard to reception and production, it is hypothesized that different nonlinguistic cues activate nonlinguistic schemata which have to do with expectations of the outside world (particularly of the communication environment) and thence flow on to language schemata and expression.

Herriot analyzes the language-thought controversy by the same token. He suggests that as egocentric speech decreases, language is internalized. Language, however, does not become thought: thought is the feedback loop from linguistic to nonlinguistic schemata that also becomes internalized (see Figures 7.7 and 7.8). As egocentric speech decreases, it tends to consist of predicates—actions and the objects of

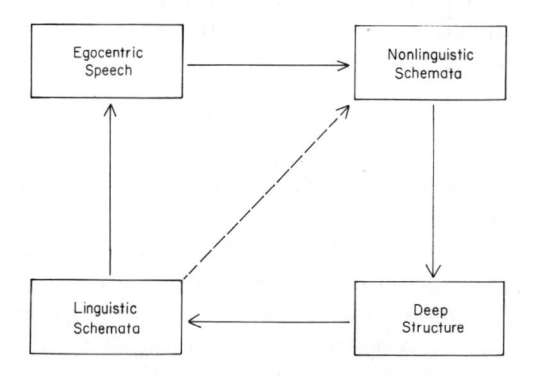

FIGURE 7.7 Language, egocentric speech, and thought

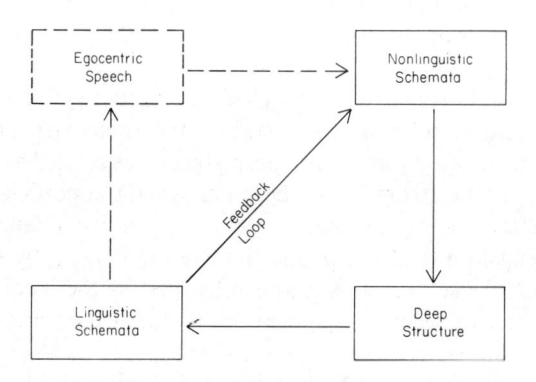

FIGURE 7.8 The internalization of egocentric speech

action (Vygotsky 1962). In Herriot's terms, when the feedback loop is not quite completely internalized, activated language schemata are inhibited before expression and only deep-structure formations, truncated predicates, are uttered as egocentric speech.[7]

Piaget asserts that language can facilitate thought only when operational structures have already evolved. Operational thinking requires that the subject represent to himself the criteria of his behavior, a complex internalized feedback, presumably in line with the internalization of the (language → nonlinguistic schemata → deep structure) feedback loop.

DEEP AND SURFACE STRUCTURE IN THE SPECTRUM OF COMPETENCIES

It is possible that all competency skills are regulated, in a way analogous to language, by deep and superficial structures that underlie performance. A psychomotor competency, such as fishing, may consist of a generalized deep intentional set—an overall plan activated by cues from other fields, for example from perceptual, linguistic, and social signals or physiological drives. The intentional set to spear a fish is then acted upon by more superficial structures until the fisherman is strategically poised, spear aloft, awaiting his prey. The tactical refinement of the actual spearing, taking into account the elements of wind, current, depth, and parallax error, represents a kind of phonological system that translates surface intention into articulated terminal performance. Bruner (1969) calls this process a *syntax of action*. Adequate performance is derived from automatized deep structures which are refined by obligatory or optional rules into performance. A boy must therefore acquire the rules. In a tribal society he does so by observation and practice. His intimate contacts with adults who fish attune him to acquire the skills (rules) without explicit training. At first his performance is wide of the mark; but, gradually, through planned trial and self-initiated perceptual feedback of goal-approximated type, his competence evolves.

Affecto-relational skills may be analyzed by the same token. Based in congenital relational schemata concerned with attachment,[8] dominance, and sexuality *inter alia*, deep structures arise that dispose the individual for action. From these, the more specific superficial structures and overt behaviors of diplomacy, love, aggressive challenge, social dialogue, persuasion, leadership, and the like are derived by the application of "rules." These "rules" have been learned by the incorporation of social norms and expectations and by individual experience. It may be

---

7. Picture the child who has not completely internalized the schemata involved in arithmetical subtraction and who sits intently working at a problem (106 − 12 = 94) and quietly mumbling: *Two from six: four; one from nought: nine and carry one....*

8. A detailed analysis of attachment systems may be found in Bowlby (1968).

that we are genetically programmed, as with language, to be especially sensitive to such social influences and to decode the "biogrammar" (Tiger and Fox 1971) of human relationships with unique facility. As with language, the strategies and tactics of expression that determine the superficial structures of human relationships will vary considerably in different cultures, but the deep affectional structures are universal and enduring.

According to Kluckhohn and Strodtbeck (1961), all people and all cultures seek answers to five basic questions that define five value orientations:

1. What is the nature of Man?
2. What is Man's relationship to Nature and Supernature?
3. What is Man's orientation to Time?
4. What is Man's orientation to Activity?
5. What is Man's relationship to other men?

There are three possible broad answers to each question. Man's relation to others, for example, can be described as linear (hierarchical), collateral (affiliative), or individual. Westerners tend to stress individuality, for example. These value orientations have a fundamental influence over the context and strategy of the expression of the profile of competencies.

SUMMARY

Competence is synchronic; realization is diachronic. The synchronic repertoire is best regarded as a spectrum of competencies in which the cognitive are inextricably interwoven with the affecto-relational.

There is a variation in the profile of competencies between individuals in the same culture and between different cultures as a whole. All cultures share the same base skills, but differ in the degree to which each is developed. Thus differences are more a matter of profile than of presence or absence. The profile is shaped predominantly by culture and to some extent by specialized individual experience. Pending further cross-cultural investigation, the specific list of basic competencies must still be speculative. It is from these basic structures that differentiation and superordination occur.

The tendency toward decentration with maturation has been overemphasized. People periodically "recenter" too by imposing personal or social figurations on reality in the form of art, ritual, fantasy, and dream. By doing so, we reintegrate our cognitive and affective life. Nevertheless, objective operational competencies are an important aspect of the profile, as are psychomotor and affecto-relational skills.

Generative linguists distinguish linguistic competence—the set of abstract rules which govern sentence production—from performance, or

CHAPTER SEVEN

rules translated into utterances. The possibility that a competence-performance model has psychological validity has stimulated useful research. In summary, there is evidence to support the theory of deep linguistic structures which are closely related to underlying competence, deep structures that are transformed, according to syntactic rules, into the surface structures of language. Herriot has pointed out the compatibility of this paradigm with the psychological model of deep hierarchical schemata or plans which are actualized according to strategies appropriate to the context. The possibility arises that the competence-performance, schema-plan-strategy, deep-surface structure model has extralinguistic relevance.

Western societies, through the medium of universal education, have greatly promoted the application of the possibilities inherent in language to the organization of knowledge. Thus hierarchies, groups, and lattices of thought are created. As a sentence itself has a structure which is subordinated to a paragraph and, beyond that, to a theme, so language aids the complex, sequential, hierarchical thought of a technological culture. It is little wonder, therefore, that schools emphasize words and psychologists devise tests saturated with language functions, thus elevating verbal comprehension and application to a superordinate pinnacle known as intelligence. Unfortunately, in doing so, psychologists have lost perspective of the broader spectrum and of the possibility of superordination in competencies other than that of verbal intelligence.

EXPRESSION AND PERFORMANCE

EXPRESSION, CONTEXT, STRATEGY, FEEDBACK

The expression of competence results in synchronic performance (see Figure 7.9). Performance is overt behavior. The expression of language competence results in more-or-less appropriate speech utterances, writing,

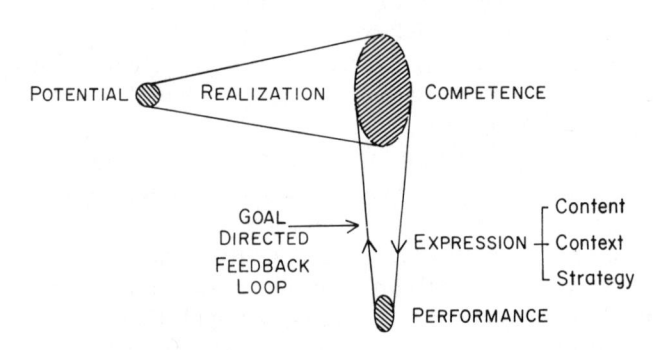

FIGURE 7.9   Expression and performance

or problem-solving behavior that has been facilitated by inner language (in which case the expression of language competence must be inferred). The expression of psychomotor competence results in more-or-less skilled acts: driving a car, cooking a meal, spearing a fish. The expression of affecto-relational competence results in a more-or-less harmonious expression and satisfaction of need (for attachment, sex, dominance, and so forth) that arises from more primitive affecto-relational schemata.

It is no accident that a woman is judged as being either "smooth," "easy," "polished," and "cool" or "clumsy," "disruptive," and "immature" in social competence, from the evidence of her repeated behavioral performances. The grief-stricken, anxious, physically ill, or fatigued man, also, may be forgiven for a temporary declension from his usual patterns. In such circumstances, speech utterances deteriorate in quality and appropriateness; inconsiderateness and lack of empathic concern are common; operational performance deteriorates; and the individual is likely to become jerky, impulsive, and poorly integrated in psychomotor performance—a menace behind the wheel of a car, for example.

The expression of a competence produces *afferent perceptual feedback*. Cues from visual, tactile, auditory, kinesthetic, and even olfactory and taste receptors are fed back into deep-competency structures for goal correction. The organism tracks its target and corrects performance synchronically and diachronically. At any point of time I can correct my tennis backhand to center the ball. I can learn, during the game, how to execute the backhand with greater force, or more control, to smash, drive up the line or across court, or drop the ball short. If my backhand is working badly, I feel discontented (disequilibrium) until and unless I can improve it or rationalize the tension away (after all, I play only for company and fresh air). If my backhand is working sweetly, I feel good (functional pleasure). Affecto-relational structures operate before, during, and after the stroke, in association with the deep and surface psychomotor structures that underlie it.[9]

Expression must be considered in terms of content, context, strategy, and tactics. Which competency will be applied? When and where will it be applied? How will it be applied? And—more broadly—why was it applied? Without these qualifications the description of performance in terms of a rating (good, poor, ...) or score (IQ 135) is thin ice, precariously thin.

CULTURAL RELATIVISM

Expression cannot be described without a discussion of cultural relativism. Different cultures develop relatively different surface com-

---

9. Affects may represent cues that indicate to the subject how close (or how far) he is from the desired goal of goal-corrected behavior.

CHAPTER SEVEN

petencies from universal bases. The occasion and manner of expression are also affected by cultural determinants. This subject has already been introduced in the sections on realization and competence. The question of favorable ("sensitive") periods for realization of potential has also been discussed. It is uncertain to what degree the relative slowness of acquisition of new cognitive material in later life is due to a neurobiological rigidity or to the operation of relatively fixed affecto-relational value structures in association with stabilized and equilibrated cognitive structures. People do not learn unless they see the relevance of doing so. They are particularly reluctant to unlearn old things or to acquire new dissonant material. In Piaget's sense, the capacity to tolerate disequilibrium seems to sclerose with age.

Cole (1973) has carried the cultural relativism argument further, and in a way different from other psychologists. He calls for the need to combine ethnographic with psychological research in order to produce a true cognitive anthropology. In the course of his argument he quotes some telling examples. He found that nonliterate Liberian Kpelle adults were strikingly poor in their ability to describe a series of sticks of different shape to other adults. In crude, bold, ethnocentric, evaluative terms the subjects appeared to be "egocentric" and "immature." This seemed a strange conclusion about members of a culture in which rhetorical and debating skills are highly valued. Cole suggests that the subjects' poor performance was related to a culturally determined interpersonal convention that constrains the Kpelle speaker to be circumspect and indirect and to rely on nuance rather than precision in ambiguous communication settings. Cole et al. (1971) quote similar results from experiments involving free recall. Kpelle nonliterates, compared with schooled Kpelle and Americans, recalled poorly and showed little ability to use structure (for example, function concepts) to aid recall of object or words; that is, until the lists to be recalled were embedded in folktales of traditional type.

In the course of a study of the development of causal thinking in a tribal Aboriginal group, a wise man gave me the following answers to a set of standard questions about the nature and origin of dreams (Laurendeau and Pinard 1962):

> Where does a dream come from?—*By thinking.*—Where are dreams made? —*In air: the universal*—Do dreams come from inside you or outside you? —*Ordinary dreams come from outside. A special dream is from inside, from one person's mind to another person's mind.*—Who makes the dream come? —*Thinking or wish for things.*—Is it you or somebody else? Who?—*I myself because my mind, my thought run to that person or the word.*—While you are dreaming, where is the dream?—*Two places. It can sit in the brain of people; the other way is in the air . . . it lands and disappears. My dream sits in my mind.*—If we could open your head while you were dreaming,

could we see the dream?—*I can't see the dream but I can see the wisdom of the dream and the picture of the world. ... The dream is air.*—What do we dream with?—*Our mind, like a very thinking, can stick quickly and things can stick on. It is just like that tape roll* [points to tape recorder]; *we got one of them in our brain.*—Then why do we have dreams?—*Suggestion. Wishing. You got telephone. Us Aboriginal people got telephone in brain and can tell things happening. Somebody is in the universal, the air; he tells you.*—Are our dreams true, then?—*No and yes. There are two. Sometimes does happen. Nearly always nothing ... just wishing for things.*

The subject describes two kinds of dream. One type comes from "outside" and is the result of day-residues or wish fulfillment, of the dreamer's association with what has occurred and what he desires. The second type of dream is a prophetic vision. An external, "universal," spiritual force to which the Aborigine is especially attuned makes contact with the dreamer. The question of exteriority or interiority is quite deliberately blurred, but not inconsistent. The dream is clearly personal, insubstantial, and in most cases internally motivated. To rate this man's level of concept development in terms of a Western scale[10] would be to destroy the incredible richness and eloquence of the material. Is the subject thinking precausally or causally? Is the causality dimension a relevant one (Nurcombe 1970a)?

Cole takes psychologists to task for their rejection of "the use of naturally occurring behavior sequences as a source of evidence about learning and thinking processes." Ethnographers characteristically reject experimentation as artificial; psychologists avoid natural behavior sequences as ambiguous. The weakest point of current cross-cultural psychological investigation is the interpretation of poor performance. Experiments can establish what children *can* do, but not what they *cannot* do.

Cole began his work by asking: (1) Which kinds of experience promote which intellectual processes? (2) Are these experiences linked to specific cultural institutions of special importance? He then shifts ground and asks: (3) Which kinds of cultural experience promote the manifestation of intellectual processes in specific experimental situations? Cultural differences reside more in the settings in which different cognitive competencies are expressed than in differences between the competencies of people in different cultures. It should be stressed that questions (1) and (2) have not been discarded. It is likely that different cultures push some cognitive processes further than others; but it is necessary to keep question (3) firmly in mind. Psychological experiments and tests should maximize the subjects' opportunity to express a competence by determining the

10. Laurendeau and Pinard (1962): 0. Incomprehension. 1. Integral realism. 2. Mitigated realism. 3. Integral subjectivism—dream personal, interior, invisible, and immaterial.

sociocultural situations in which the competence is regularly or conventionally expressed.

Australian Aborigines are characterized by a marked lack of interpersonal intrusiveness. In this, their culture contrasts with the evangelical educating and organizing attitudes of Westerners. If an Aboriginal girl has a tantrum, the parents either wait until it blows over or provide the distraught one with whatever it was she wanted. The Aboriginal man cannot be convinced to shake another man to wake him up. He will not offer cigarettes or blankets unless asked; in which event he will provide them to those toward whom he has reciprocal obligations. In the phrase of American hippies, each person "does his own thing," within sanctioned limits, and allows others to do theirs. How, therefore, does the Aborigine perceive the eager psychologist who asks a series of apparently irrelevant or exceedingly personal questions as part of a test? What effect does such a violation of cultural norms have upon the performance sampled and scored? An entertaining description of how a set of rather dreary maze tests was made relevant and entertaining is offered by Bochner (Porteus et al. 1967), who told his Aboriginal subjects that the center of the maze was a jail from which the subject had to escape. Hilarious memories of many such situations were common among the hard-drinking subjects—who applied themselves to the abstract task with evident enthusiasm and produced higher scores on this text than had ever been found among Aborigines.

ECOLOGICAL FUNCTIONALISM

Berry and Dasen's (1973) concepts of radical cultural relativism and ecological functionalism have already been described. The child-rearing practices, socialization procedures, and cultural institutions that affect cognitive realization and competencies also affect the mode and context of the expression of those competencies. Values, motives, and attitudes activate and shape the development and expression of psychomotor and cognitive competence. These social forces are themselves cultural adaptations to the ecological pressures upon a society. Putting it quite simply: People express competence when it makes adaptive sense to do so.

In 1971, we attempted to apply a choice-reaction time experiment to tribal Aboriginal adolescents (Davidson 1971). The results were then compared with the reactions of white Brisbane adolescents. Despite the fact that the key stimuli were shapes associated with two different types of dugong head and turtle shell (specifically coded in the Aboriginal society and not coded by Europeans), Aborigines were markedly slower in pressing buttons than whites. This is in contrast to their grace and split-second timing in dodging spears or catching fish. The purpose of the experiment was at best meaningless to the subjects.

Ask the impassive, glassy-eyed Aboriginal schoolgirl to leave the classroom and go out into the bush to bring back five leaves, six edible fruits, and four objects you can make something from. Better still, ask her to take you and show you. Her face lights up and her desire to teach you produces an unexpectedly animated performance. Praise her and at first she is uncertain, then gratified—provided she is not made too conspicuous. Criticism for poor performance crushes her—far more so than with a European child, for ridicule is a prominent aspect of Aboriginal social control.

The need for achievement in contrast to the need for affiliation has already been discussed in the section on realization. The Aboriginal adolescent boy expresses his need for competitive success in hunting and weapon use rather than in school, which tends to be viewed as a feminine place. Where traditional customs have lost their relevance, he may express his need for masculine dominance by sniffing petrol or drinking alcohol (Nurcombe et al. 1970).

SUMMARY

The expression of competence results in synchronic performance. Quality of performance may be disrupted by transient affective or motivational factors. Competence and performance are coordinated, and the performance target tracked, by the operation of a goal-directed feedback that leads to both synchronic approximation of aim and diachronic refinement of performance.

Expression must be considered in terms of content, strategy, and context. The concept of cultural relativism indicates that different cultures will (1) emphasize different aspects of the base competency spectrum and (2) foster the expression of these competencies in different sociocultural contexts by (3) different strategies and tactics. Crude cross-cultural comparisons of competence are invalid unless the ethnography of the groups involved is understood and a satisfactory maximization of the expression of competence has been attained. Psychologists should try to understand naturally occurring behavior sequences before designing experiments in other cultures.

Competence, expression, and performance are molded by sociocultural pressures that are a response to ecological forces. People will not express a competence fully, if at all, unless it is adaptive. People do not learn new things or unlearn old things unless it makes sense to them to do so.

The question of whether or not there is a genetic difference in cognitive potential between races is not answerable at this time. It may be a theoretically sterile cul-de-sac that distracts attention from more fruitful areas of research. Premature conclusions about heredity could have unfortunate social results. At this point, psychologists would do better to delineate the spectrum of competencies and to determine valid, socially congruent methods for evaluating it.

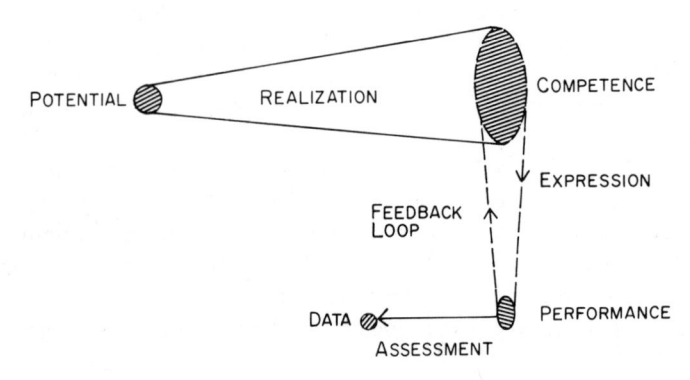

FIGURE 7.10 Evaluation

ASSESSMENT AND EVALUATION

The problems of reliably and validly sampling and measuring performance have already been considered in chapter 1. The process is illustrated in Figure 7.10.

Motivational factors affect the evaluation of performance in the same way they determine the expression of competence generally. Certain prerequisites have to be met before tested samples of performance can be regarded as satisfactory. The prerequisites have to do with content validity, predictive validity, standardization, reliability, the maximization of performance, and construct validity. Contemporary intelligence tests are unsatisfactory as tests of competence since they are not based on empirically derived laws of behavior but, rather, are validated in circles against each other and against school performance. Until cross-cultural research has enabled us to define the basic profile of competencies, valid tests of competence are visions of the future. It is premature to compare the innate potentials of different races in view of the fact that such inferences are derived from instruments the validity of which varies unpredictably in different cultural groups.

A final comment. The reader will have noticed that in describing potential I have spent much of the time speaking about realization, that realization was inextricable from competence, that competence could be inferred only after its expression as performance, and that performance (and the evaluation of performance) reflected back to competence. That is as it should be. The conceptual framework I have proposed is an artificial freezing of dynamic synchronic and diachronic processes. The value of the configuration will be determined by the degree to which it generates operations, that is, applications to research and practice. Its most important application, hopefully, will be in interdisciplinary research, communication, and coordination.

CHAPTER 8
QUESTIONS AND ASSUMPTIONS

In the welter of conflicting fanaticisms, one of the few unifying forces is scientific truthfulness, by which I mean the habit of basing our beliefs upon observations and inferences as impersonal, and as much divested of local and temperamental bias, as is possible for human beings.

Bertrand Russell

QUESTIONS

A great deal of research has been done into the development of human competence. Cognitive psychologists, stimulus-response theorists, linguists, psychometricians, and anthropologists have all been prominent in their contribution. The time has come for a comprehensive review. This book aims to provide that review by organizing its discussion around a broad theoretical framework. The potential of the framework for illuminating applied research has already been demonstrated in chapters 3 to 6. Action research affords the opportunity to apply hypotheses in the field and to test the utility of theoretical models. It may also generate fresh hypotheses away from the somewhat restrictive conditions of laboratory work—hypotheses that can be tested later by more fully controlled experimentation. One of the problems in this field is the degree of specialization of many workers and the relative lack of communication between them; for example, between developmental psychologists and educationists. It is hoped that the theoretical model in this book will provide a framework for better interdisciplinary cooperation and planning. Ultimately, like all models, if it is useful it will generate ideas that will lead to its modification, refinement, and replacement. Reference to the model makes clear that there are major gaps in our knowledge, some of them glaring.

What are the inherent potentials? What is the degree of genetically determined variation in these potentials in biologically intact individuals? Are there racially determined differences in innate potentials? Can particular innate potentials be reduced by intrauterine or perinatal traumata or privation? If so, what is the mechanism of the damage? Which potentials are particularly vulnerable to such damage? At which age is protein-calorie deprivation most likely to cause growth arrest? Is this growth arrest ever irreversible in terms of a reduction of brain-cell population? Which areas of the brain are most vulnerable and at what periods in development? Are other nutritional elements involved apart from protein? How? What is the effect of protein-calorie restriction on brain biochemistry and particularly on nucleic acid synthesis?

Are there critical or sensitive periods for the realization of certain potentials? If so, is there a neurophysiological correlate for such sensitive periods? Are the developmental stages described by Piaget invariant? If so, what are the anatomical and physiological correlates of stage? What is the function of memory in the realization of congenital schemata, and how do memory functions change and develop in the first five years?[1] What is the relation between the development of memory and perception and the development of the cognitive structures underlying invariance? What is the influence of lexical (semantic) features on the acquisition of grammatical competence? What are the primordial schemata from which language develops? Does it evolve from sensorimotor schemata or is it, in one sense, a separate system that eventually interrelates with sensorimotor schemata?

How pertinent, psychologically, is the separation between semantic and syntactic systems in Chomsky's ideal model? If native speakers can intuit the complex rules of language, why do they not necessarily do so for other epistemological domains? And what is the neurological substrate of such a difference, if there is a difference? What are the most pertinent aspects of the linguistic environment that allow the child to realize language competence? Which aspects of the environment are most effective in fostering the development of other cognitive, psychomotor, and affecto-relational competencies? How does disturbance in affecto-relational schemata—for example, as a result of psychological trauma following separation—affect realization? What aspects of competency are most vulnerable to psychic trauma, and at what time?

How can the basic competencies of immature and mature individuals be described? What are the irreducible structural abstractions that can account for function? In Mehler's (1971) terms: (1) What is the *vocabulary* that exhaustively enumerates the elements of competency

---

1. This subject has been investigated by Mehler (1971).

structure? (2) What is the set of *formation rules* that permit the determination of all expressions of the structure? (3) What is the set of *axioms* comprising the terminal performance behavior strings and the irreducible parameters that require no further proof? (4) What is the set of *inference rules* that determine the *set of theorems* with respect to the set of axioms? Is it possible to describe cognitive competence in terms of an axiomatic system? If so, the structures of cognitive and linguistic competence would overlap. The model is elegant and parsimonious; but does it correspond to psychological reality?

What is the evidence for deep and surface structure and rules of transformation in cognitive, psychomotor, and affecto-relational domains, as in the linguistic? What are the transformational rules for the different domains and in relation to specific skills? How do the domains interact in expression? For example, how do transient vicissitudes in affect cause declensions of psychomotor expression? What are the contextual rules for the expression of competencies in different cultures? What is the neurophysiological correlate of deep structure and its extralinguistic (or extrarelational or extrapsychomotor) antecedents?

What are the superordinate competencies? What are the laws of their operation? What are the operational definitions of competency expression that can be derived from these laws? What are the different manifestations of the basic competencies in different cultures?

How can performance be sampled and evaluated in a valid and reliable way? How can evaluation techniques be refined to tap competence in different cultural settings? How can the evaluation of performance be quantified, for comparison, according to the derived laws of competency expression?

The questions are innumerable. Answers to them will generate more questions and stimulate the framing of more precise, more pertinent hypotheses and experiments. Information from controlled experimentation will enrich and be vitalized by experience in the field with naturally occurring sequences of behavior. The theoretical framework clearly owes much to Piaget and to Chomsky. Both these writers, however, idealize their fields. Piaget, like Spearman, searches for abstract quintessences; and so, in a different way, does Chomsky. Theories can sometimes develop a life of their own that may become divorced from actuality. Applied research may help to provide the plasma that desiccated, abstract models lack.

ASSUMPTIONS

In the following description of the eight assumptive qualities of the model, my debt to Piaget and Chomsky will become even clearer.

First: the model is *nativist* and *rationalist*. The individual is described as born with certain universally human, species-specific, cognitive, psychomotor, and relational potentials that are applied from the outset, to the world, in the service of adaptation.

Second: the model is *structural*. It proposes that innate, genetically programmed potentials are already organized at birth in the form of schemata. The potentials evolve with maturation and experience (by superordination, subordination, differentiation, and decentration) and are realized as more stable structures that impose a hierarchical pattern upon perception and the expression of competence.

Third: ontogenetic evolution is seen as *interactive*, as a spiral interaction between innate structure, biological maturation, and experience. It is termed *realization*.

Fourth: the model is *generative*. From deep superordinate competencies, by the application of rules, an infinite series of terminal behavioral strings can be derived. The degree to which the rules are based in innate structure and to which they are learned by intuition, reinforcement, or formal instruction is left open.

Fifth: in this model the organism is *active*. It actively scans the exterior for new data. It actively assimilates, or accommodates its structures to, new data. It operates to grasp and adapt to environmental novelty and also to keep internal disequilibrium within tolerable limits. Cognitive, psychomotor, and affecto-relational structures are self-regulating systems which operate by goal-approximated feedback and which are more complex than biochemical and physiological systems. The system is equilibratory rather than homeostatic.

Sixth: the *competence* aspect of the model is seen as operating, by analogy with Chomsky's theory, according to deep and more superficial structures. The dispositional sets incorporated in deep structure are translated, by means of obligatory or optional rules, into performance. The rules take into account not only the formal requirements of the aim (for example, how to hold a fish spear, how to place the feet, and so on, before releasing the weapon at a target) but also the contextual (for example, socially determined) restrictions in which the individual operates. Certain competencies, ideally, will be expressed only in certain contexts; others will be modified in expression according to context.

Seventh: *competence* and *performance* are separated theoretically for the purpose of analysis. Competence implies both structure and strategies of application (expression). Competence can only be inferred from behavioral performance.

And eighth: the model is *holistic*. Cognitive, psychomotor, and perceptual structures do not operate *in vacuo*. The speaker, like Chomsky, does not say *colorless green ideas sleep furiously* unless he is motivated through affecto-relational structures to make a logical point with the listener. The logical thinker, like Piaget, will not employ combinatorial operations unless there is a good adaptational reason for doing so; for example, achieving on a test that will determine whether or not she gets into college.

IN CONCLUSION

Intelligence is a protean concept. The behavior that a Ugandan perceives as "intelligent" would not fit Spearman's definition of the term. Undoubtedly, there are common features that underlie skilled, adaptive behavior in Alaska, central Australia, and Geneva; but these have yet to be defined. We know little of the basic spectrum of competencies and the way it has been realized in different cultures. Until we set to work to elucidate these problems, operational definitions of intelligence and the search for its factorial quintessence are premature, culture-bound, and damagingly ethnocentric. When social scientists have appreciated this point, the current excessive reliance on that utilitarian but limited statistic, the IQ, will be a subject mainly for historians.

Genetically based biological change is gradual and evolutionary; culturally based change may be sudden and disintegrative. Much of the world today is in the process of a rapid, potentially disruptive, transformation. Education will have an increasing part to play in helping people adapt to, and get the most from, the challenges of technological change without losing a grip of their cultural roots; but education must begin from an understanding of the universal spectrum of human competencies and the particular profile of competencies and expressive strategies that characterize each cultural group. The exportation of Western educational systems and their imposition, without modification, on other people has had damaging educational, social, and political consequences. The time has come for educational research and practice to respect and take account of these facts, to help people define their own individual, social, and educational goals, and to design teaching strategies that complement, rather than violate, social and motivational characteristics. It has become increasingly clear that these considerations apply in all situations, Western and non-Western. The most pressing educational question of the next twenty-five years is whether our institutions have the flexibility to respond to the growing demands of cultural pluralism and diversity.

APPENDIX

EXTENDED EXPERIENCE PROGRAM: 1973–1974

It should be noted that teachers are free to spend more or less time on any section of the program as the need arises.

TERM I

Week 1: orientation. Identification of familiar objects (insects, animals, houses, trees) in the environment, emphasizing naming and description.

Week 2: continued orientation. Self-concept development. Children to introduce themselves (*I am Rodney; I am Ruth*) using mirror. Children to describe their own and others' actions (*Ruth is jumping; I am walking*).

Free play with blocks, toys, pencils, crayons, paints, and felt pens to familiarize children with preschool and its equipment.

Week 3: introduction of structure. Identification of objects in preschool. Children to construct objects with blocks, cardboard, colored paper, and paste.

Further introduction of action words in relation to self, other children, and animals (*jumping, running, walking, sitting, standing*), using mirror, songs, finger play, and games. Emphasis on activities in the immediate environment and on season, water, soil, wind, heat, light, shade, family, schoolroom, and playground; stories to be told to children about these things with focus on identification and action words. Child to be encouraged to describe own action as it is in operation; other children to reinforce it at the same time (*I am, Rodney is, jumping*). This should be continued until week 6, by which time children should be able to think of, perform, and describe an action.

At the end of each day, recapitulation of the day's activities:

APPENDIX

children to describe their actions for the day. Each day, one or two children to describe something they did at home in the previous evening (each child to have one turn per week).

Weeks 4–7: attributes. Attributes of objects to be discriminated and identified; for example, weight, color, size, temperature, shape, texture. Objects to be described in terms of more than one dimension.

Colors to be discriminated: red, yellow, green, blue, purple. One color to be emphasized each day to begin with. Use objects made by children to illustrate colors: *This is a red house ... a yellow balloon ... a green ball ...* and so forth. Give many examples. Children to construct objects with blocks using different colors. Negative identity statements to be introduced: *This is a blue ball. It is not a red ball.* Homework to deal with construction of differently colored objects.

Week 8: shapes. Concentration on square and circle to begin with in first two days; then rectangle and triangle. Concepts of squareness and so on to be derived from concrete activity with shapes from multiattribute block sets. Homework to emphasize shapes; for example, cutouts.

Week 9: color and shape. Extension of week 8 to cover both color and shape; for example, red squares, blue circles, green triangles. Homework to deal with color and shape attribution.

Week 10: sizes. Experience with concrete objects emphasizing polar opposites: big-little, large-small, long-short, fat-thin. Have one subgroup of children build a big house and another a small house, for example. Homework to deal with sizes.

Weeks 11–12: review and consolidation. Color, size, shape, multiple attribution, and negative identity statements.

Week 13: directional orientation. High-low, up-down, in-out, right-left, through, over-under—based on concrete experience and description of own and others' actions. Homework to reinforce preschool experiences.

TERM II

Details of the specific sequence of learning activities for terms II and III will depend upon the rate of progress of the classes. Further experience with combinations of attributes to be arranged. Prepositions to be introduced, based upon concrete activities. In general, term II will review and broaden term I experience. The following trips to be arranged and experiences during and after the experience to be utilized to reinforce concept learning: to river and weir; to irrigated vegetable farm; to town shops; to meat-works; to airport; to buildings under construction.

New concepts to be introduced in term II: alternatives (*or*); comparatives and superlatives (*big, bigger, biggest*). New colors to be introduced: pink, brown, gray, white, black. Experience with conservation and seriation of concrete objects (for example, colored beads) and activities to be introduced, along with representation and deduction. A suggested sequence of learning activities in term II follows.

Week 1: review. Review term I materials and concepts. Colors, shapes, sizes, directions, singly and in combination, using examples from inside and outside the classroom.

Week 2: conservation. Promotion of the idea that quantities stay the same, if nothing is added or subtracted, despite change of shape; using water play with clear plastic containers and concepts of more, less, same. Demonstration of concepts of heavy and light, using scales.

Week 3: seriation. Building on concepts of polar opposites and alternatives by introduction of concepts of comparatives and superlatives. Color seriation: for example light, medium, and deep blue. Seriation of size using concrete objects: big, bigger, biggest, tall ... tallest, small ... smallest. Draw upon cardboard shapes of differing size and colors and use photographs of different-size children in class.

Week 4: representation. Promotion of the realization that a picture or drawing can represent a concrete object (for example, a photograph of a member of the class) and a model can represent an original (for example, a toy bus can stand for a real bus).

Week 5: Continued emphasis on themes of self-concept, personal competence, home and family, the work people do, transport, the world around us.

Weeks 6–7: labeling. Parts of body, laterality, and a select vocabulary (see *A Word List for Australian Schools* [Australian Council for Educational Research, 1960]). More experience with recounting events after lengthening periods of time.

Week 8: deduction. Guessing games introduced; for example, *What is an animal that flies ... swims ... hops?* Reinforced by games in which children play role of the animal.

Weeks 9–10: consolidation. Reinforced by field trips and homework.

APPENDIX

TERM III

In term III, further emphasis on representation will be arranged; creative play and the alphabet and number concepts will be introduced. Further excursions will be arranged: to post office; to zoo; on railway; to orchard; and to high school. In the last three weeks of the preschool year the elementary school's infant teachers will visit and be introduced and the children will visit the infants' department of the elementary school. In more detail, the sequence is as follows:

Weeks 1–2: revision and consolidation of term II.

Weeks 3–12: creative play to foster spontaneous expression. Further emphasis on representation: using pictures and photographs taken in the preschool and on excursions; using flashcards of a selection of words encountered in Bourke and on excursions (for example: *entrance*, *exit*, *go*) and in the preschool (*wall*, *window*); and using flashcards of numbers from 1 to 10 to reinforce elementary counting.

The purpose of these representational exercises is not to teach counting and reading but to foster the concept that spoken words can be represented in printing and to provide a small, basic (but unstable) nucleus of specific representations.

Further experience with seriation: from *big, bigger, biggest* to constructing series of four to five elements graduated by size or number.

Parent activity to reinforce school experiences in homework and to provide cardboard and paper for classroom cutout activity.

CREATIVE PLAY

The purpose of creative play is to stimulate spontaneous, imaginative activity in such a way as to promote divergent thought and problem-solving. Creative play is derived from Piaget's contention that mental operations have their genesis in sensorimotor experience.

The teacher may begin, for example, by asking each child to find his or her own space in the room. The teacher may then suggest that the children should move like animals. To begin with the teacher may show a picture of an animal and demonstrate its movements. With further experience the cues can be reduced from physical movement plus verbal suggestion to verbal suggestion alone to naming the animal alone.

APPENDIX

Later, polar-opposite concepts can be introduced (*Be little ants ... Be big kangaroos*). Children may be encouraged to dance to music expressing what the melody reminds them of (wind, sea, animals). Later, nursery rhymes and stories can be cast, and enacted in costume, in sociodramatic play.

BIBLIOGRAPHY

Anastasi, A. Culture-fair testing. *Educational Horizons*, 1964, Fall, 26–30.
Ball, S., and Bogatz, G. A. Research on Sesame Street: some implications for compensatory education. In: J. C. Stanley (ed.), *Compensatory Education for Children, Ages 2 to 8*. Baltimore: Johns Hopkins, 1973.
Baratz, J. C. Teaching reading in an urban Negro school system. In: J. C. Baratz and R. Shuy (eds.), *Teaching Black Children to Read*. Washington, D.C.: Center for Applied Linguistics, 1969a.
Baratz, J. C. *Language in the Economically Disadvantaged Child: A Perspective*. Washington, D.C.: Center for Applied Linguistics, 1969b.
Baratz, J. C. Teaching reading in an urban Negro school system. In: F. Williams (ed.), *Language and Poverty: Perspectives on a Theme*. Chicago: Markham, 1970.
Baratz, J. C., and Povich, E. *Grammatical Constructions in the Language of the Negro Preschool Child*. Washington, D.C.: Center for Applied Linguistics, 1967.
Baratz, J. C., and Shuy, R. (eds.). *Teaching Black Children to Read*. Washington, D.C.: Center for Applied Linguistics, 1969.
Barry, H., Child, I. L., and Bacon, M. K. Relations of child training to subsistence economy. *American Anthropologist*, 1959, *61*, 51–63.
Bayley, N. Comparison of mental and motor test scores for ages 1–15 months by sex, birth order, race, geographic location, and education of parents. *Child Development*, 1965, *36*, 379–411.
Beckett, J. R. Marginal men: a study of two half caste Aborigines. *Oceania*, 1958, *29*, 91–108.
Beckett, J. R. Aborigines, alcohol and assimilation. In: M. Reay (ed.), *Aborigines Now*. Sydney: Angus and Robertson, 1964a.
Beckett, J. R. The land where the crow flies backward. *Quadrant*, 1964b, May.
Beckett, J. R. Kinship, mobility and community among part-Aborigines in rural Australia. *International Journal of Comparative Sociology*, 1965, *6*, 7–23.
Beilin, H. The status and future of preschool compensatory education. In: J. C. Stanley (ed.), *Preschool Programs for the Disadvantaged*. Baltimore: Johns Hopkins, 1972.
Bereiter, C. A nonpsychological approach to early compensatory education. In: M. Deutsch, I. Katz, and A. R. Jensen (eds.), *Social Class, Race and Psychological Development*. New York: Holt, Rinehart and Winston, 1968.
Bereiter, C. Genetics and educability: educational implications of the Jensen debate. In: J. Hellmuth (ed.), *The Disadvantaged Child*. Volume III. New York: Brunner-Mazel, 1970.
Bereiter, C. An academic preschool for disadvantaged children: conclusion from evaluation

Bibliography

studies. In: J. C. Stanley (ed.), *Preschool Programs for the Disadvantaged.* Baltimore: Johns Hopkins, 1972a.

Bereiter, C. Moral alternatives to education. *Interchange: A Journal of Educational Studies,* 1972b, *3,* 25–41.

Bereiter, C., and Engelmann, S. *Teaching Disadvantaged Children in the Preschool.* Englewood Cliffs, N.J.: Prentice-Hall, 1966.

Bernstein, B. B. Social structure, language and learning. *Educational Research,* 1961, *3,* 163–176.

Bernstein, B. B. Linguistic codes, hesitation phenomena and intelligence; and Social class, linguistic codes and grammatical elements. *Language and Speech,* 1962a and 1962b, *5,* 31–46 and 221–240.

Bernstein, B. B. A critique of the concept of compensatory education. In: C. B. Cazden, V. P. John, and D. Hymes (eds.), *Functions of Language in the Classroom.* New York: Teachers College Press, Columbia University, 1972.

Berry, J. W. Temne and Eskimo perceptual skills. *International Journal of Psychology,* 1966, *1,* 207–229.

Berry, J. W. Ecological and cultural factors in spatial perceptual development. *Canadian Journal of Behavioral Science,* 1971, *3,* 324–336.

Berry, J. W. Marginality, stress and ethnic identification. In: G. E. Kearney, P. R. de Lacey, and G. R. Davidson (eds.), *The Psychology of Aboriginal Australians.* Sydney: Wiley, 1973a.

Berry, J. W. Radical cultural relativism and the concept of intelligence. In: J. W. Berry and P. R. Dasen (eds.), *Readings in Cross-Cultural Psychology.* London: Methuen, 1973b.

Berry, J. W., and Dasen, P. R. (eds.). Introduction in: *Readings in Cross-Cultural Psychology.* London: Methuen, 1973.

Binet, A., and Simon, T. Methodes nouvelles pour le diagnostic du niveau intellectuel des anormaux. *Année Psychologique,* 1905, *11,* 191–244.

Bissell, J. S. Planned variation in Head Start and Follow Through. In: J. C. Stanley (ed.), *Compensatory Education for Children, Ages 2 to 8.* Baltimore: Johns Hopkins, 1973.

Blank, M., and Solomon, F. A tutorial language program to develop abstract thinking in socially disadvantaged pre-school children. *Child Development,* 1968, *39,* 379–390.

Bloom, B. S. *Stability and Change in Human Characteristics.* New York: Holt, Rinehart and Winston, 1964.

Bloom, B. S., Davis, A., and Hess, R. *Compensatory Education for Cultural Deprivation.* New York: Holt, Rinehart and Winston, 1965.

Bodmer, W. F. Race and IQ: the genetic argument. In: K. Richardson and D. Spears (eds.), *Race, Culture and Intelligence.* Harmondsworth: Penguin, 1972.

Boehm, A. E. The development of comparative concepts in primary school children. New York: Columbia University, unpublished doctoral dissertation, 1966.

Bowlby, J. *Attachment and Loss.* Volume I. New York: Basic Books, 1968.

Braine, M. D. S. The ontogeny of English phrase structure: the first stage. *Language,* 1963, *39,* 129–151.

Brislin, R. W. Interaction among members of nine ethnic groups and belief-similarity hypothesis. *Journal of Social Psychology,* 1971, *85,* 171–179.

Brislin, R. W., Lonner, W. J., and Thorndike, R. M. *Cross-Cultural Research Methods.* New York: Wiley, 1973.

Brown, R. W., and Lenneberg, E. H. A study in language and cognition. *Journal of Abnormal and Social Psychology,* 1954, *49,* 454–462.

BIBLIOGRAPHY

Bruce, D. W., Hengeveld, M., and Radford, W. C. Cognitive abilities of Aboriginal children in primary school. *Australian Council for Educational Research, Forty-First Annual Report.* Melbourne: ACER, 1970-1971.
Bruner, J. S. The course of cognitive growth. *American Psychologist,* 1964, *19,* 1-15.
Bruner, J. S. *Ninth Annual Report.* Cambridge, Mass.: Harvard Center for Cognitive Studies, 1969.
Bruner, J. S., Olver, R. R., and Greenfield, P. M. *Studies in Cognitive Growth.* New York: Wiley, 1966.
Bruner, J. S., and Olver, R. R. Development of equivalence transformations in children. In: *Cognitive Development in Children: Five Monographs of the Society for Research in Child Development.* Chicago: University of Chicago Press, 1970.
Burt, C. The inheritance of mental ability. *American Psychologist,* 1958, *13,* 1-15.
Butcher, H. J. *Human Intelligence.* London: Methuen, 1968.
Cabak, V., and Najdanvic, R. Effect of undernutrition in early life on physical and mental development. *Archives of Diseases of Childhood,* 1965, *40,* 532-540.
Caldwell, B. M. Descriptive evaluation of child development and of developmental settings. *Paediatrics,* 1967, *40,* 46-54.
Caldwell, B. M., and Richmond, J. S. The children's center in Syracuse, New York. In: C. A. Chandler, R. S. Lourie, and A. de H. Peters (eds.), *Early Child Care: New Perspectives.* New York: Atherton Press, 1968.
Cameron, W. J. (ed.). *The History of Bourke.* Volume II. Bourke, NSW: Bourke and District Historical Society, 1968.
Campbell, D., and Erlebacher, A. How regression artefacts in quasi-experimental evaluations can mistakenly make compensatory education look harmful. In: J. Hellmuth (ed.), *The Disadvantaged Child.* Volume III. New York: Brunner-Mazel, 1970.
Campbell, D. T., and Stanley, J. C. *Experimental and Quasi-Experimental Designs for Research.* Chicago: Rand McNally, 1973.
Caplan, G. *Principles of Preventive Psychiatry.* London: Tavistock, 1964.
Carlisle, F. Personal communication, 1973.
Carver, R. P. Special problems in measuring change with psychometric devices. In: B. Baxter (ed.), *Evaluative Research: Strategies and Methods.* Pittsburgh: American Institute for Research, 1970.
Cattell, R. B. Theory of fluid and crystallized intelligence: a critical experiment. *Journal of Educational Psychology,* 1963, *54,* 1-22.
Cavalli-Sforza, L. L. Problems and prospects of genetic analysis of intelligence at the intra- and inter-racial level. In: J. Hellmuth (ed.), *The Disadvantaged Child.* Volume III. New York: Brunner-Mazel, 1970.
Cawte, J. E. Racial prejudice and Aboriginal adjustment: the social psychiatric views. In: F. H. Stevens (ed.), *Racism, the Australian Experience.* Volume II. Sydney: Australian and New Zealand Book Co., 1972.
Cawte, J. E. *Medicine Is the Law: A Sourcebook of an Aboriginal Society.* Honolulu: University Press of Hawaii, 1974.
Cazden, C. B. Subcultural differences in child language. In: J. Hellmuth (ed.), *The disadvantaged Child.* Volume II. New York: Brunner-Mazel, 1968.
Chase, A. K., and von Sturmer, J. R. "Mental man" and social evolutionary theory. In: G. E. Kearney, P. R. de Lacey, and G. R. Davidson (eds.), *The Psychology of Aboriginal Australians.* Sydney: Wiley, 1973.
Cheek, D. B., Holt, A. B., and Mellits, E. D. Malnutrition and the nervous system. In: A. L. Fitzgibbon (ed.), *Malnutrition in Early Life and Subsequent Mental Development.* Washington, D. C.: Pan-American Health Organization, 1973.

Bibliography

Chomsky, N. *Syntactic Structures*. The Hague: Mouton, 1957.
Chomsky, N. Review of Skinner's *Verbal Behavior*. *Language*, 1959, *35*, 26–58.
Chomsky, N. *Aspects of the Theory of Syntax*. Cambridge, Mass.: M.I.T. Press, 1965.
Chomsky, N. The formal nature of language. In: E. H. Lenneberg, *Biological Foundations of Language*. New York: Wiley, 1967.
Chomsky, N. *Language and Mind*. New York: Harcourt Brace Jovanovich, 1968.
Cicero, Marcus Tullius. *Letters to Atticus*, I:324. Translated and edited by E. O. Winstedt. Cambridge, Mass.: Loeb Classical Library, 1920.
Cleaver, E. *Soul on Ice*. New York: McGraw-Hill, 1967.
Clough, J. R. Compensatory education programs: a review of research. *Australian Journal of Education*, 1972, *16*, 262–278.
Cole, M. An ethnographic psychology of cognition. Paper delivered at the Conference on the Interface between Culture and Learning, East-West Culture Learning Institute, Honolulu, February 1973.
Cole, M., and Bruner, J. S. Cultural differences and inferences about psychological processes. In: J. W. Berry and P. R. Dasen (eds.), *Culture and Cognition: Readings in Cross-Cultural Psychology*. London: Methuen, 1973.
Cole, M., Gay, J., Glick, J. A., and Sharp, D. W. *The Cultural Context of Learning and Thinking*. London: Methuen, 1971.
Coleman, J. S., et al. *Equality of Educational Opportunity*. Washington, D. C.: Department of Health, Education, and Welfare, 1966.
Coles, R. *The Desegregation of Southern Schools: A Psychiatric Study*, New York: Anti-Defamation League, 1963.
Coolican, R. E. *Australian Rural Practice*. Sydney: Australian Medical Association, Mervyn Archdall Medical Monograph No. 9, 1973.
Cravioto, J., and Robles, B. Evolution of adaptive and motor behavior during rehabilitation from kwashiorkor. *American Journal of Orthopsychiatry*, 1965, *35*, 449–458.
Dale, P. S. *Language Development: Structure and Function*. Hinsdale, Ill.: Dryden, 1972.
Dasen, P. R. Piagetian research in central Australia. In: G. E. Kearney, P. R. de Lacey, and G. R. Davidson (eds.), *The Psychology of Aboriginal Australians*. Sydney: Wiley, 1973.
Dasen, P. R., de Lacey, P. R., and Seagrim, G. N. Reasoning ability in adopted and fostered Aboriginal children. In: G. E. Kearney, P. R. de Lacey, and G. R. Davidson (eds.), *The Psychology of Aboriginal Australians*. Sydney: Wiley, 1973.
Dave, R. H. The identification and measurement of environmental process variables that are related to educational achievement. Chicago: University of Chicago, unpublished doctoral dissertation, 1963.
Davidson, G. R. Brisbane: Department of Psychology, University of Queensland, 1971.
Dawe, H. C. A study of the effect of an educational program upon language development and related mental functions in young children. *Journal of Experimental Education*, 1942, *11*, 200–209.
Dawson, J. L. M. Cultural and physiological influence upon spatial-perceptual processes in West Africa. *International Journal of Psychology*, 1967, *2*, 115–128 and 171–185.
de Lacey, P. R. Classificatory ability. *Journal of Cross-Cultural Psychology*, 1970, *1*, 293–304.
de Lacey, P. R. Verbal intelligence, operational thinking and environment in part-Aboriginal children. *Australian Journal of Psychology*, 1971, *23*, 145–149.
de Lacey, P. R., and Taylor, L. J. *Three dimensions of Aboriginal Intelligence*. Paper presented to the General Meeting of the Australian Institute of Aboriginal Studies, Canberra,

Bibliography

May 1972.

de Lacey, P. R., Taylor, L. J., and Nurcombe, B. An assessment of the reliability of the Peabody Picture Vocabulary Test. *Australian Psychologist*, 1972, *7*, 167–169.

de Lacey, P. R., Nurcombe, B., Taylor, L. J., and Moffitt, P. F. Effects of enrichment preschooling: an Australian followup study. *Exceptional Children*, 1973, *40*, 171–176.

de Las Casas, B. Quoted in: L. Hanke, *Aristotle and the American Indians*. Chicago: Regnery, 1959.

De Lemos, M. M. The development of conservation. *International Journal of Psychology*, 1969, *4*, 255–269.

Deutsch, M. The disadvantaged in the learning process. In: A. H. Passow (ed.), *Education in Depressed Areas*. New York: Teachers College Press, Columbia University, 1963.

Deutsch, M. (ed.). *The Disadvantaged Child*. New York: Basic Books, 1967.

Deutsch, M., Levinson, A., Brown, B. R., and Peisach, E. C. Communication of information in the elementary school classroom. In: M. Deutsch (ed.), *The Disadvantaged Child*. New York: Basic Books, 1967.

Dickie, J. P. Effectiveness of structured and unstructured (traditional) methods of language training. In: M. A. Brottman (ed.), *Language Remediation for the Disadvantaged Preschool Child*. Monographs of the Society for Research in Child Development, 1968, *124*, 62–79.

Di Lorenzo, L. T., and Salter, R. An evaluative study of pre-kindergarten programs for educationally disadvantaged children: follow-up and replication. *Exceptional Children*, 1968, *35*, 111–119.

Dobzhansky, T. *Genetic Diversity and Human Equality*. New York: Basic Books, 1973.

Duffy, B. Unpublished research data. Sydney: School of Paediatrics, University of New South Wales, 1973.

Duffy, B., and Nurcombe, B. Unpublished research data. Sydney: School of Paediatrics, University of New South Wales, 1969.

Duncan, A. T. Paper delivered to the Australian Conference on Cognitive Development, Canberra, February 1973.

Dunn, L. M. *The Peabody Picture Vocabulary Test*. Circle Pines, Minn.: American Guidance Service, 1965.

Eckermann, A.-K. Group identity and urban Aborigines. Paper delivered to the Forty-Third Annual Congress of the Australian and New Zealand Association for the Advancement of Science, Brisbane, May 1971.

Eckermann, A.-K. Value orientation. In: G. E. Kearney, P. R. de Lacey, and G. R. Davidson (eds.), *The Psychology of Aboriginal Australians*. Sydney: Wiley, 1973.

Eels, K., Davis, A., and Havighurst, R. J. *Intelligence and Cultural Differences*. Chicago: University of Chicago Press, 1951.

Eiferman, R. *School Children's Games*. Washington, D. C.: Department of Health, Education, and Welfare, 1968.

Engelmann, S. The effectiveness of direct instruction on IQ performance and achievement in reading and arithmetic. In: J. Hellmuth (ed.), *The Disadvantaged Child*. Volume III. New York: Brunner-Mazel, 1970.

Entwisle, D. T. Semantic systems of children: some assessments of social class and ethnic differences. In: F. Williams (ed.), *Language and Poverty: Perspectives on a Theme*. Chicago: Markham, 1970.

Erickson, E. L., McMillan, J., Bennell, J., Hoffman, L., and Callaghan, O. D. *Experiments in Head Start and Early Education*. Washington, D. C.: Office of Economic

Bibliography

Opportunity, 1969.
Erlenmeyer-Kimling, L., and Jarvik, L. F. Genetics and intelligence. *Science*, 1964, *142*, 1477–1479.
Evans, E. E. *Contemporary Influences in Early Childhood Education*. New York: Holt, Rinehart and Winston, 1971.
Eysenck, H. J. *Race, Intelligence and Education*. Melbourne: Sun Books, 1971.
Fanon, F. *The Wretched of the Earth*. Translated by C. Farrington. New York: Grove Press, 1965.
Fink, R. A. The caste-barrier—an obstacle to the assimilation of part-Aborigines in north-west New South Wales. *Oceania*, 1957, *28*, 100–110.
Fiske, J. *Man's Destiny*. London: Macmillan, 1893.
Flavell, J. H. *The Developmental Psychology of Jean Piaget*. New York: Van Nostrand, 1963.
Flint, E. H. *Aboriginal English*. Brisbane: University of Queensland, 1970.
Frazer, J. G. Types of magic. In: T. Parsons, E. Shils, K. O. Naegele, and J. R. Pitts (eds.), *Theories of Society*. Volume II. New York: Free Press, 1961.
Freeman, F. N. The meaning of intelligence. *Yearbook of the National Society for the Study of Education*, 1940, *39*, 11–20.
Fries, C. C. *American English Grammar*. New York: Appleton Century Crofts, 1940.
Frostig, M., and Horne, D. *The Frostig Program for the Development of Visual Perception*. Chicago: Follett, 1964.
Furth, H. G. On language and knowing in Piaget's developmental theory. *Human Development*, 1970, *13*, 241–257.
Furth, H. G., and Youniss, J. Formal operations and language: a comparison of deaf and hearing adolescents. *International Journal of Psychology*, 1971, *6*, 49–64.
Galton, F. *Hereditary Genius*. London: Macmillan, 1869.
Garrow, J. S., and Pike, M. C. Long-term prognosis of severe infantile malnutrition. *Lancet*, 1967, *1*, 1–8.
Ghiselin, B. *The Creative Process*. New York: Mentor Books, 1955.
Ginsburg, B. E. Developmental behavioral genetics. In: N. B. Talbot, J. Kagan, and L. Eisenberg (eds.), *Behavioral Science in Pediatric Medicine*. Philadelphia: Saunders, 1971.
Golden, M., Birns, B., Bridger, W., and Moss, A. Social class differentiation in cognitive development among black preschool children. *Child Development*, 1971, *42*, 37–45.
Gordon, E. W. Problems in the determination of educability in populations with differential characteristics. In: J. Hellmuth (ed.), *The Disadvantaged Child*. Volume III. New York: Brunner-Mazel, 1970.
Gordon, I. J. Stimulation via parent education. *Children*, 1969, *16*, 57–59.
Graham, G. G. Environmental factors affecting the growth of children. *American Journal of Clinical Nutrition*, 1972, *25*, 1184–1193.
Gray, S. W. Selected longitudinal studies of compensatory education: a look from the inside. Paper presented at the 77th Annual Meeting of the American Psychological Association, Washington, D. C., 1969.
Gray, S. W., and Klaus, R. A. *Before First Grade: The Early Training Project for Culturally Disadvantaged Children*. New York: Teachers College Press, Columbia University, 1968.
Gray, S. W., and Klaus, R. A. The early training project: a seventh year report. *Child Development*, 1970, *41*, 909–924.
Grey, A. Aboriginal education through supported Aboriginal responsible involvement. Paper presented at the Education Section of the Forty-First Congress of the

BIBLIOGRAPHY

Australian and New Zealand Association for the Advancement of Science, Adelaide, 1969.
Griffiths, R. *The Abilities of Babies: A Study in Mental Measurement*. London: University of London Press, 1954.
Guilford, J. P. *The Nature of Human Intelligence*. New York: McGraw-Hill, 1967.
Guthrie, G. Structure of abilities in a non-western culture. *Journal of Educational Psychology*, 1963, *54*, 94–103.
Harrell, R. F., Woodyard, E., and Gates, A. I. *The Effect of Mother's Diet on the Intelligence of Offspring*. New York: Teachers College, Columbia Bureau of Publications, 1955.
Harries, W. T. The effect of a traditional preschool programme on the intelligence and psycholinguistic abilities of mixed blood Aboriginal children. Paper presented at the Sixth Annual Conference of the Australian Psychological Society, Melbourne, 1971.
Harris, D. B. *Children's Drawings as Measures of Intellectual Maturity: A Revision and Extension of the Goodenough Draw-A-Man Test*. New York: Harcourt Brace Jovanovich, 1963.
Hart, N. W. M. A task-analysis approach to language programming. In: G. E. Kearney, P. R. de Lacey, and G. R. Davidson (eds.), *The Psychology of Aboriginal Australians*. Sydney: Wiley, 1973.
Hawkins, P. R. Social class, the nominal group and reference. *Language and Speech*, 1969, *12*, 125–135.
Hebb, D. O. *The Organization of Behavior*. New York: Wiley, 1949.
Henderson, D. Social class differences in form class usage among five-year-old children. In: W. Brandis and D. Henderson (eds.), *Social Class, Language and Communication*. London: Routledge & Kegan Paul, 1970.
Herriot, P. *An Introduction to the Psychology of Language*. London: Methuen, 1970.
Herrnstein, R. J. IQ. *The Atlantic Monthly*, 1971, *228*, 43–64.
Hess, R. D., and Shipman, V. C. Early experience and the socialization of cognitive modes in children. *Child Development*, 1965, *36*, 869–886.
Hiatt, L. *Kinship and Conflict*. Canberra: Australian National University Press, 1965.
Hirsch, G. Behavior-genetic analysis and its biosocial consequences. In: R. Cancro (ed.), *Intelligence: Genetic and Environmental Influences*. New York: Grune & Stratton, 1971.
Hockett, C. F. The origin of speech. *Scientific American*, 1960, *203*, 89–96.
Hockett, C. F., and Ascher, R. The human revolution. *Current Anthropology*, 1964, *5*, 135–147.
Hodges, N., McCandless, B., and Spicker, H. *The Development and Evaluation of a Diagnostically Based Curriculum for Pre-School Psychologically Deprived Children*. Washington, D.C.: U.S. Office of Education, 1967.
Horner, V. M., and Gussow, J. D. John and Mary: a pilot study in linguistic ecology. In: C. B. Cazden, V. P. John, and D. Hymes (eds.), *Functions of Language in the Classroom*. New York: Teachers College Press, Columbia University, 1972.
Hunt, J. McV. *Intelligence and Experience*. New York: Ronald Press, 1961.
Hymes, D. Introduction. In: C. B. Cazden, V. P. John, and D. Hymes (eds.), *Functions of Language in the Classroom*. New York: Teachers College Press, Columbia University, 1972.
Inhelder, B., and Sinclair, H. Learning cognitive structures. In: P. H. Mussen, J. Lange, and M. Covington (eds.), *Trends and Issues in Developmental Psychology*. New York: Holt, Rinehart and Winston, 1969.

BIBLIOGRAPHY

Irvine, S. H. Towards a rationale for testing abilities and attainments in Africa. *British Journal of Educational Psychology*, 1966, *36*, 24–32.
Irvine, S. H. Contributions of ability and attainment testing in Africa to a general theory of intellect. *Journal of Biosocial Science*, 1969a, Supplement No. 1, 91–102.
Irvine, S. H. Culture and mental ability. *New Scientist*, 1969b, 1 May, 230–231.
Irvine, S. H. Factor analysis of African abilities and attainments: constructs across cultures. *Psychological Bulletin*, 1969c, *71*, 20–32.
Irwin, O. C. Infant speech: the effect of family occupational status and of age on use of sound types. *Journal of Speech and Hearing Disorders*, 1948, *13*, 224–226 and 320–323.
Jencks, C., et al. *Inequality: A Reassessment of the Effects of Family and Schooling in America*. New York: Basic Books, 1972.
Jensen, A. R. Learning abilities in Mexican-American and Anglo-American children. *California Journal of Educational Research*, 1961, *12*, 147–159.
Jensen, A. R. Learning abilities in retarded, gifted and average children. *Merrill-Palmer Quarterly*, 1963, *9*, 123–140.
Jensen, A. R. Verbal mediation and educational potential. *Psychology in the Schools*, 1966, *3*, 99–109.
Jensen, A. R. Estimation of the limits of heritability of traits by comparison of monozygotic and dizygotic twins. *Proceedings of the National Academy of Sciences*, 1967, *58*, 149–157.
Jensen, A. R. The culturally disadvantaged and the heredity-environment uncertainty. In: J. Hellmuth (ed.), *The Disadvantaged Child*. Volume II. New York: Brunner-Mazel, 1968a.
Jensen, A. R. Social class and verbal learning. In: M. Deutsch, I. Katz, and A. R. Jensen (eds.), *Social Class, Race and Psychological Development*. New York: Holt, Rinehart and Winston, 1968b.
Jensen, A. R. How much can we boost IQ and educational achievement? *Harvard Educational Review*, 1969a, *39*, 1–123.
Jensen, A. R. Reducing the heredity-environment uncertainty: a reply. *Harvard Educational Review*, 1969b, *39*, 449–483.
Jensen, A. R. Another look at culture-fair testing. In: J. Hellmuth (ed.), *The Disadvantaged Child*. Volume III. New York: Brunner-Mazel, 1970a.
Jensen, A. R. Can we and should we study race-differences? In: J. Hellmuth (ed.), *The Disadvantaged Child*. Volume III. New York: Brunner-Mazel, 1970b.
Jensen, A. R. The race × sex × ability interaction. In: R. Cancro (ed.), *Intelligence: Genetic and Environmental Influences*. New York: Grune & Stratton, 1971a.
Jensen, A. R. The role of verbal mediation in mental development. *Journal of Genetic Psychology*, 1971b, *118*, 39–70.
Jensen, A. R. The IQ controversy: a reply to Layzer. *Cognition: International Journal of Cognitive Psychology*, 1973a, *4*, 427–452.
Jensen, A. R. The differences are real. *Psychology Today*, December 1973b, *7*, 80–86.
Jensen, A. R. *Educability and Group Differences*. New York: Harper & Row, 1973c.
Jensen, A. R. Review of T. Dobzhansky: *Genetic Diversity and Human Equality*. *Perspectives in Biology and Medicine*, 1974a, 17(3), 430–434.
Jensen, A. R. Interaction of Level I and Level II abilities with race and socioeconomic status. Unpublished manuscript, 1974b.
Jensen, A. R. The effect of race of examiner on the mental test scores of white and black pupils. *Journal of Educational Measurement*, 1974c, *11*, 1–14.
Jensen, A. R., Collins, C. C., and Vreeland, R. W. A multiple S-R apparatus for human

learning. *American Journal of Psychology*, 1962, *75*, 470–476.
Jessor, R., and Richardson, S. Psychosocial deprivation and personality development. In: *Perspectives on Human Deprivation: Biological, Psychological and Social*. Washington, D.C.: Department of Health, Education, and Welfare, 1968.
John, V. P. The intellectual development of slum children: some preliminary findings. *American Journal of Orthopsychiatry*, 1963, *33*, 813–822.
John, V. P., and Goldstein, L. S. The social context of language acquisition. *Merrill-Palmer Quarterly*, 1964, *10*, 265–276.
Kagan, J. Personality development. In: N. B. Talbot, J. Kagan, and L. Eisenberg (eds.), *Behavioral Science in Pediatric Medicine*. Philadelphia: Saunders, 1971.
Karnes, M. B. Evaluation and implications of research with young handicapped and low-income children. In: J. C. Stanley (ed.), *Compensatory Education for Children, Ages 2 to 8*. Baltimore: Johns Hopkins, 1973.
Karnes, M. B., Studley, W. M., Wright, W. W., and Hodgins, A. S. An approach for working with mothers of disadvantaged preschool children. *Merrill-Palmer Quarterly*, 1968, *14*, 174–184.
Karnes, M. B., Teska, J. A., and Hodgins, A. S. The effects of four programs of classroom intervention on the intellectual and language development of four-year-old disadvantaged children. *American Journal of Orthopsychiatry*, 1970a, *1*, 58–76.
Karnes, M. B., Teska, J. A., Hodgins, A. S., and Badger, E. D. Educational intervention at home by mothers of disadvantaged infants. *Child Development*, 1970b, *41*, 925–935.
Katz, I. Review of evidence relating to effects of desegregation on the intellectual performance of Negroes. In: A. H. Passow, M. Goldberg, and A. J. Tannenbaum (eds.), *Education of the Disadvantaged*. New York: Holt, Rinehart and Winston, 1967.
Katz, I. Factors influencing Negro performance in the desegregated school. In: M. Deutsch, I. Katz, and A. R. Jensen (eds.), *Social Class, Race and Psychological Development*. New York: Holt, Rinehart and Winston, 1968.
Kawi, A. A., and Pasamanick, B. The continuum of reproductive casualty. *Journal of the American Medical Association*, 1958, *166*, 1420–1425.
Kearney, G. E. Some aspects of the general cognitive ability of various groups of Aboriginal Australians as assessed by the Queensland Test. Brisbane: University of Queensland, unpublished doctoral dissertation, 1966.
Kelly, M. *Report to the Department of Education, Papua New Guinea: An Ongoing Educational Research Project Involving Cognition, Classroom Interaction and Attitudes in a Developmental Framework*. Sydney: MacQuarie University, 1973.
Kelly, M., and Nurcombe, B. Unpublished research data. Bourke, NSW: Project Enrichment of Childhood, 1973.
Kerr, C. Race, intelligence and education—continued. *Medical Journal of Australia*, 1973, *1*, 199.
Kirk, S., McCarthy, J., and Kirk, W. *The Illinois Test of Psycholinguistic Abilities*. Urbana: University of Illinois, 1968.
Kirke, K. Morbidity, mortality and malnutrition in Aboriginal children. In: G. M. Maxwell (ed.), *The Australian Aboriginal Child*. Sydney: Ross Laboratories, 1972.
Klaus, R., and Gray, S. The early training program for disadvantaged children: a report after five years. *Monographs of the Society for Research in Child Development*, *33*, No. 4, 1968.
Klineberg, O. *Race and Psychology*. Paris: UNESCO, 1951.
Kluckhohn, F., and Strodtbeck, F. *Variants in Value Orientations*, New York: Row, Peterson, 1961.

Bibliography

Kochman, T. Black American speech events and a language program for the classroom. In: C. B. Cazden, V. P. John, and D. Hymes (eds.), *Functions of Language in the Classroom*. New York: Teachers College Press, Columbia University, 1972.

Labov, W. *The Study of Non-Standard English*. Washington, D.C.: National Council of Teachers of English and Center for Applied Linguistics, 1970a.

Labov, W. The logic of nonstandard English. In: F. Williams (ed.), *Language and Poverty: Perspectives on a Theme*. Chicago: Markham, 1970b.

LaCivita, A. F., Kean, J. M., and Yamamoto, K. Socioeconomic status of children and acquisition of grammar. *Journal of Educational Research*, 1966, *60*, 71–74.

Lantz, D. L., and Stefflre, V. Language and cognition revisited. *International Journal of Abnormal and Social Psychology*, 1964, *69*, 472–481.

Lantz, D. L., and Lenneberg, E. H. Verbal communication and color memory in the deaf and hearing. *Child Development*, 1966, *37*, 765–779.

Lashley, K. The problem of serial order in behavior. In: L. Jeffress (ed.), *Cerebral Mechanisms in Behavior*. New York: Wiley, 1951.

Laurendeau, M., and Pinard, A. *Causal Thinking in the Child*. New York: International Universities Press, 1962.

Lawton, D. Social class language differences in group discussions. *Language and Speech*, 1964, *7*, 183–204.

Lawton, D. *Social Class, Language and Education*. London: Routledge & Kegan Paul, 1968.

Layzer, D. Science or superstition? A physical scientist looks at the IQ controversy. *Cognition: International Journal of Cognitive Psychology*, 1972, *1*, 265–309.

Layzer, D. Heritability analyses of IQ scores: science or numerology? *Science*, 1974, *183*, 1259–1266.

Leacock, E. B. (ed.), *The Culture of Poverty: A Critique*. New York: Simon & Schuster, 1971.

Leacock, E. B. Abstract versus concrete speech: a false dichotomy. In: C. B. Cazden, V. P. John, and D. Hymes (eds.), *Functions of Language in the Classroom*. New York: Teachers College Press, Columbia University, 1972.

Lenneberg, E. H. Cognition and ethnolinguistics. *Language*, 1953, *29*, 463–471.

Lenneberg, E. H., *Biological Foundations of Language*. New York: Wiley, 1967.

Lenneberg, E. H., and Roberts, J. M. The language of experiment: a study in methodology. *International Journal of American Linguistics*, 1956a, *22*, Supplement.

Lenneberg, E. H., and Roberts, J. M. *The Language of Experience*. Indianapolis: Indiana University Press, 1956b.

Lesser, G. S., Fifer, G., and Clark, D. H. Mental abilities of children in different social and cultural groups. *Monographs of the Society for Research in Child Development*, 1965, *30*, Whole Number 4.

Levin, T. Preschool education and the communities of the poor. In: J. Hellmuth (ed.), *The Disadvantaged Child*. Volume I. New York: Brunner-Mazel, 1967.

Lévi-Strauss, C. *The Savage Mind*. New York: Random House, 1962.

Lewis, O. *Five Families: Mexican Case Studies in the Culture of Poverty*. New York: Basic Books, 1959.

Lewis, O. *The Children of Sanchez*. New York: Random House, 1961.

Lewis, O. *Pedro Martinez*. New York: Random House, 1964.

Lewis, O. *La Vida*. New York: Random House, 1966.

Li, C. C. A tale of two thermos bottles: properties of a genetic model for human intelligence. In: R. Cancro (ed.), *Intelligence: Genetic and Environmental Influences*. New York: Grune & Stratton, 1971.

Lloyd, B. B. *Perception and Cognition*. Harmondsworth: Penguin, 1972.

Loban, W. D. *The Language of Elementary School Children*. Champaign, Ill.: National

BIBLIOGRAPHY

Council of Teachers of English, 1963.
Lunzer, E. A. *The Regulation of Behavior*, London: Staples, 1968.
Luria, A. R. The directive function of speech in early childhood. *Word*, 1959, *15*, 341–352.
Lyons, J. *Chomsky*. London: Fontana, 1970.
McAfee, O. An integrated approach to early childhood education. In: J. C. Stanley (ed.), *Preschool Programs for the Disadvantaged*. Baltimore: Johns Hopkins, 1972.
McCandless, B. R., Smock, C. D., Noll, V. H., and others. Reviews of the Boehm Test of Basic Concepts. In: O. Buros (ed.), *The Seventh Mental Measurements Yearbook*. Volume I. Highland Park, N.J.: Gryphon Press, 1972.
McClelland, D. C. Testing for competence rather than intelligence. *American Psychologist*, 1973, *28*, 1–14.
Maccoby, E. E., and Zellner, M. *Experiments in Primary Education: Aspects of Project Follow-Through*. New York: Harcourt Brace Jovanovich, 1970.
McConnell, F., Horton, K. B., and Smith, B. R. Language development and cultural disadvantagement. *Exceptional Children*, 1969, *35*, 597–606.
McElwain, D. W., and Kearney, G. E. Intellectual development. In: G. E. Kearney, P. R. de Lacey, and G. R. Davidson (eds.), *The Psychology of Aboriginal Australians*. Sydney: Wiley, 1973.
Maclay, H. An experimental study of language and non-linguistic behavior. In: J. W. Berry and P. R. Dasen (eds.), *Culture and Cognition: Readings in Cross-Cultural Psychology*. London: Methuen, 1973.
McNeill, D. The creation of language. *Discovery*, 1966, *27*, 34–38.
Marans, A. E., and Lourie, R. Hypotheses regarding the effects of child-rearing patterns on the disadvantaged child. In: J. Hellmuth (ed.), *The Disadvantaged Child*. Volume I. New York: Brunner-Mazel, 1967.
Marsella, A. J., and Golden, C. G. The structure of cognitive abilities in Americans of Japanese and of European ancestry in Hawaii, 1973. Honolulu: Department of Psychology, University of Hawaii, unpublished manuscript, 1973.
Marsella, A. J., and Higgenbottham, H. N. *Sensory Types: Towards an Interactionist Model of Human Behaviour*. Honolulu: Department of Psychology, University of Hawaii, Ethnopsychology Laboratory, Working Paper No. 1, 1973.
Mehler, J. Studies in language and thought development. In: R. Huxley and E. Ingram (eds.), *Language Acquisition: Models and Methods*. London: Academic Press, 1971.
Meier, J. H., Nimnicht, G., and McAfee, O. An autotelic responsive environment for deprived children. In: J. Hellmuth (ed.), *The Disadvantaged Child*. Volume II. New York: Brunner-Mazel, 1968.
Mercer, J. R. Pluralistic diagnosis in the evaluation of black and Chicano children: a procedure for taking sociocultural variables into account in clinical assessment. Paper presented at the Annual Conference of the American Psychological Association, Washington, D.C., 1971.
Miller, G. A., Galanter, E., and Pribram, K. H. *Plans and the Structure of Behavior*. New York: Holt Dryden, 1960.
Miller, G. A., and McNeill, D. Psycholinguistics. In: G. Lindzey and E. Aronsen (eds.), *The Handbook of Social Psychology*. Volume III. New York: Addison-Wesley, 1969.
Miller, L. B., and Dyer, J. L. *Two Kinds of Kindergarten after Four Types of Head Start*. Louisville, Ky.: University of Louisville, 1971.
Moffitt, P. F., and Nurcombe, B. Action research—a preschool for rural Aborigines and Europeans. *Australian Psychologist*, 1970, *5*, 243–248.

Bibliography

Moffitt, P. F., Nurcombe, B., Passmore, M., and McNeilly, A. Intervention in cultural deprivation. *Australian Psychologist*, 1971, *6*, 51–61.

Moore, O. K. Autotelic responsive environments for learning. In: R. Gross and J. Murphy (eds.), *The Revolution in the Schools*. New York: Harcourt Brace Jovanovich, 1964.

Moynihan, D. P. *The Negro Family: The Case for National Action*. Washington, D.C.: Department of Labor, 1965.

Moynihan, D. P., and Schelling, C. S. (eds.). *On Understanding Poverty: Perspectives for the Social Sciences*. New York: Basic Books, 1969.

Nimnicht, G., McAfee, O., and Meier, J. *The New Nursery School*. New York: General Learning Corporation, 1969.

Nixon, M. C. Development of classification skills in young children. Melbourne: University of Melbourne, unpublished doctoral dissertation, 1967.

Nurcombe, B. Precausal and paracausal thinking: concepts of causality in Aboriginal children. *Australian and New Zealand Journal of Psychiatry*, 1970a, *4*, 70–81.

Nurcombe, B. Deprivation. *Medical Journal of Australia*, 1970b, *2*, 87–92.

Nurcombe, B. Morningstar. Sydney: School of Psychiatry, University of New South Wales, unpublished manuscript, 1973.

Nurcombe, B., Bianchi, G. M., Money, J., and Cawte, J. E. A hunger for stimuli: petrol inhalation. *British Journal of Medical Psychology*, 1970, *43*, 367–374.

Nurcombe, B., and Moffitt, P. F. Cultural deprivation and language deficit. *Australian Psychologist*, 1970, *5*, 249–259.

Nurcombe, B., de Lacey, P. R., Moffitt, P. F., and Taylor, L. J. The question of Aboriginal intelligence. *Medical Journal of Australia*, 1973, *2*, 625–630.

Nurcombe, B., de Lacey, P. R., and Taylor, L. J. The Bourke experiment: 1972. Structured and semi-structured language programs in a rural preschool. Sydney: University of New South Wales, unpublished manuscript, 1973.

Osborne, R. T., and Gregor, A. J. Racial differences in heritability estimates for tests of spatial ability. *Perceptual and Motor Skills*, 1968, *27*, 735–739.

Osborne, R. T., Gregor, A. J., and Miele, F. Heritability of factor V: verbal comprehension. *Perceptual and Motor Skills*, 1968, *26*, 191–202.

Osborne, R. T., and Miele, F. Racial differences in environmental influences on numerical ability as determined by heritability estimates. *Perceptual and Motor Skills*, 1969, *28*, 535–538.

Osser, H., Wang, M. D., and Zaid, F. The young child's ability to imitate and comprehend speech. *Child Development*, 1969, *40*, 1063–1075.

Painter, G. The effect of a structured tutorial program on cognitive and language development of culturally disadvantaged infants. *Merrill-Palmer Quarterly*, 1969, *15*, 279–294.

Palmer, F. H. Learning at two. *Children*, 1969, *16*, 55–57.

Pasamanick, B. Socioeconomic status: some precursors of neuropsychiatric disorder. *American Journal of Orthopsychiatry*, 1956, *26*, 594–603.

Pavlov, I. P. *Conditioned Reflexes*. Oxford: Clarendon Press, 1927.

Piaget, J. *Le Structuralisme*. Paris: Universitaires de France, 1968.

Piaget, J. *Genetic Epistemology*. Translated by E. Buckworth. New York: Columbia University Press, 1970.

Popham, J. Probing the validity of arguments against behavioral goals. In: R. J. Kibler, L. L. Barker, and D. T. Miles (eds.), *Behavioral Objectives and Instruction*. Boston: Allyn and Bacon, 1970.

Porteus, S. D. Ethnic group differences. *Mankind Quarterly*, 1961, *1*, 187–200.

Bibliography

Porteus, S. D., Bochner, S., Russell, J., and David, K. Age as a factor in Australid mentality. *Perceptual and Motor Skills*, Monograph Supplement 1-V25, 1967, *25*, 3–16.
Provence, S. A three-pronged project. *Children*, 1969, *16*, 53–55.
Rapier, J. L. The learning abilities of normal and retarded children as a function of social class. *Journal of Educational Psychology*, 1968, *59*, 102–114.
Reay, M. Native thought in rural New South Wales. *Oceania*, 1949, *20*, 89–118.
Reay, M., and Sitlington, G. Class and status in a mixed-blood community (Moree, N.S.W.). *Oceania*, 1948, *18*, 179–207.
Robinson, H. B. The Frank Porter Grahame Child Development Center. In: C. A. Chandler, R. S. Lourie, and A. de H. Peters (eds.), *Early Child Care: New Perspectives*. New York: Atherton Press, 1968.
Robinson, W. P. Where do children's answers come from? In: B. Bernstein (ed.), *Class, Codes and Control*. London: Routledge & Kegan Paul, 1973.
Robinson, W. P., and Rackstraw, S. J. *A Question of Answers*. London: Routledge & Kegan Paul, 1972.
Roget, P. M. *Thesaurus of English Words and Phrases*. Abridged edition with additions by J. L. Roget and S. R. Roget. Harmondsworth: Penguin, 1965.
Rohwer, W. D. Prime time for education: early childhood or adolescence? *Harvard Educational Review*, 1971, *41*, 316–341.
Rosenthal, R., and Jacobsen, L. *Pygmalion in the Classroom*. New York: Holt, Rinehart and Winston, 1968.
Ross, B. M., and Cawte, J. E. Unpublished research data. Sydney: University of New South Wales, 1969.
Rowley, C. D. *The Destruction of Aboriginal Society*. Volume I. Canberra: Australian National University Press, 1970.
Russell, B. *A History of Western Philosophy*. New York: Simon & Schuster, 1945.
Sanday, P. R. On the causes of IQ differences between groups and implications for social policy. *Journal of the Society for Applied Anthropology*, 1972, *31*, 411–423.
Sapir, E. *Language: An Introduction to the Study of Speech*. New York: Harcourt, Brace and World, 1921.
Sarason, S. B. Jewishness, blackishness and the nature-nurture controversy. *American Psychologist*, 1973, *28*, 962–971.
Scarr-Salapatek, S. Race, social class, and IQ. *Science*, 1971, *174*, 1285–1295.
Schaefer, E. S. A home-tutoring program. *Children*, 1969, *16*, 59–61.
Schoggen, M. *An Ecological Study of Three-Year-Olds at Home*. Nashville: George Peabody College for Teachers, 1969.
Scrimshaw, N. S., and Gordon, J. E. (eds.). *Malnutrition, Learning and Behavior*. Proceedings of an International Conference Cosponsored by the Nutrition Foundation Incorporated and the Massachusetts Institute of Technology. Cambridge, Mass.: M.I.T. Press, 1968.
Semler, I. J., and Iscoe, I. Comparative and developmental study of the learning abilities of Negro and white children under four conditions. *Journal of Educational Psychology*, 1963, *54*, 38–44.
Shatzman, L., and Strauss, A. Social class and modes of communication. *American Journal of Sociology*, 1955, *60*, 329–338.
Shriner, T. H., and Miner, L. Morphological structures in the language of advantaged and disadvantaged children. *Journal of Speech and Hearing Research*, 1968, *11*, 605–610.
Shuey, A. M. *The Testing of Negro Intelligence*. New York: Social Science Press, 1966.
Sigel, I. E. Reflections. In: I. E. Sigel and F. H. Hooper (eds.), *Logical Thinking in Children*.

Bibliography

New York: Holt, Rinehart and Winston, 1968a.
Sigel, I. E. The distancing hypothesis: a causal hypothesis for the acquisition of representational thought. In: M. R. Jones (ed.), *Miami Symposium on the Prediction of Behavior*. Coral Gables: University of Miami Press, 1968b.
Sigel, I. E. Where is preschool education going: or are we en route without a road map? In: *Proceedings of the 1972 Invitational Conference on Testing Problems—Assessment in a Pluralistic Society*. Princeton, N.J.: Educational Testing Service, 1973.
Sigel, I. E., and McBane, B. Cognitive competence and level of symbolization among five-year-old children. In: J. Hellmuth (ed.), *The Disadvantaged Child*. Volume I. New York: Brunner-Mazel, 1967.
Sigel, I. E., and Olmstead, P. Modification of classificatory competence and level of representation among lower-class Negro kindergarten children. In: A. H. Passow (ed.), *Reaching the Disadvantaged Learner*. New York: Teachers College Press, Columbia University, 1970a.
Sigel, I. E., and Olmsted, P. Modification of cognitive skills among lower-class black children. In: J. Hellmuth (ed.), *The Disadvantaged Child*. Volume III. New York: Brunner-Mazel, 1970b.
Sigel, I. E., Secrist, A., and Forman, G. Psycho-educational intervention beginning at age two: reflections and outcomes. In: J. C. Stanley (ed.), *Compensatory Education for Children, Ages 2 to 8*. Baltimore: Johns Hopkins, 1973.
Sigelman, C. K. Social class and ethnic differences in language development. In: L. S. Wrightsman (ed.), *Social Psychology in the Seventies*. Monterey: Brooks-Cole, 1972.
Sinclair-De-Zwart, H. Developmental psycholinguistics. In: D. Elkind and J. H. Flavell (eds.), *Studies in Cognitive Development: Essays in Honor of Jean Piaget*. New York: Oxford University Press, 1969.
Skeels, H. M. Adult status of children with contrasting early life experiences: a follow-up study. *Monographs of the Society for Research in Child Development*, 1966, *31*, 1-65.
Skinner, B. F. *Verbal Behavior*. New York: Appleton Century Crofts, 1957.
Smilansky, S. The effect of certain learning conditions on the progress of disadvantaged children of kindergarten age. *Journal of School Psychology*, 1968, *4*, 68-81.
Smilansky, S., and Smilansky, M. The role and program of pre-school education for socially disadvantaged children. *International Review of Education*, 1970, *16*, 45-65.
Smith, M. S., and Bissell, J. S. Report analysis: the impact of Head Start. *Harvard Educational Review*, 1970, *40*, 51-104.
Sommerlad, E. A., and Berry, J. Role of ethnic identification in distinguishing between attitudes towards assimilation and integration of a minority racial group. *Human Relations*, 1970, *23*, 23-29.
Sonquist, H. D., and Kamii, C. K. Applying some Piagetian concepts in the classroom for the disadvantaged. In: J. L. Frost (ed.), *Early Childhood Education Re-discovered*. New York: Holt, Rinehart and Winston, 1968.
Sontag, M., Sella, A. P., and Thorndike, R. L. The effect of Head Start training on the cognitive growth of disadvantaged children. *Journal of Educational Research*, 1969, *62*, 387-389.
Spearman, C. *The Abilities of Man*. New York: Macmillan, 1927.
Spencer, H. *The Principles of Psychology*. Third edition. New York: Appleton, 1895.
Staats, A. W. *Learning, Language and Cognition*. New York: Holt, Rinehart and Winston, 1968.

Stanford-Binet Intelligence Scale. New York: Houghton Mifflin, 1960.

Stanley, J. C. (ed.). *Preschool Programs for the Disadvantaged: Five Experimental Approaches to Early Childhood Education.* Baltimore: Johns Hopkins, 1972.

Stanley, J. C. (ed.). *Compensatory Education for Children, Ages 2 to 8: Recent Studies of Educational Intervention.* Baltimore: Johns Hopkins, 1973.

Stevens, F. H. *Racism: The Australian Experience.* Volumes I to III. Sydney: Australian and New Zealand Book Company, 1971-1972.

Stewart, W. A. (ed.). *Non-Standard Speech and the Teaching of English.* Washington, D.C.: Center for Applied Linguistics, 1964.

Stoch, M. B., and Smythe, P. M. Does undernutrition during infancy inhibit brain growth and subsequent intellectual development? *Archives of Diseases of Childhood,* 1963, *38,* 546-554.

Stodolsky, S. S., and Lesser, G. Learning patterns in the disadvantaged. *Harvard Educational Review,* 1967, *37,* 546-593.

Strodtbeck, F. L. The hidden curriculum of the middle-class home. In: C. W. Hunnicutt (ed.), *Urban Education and Cultural Deprivation.* Syracuse: Syracuse University Press, 1964.

Taplin, G. The Narrinyeri. In: J. D. Woods (ed.), *The Native Tribes of South Australia.* Adelaide: Wigg, 1879.

Taylor, L. J., de Lacey, P. R., and Nurcombe, B. An assessment of the reliability of the Peabody Picture Vocabulary Test. *Australian Psychologist,* 1972, *7,* 167-169.

Taylor, L. J., Nurcombe, B., and de Lacey, P. R. Research note: classification ability in Aboriginal children: a re-evaluation. *Australian Psychologist,* 1973, *8,* 246-249.

Taylor, L. J., Nurcombe, B., and de Lacey, P. R. The ethics of preschool intervention: Project Enrichment of Childhood, Bourke, N.S.W. *Australian Journal of Social Issues,* 1974, *9,* 29-34.

Teasdale, G. R., and Katz, F. M. Psycholinguistic abilities. *Australian Journal of Psychology,* 1968, *20,* 155-159.

Templin, M. C. *Certain Language Skills in Children: Their Development and Interrelationships.* Minneapolis: University of Minnesota Press, 1957.

Terman, L. M., and Oden, M. H. *The Gifted Group at Midlife: Thirty-Five Years Follow Up of the Superior Child.* Stanford: Stanford University Press, 1959.

Thorndike, E. L. *The Measurement of Intelligence.* New York: Teachers College Press, Columbia University, 1927.

Thorndike, R. L. Review of R. Rosenthal and L. Jacobsen, *Pygmalion in the Classroom. American Educational Research Journal,* 1968, *5,* 708-711.

Thurstone, L. L. *The Differential Growth of Mental Abilities.* Chapel Hill: University of North Carolina Press, Psychometric Laboratory, 1955.

Tiger, L., and Fox, R. *The Imperial Animal.* New York: Holt, Rinehart and Winston, 1971.

Turner, T. Piaget's structuralism. A review of *Genetic Epistemology* and *Le Structuralisme. American Anthropologist,* 1973, *75,* 351-373.

Vandenberg, S. G. The primary mental abilities of South American students: a second comparative study of the generality of a cognitive factor structure. *Multivariate Behavior Research,* 1967, *2,* 175-189.

Vandenberg, S. G. A comparison of heritability estimates of U.S. Negro and white high school students. *Acta Geneticae Medicae et Gemellologiae,* 1970, *19,* 280-284.

Vandenberg, S. G. What do we know today about the inheritance of intelligence and how do we know it? In: R. Cancro (ed.), *Intelligence: Genetic and Environmental Influences.* New York: Grune & Stratton, 1971.

Van De Reit, V., and Van De Reit, H. An evaluation of the effects of a unique sequential

BIBLIOGRAPHY

learning program on culturally deprived preschool children: final report. Washington, D.C.: ERIC, 1968.
Van De Reit, V., Van De Reit, H., and Sprigle, H. The effectiveness of a new sequential learning program with culturally disadvantaged preschool children. *Journal of School Psychology*, 1969, 7, 5-14.
van Lawick-Goodall, J. *In the Shadow of Man*. Boston: Houghton Mifflin, 1971.
Vernon, P. E. *Intelligence and Cultural Environment*. London: Methuen, 1969.
Vygotsky, L. S. *Thought and Language*. Translated by E. Haufmann and G. Vakar. Cambridge, Mass.: M.I.T. Press, 1962.
Wake, C. S. The mental characteristics of primitive man as exemplified by the Australian Aborigines. *Journal of the Anthropological Institute*, 1872, *1*, 74-84.
Watts, B. H. Personality factors in the academic success of adolescent girls. In: G. E. Kearney, P. R. de Lacey, and G. R. Davidson (eds.), *The Psychology of Aboriginal Australians*. Sydney: Wiley, 1973.
Wechsler, D. *The Measurement and Appraisal of Adult Intelligence*. Fourth edition. Baltimore: Williams & Wilkins, 1958.
Wechsler, D. *The Wechsler Preschool and Primary Scale of Intelligence*. New York: The Psychological Corporation, 1963.
Weikart, D. P. (ed.). *Preschool Intervention: A Preliminary Report of the Perry Preschool Project*. Ann Arbor: University of Michigan Press, 1967.
Weikart, D. P. Relationship of curriculum, teaching and learning in preschool education. In: J. C. Stanley (ed.), *Preschool Programs for the Disadvantaged*. Baltimore: Johns Hopkins, 1972.
Weikart, D. P., Deloria, D., Lawser, S., and Weigarink, R. *Longitudinal Results of the Ypsilanti Perry Preschool Project*. Ypsilanti, Mich.: High Scope Educational Research Foundation, 1971.
Westinghouse Learning Corporation and Ohio University. *The Impact of Head Start: An Evaluation of the Effects of Head Start on Children's Cognitive and Affective Development*. Volumes I and II. Washington, D.C.: Office of Economic Opportunity, 1969.
White, S. H. The national impact study of Head Start. In: J. Hellmuth (ed.), *The Disadvantaged Child*. Volume III. New York: Brunner-Mazel, 1970.
Williams, D. The Aboriginal child: at school, at home, and at play. Brisbane: University of Queensland, unpublished doctoral dissertation, 1971.
Williams, F., and Naremore, R. C. Social class differences in children's syntactic performance: a quantitative analysis of a field-study. *Journal of Speech and Hearing Research*, 1969, *12*, 778-793.
Winick, M. Malnutrition and brain development. *Journal of Paediatrics*, 1969, *74*, 667-679.
Winschel, J. F. In the dark...reflections on compensatory education 1960-1970. In: J. Hellmuth (ed.), *The Disadvantaged Child*. Volume III. New York: Brunner-Mazel, 1970.
Wiseman, S. *Education and Environment*. Manchester: University of Manchester Press, 1964.
Witkin, H. A. Cognitive styles across cultures. *International Journal of Psychology*, 1967, *2*, 233-250.
Wober, M. Sensotypes. *Journal of Social Psychology*, 1966, *70*, 181-189.
Wolf, R. M. The identification and measurement of environmental process variables related to intelligence. Chicago: University of Chicago, unpublished doctoral dissertation, 1963.
Wolff, P. The developmental psychologies of Jean Piaget and psychoanalysis. *Psychological Issues*, 1960, *2*, No. 1, Monograph 5.

Woods, J. D. (ed.). *The Native Tribes of South Australia.* Adelaide: Wigg, 1879.
Zigler, E. Mental retardation: current issues and approaches. In: L. W. Hoffman and M. L. Hoffman (eds.), *Review of Child Development Research.* New York: Russell Sage Foundation, 1966.
Zigler, E., and Butterfield, E. Motivational aspects of changes in IQ test performances of culturally deprived nursery school children. *Child Development,* 1968, *39*, 1–14.

INDEX

Aborigines, Australian
  alcohol and, 109, 229
  assimilation policies for, 104
  caricature of, 23
  census of in Bourke in 1970, 107
  choice-reaction time experiment and, 228
  concepts of the dream, 226–227
  considered to be a Darwinian relic, 22
  considered to be a dying race, 104
  and culture of poverty, 111–114
  degeneration hypothesis concerning languages of, 23
  diglossia, 116–119
  "doing their own thing," 228
  early history of, 105–107, 182–183
  early history of contact with whites, 182–183
  English dialect of, 116–119, 185–186
  high infant and adult mortality and morbidity of, 104, 123, 184
  increase in birth-rate of, 104
  "intelligent parasitism" of, 107
  lower intellectual faculties of, 23
  language and cognitive competence of, 114–119, 184–188
  marginality of, 108–114, 123
  marriage, 108–109
  matrifocal family of, 108–110
  need for affiliation versus need for achievement of, 229
  need to separate children from parents, 23
  notions concerning conception, 13, 104
  petrol inhalation and, 229
  physical deprivation and, 53, 104, 182–188
  rationale of intervention with, 182–188
  reaffirmation of identity, 110
  recent psychological studies of, 42–44
  reciprocity in, 108–109, 110
  scholastic disadvantage of, 114–121
  sorcery and, 107
  traditional social organization of, 182–183
  tribes of the Bourke district, 106–107
Accommodation, 201, 235
Anastasi, A., 11
Arid Zone, survey of, 122–124
Ascher, R., 192
Assimilation, recognitory and generalizing, 195, 201, 235
Autotelic responsive environment, 95

Bacon, M. K., 207
Ball, S., 95
Baratz, J. C., 67, 69, 118
Barry, H., 207
Bayley, N., 35
Beilin, H., 100
Bereiter, C., 63, 68
  DISTAR, 90–92, 95–100, 133–134, 137–139, 143–180 passim
Bernstein, B., 34
  concept of language code, 63–67
  criticism of deprivation concept, 70–71, 186
Berry, J. W., 17–18, 110–111, 185
  theory of ecological functionalism, 207, 228

INDEX

Binet, A.
  attempt to measure intelligence directly, 6
  eclectic construction of intelligence test, 5–7
  failure of, to define intelligence, 7
Biogrammar, 223
Bissell, J. S., 80, 96
black, American
  aspirations, 59
  caricature of, 23
  cognitive disadvantage of, 59–63
  cultural deprivation of, 56–63
  impulsivity of, 59
  low self-esteem of, 57
  and lack of basic trust, 58–59
  matrifocal family and, 57–58
  and stigma, 58
Blank, M., 61, 92–93
Bloom, B., xxii, 52, 61
Bochner, S., 228
Bodmer, W. F., 36
Boehm, A. E., test of basic concepts, 114–142, 143
Bogatz, G. M., 95
Bourke. *See also* Enrichment of Childhood, Project.
  Aboriginal tribes of, 106–107
  depression and recovery of, 106
  development of, 105–107
  ecology of, 105
  history of, 105–107
  introduction of myxomatosis to, 106 and n
  Preschool, 122–188
  social organization of part-Aboriginal community in, 107–114
Bowlby, J., 208
Brain, effect of starvation on, in animal and clinical studies, 53–56
Braine, M. D. S., 117
Brislin, R., 14, 179 n
Bruce, D. W., 115
Bruner, J. S.
  concept of implicit and explicit learning, 206
  criticism of deprivation theory, 68–69
  on evolution by prosthesis, 199
  on syntax and thought, 199
  syntax of action, 222
  theory of as to the integral role of language in thought, 198–199
Burt, C., 27
Butcher, H., 9
Butterfield, E., 61

Caldwell, B., 89
Campbell, D. T., 33 n, 79 n, 129
Caplan, G., 53
Carlisle, F., 210
Carver, R. P., 101
Cattell, R. B., 11, 17, 45
Cavalli-Sforza, L. L., 36
Cawte, J. E., 114, 122, 183
Cazden, C. B., review of literature on language competence in disadvantaged children, 61–62
Chase, A. K., 22
Cheek, D. B., 55–56, 204
Chauvinism, cultural, 21
Child, I. L., 207
Chomsky, N.
  quoted, 189–190, 196 n
  theory of a generative grammar, 216–219, 220 n, 233
Clark, D. H., 31, 214
Class system in part-Aboriginal communities, 108–111
Cleaver, E., 58
Clough, J. R., 88
Codes, language. *See* Language
Cognitively oriented curriculum, 98
Cole, M., 13, 17
  discussion of difficulties in expression of competence in culturally different child, 68–70, 206, 209, 212, 226, 227
Coleman, J. S., 31, 35, 51, 58
Coles, R., 59
Competence
  affective domain of, 214
  axioms of, 233
  Chomsky's notion of, 216
  conceptual framework of, 189–231 passim
  deep and surface structure in the spectrum of, 217–225
  definition of, 18
  different intellectual factors in different ethnic groups, 215–216

different profiles of in different ethnic groups, 215
formation rules of, 233
generative grammar and, 216–222
inference rules of, 233
and language, 189–225 passim
and paralogical thought styles, 212
psychomotor domain of, 213–214
rules of expression of, 68–72
spectrum of competencies, 211–216; 222–224; 229–230
a suggested spectrum of psychomotor and operational structures, 213–214
and synchronicity, 211
syntactic, semantic, and phonological, 217
theorems of, 233
unresolved questions concerning, 233–234
value orientations and, 223
vocabulary of, 233
Convergent thinking, 83 n
Coolican, R. E, 104, 122–123
Cooperation, interdisciplinary, need for, xxiv, 232
Criterion, contamination of, 180
Criterion-referenced testing, 180
Cultural relativity, 17–20, 67–76, 225–230
  effect on teaching of approach based on, 70–71

Dasen, P. R., 17, 43, 44, 205, 228
Dave, R. H., 60
Davidson, G. R., 228
Davis, A., 52
Dawe, H. C., 94
Dawson, J. L. M., 207
de Lacey, P. R., 43–44, 47, 116, 185
De Lemos, M. M., 42
Deprivation, physical
  caused by exposure to adverse antenatal, perinatal, and postnatal factors, 53–54
  clinical studies of, 55–56
  continuum of reproductive casualty, 53
  defined, 53
  in Northern Australia, 53
  subnutrition and, in animal studies, 54

Deprivation, psychosocial, defined, 53
Deprivation, sensory, 60–61
Deprivation, (socio-) cultural, 52
  aspirations and values in, 59
  associated with lack of maternal guidance in cognitive strategies, 61
  association with low self-esteem, 57
  association with matrifocal family structure, 58
  association with stigma, 58
  cognitive disadvantage in, 59–63
  confused background noise and, 61
  correlation with environmental variables, 60
  deficiency in verbal abstractions and, 61
  definition, 53
  difficulty in distancing and, 73–74
  difficulty in representational thinking and, 61, 73–74
  "distal" and "proximal" variables in, 57
  giant word units and, 63
  improverishment of language in, 61–63
  importance of historical background, 56
  impulsivity and, 59
  lack of basic trust in, 58–59
  and language code, 63–67
  linguistic criticisms of deprivation theory, 67–73
  mediating variables in language acquisition, 62
  misleading nature of term, 56
  mother-child interaction in, 67
Deoxyribonucleic acid (DNA), 54
Descent groups, unilateral and bilateral, 111 and n
Deutsch, M., xxii, 61, 66, 94–95
Dialect
  and contextual rules, 70
  relation of to cultural difference, 67–73
  standard and nonstandard, 67–73
  and teaching techniques, 70
Dickie, J. P., 93
Difference, cultural
  and communicative repertoire, 72
  criticism of deprivation theory, 67–73
  and dialect, 67–73

INDEX

and distancing, 73–74
and education, 70–71
Di Lorenzo, L. T., 95–96
Distancing, Sigel's hypothesis of, in relation to language, 73–74
Divergent thinking, 83 n
DISTAR program, 90–92
Dobzhansky, T., 28
Draw-a-Person Test (DAP), 141
Duffy, B. J., 54
Duncan, A. T., 114
Dunn, L. M., 114
Dyer, J. L., 96

Eckermann, A. K, 110
Eeels, K., 52
Eiferman, R., 61
Engelmann, S., 63–68
 DISTAR, 90–92, 97, 125
Enrichment of Childhood, Project
 attendance, 128–129
 behavioral objectives, 126–127
 BEP and EEP contrasted, 138–139
 Bereiter-Engelmann structured program used in, 133–134
 Bourke Perceptual-Motor Program used in, 135–136
 children in, 177–178
 community desire for an integrated preschool, 124
 contrast of programs in methodology, 125
 durability of results, 180
 effect of program on, 178
 effect of program on contextual rules of expression, 178
 ethnic integration in, 178–179
 evaluation, 139–143
 Extended Experience, semistructured program, 136–139
 follow-up, 165–172
 Frostig perceptual program used in, 134–135
 future needs of, 181–182
 history, 122–127
 home-school liaison teaching, 139
 horizontal and vertical transfer of gains, 181
 parents, 175–177
 rationale and ethics of, 182–188

research design, 126–143
results, 143–174
selection of participants, 128
staff, 174–175
structure of preschool, 124
teaching strategies, 132–139
tests used, 139–143
traditional unstructured child-centered program used in, 132–133
validity of results, 179–180
Entwisle, D. R., 35
Equilibration, 201, 204–206, 235
Erickson, E. L., 92
Erikson, E., 208
Erlebacher, A., 33 n, 79 n
Erlenmeyer-Kimling, L., 26
Evaluation
 conceptual framework of, 230
 definition of, 18–19
Evans, E. E., 80, 88
Expression. *See also* Performance
 conceptual framework of, 189–231 passim
 context, strategy, and feedback of, 224–229, 235
 contextual rules and strategies of, 224–229, 235
 cultural relativism and, 225–229
 definition of, 18–19
 ecological functionalism and, 228–229
 tactics of, 225
 unresolved questions and assumptions concerning, 232–236
Eysenck, H. J., 24, 42

Fanon, F., 58
Feedback, goal-approximate, 213–214, 235
Fifer, G., 31, 214
Fiske, J., quoted, 22
Flint, E. H., 116–117
Forman, G., 89
Fox, R., 223
Frazer, J. G., quoted, 22
Freeman, F. N., 10
Fries, C. C., 65
Frostig, M., 134–135
Functionalism, ecological, 17–18, 72, 228–229
Furth, H., 198, 200, 201

INDEX

Galanter, E., 220
Galton, F., 5
Gay, J., 205, 206, 209, 212
Ghiselin, B., 208
Ginsburg, B. E., 37
Glick, J. A., *See* Gay, J.
Golden, C. G., 216
Golden, M., 38
Goldstein, L. S., 63
Gordon, E. W., 59
Gordon, I. J., 90
Gray, S., 61, 95
Grey, A., xxiv, 102 n, 184
Gregor, A. J., 30, 38
Griffiths, R., 53 n
Growth, arrest of in subnutrition, 54
Guilford, J. P., 7, 8
   structural theory of intelligence, 214–215
Gussow, J. D., 59
Guthrie, G., 216

Harries, W. T., 131
Harris, D. B., 141
Hart, N. M., 115, 117–119, 185
Havighurst, R. J., xxii, 52
Hawkins, P. R., 66
Hawthorne effect, 100 and n, 179–180
Head Start, Project
   origin, 78
   Westinghouse Learning Corporation, evaluation by, 79–80
Herriot, P., 199, 217
   review of evidence for Chomsky's theory, 220, 222
   theory as to internalization of speech, 221
Hebb, D., 16, 45
Henderson, D., 66
Heritability (h^2)
   definition and formulas for derivation of, in regard to intelligence, 25–28
   problems in application to human populations, 36–42
Hess, R. D., 34, 67, 69, 206
Hiatt, L., 183
Higgenbottham, H. N., 72
Hirsch, J., 37
Hockett, C. F., 192
Hodgins, S., 93–94

Horne, D., 134
Horner, V., 59
Horton, K. B., 89
Hunt, J. McV., xxii, 52, 60
Hymes, D., 72

Illinois Test of Psycholinguistic Abilities (ITPA), 114–116, 118, 139–140, 142, 143, 180
   scores of Aborigines and whites on
      Wave I (1970), 145–149
      Wave II (1971), 151–152
      Wave III (1972), 153–158
      Wave IV (1973), 159–163
      follow-up comparison of, 166–171, 173–174
Intelligence
   attempts to define, 9–10
   attempts to measure via sensory discrimination, 5
   basis for IQ deficits in early childhood of disadvantaged child, 59–63
   circularity of validation of intelligence tests, 45
   circularity of rationale concerning validity, 16
   concept of a universal g as an ethnocentric artefact, 18
   cross-cultural applications of, 11–16
   cultural relativism, ecological functionalism and, 17–19
   cultural variations in definition of, 3–4
   different types of, A, B, C, g_f, g_c, level 1, level 2, 16–17
   differential patterns of, 31
   direct measurement of, 5–6
   and distancing ability, 73–74
   effect of race of examiner on IQ score, 34–35
   effect of universal education on notion of, 4–5
   environmentalist studies of, 29
   establishment of norms for children of different ages, 6
   general or specific nature of, 8–9
   heritability of, 25–33, 36–42
   hierarchial theories and resulting controversy, 8–9
   Jensen's threshold hypothesis, 29, 31–32, 41–42

INDEX

multidimensional nature of, 19
Negro sex differences in, 30
normal distribution and regression to the mean of IQ scores, 25
polymorphous nature of, 236
potential, competence, performance, and evaluation, 18–19
and potential, competence and performance, 232–236
problems in implementation of tests cross-culturally, 12–16
racial difference in, 21–50
racial difference in IQ, 30
recent studies of, in Australia, 42–44
separation of personality and cognition in Western concepts of intelligence, 45
status- and culture-fairness, 11–16
subnutrition and, 36
synonyms for, 3–4
twin studies concerning, 26–27
unsatisfactory nature of operational definition of, 10
validity and reliability of tests for, 13–16
Wechsler's scales for, 7
Intelligence quotient, concept of, 6 and n
Irvine, S. H., 4, 17, 45, 201, 215
Irwin, O. C., 61

Jacobsen, L., 30, 57
Jarvik, J. F., 26
Jencks, C., summary of report, 51–52
Jensen, A.
 arbitrary nature of his operational definition of intelligence, 17, 25
 attacks upon, 24
 concept of intelligence, 25
 consideration of assertative and selective breeding, dominance, epistasis, interactive effects, attenuation, error factor, and nongenetic differentiating factors in twin studies, 28–29
 consideration of black sex differences in IQ, 33
 consideration of reaction range of phenotype, 28
 consideration of effect of race of examiner on IQ score, 34–35
 criticism of compensatory programs, 30
 criticism of environmentalist arguments, 33–35
 criticisms of Jensen's heritability argument, 36–42
 definition of race, 30
 differential abilities in different ethnic groups, 31–32
 formula for derivation of h^2, 27–28
 his reply to Layzer's critique, 39–41
 postulation of an environmental threshold effect, 29
 racial differences in IQ, 30
 review of criteria of culture- and status-fair testing, 11–12
 summary of the Jensen controversy, 48–50
 and social responsibility, 45–48
 threshold hypothesis, 29, 31–32, 41–42
 two levels of intelligence distinguished by, 17, 31–32, 41
 viewpoint concerning possible racially determined differences in intelligence, 24–50
John, V. P, 62–63

Kagan, J., 201 n
Kamien, M., 123, 176
Kamii, C. K., 98 n
Karnes, M., 90, 93, 96–97
Katz, F. M., 114
Katz, I., 34
Kawi, A. A., 36
Kearney, G. E., 43, 212
Kirk, S., 114, 139
Kirk, W., 114, 139
Kirke, K., 104
Klaus, R., 61–95
Klineberg, O, quoted, 24
Kluckhohn, F., 223
Kochman, T., 71

Labov, W., 34, 67–70, 118
La Civita, A. F., 66
Language
 acquisition of, 196
 central importance of in cultural identity and in intervention programs, 185–187

Chomsky's theory of, 216–220
closed and open call systems in, 192
and communicative repertoire, 72
concept of code-switching, 65
and conservation, 202
and creative function, 195
deep and surface structure in, 217–222, 224
dialect, cultural deprivation, and difference, 67–73
and distancing, 197
distancing function of. 73–74
distinguishing features of human language, 192
and figurative and operative thought, 202
importance of, in differentiation and association, 197
impoverishment of in cultural deprivation, 60–63
inability of reinforcement theory to account for acquisition, 196
"language acquisition device," 196
language code and universal meanings, 70–71
learning of, by hypothesis formation and testing, 217
levels of language behavior, 62–63
mediating variables in acquisition of, 61–62
metalanguages and abstract thinking in cultural difference, 73
phrase-structure grammar, 218
phyletic origins of, 192, 196
Piaget's theory as to function of, 200–203
programs, 186–187
relation of to tool use and communication, 193–195
and representation, 197
restricted and elaborated codes, 63–67
and second-signal system, 199
sensitive periods for acquisition of, 210
and spatial ability, 197
syntactic, semantic, and phonological components of, 217–218
syntax and thought, 199
transformations, 217–222, 224
Lashley, K., 220

Laurendeau, M., 226, 227
Lawton, D., 65, 66
Layzer, D.
critique of Jensen's theory, 39–42
quoted, 7
Leacock, E. B., 71
Lenneberg, E. H., 197, 198
Lesser, G. S., 31, 35, 61, 214–215
Lester, M., 118
Lévi-Strauss, C., 212
Lewis, O., 104, 111
concept of culture of poverty, 111–114
in relation to Bourke, 112, 114
Li, C. C., 37
Loban, W. C., 61
Lonner, W., 14
Lowrie, R., 58–59
Lunzer, E. A., 220
Luria, A.R., 119
Lyons, J., 217

McAfee, O., 95
McBane, B., 73
McCarthy, J., 114, 139
Maccoby, E., 80, 83
McCandless, B., 141
McClelland, D., 16 and n
McConnell, F., 89
McElwain, D. W., 43, 212
McNeill, D., 196
Mager, R., 83
Marans, A. E., 58
Marsella, A. J., 215
Maturation, 204–205
Mehler, J., 233
Meier, J. H., 95
Mental age, Binet's establishment of, 6 and n
Mercer, J. R., 38
Miller, G. A., 220
Miller, L. B., 96
Mitchell, Sir Thomas, 105
Miner, L., 66
Moffitt, P. F., 115, 185, 210
Montessori, M., perceptual training techniques, use of by others, 78, 92, 95, 96, 97
Moore, O. K., 95
Moynihan, D. P., 57–58
Myelin, 54

Index

Naremore, R. C., 65
Negro, American. *See* black, American
Nimnicht, G., 95
Nixon, M. C., 141
Nixon test of reclassification, 141
Norm (s), in the development of the Binet test, 6
Norm-referenced testing, 180
Nurcombe, B., 53, 115, 141, 184, 209 n, 210, 212, 226, 227, 229
Nutrition, deficiency of in physical deprivation, 36, 53–58

Objectives, behavioral, 84–86
  of Bourke Project Enrichment of Childhood, 126–127
Olmstead, P., 73
Operational thinking, 200, 213
Osborne, T. R., 30, 38
Osser, H., 67

Painter, G., 89
Palmer, F. H., 59
Parents
  need to involve in preschool programs, 87–88, 102
  use of as educators, 90
Pasamanick, B., 36, 53
Pattern drill, technique of, 91
Pavlov, I. P.,
  theory of second signal system, 199
Peabody Picture Vocabulary Test (PPVT), 114–116, 118
  correlation with scores on Nixon Test, 141–142
  described, 140
  scores of Bourke children on, 115, 116, 144, 146–149, 150–151, 153–164, 166–169, 171–172
  use of in Bourke, 128–130, 134, 139, 142–143
Performance. *See also* Expression
  Chomsky's notion of, 216, 218
  conceptual framework of, 189–231
  definition of, 18
  expression and, 224–231
  and language, 190
  and reinforcement theory, 196 n
  unresolved questions and assumptions concerning, 232–236

Perry Preschool Project. *See* Weikart
Piaget, J., 9–10, 185, 195, 196, 198, 199, 211
  figurative and operative thought, 202, 208
  nonhomeostatic model of, 205–206, 208
  operational thought, 209, 213, 234–235
  and psychoanalytic theory, 208
  stages of development described by, 205–206
  theory of accommodation and assimilation, 200–201
  theory as to decentering, representation, signal, sign, and significate, 200–203
Pinard, A., 226, 227 n
Pluralism, cultural, 236
Porteus, S. D., quoted, 23
Potential
  association of with language, 192–196
  biological rudiment of, 190–196
  comparator for association and differentiation, 195
  conceptual framework of, 189–231
  definition of, 18
  relation of to tool-use in man, 192–196
  and sensorimotor intelligence, 195
  unresolved questions concerning, 233–234
Potential, competence, and performance, theoretical framework of
  defined, 17–20
  elaborated, 189–231
  questions and assumptions concerning, 232–236
Poverty, (sub-)culture of, 111–114
Preschool programs
  Bereiter-Engelmann technique, 83
  children in, selection, commencement, duration of school day, and total program for, 87
  child-centered programs reviewed, 95
  cognitively oriented program, 83
  conclusions and predictions, 100–102
  criteria for evaluation of, 81–82
  description of typical Australian preschool, 78
  DISTAR, 83
  educational philosophy of, 82–84
  infant education programs, 89–90
  Karnes ameliorative program, 93–94

Montessori technique, 78, 92, 95, 96, 97
multiple programs compared, 95–98
need for collaboration with primary schools, 88
need to involve parents in, 87–88, 102
need to train professionals from the indigenous group, 102
origin of preschool movement, 77
Project Head Start, 78–80
reciprocal linkage of objectives, strategies, and evaluation in, 85–86 and Fig. 4.2
semistructured programs reviewed, 94–95
staff in, 86–87
structured, semistructured, child-centered and custodial programs, 82–84, and Fig. 4.1
structured programs reviewed, 90–94
systematic planning for, 85–86
use of behavioral objectives in, 84–85
Pribram, K. H., 7, 51
Provence, S., 89

Race, definition of, by Jensen, 30
Rapier, J. C., 31
Reaction range, of phenotype, 28
Realization
adaptation and, 205
and affective schemata, 207–208
conceptual framework of, 189–231
cultural differences in, 205
definition of, 18
description of, as a process, 203–211
and diachronicity, 211
and ecological pressures, 209–211
environment and, 206–208
equilibration and, 205–206
functional pleasure and, 206
maturation and, 204–205
modal cultural themes, 208–210
objectivity, relativity, and reciprocity, 204
sensitive periods for, 210
stages of development; 205
unresolved questions concerning, 233, 235
Reay, M., 107
Relativity, cultural. *See* Cultural relativity
Repertoire, communicative, 72

Representation, 202, 203, 213
development of potential for, 195, 213
enactive, iconic, and symbolic modes of, 198–199
its relationship to language, 196, 200, 203, 213
Sigel's theory of representational thought and its promotion, 73–74, 197
Richardson, S., 56–57
Richmond, J. S., 89
Robinson, W. P., 66
Roget, P. M., 3–4
Rosenthal, R., 30, 57
Ross, B., 122–123

Salter, R., 95
Sanday, P., 38–39
explanatory model alternative to Jensen's, 39
Sapir, E., 198
Scarr-Salapatek, S., 30
Schaefer, E. S., 89–90
Schema(ta), mental, 9–10, 193
affective, 208, 210, 220–226, 235
Schoggen, M., 61
Seagrim, G. N., 44
Secrist, A., 89
Sensitive periods, 210
Sensorimotor intelligence, 195
Sesame Street, 95
Sharp, O. W., 205, 206, 209, 212
Shatzman, I., 65
Shipman, V. C., 34, 67, 69
Shockley, R. D., 46
Shriner, T. H., 66
Shuey, A. M., 30, 38, 58
Sigel, I., 61
distancing hypothesis of, 73, 89, 101, 197
theory of representational competence, 73–74, 197
Sigelman, C., 61
Sinclair-De-Zwart, H., 196, 202
Skeels, H. M., 29, 94
Skinner, B. F., 83, 196
Smilansky, S. and M., 61, 94
Smith, B. R., 89
Solomon, F., 61, 92–93
Sommerlad, E., 110–111
Sonquist, H. D., 98 n

269

Index

Spearman, C.,
  Use of factorial analysis by, 8–9, 236
Speech community, 72
Spencer, H., 5, 8
Staats, A. W., 88 n
Stanley, J. C., 88, 129
Stern, W., 6
Stewart, W., 67
Stodolsky, S. S., 214
Strategy, mental, 220, 222–223
Strauss, A., 65
Strodtbeck, F. I., 52, 223
Structure(s), mental, 10
  affecto-relational, 214
  deep and surface, 217–224, 235
  definition of, 200–201, 207, 210
  psychomotor, 213
  a suggested spectrum of, 212–214
Studley, W. M., 90
Sturt, C., 105
Subnutrition and brain growth, studies of, summarized, 54–56, 204

Taplin, G., quoted, 23
Taylor, L. J., 141
Teasdale, G. R., 114
Templin, M. C., 61
Terman, L., 16
Thorndike, E. L., 9
Thorndike, R. L., 30
Thurstone, L., 10
Tiger, L., 223
Transformations, theory of, 217–224
Turner, T., 201
  his concept of recentration, 213
Twins, studies of in regard to heritability, 26–28, 36

Tyler, R., 83

Vandenberg, S. G., 30, 37, 216
Van de Reit, V. and H., 93
van Lawick-Goodall, J., 192
Van Leer Foundation, 102 n, 115, 117, 180
Variance, definition of, 26
Vernon, P. E., 8, 9, 16, 24, 44–45, 206
von Sturmer, J. R., 22
Vygotsky, L. S., theory as to
  internalization of egocentric
  speech, 199, 222

Wake, C. S., quoted, 23
Wang, M. D., 67
Watts, B. H., 114, 209–210
Wechsler, D.
  introduction of new intelligence scale, 7
  nature of tests, 7–8
  Preschool and Primary Scale of
    Intelligence (WPPSI), 141
Weikart, D., 82, 98–99
Westinghouse Learning Corporation,
  evaluation of Head Start by, 79–80
White, S. H., 79
Williams, F., 65
Winick, M., 54–56, 204
Wiseman, S., 60
Witkin, H. A., 72, 207
Wober, M. A., 72
Wolf, R. M., 34
Wolff, P., 208
Woods, J. D., quoted, 22

Zaid, F., 67
Zellner, M., 80
Zigler, E., 59, 61

ABOUT THE AUTHOR

Barry Nurcombe is Associate Professor of Child Psychiatry in the Schools of Psychiatry and Paediatrics, University of New South Wales, Australia.

NOV 28 1988

JUL 4 1979
FEB 18 1980
DISCHARGED

NOV 9 1981
DISCHARGED

JUL 9 1985
DISCHARGED

DISCHARGED

DEC 1 1989

FEB 2 1994

FEB 2 3 1994
DEC 0 5 2000